Get Togethers

A Cookbook Celebrating
Friends, Family & Food

Beta Sigma Phi

EDITORIAL STAFF

P.O. Box 305141, Nashville, Tennessee 37230

ISBN: 0-87197-515-7

Manufactured in the United States of America

First Printing 2004

Contents

Beta Sigma Phi

Dear Friends,

We thank you for purchasing this cookbook. This cookbook is one of the many that we have published over the years. Each cookbook is unique in every way, and the recipes included in this book are exceptional. You will enjoy them!

Bill and Marilyn Ross

By the purchase of this cookbook, you have allowed the members of Beta Sigma Phi to raise money for worthy causes and contribute to their favorite charities.

"Get Togethers" are a Beta Sigma Phi tradition. They have been getting together for 72 years, and each year they want to do something special for you. I strongly believe that this cookbook is extra special; you and your friends will enjoy it.

Gratefully yours,

Bill Ross

Walter W. Ross, III

Let's Get Together

How often have you said to friends, family, and Beta Sigma Phi sisters, "Let's get together?" This saying is steeped in a tradition revolving around wonderful food and great conversation. Whether it is a church social, a backyard barbecue, or a tailgate party at a favorite sporting event, Beta Sigma Phi sisters love to get together for food and fellowship.

As a tribute to this time-honored tradition, we have compiled some of our favorite recipes in our latest cookbook, *Get Togethers*. We invite you to share with us the love of friends, family, and food. After testing countless recipes from this collection, we have confirmed, once again, that Beta Sigma Phi sisters are the best cooks around. Try one or two of these recipes, and you will find yourself calling friends and family and saying, "Let's get together!"

Appetizers

SWISS PARMESAN CANAPES

The topping for this delectable appetizer can be made ahead of time and stored in the refrigerator for 5 to 7 days. Stir before using.

3/4 cup mayonnaise
1/2 cup minced onion
Tabasco sauce to taste
1/2 cup grated Parmesan cheese
1/2 cup shredded Swiss cheese
1 loaf party rye bread, or any thinly sliced bread

Combine the mayonnaise, onion, Tabasco sauce, Parmesan cheese and Swiss cheese in a bowl and mix well. Spread the cheese mixture evenly over bread slices. Broil 6 inches from the heat source for 2 to 3 minutes or until light brown and bubbly. Serve hot. Yield: 1 1/2 dozen.

Linda Gallose, Preceptor Beta Delta
Sayville, New York

CHEESY ONION CANAPES

Many people think there is crab in the mix—it is the onion that fools them.

1 cup mayonnaise-type salad dressing
1 tablespoon milk
1/2 cup grated Parmesan cheese
1/2 cup shredded Romano cheese
2 tablespoons minced parsley
1/2 cup chopped onion
1 loaf party pumpernickel or rye

Combine the salad dressing, milk, Parmesan cheese, Romano cheese, parsley and onion in a bowl and mix well. Spread the cheese mixture evenly over bread slices. Broil 6 inches from the heat source for 2 to 3 minutes or until light brown and bubbly. Serve hot. Yield: 1 1/2 dozen.

Joan E. Tebbenhoff, Alpha Delta Omicron
Bonne Terre, Missouri

CHILE CHEESE PUFF

I first tasted this appetizer at a Young Homemakers meeting almost thirty years ago, and it has become a favorite at my own sorority meetings and family gatherings.

6 frozen patty shells, thawed
12 ounces Cheddar cheese, shredded
1 (4-ounce) can chopped green chiles, drained

Stack the patty shells two at a time on a lightly floured surface and roll with a rolling pin to make 3 paper-thin circles. Place 1 circle on a pizza pan. Layer the cheese, chiles and remaining paper-thin circles 1/2 at a time over the first circle. Freeze, tightly wrapped with foil. At serving time, bake at 450 degrees for 10 minutes. Remove foil, reduce heat to 400 degrees and bake for 10 minutes longer or until lightly browned. Serve hot. Yield: 12 servings.

Nancy L. Barton, Laureate Xeta Xi
Austin, Texas

CRISP CHEDDAR NIBBLES

1/2 cup butter
1 cup flour
1 cup crisp rice cereal
1 1/2 cups shredded sharp Cheddar cheese
1 egg, well beaten

Cut the butter into the flour in a bowl until mixture resembles coarse crumbs. Stir in the cereal and cheese. Mix in the egg. Shape into 3/4-inch balls. Arrange balls on an unbuttered cookie sheet and flatten with a fork. Bake at 350 degrees for 15 minutes or until golden. Cool and store in tins. Yield: 4 dozen.

Donna Wyatt, Laureate Alpha Delta
Duncan, British Columbia, Canada

BROILED CRAB MELTAWAYS

Quick, easy to prepare, and delicious. These appetizers are great to keep in the freezer ready to broil for unexpected guests or to take to a potluck.

6 English muffins
1/2 cup margarine, softened
2 tablespoons mayonnaise
1/4 teaspoon garlic salt
1 (7-ounce) can flaked crab meat, drained
1 (5-ounce) jar Old English sharp Cheddar cheese spread

Split the English muffins and arrange the halves on a baking sheet. Combine the margarine, mayonnaise, garlic salt, crab meat and cheese spread in a bowl; mix well. Spread the crab mixture evenly over the English muffin halves. Store in a resealable freezer bag until ready to use. When ready to use, arrange on baking sheets and thaw slightly. Broil 4 inches from heat for 5 minutes or until bubbly, puffy and slightly golden brown. Cut each muffin half into quarters and serve. Yield: 48 pieces.

Dorothy Pierce, Laureate Gamma Zeta
San Bernardino, California

CREAM CHEESE CRAB WRAPS

These wraps are great for taking to work for snacks, and they work well for Super Bowl parties and summer barbecues.

12 ounces whipped cream cheese
1 (6-count) package burrito-size flour shells
1 (8-ounce) bottle cocktail sauce
1 bunch green onions, chopped
1 (8-ounce) package imitation crab meat, chopped or shredded

Spread the cream cheese evenly over the burrito shells. Spread cocktail sauce evenly over the cream cheese layer. Sprinkle the green onions evenly over the cocktail sauce and layer the crab over the top. Roll each tortilla tightly and wrap in plastic wrap or waxed paper. Chill for 8 to 10 hours or until firm. Cut into 3/4-inch slices and serve. Yield: 6 to 10 servings.

Eileen Shore, Preceptor Omicron
Casper, Wyoming

CRAB QUESADILLAS

1/4 cup finely chopped onion
1 tablespoon vegetable oil
8 ounces Cheddar cheese, shredded (2 cups)
1 (6-ounce) can flaked crab meat, drained
2 to 3 tablespoons finely chopped jalapeños
2 tablespoons mayonnaise
2 to 3 tablespoons sour cream
1 teaspoon Worcestershire sauce
1/4 teaspoon pepper
4 (8- to 9-inch) flour tortillas

Sauté the onion in hot oil for 5 minutes; remove from heat. Combine the onion mixture, cheese, crab meat, jalapeños, mayonnaise, sour cream, Worcestershire sauce and pepper in a medium bowl; mix well. Spread the cheese mixture evenly over 1/2 of each tortilla; fold over to make 4 half-circles. Arrange the half-circles on a baking sheet that has been sprayed with nonstick cooking spray. Bake at 375 degrees for 15 minutes or until cheese is melted. Cut into wedges and serve. Yield: 8 (2-wedge) servings.

Judy Eppley, Xi Omicron
Norfolk, Massachusetts

ARMADILLO EGGS

Great tailgate party fare, Armadillo Eggs are especially popular with those who enjoy hot, spicy finger foods. Jalapeño pepper seeds are very hot. Wear rubber gloves and be sure to keep hands away from face and eyes when working with them.

1 (26-ounce) can pickled whole jalapeños
10 ounces Monterey Jack cheese
1 pound bulk pork sausage
1 cup baking mix
3 eggs, beaten
1 (6-ounce) package extra-crispy Shake'n Bake for pork

Remove stem end and seeds from each jalapeño pepper. Cut 8 ounces of the cheese into 2 dozen narrow pieces; shred the remaining cheese. Stuff each pepper with a slice of cheese. Combine the uncooked sausage, baking mix and shredded cheese in a large bowl and mix well. Shape the sausage mixture into 2 dozen thin patties. Wrap each stuffed jalapeño pepper in a sausage patty and pinch to enclose. Dip each Armadillo Egg into the real eggs and coat with Shake'n Bake. Arrange on an oiled baking sheet. Bake at 350 degrees for 30 minutes or until brown and sausage is cooked through. Yield: about 2 dozen.

Rita Robertson, Xi Xi Psi
Benbrook, Texas

CLASSIC DEVILED EGGS

For variety, make Shrimp and Olive Deviled Eggs by adding 1/2 cup mashed cooked shrimp, 1/2 cup chopped black olives, 2 tablespoons minced parsley, and horseradish and lemon juice to taste.

12 hard-cooked eggs, peeled
1/4 cup mayonnaise
2 tablespoons Dijon mustard
Salt and pepper to taste

Halve the eggs lengthwise and remove the yolks. Mash the yolks in a bowl with a fork. Stir in the remaining ingredients. Fill the egg white halves with yolk mixture and garnish to taste. Serve immediately, or chill, covered, in the refrigerator for up to 3 days. Yield: 2 dozen.

Pat Pelosse, Laureate Beta Pi
Chilliwack, British Columbia, Canada

SAVORY DEVILED EGGS

6 hard-cooked eggs, peeled
2 tablespoons sour cream
2 tablespoons mayonnaise
2 tablespoons dry ranch salad dressing mix
1 tablespoon sweet pickle relish

Halve the eggs lengthwise and remove the yolks. Mash the yolks in a bowl with a fork. Stir in the sour cream, mayonnaise, dressing mix and pickle relish. Fill the egg white halves generously with yolk mixture. Yield: 1 dozen.

Marciell Johnson, Preceptor Zeta
Edina, Minnesota

SCOTCH EGGS

This unusual dish is a favorite at our English teas.

1/2 cup bread crumbs
1 tablespoon dried minced onion
1/4 cup hot milk
Salt and pepper to taste
1 egg, separated
1 pound bulk pork sausage
5 hard-cooked eggs, peeled

Combine 1/4 cup of the bread crumbs, dried onion, hot milk, salt, pepper and uncooked egg yolk in a bowl and mix well. Mix in the sausage. Shape the sausage mixture evenly around the hard-cooked eggs, pressing to enclose. Roll in uncooked egg white and coat with additional bread crumbs. Arrange on a rack in a baking pan. Bake at 350 degrees for 30 minutes or until browned and sausage is cooked through, turning once. Let stand until cool. Cut the eggs into halves and arrange over a bed of lettuce or parsley on a serving tray. Yield: 10 pieces.

Diana O'Conor, Alpha Zeta
Wallkill, New York

SMOKED EGGS

1 dozen hard-cooked large eggs, peeled, shredded
2 tablespoons margarine, softened
1 tablespoon fresh lemon juice
2 1/2 teaspoons liquid smoke
2 teaspoons prepared mustard
1 teaspoon Worcestershire sauce
1 teaspoon minced onion
1 teaspoon pepper
3/4 cup mayonnaise
2 drops Tabasco sauce
Salt to taste

Combine the shredded eggs, margarine, lemon juice, liquid smoke, mustard, Worcestershire sauce, onion, pepper, mayonnaise, Tabasco sauce and salt in a bowl and mix well. Chill, covered, for at least 4 hours. Beat with a fork and serve over crackers or in sandwiches. Yield: 1 to 2 dozen servings.

Carolyn Dunlop, Iota Iota
Parker, Kansas

SWEET-AND-SOUR MEATBALLS

2 pounds ground beef
1 egg, beaten
3/4 cup bread crumbs
1 1/2 teaspoons garlic salt
1/2 teaspoon pepper
2 cups brown sugar
8 teaspoons flour
1/2 cup apple cider vinegar
4 tablespoons water
2 tablespoons soy sauce
1 tablespoon ketchup

Combine the ground beef, egg, bread crumbs, garlic salt and pepper in a large bowl and mix well. Shape the ground beef mixture into 1 1/4-inch balls. Brown in a skillet for 15 minutes or until cooked through; drain. Place in a 2-quart casserole. Combine the brown sugar and flour in a saucepan and mix well. Stir in the vinegar, water, soy sauce and ketchup. Bring to a boil over medium heat, stirring constantly. Pour the ketchup mixture evenly over the meatballs. Bake, covered, at 350 degrees for 20 minutes or until done. Yield: 30 meatballs.

Johnell Knoop, Xi Delta Phi
Cleveland, Tennessee

WHISKEY MEATBALLS

3 pounds ground beef
2 cups firmly packed brown sugar
2 cups whiskey
2 cups ketchup

Roll the ground beef into 1-inch balls. Place in a large baking dish. Combine the brown sugar, whiskey and ketchup in a bowl and whisk until smooth. Pour the whiskey mixture over the meatballs. Bake, covered, at 325 degrees for 2 hours. Yield: 48 meatballs.

Marjorie Meyers, Alpha Zeta
Holland, Michigan

CHEESY STUFFED MUSHROOMS

2 pounds large mushrooms
6 tablespoons margarine
8 ounces cream cheese, softened
1/2 cup crumbled bleu cheese
2 tablespoons finely chopped onion

Remove stems from mushrooms. Chop enough stems to measure 1/2 cup. Sauté half the mushroom caps over medium heat in half the margarine for 5 minutes; drain. Repeat with the remaining mushroom caps and margarine. Combine the cream cheese and bleu cheese in a bowl and mix well. Stir in the sautéed mushroom stems and onion. Fill the mushroom caps and arrange in a 9×13-inch baking pan. Bake at 425 degrees for 20 minutes or until golden brown. Yield: about 2 1/2 dozen.

Darla Gaus, Epsilon Gamma
Canton, Missouri

✣ MUSHROOM CROUSTADES

Croustades are little bread cases made with round slices of soft white bread that are pressed into tiny muffin cups and toasted slowly to hold their shape, then filled with a creamy mixture. If you use a small cookie cutter that yields two circles per bread slice, use a miniature muffin pan.

2 tablespoons very soft butter
24 thin slices fresh white bread
3 tablespoons (very) finely chopped sweet white onion
1/2 pound mushrooms, very finely chopped
4 tablespoons butter
2 level tablespoons flour
1 cup heavy cream
1/2 teaspoon salt
1/8 teaspoon cayenne pepper
1 tablespoon finely chopped parsley
1 1/2 tablespoons finely chopped chives
1/2 teaspoon lemon juice
2 tablespoons grated Parmesan cheese

Prepare 24 muffin cups (each about 1 3/4 inches wide at the top) by using a pastry brush to coat the bottoms and sides heavily with the 2 tablespoons butter. Cut a round from each bread slice with a 2 1/2-inch plain or fluted biscuit or cookie cutter. Fit the rounds carefully into the muffin cups. Form a perfect little cup by pushing the center of the bread into the well and molding it around the bottom; a wooden pestle or a round bottle slightly smaller than the bottom of each cup works well for this task. Bake the croustades at 400 degrees for about 10 minutes or until lightly browned on the rims and outsides; watch closely. Remove from the muffin cups and cool on a wire rack. Melt the 4 tablespoons butter in a heavy 10-inch skillet over moderate heat. Add the onion before the foam subsides and sauté for 4 minutes without letting it brown. Stir in the mushrooms; make sure they are well coated with butter. Cook for 10 to 15 minutes or until all moisture has evaporated, stirring occasionally. Remove from heat. Sprinkle the flour over the mushroom mixture and stir well until not a trace of flour is visible. Return skillet to heat and add the cream, stirring constantly. Bring to a boil, stirring constantly; mixture will be very thick. Reduce heat and simmer for a minute or two to remove any taste of raw flour. Remove from heat and stir in the salt, cayenne pepper, parsley, chives, lemon juice and Parmesan cheese. Remove the mushroom filling to a bowl and let stand until cool. Chill, covered, until ready to use. Use a small spoon to fill the Croustades, mounding the filling slightly. Sprinkle each with a few grains of Parmesan cheese, and arrange on a jelly roll pan or baking sheet. Bake in a preheated 350-degree oven for 10 minutes or until beginning to brown; watch closely, for they burn easily. Yield: 2 dozen.

Sharon Haworth, Laureate Gamma Xi
Shelton, Washington

MUSHROOM LOGS

2 (8-count) cans crescent rolls
8 ounces cream cheese, softened
1 (8-ounce) can chopped mushrooms, drained
1 teaspoon seasoned salt
1 egg, beaten
1 to 2 tablespoons poppy seeds

Unroll the dough. Separate into 8 rectangles, pressing the perforations to seal. Combine the cream cheese, mushrooms and seasoned salt in a bowl and mix well. Spread the cream cheese mixture over the dough rectangles. Roll into logs and press to seal the lengthwise seam. Cut into 1-inch sections and arrange seam side down on a nonstick baking sheet. Brush with beaten egg and sprinkle with poppy seeds. Bake at 375 degrees for 10 to 12 minutes or until golden brown. Yield: 4 dozen.

Diana Ayers, Preceptor Gamma Omicron
Forest, Virginia

Jolene Varese, Laureate Eta Gamma, Horseshoe Bay, Texas, prepares ***Bourbon Meatballs*** *by pouring a mixture of 1 cup ketchup, 3/4 cup brown sugar, and 1/2 cup bourbon over a 2-pound package of frozen meatballs in a baking dish. Bake, uncovered, at 300 degrees for 1 hour, stirring occasonally.*

ZUCCHINI-STUFFED MUSHROOMS

20 large or 30 medium mushrooms
1 small zucchini, shredded
2 tablespoons sliced green onion
2½ tablespoons grated Parmesan cheese
4 (¾-ounce) wedges light creamy cheese

Remove the stems from the mushrooms and arrange the caps in a 9×13-inch baking dish. Finely chop the stems. Combine the chopped stems, zucchini and green onion in a saucepan over medium heat. Cook for 5 to 10 minutes or until tender, stirring constantly; add 1 tablespoon white wine if necessary to prevent sticking. Stir the Parmesan cheese and light cheese into the zucchini mixture with a fork. Remove from heat. Fill the mushroom caps with the zucchini mixture. Bake at 375 degrees for 8 to 10 minutes or until brown and bubbly. Yield: 20 to 30 pieces.

Frances A. Brinkerhoff, Alpha Kappa Master
Redding, California

OLIVE BALLS

4 ounces sharp Cheddar cheese, shredded (1 cup)
¼ cup soft butter
½ rounded cup flour
¼ teaspoon salt
¼ teaspoon pepper
½ teaspoon paprika
35 small stuffed green olives

Combine the cheese, butter, flour, salt, pepper and paprika in a large bowl and use your hands to mix into a smooth dough. Shape a small piece of dough around each olive, pinching edges to enclose. Chill or freeze, covered, until serving time. Bake at 400 degrees for 12 to 16 minutes or until beginning to brown. Serve immediately. Yield: 35 pieces.

Mary Jean Reeves, Iota
Alabaster, Alabama

OLIVE PEPPER PINWHEELS

8 ounces light cream cheese, softened
1 (2-ounce) can chopped black olives, drained
2 tablespoons ranch salad dressing mix
⅓ cup each chopped red, green and yellow bell peppers
4 to 6 (8-inch) flour tortillas

Mix the cream cheese, olives, dry salad dressing and peppers in a bowl. Spread the olive mixture evenly over each tortilla. Roll up tightly. Chill, tightly wrapped in plastic wrap, for at least 2 hours. Cut into 1-inch slices and serve. Yield: 3 dozen.

Mary Strohmeyer, Xi Theta Sigma
Farmington, Missouri

BROCCOLI HAM ROLL-UPS

1 (10-ounce) package frozen chopped broccoli
1 (10-ounce) can cream of mushroom soup
1 cup dry bread crumbs
¼ cup shredded Cheddar cheese
1 tablespoon chopped onion
1½ teaspoons chopped pimentos
⅛ teaspoon rubbed sage
⅛ teaspoon crushed dried rosemary
⅛ teaspoon dried thyme
12 (⅛-inch-thick) slices fully cooked ham

Cook broccoli using package directions; drain. Combine the soup, bread crumbs, cheese, onion, pimentos, sage, rosemary and thyme in a large bowl and mix well. Mix in the broccoli. Spoon ¼ cup broccoli mixture over each ham slice. Roll up tightly and arrange in an ungreased 9×13-inch baking dish. Bake, covered, at 350 degrees for 40 minutes or until heated through. Yield: 12 roll-ups.

Faye A. Magers, Alpha Upsilon Master
Chester, Illinois

CURRIED CHICKEN AND ALMOND ROLLS

1 cup finely chopped cooked chicken
1 cup mayonnaise
¾ cup shredded Monterey Jack cheese
⅓ cup finely chopped almonds
¼ cup chopped fresh parsley
1 small onion, finely chopped
2 teaspoons curry powder
2 teaspoons lemon juice
½ teaspoon salt
½ teaspoon pepper
18 sliced whole wheat sandwich bread, crusts trimmed
¼ cup butter, melted

Combine the chicken, mayonnaise, Monterey Jack cheese, almonds, parsley, onion, curry powder, lemon juice, salt and pepper in a bowl and mix well. Chill, covered, for 30 minutes. Flatten the bread slices with a rolling pin. Spread 2 tablespoons chicken mixture over each bread slice and roll tightly. Cut each roll in half and secure with wooden picks. Arrange on an ungreased baking sheet and brush with melted butter. Bake at 375 degrees for 15 minutes. Cool and serve, or freeze. At serving time, bake frozen rolls at 400 degrees for 10 minutes. Yield: 36 rolls.

Joyce Auger, Laureate Omega
Guelph, Ontario, Canada

BACON-WRAPPED DOGS

1 pound sliced bacon
1 pound bite-size hot dogs
2 cups packed brown sugar

Cut bacon slices into thirds. Wrap a piece of bacon around each miniature hot dog and arrange seam side down in a 9×12-inch baking dish, placing them in tight rows. Layer the brown sugar over the wrapped hot dogs. Bake, uncovered, at 350 degrees for 45 to 60 minutes or until bacon is cooked and brown sugar and hot dog liquid have made a sweet glaze. Serve in a warming dish.
Yield: 6 to 10 servings.

Ruth Becker, Xi Gamma Alpha
Norfolk, Nebraska

CHEESY SAUSAGE STROMBOLI

You may use 2 loaves of frozen bread dough if desired. Hot Italian sausage adds a special kick.

5 cups all-purpose flour
2 tablespoons sugar
2 teaspoons salt
2 envelopes dry yeast
1/2 cup warm milk
2 tablespoons melted margarine
2 pounds bulk pork sausage
4 cups shredded mozzarella cheese
3 eggs
1 teaspoon minced fresh basil, or 1/4 teaspoon dried
2 tablespoons grated Parmesan cheese

Combine the flour, sugar, salt and yeast in a bowl and mix well. Combine 1 1/2 cups warm water, milk and margarine in a large saucepan and heat, stirring until smooth. Stir into the flour mixture. Turn onto a well-floured surface. Knead for 6 to 8 minutes or until smooth and elastic. Place in a greased bowl, turning once to grease the top. Let rise, covered, in a warm place for about an hour or until doubled in bulk. Brown the sausage in a skillet, stirring until crumbly; drain. Combine the sausage, mozzarella cheese, 2 of the eggs and basil in a large bowl and mix well. Punch down the risen dough and divide in half. Roll one half into a 10×15-inch rectangle and place on a greased baking sheet. Spoon half the sausage mixture evenly over half the dough rectangle to within 1 inch of the edges. Fold dough in half and pinch edges to seal. Cut 4 diagonal slits in the top of the dough. Repeat with the remaining sausage mixture and dough. Beat the remaining egg and brush over top of dough. Sprinkle with Parmesan cheese. Let rise, covered, in a warm place for about 45 minutes or until doubled in bulk. Bake at 375 degrees for 20 to 25 minutes or until golden brown. Slice, and serve warm. The Stromboli freezes well and can be reheated in the oven or toaster oven. Yield: 2 loaves.

Cheryl Worr, Xi Eta Tau
Windsor, Ontario, Canada

INDIVIDUAL SAUSAGE PIZZAS

1 pound bulk pork sausage
1/2 cup drained canned mushrooms
1/2 cup chopped onion
1/2 cup chopped green bell pepper
1 (6-ounce) can tomato paste
1 (10-ounce) can tomato soup
1/4 teaspoon garlic salt
1/4 teaspoon chili powder
Salt and pepper to taste
1/2 cup grated Parmesan cheese
12 small dinner rolls, halved

Brown the sausage in a skillet with the mushrooms, onion and bell pepper, stirring until crumbly; drain. Add the tomato paste, tomato soup, garlic salt, chili powder, salt and pepper; simmer over medium-low heat until thickened. Arrange dinner roll halves on a baking sheet. Spread sausage mixture over dinner roll halves and sprinkle with Parmesan cheese. Broil until bubbly. Yield: 2 dozen.

Arlene Hamilton, Xi Delta Alpha
Hamilton, Ontario, Canada

SAUSAGE CHEESE BALLS

These sausage balls may be frozen uncooked and then baked before serving time. If you like a firmer texture, use 3 cups baking mix and an additional 2 cups shredded cheese.

2 pounds bulk pork sausage
1 1/2 cups baking mix
16 ounces sharp Cheddar cheese, shredded (4 cups)
1/2 cup finely chopped onion
1/2 cup finely chopped celery
1/2 teaspoon garlic powder

Combine the sausage, baking mix, cheese, onion, celery and garlic powder in a bowl and mix well. Shape sausage mixture into 1-inch balls and arrange on an ungreased baking sheet. Bake in a preheated 375-degree oven for 15 minutes or until golden brown. Yield: about 6 dozen.

Doni Helser, Xi Mu Pi
Edwardsville, Illinois

SAUSAGE WON TON STARS

1 (12-ounce) package won ton wrappers
1 pound bulk pork sausage
1/2 medium green bell pepper, chopped
1/2 medium red bell pepper, chopped
2 cups shredded Colby cheese (8 ounces)
2 bunches green onions, sliced
1/2 cup ranch salad dressing

Press the won ton wrappers lightly against the bottoms and up the sides of greased miniature muffin cups. Bake in a preheated 350-degree oven for about 5 minutes or until lightly browned. Brown the sausage in a large skillet over medium heat, stirring until crumbly; drain. Stir in the bell peppers, cheese, green onions and salad dressing. Remove from heat. Spoon a rounded tablespoon of sausage mixture into each won ton cup. Bake for 6 to 7 minutes or until heated through. Yield: 4 dozen.

Cynthia Moore, Alpha Rho Master
Brooksville, Florida

BAKED SAUSAGE AND APPLES

I first tasted this dish at a church event, and was so impressed by its savory flavor. It was served so many times by church members that it became known as St. Anne's Sausage.

2 pounds cocktail frankfurters
6 Granny Smith or McIntosh apples, peeled and finely chopped
1 large onion, finely chopped
1 cup packed brown sugar

Combine the cocktail frankfurters, apples, onion and brown sugar in a Dutch oven and mix well. Bake, covered, at 250 degrees for 4 to 5 hours, stirring halfway through the baking time.
Yield: 20 to 30 servings.

Anne M. Copeland, Xi Alpha Upsilon
West Lafayette, Indiana

GINGER SHRIMP TOAST

1 loaf white bread, thinly sliced
3/4 pound fresh medium shrimp, boiled, peeled, deveined
6 tablespoons unsalted butter, at room temperature
1/4 teaspoon salt
1 garlic clove, minced
2 tablespoons minced fresh parsley
1 teaspoon grated fresh gingerroot

Cut the bread slices into rounds with a 1 1/2- to 2-inch cookie cutter. Arrange on a baking sheet and broil briefly to toast one side. Turn bread rounds untoasted side up. Finely chop the shrimp. Cream the butter and salt in a medium bowl until light and fluffy. Add the shrimp, garlic, parsley and ginger and mix well. Spread the shrimp mixture over the bread rounds and broil until lightly browned. Serve immediately. Yield: 60 pieces.

Evalynn Christiansen, Laureate Eta Nu
Houston, Texas

MARTINI SHRIMP

1 1/2 pounds (30 to 40) raw shrimp
1 cup stuffed green olives
1/2 cup vodka
2 tablespoons vermouth
3 tablespoons finely diced white onion
3 garlic cloves, minced
3 tablespoons butter

Place the shrimp and olives in a glass dish. Add a mixture of the vodka and vermouth and marinate for 2 hours. Sauté the onion and garlic in butter in a 10-inch skillet over medium-low heat for about 5 minutes. Add the shrimp mixture and sauté for 4 to 5 minutes or until shrimp turn pink. Pour into martini glasses or a large bowl and garnish with freshly ground pepper. Serve with baguette slices for soaking up the juices. Yield: 4 to 6 servings.

Alisa McGregor, Xi Nu
Rosetown, Saskatchewan, Canada

MUSTARD SHRIMP

1/4 cup finely chopped parsley
1/4 cup finely chopped shallots
1/4 cup tarragon vinegar
1/4 cup wine vinegar
1/2 cup olive oil
4 tablespoons Dijon mustard
2 teaspoons crushed red chile peppers
Salt and pepper to taste
2 pounds frozen cooked shrimp, thawed

Combine the parsley, shallots, tarragon vinegar, wine vinegar, olive oil, Dijon mustard, chile peppers, salt and pepper in a small bowl and mix well. Place the shrimp in a glass dish and cover with the parsley mixture. Marinate, covered, in the refrigerator for 8 to 10 hours, stirring once or twice. Serve over a bed of lettuce and garnish with parsley sprigs.
Yield: up to 70 large or 40 extra-large pieces.

Edy Mohler, Laureate Alpha Upsilon
Tucson, Arizona

SPICY TOMATO SHRIMP

Add kalamata olives or capers or both if desired. This delectable appetizer may also be used as a topping for pasta.

1/2 cup Frank's RedHot Sauce or hot pepper sauce of choice
1/2 cup melted butter or margarine
4 garlic cloves, crushed
1 to 2 pints cherry tomatoes, halved
2 cups uncooked shrimp (1 pound)

Combine the hot pepper sauce, butter and garlic in a small bowl and beat until smooth. Layer the cherry tomato halves in a 9×13-inch baking dish. Layer the shrimp over the tomatoes and drizzle evenly with the hot sauce mixture. Bake, uncovered, at 450 degrees for 10 minutes and broil for 2 minutes or until shrimp are cooked. Serve with chunks of bread. Yield: 24 to 32 pieces.

Jean Wilson, Xi Eta Tau
Windsor, Ontario, Canada

BLT BITES

16 to 20 cherry tomatoes
1 pound bacon, crisp-cooked, crumbled
1/2 cup mayonnaise or salad dressing
1/3 cup chopped green onions
3 tablespoons grated Parmesan cheese

Remove a thin slice from each tomato top. Scoop out the tomato pulp with a small spoon and discard. Invert the tomatoes over a paper towel to drain. Combine the bacon, mayonnaise, green onions and Parmesan cheese in a small bowl; mix well. Spoon the bacon filling into the tomato shells. Chill, covered, for at least 2 hours. Yield: 16 to 20 pieces.

Kim LaFollette, Nu Epsilon
Holiday, Florida

GUACAMOLE-STUFFED CHERRY TOMATOES

1 medium avocado, very ripe
2 tablespoons medium salsa
12 to 16 cherry tomatoes (1 pint)

Mash the avocado in a bowl; mix in the salsa. Remove a thin slice from each tomato top. Scoop out the tomato pulp with a small spoon and discard. Invert the tomatoes over a paper towel to drain. Spoon the avocado mixture into the tomato shells and garnish each with a cilantro leaf. Chill, covered, until serving time. Yield: 6 to 8 servings.

Joanne Rivest, Xi Kappa
Calgary, Alberta, Canada

TOMATO BACON CUPS

1 (10-count) can "flaky layers" biscuits
8 slices bacon, crisp-cooked, crumbled
1 medium tomato, chopped
1 teaspoon dried basil
1 cup shredded Monterey Jack cheese
1/2 cup mayonnaise

Separate each biscuit into 3 layers. Press each layer into a lightly greased miniature muffin cup. Combine the bacon, tomato, basil, cheese and mayonnaise in a medium bowl; mix well. Spoon the bacon mixture into the lined muffin cups. Bake at 375 degrees for 10 to 12 minutes or until golden brown.
Yield: 30 pieces.

Susan Treece, Psi Xi
Carterville, Illinois

SPINACH AND ARTICHOKES IN PUFF PASTRY

1 (10-ounce) package frozen spinach, thawed
1 (14-ounce) can artichoke hearts, drained, chopped
1/2 cup mayonnaise
1/2 cup grated Parmesan cheese
1 teaspoon onion powder
1 teaspoon garlic powder
1/2 teaspoon pepper
1 (18-ounce) package frozen puff pastry

Press the spinach between layers of paper towels to drain well. Combine the spinach, artichokes, mayonnaise, Parmesan cheese, onion powder, garlic powder and pepper in a bowl and mix well. Thaw the puff pastry at room temperature for 30 minutes. Unfold the pastry and place 1 sheet on a lightly floured surface. Spread 1/4 of the spinach mixture evenly over the pastry sheet to within 1/2 inch of the edges. Roll as for a jelly roll and press seam to seal. Repeat with the remaining spinach mixture and pastry sheets. Freeze for 30 minutes; cut into 1/2-inch-thick slices. Arrange the slices on a nonstick baking sheet. Bake at 400 degrees for 20 minutes or until golden. Yield: 4 dozen.

LuAnn Throgmorton, Theta Psi
Cookeville, Tennessee

Florence Santarsieri, Xi Mu Eta, Jacksonville, Florida, makes ***Easy BLT Dip*** *by combining 2 large chopped seeded tomatoes with 1 1/4 cups mayonnaise, 1 cup sour cream, and a 4-ounce jar of bacon bits. Chill. Serve with crackers.*

MEXICAN PINWHEELS

1 cup sour cream
8 ounces cream cheese, softened
1 (4-ounce) can chopped green chiles, drained
1 (4-ounce) can chopped black olives, drained
1 cup shredded Cheddar cheese
1/2 cup chopped green onions
Garlic powder and seasoned salt to taste
5 (10-inch) flour tortillas

Combine the sour cream, cream cheese, green chiles, olives, Cheddar cheese, green onions, garlic powder and seasoned salt in a bowl; mix well. Spread 1/5 of the cream cheese mixture evenly over each tortilla. Roll as for a jelly roll. Chill, wrapped tightly in plastic wrap, for 3 to 10 hours. Remove plastic wrap and cut into 1/2- to 3/4-inch-thick slices. Serve with salsa if desired. Yield: about 4 dozen.

Sharon Weaver, Preceptor Alpha
Carson City, Nevada

VEGETABLE BARS

Use any combination of broccoli, celery, cauliflower, olives, green onions, or bell peppers.

2 (8-count) cans crescent rolls
16 ounces cream cheese, softened
2 envelopes ranch salad dressing mix
1 cup mayonnaise
3/4 cup each chopped fresh vegetables (2 or 3 kinds)
3/4 cup shredded carrots
3/4 cup shredded Cheddar cheese

Unroll the dough. Separate into 2 rectangles, pressing the perforations to seal. Press onto a baking sheet. Bake at 350 degrees for 7 to 8 minutes. Cool for 10 to 12 minutes. Combine the cream cheese, dry salad dressing mix and mayonnaise in a small bowl and mix until smooth. Spread the cream cheese mixture evenly over the cooled crust. Layer the vegetables, including carrots, evenly over the cream cheese mixture and press lightly. Top with Cheddar cheese. Cut into bars. Yield: 15 to 20 servings.

Betsy Asay, Laureate Gamma Phi
Ridgefield, Washington

SPICY CHICKEN WINGS

24 whole chicken wings (about 5 pounds)
1 cup barbecue sauce
1 cup honey
1 cup soy sauce

Disjoint the wings and arrange in a greased 9×13-inch baking dish. Combine the barbecue sauce, honey and soy sauce in a small bowl and whisk until smooth. Pour the honey mixture evenly over the wings. Bake, uncovered, at 350 degrees for 50 to 60 minutes or until juices run clear. Yield: 8 servings.

Trina Good, Preceptor Zeta
Yakima, Washington

SPICY SUPER BOWL WINGS

1 1/2 pounds chicken wings, disjointed
1 egg, lightly beaten
1/2 cup flour
1/2 cup vegetable oil
1/4 cup packed brown sugar
1/4 cup honey
2 tablespoons white vinegar
2 tablespoons Worcestershire sauce
1 to 2 tablespoons Tabasco sauce, or to taste
1/4 teaspoon salt
1/4 teaspoon crushed black pepper

Dip the wings in the egg and coat with flour. Heat the vegetable oil in a large skillet over medium-high heat. Brown the wings in the hot oil for 5 to 10 minutes or until crisp on both sides, turning once; drain. Arrange in an 8×11-inch baking dish. Combine the brown sugar, honey and vinegar in a small bowl; whisk until smooth. Stir in the Worcestershire sauce, Tabasco sauce, salt and pepper. Drizzle over the chicken wings. Bake, uncovered, at 350 degrees for about 40 minutes or until done, turning and basting wings occasionally. Yield: 10 to 20 servings.

Erin Nelson, Sigma Zeta
Gladstone, Missouri

✣ CAJUN PORK SOUTACHE

The word soutache, a narrow braided trim, is also used in the garment industry.

1 pound ground lean pork or beef
1/2 cup chopped onion
1/4 cup chopped celery
1/4 cup chopped green bell pepper
1 garlic clove, minced
1/2 teaspoon salt
1/4 teaspoon cayenne pepper
8 ounces cream cheese, cubed
2 tablespoons chopped green onions
2 tablespoons chopped fresh parsley
2 (8-count) cans crescent rolls
1 egg, beaten

Brown the ground pork in a skillet, stirring until crumbly; drain. Add the onion, celery, bell pepper, garlic, salt and cayenne pepper and cook over low heat for 5 minutes, stirring occasionally. Add the cream cheese, green onions and parsley and cook until the cream cheese is melted, stirring constantly. Unroll half the dough on a lightly greased baking sheet. Use a floured rolling pin to roll the dough into

a 10×12-inch rectangle. Spoon half the pork mixture down the center, leaving 1 inch on each end and 3 inches on each side of the rectangle uncovered. Cut each side into 14 (3/4-inch) diagonal strips; brush strips with beaten egg. Fold the dough strips alternately over the center to enclose the filling; brush top with beaten egg. Repeat with the remaining dough and pork mixture. Bake at 350 degrees for 25 minutes or until golden brown. Serve hot. The second loaf may be frozen for later use.
Yield: 6 to 8 servings per loaf.

Dianne Daniel, Xi Delta Rho
Covington, Louisiana

HOLIDAY CORNUCOPIAS

20 slices white bread
2 tablespoons melted butter or margarine
3 ounces cream cheese, softened
3 tablespoons minced onion
1 1/2 teaspoons prepared horseradish, drained
1 (4-ounce) can deviled ham
1/8 teaspoon celery seed
Salt and pepper to taste

Cut a circle from each bread slice with a 3-inch cookie cutter. Flatten circles with a rolling pin and brush both sides with melted butter. Roll to form cornucopia shapes and secure with wooden picks. Arrange on a baking sheet. Bake at 350 degrees for 12 minutes. Combine the cream cheese, onion, horseradish, deviled ham, celery seed, salt and pepper in a bowl; mix well. Place 1 teaspoon of the deviled ham mixture in each cornucopia. Garnish with fresh parsley and serve. Yield: 20 servings.

Elaine Barnicoat, Xi Eta Tau
Windsor, Ontario, Canada

RYE PARTY PUFFS

1/2 cup butter
1/2 cup all-purpose flour
1/2 cup rye flour
2 teaspoons dried parsley flakes
1/2 plus 1/8 teaspoon garlic powder
1/4 teaspoon salt
4 eggs
Caraway seeds to taste
16 ounces cream cheese, softened
2 (3-ounce) packages cooked corned beef, finely chopped
1/2 cup mayonnaise
2 tablespoons minced chives
1 teaspoon Dijon mustard
1/4 cup sour cream
2 tablespoons finely chopped onion
10 small stuffed green olives, finely chopped

Combine the butter and 1 cup water in a saucepan over medium heat; bring to a boil. Add the flours, parsley flakes, the 1/2 teaspoon garlic powder and salt all at once; stir until a smooth ball forms. Remove from heat and let stand for 5 minutes. Add the eggs 1 at a time, beating constantly until smooth. Drop the dough by rounded teaspoons 2 inches apart on a greased baking sheet. Sprinkle with caraway seeds. Bake at 400 degrees for 18 to 20 minutes or until golden brown. Combine the cream cheese, corned beef, mayonnaise, chives, Dijon mustard, sour cream, onion and the 1/8 teaspoon garlic powder in a bowl; mix well. Stir in the olives. Split the puffs and fill with the cream cheese mixture. Chill, covered, until serving time. Top with olive slices if desired.
Yield: 4 1/2 dozen.

Donna Oden, Xi Alpha Tau
Kemmerer, Wyoming

BASIC CALIFORNIA ROLL

I persuaded my adult son to take a sushi-making course with me several years ago, and now it's a mother-son get-together whenever we prepare it. You may substitute shrimp for the imitation crab meat.

1 1/2 cups uncooked short-grain rice
3 tablespoons rice vinegar
1 1/2 tablespoons sugar
1 1/2 teaspoons salt
1 (1-ounce) package nori sheets
1 peeled ripe avocado, cut into wedges (optional)
3/4 cup imitation crab meat (optional)
Thin strips of vegetables such as green onion, green or red bell pepper, cucumber, carrot, cooked asparagus (optional)
Strips of smoked salmon (optional)

Combine the rice and 1 3/4 cups cold water in a saucepan over medium heat. Cook, covered, until rice is tender and liquid is absorbed. Combine the rice vinegar, sugar and salt in a small saucepan and bring to a boil, stirring constantly; remove from heat and let cool. Place the cooked rice in a large shallow bowl. Stir in the vinegar mixture with a spatula, using slicing motions and fanning rice at the same time. Cover a small flexible bamboo mat with plastic wrap. Place a sheet of nori over the plastic wrap. Moisten your hands and scoop up 1/3 of the rice mixture; spread over the nori, leaving a 1-inch strip at the top of the sheet. Select three of the optional ingredients. Working from left to right, place the selected three fillings in a line, 1/3 of the way up the sheet of nori. Roll the mat away from you, compacting rice, making sure the plastic stays outside. Cut into 8 pieces. Repeat with 2 nori sheets, the remaining rice mixture and the selected fillings. Serve with pickled ginger, soy sauce and horseradish. Yield: 2 dozen.

Margaret-Ann Smith, Alpha Eta Master
Victoria, British Columbia, Canada

CHEESY POTATO BITES

2 tablespoons butter
1/2 teaspoon salt
2 1/3 cups plain mashed potato mix
2 eggs
1/4 cup chopped fresh chives
24 (1/2-inch) cubes pasteurized process cheese

Combine 1 cup water, butter and salt in a medium saucepan and bring to a boil. Stir in 1 1/3 cups of the dry mashed potato mix, 1 of the eggs and chives; mix well. Remove from heat and let stand for 30 seconds; stir. Let cool for 10 minutes. Spoon the mashed potatoes into twenty-four 1-tablespoon mounds on an ungreased baking sheet. Flatten the mounds into disks. Use a spatula to remove each potato disk and shape each around a cube of cheese, pinching to enclose. Combine the remaining egg and 1 tablespoon water in a small bowl; beat well. Place the remaining 1 cup dry mashed potato mix in a shallow dish. Roll the wrapped cheese cubes in the dry mashed potato mix to coat. Dip in the egg mixture, then again in the mashed potato mix. Arrange on an ungreased baking sheet. Just before baking, spray the coated balls with butter-flavor nonstick cooking spray. Bake at 400 degrees for 12 minutes or until potato coating begins to brown. Yield: 2 dozen.

Linda Hoffman, Xi Theta Sigma
Farmington, Missouri

SPINACH BALLS

The spinach balls may be frozen on the baking sheet until hard, then removed to airtight freezer bags to be kept frozen until serving time. To serve, thaw slightly and bake at 350 degrees for 20 to 25 minutes.

2 (10-ounce) packages frozen spinach
2 cups herb-flavored stuffing mix
1 large onion, finely chopped
6 eggs, well beaten
1 1/2 teaspoons garlic salt
3/4 teaspoon black pepper
3/4 teaspoon cayenne pepper (optional)
1 to 2 teaspoons creole seasoning (optional)
1/4 cup grated Parmesan cheese

Prepare spinach using the package directions; drain well and squeeze to remove excess moisture. Combine the spinach, stuffing mix, onion, eggs, garlic salt, black pepper, cayenne pepper, creole seasoning and Parmesan cheese in a bowl; mix well. Shape into 3/4-inch balls; arrange on a lightly greased baking sheet. Bake at 350 degrees for 15 to 20 minutes or until firm and fragrant. Yield: 2 dozen.

Lyn Anderson, Xi Epsilon Upsilon
Allen, Oklahoma

SWEET BACON PARTY PEPPERS

1 (26-ounce) can whole jalapeño peppers, drained, halved
8 ounces cream cheese, softened
1 pound sliced bacon
2 cups packed brown sugar

Scoop the seeds from the jalapeño pepper halves and wash the peppers. Pack each jalapeño half with cream cheese, allowing the cream cheese to extend slightly from the end of the pepper. Wrap each stuffed pepper evenly with a slice of bacon. Arrange in a 9×13-inch baking pan and cover evenly with the brown sugar. Bake, covered, at 400 degrees for 40 to 45 minutes or until bacon is well cooked. Place a wooden pick in each pepper and serve warm.
Yield: 12 to 15 servings.

Bridget D. Stifflemire, Omega Gamma
Winnie, Texas

TOMATO CREAM CHEESE TARTS

3 sheets phyllo dough
1 egg white
4 ounces cream cheese, softened
Salt and pepper to taste
1 dozen fresh basil leaves, or dried basil to taste
3 plum tomatoes, thinly sliced

Separate the phyllo sheets and keep covered with a moist cloth to prevent drying. Beat the egg white until frothy. Work with 1 sheet of phyllo at a time, keeping remaining phyllo covered. Brush the phyllo with the beaten egg white and cut into 4-inch squares. Press 2 squares into each of 12 small muffin cups to make pastry cases. Beat the cream cheese until spoonable. Spoon the cream cheese into the pastry cases. Season with salt and pepper and top with basil leaves and tomato slices. Bake at 400 degrees for 10 to 12 minutes or until golden. Remove the tarts to a wire rack immediately to avoid a soggy crust.
Yield: 1 dozen.

Florence M. Short, Preceptor Alpha Epsilon
Melbourne, Florida

Stacey Wright, Beta Tau, Newport News, Virginia, prepares ***Chicken Won Tons*** *that are a big hit at any party. She presses won ton wrappers into miniature muffin cups and bakes them at 350 degrees for 4 minutes. Fill the wrappers with a mixture of 3 cups finely chopped, cooked chicken and 1 cup ranch salad dressing. Top with 1 pound shredded Monterey Jack cheese and a sprinkle of chili powder. Bake for an additional 6 to 7 minutes at 350 degrees.*

HOT ARTICHOKE DIP

1 (14-ounce) can artichoke hearts, drained and chopped
1 (4-ounce) can chopped green chiles, drained
1 cup mayonnaise
$1^1/_4$ cups shredded Monterey Jack cheese
2 garlic cloves, minced

Combine the artichokes, green chiles, mayonnaise, Monterey Jack cheese and garlic in a 1-quart baking dish and mix lightly. Bake, uncovered, at 350 degrees for 22 minutes or until heated through. Serve with crackers or tortilla chips. Yield: about $2^1/_2$ cups.

Dean Jones, Preceptor Alpha Epsilon
Bowling Green, Kentucky

✣ PECAN-TOPPED ARTICHOKE DIP

2 tablespoons butter
$^1/_2$ cup finely chopped onion
3 garlic cloves, minced
1 (10-ounce) package chopped spinach, thawed and well drained
1 (14-ounce) can artichoke hearts, drained and chopped
8 ounces cream cheese, softened
$^1/_2$ cup mayonnaise
2 cups shredded Cheddar cheese
$^1/_2$ cup grated Parmesan cheese
3 to 4 dashes hot red pepper sauce
$^1/_3$ cup chopped pecans

Melt the butter in a skillet over medium heat. Sauté the onion and garlic in the butter for 3 to 4 minutes. Add the spinach and cook for 5 minutes longer, stirring frequently. Remove from heat. Stir in the next 6 ingredients. Spoon the spinach mixture into a greased $1^1/_2$-quart baking dish. Bake, covered, at 350 degrees for 40 minutes. Top with pecans. Bake, uncovered, for 10 minutes longer. Serve warm with crackers. Yield: 12 to 15 servings.

Carol Darlington, Nu Eta
Asbury, Missouri

SPICY ARTICHOKE DIP

3 (14-ounce) cans artichoke hearts, rinsed, drained, coarsely chopped
1 cup mayonnaise
1 cup grated Parmesan cheese
1 (4-ounce) can chopped green chiles
2 tablespoons chopped jalapeño pepper
3 garlic cloves, minced
$^1/_2$ teaspoon cumin

Place the artichokes, mayonnaise, Parmesan cheese, green chiles, jalapeño pepper, garlic and cumin in a large mixing bowl; stir well to combine. Spoon the artichoke mixture into an ungreased $1^1/_2$-quart baking dish. Sprinkle with paprika. Bake, uncovered, at 350 degrees for 30 minutes or until hot and bubbly. Remove from oven and let stand for 10 minutes. Serve warm with tortilla chips, crackers or toasted baguette slices. Yield: 8 cups.

Linda Howard, Gamma Xi
Yakima, Washington

*For her version of **Artichoke Dip**, Cheryl Adamick, Epsilon Epsilon, Brooksville, Florida, chops 1 can of artichoke hearts into bite-size pieces and adds 1 cup each Parmesan cheese and mayonnaise. Bake at 350 degrees in a 5×9-inch pan for 45 minutes or until the top is brown.*

TACO BEAN DIP

1 (15-ounce) can refried beans
1 cup low-fat sour cream
2 to 4 tablespoons taco seasoning
1 cup salsa
2 cups shredded Colby cheese

Spread the refried beans in a deep-dish pie plate. Spread a mixture of the sour cream and taco seasoning over the bean layer. Spoon the salsa over the sour cream layer. Top with the Colby cheese. Bake, uncovered, at 350 degrees for 20 to 30 minutes until heated through and cheese is melted. Garnish with chopped tomatoes, sliced black olives and pickled jalapeños if desired. Serve with tortilla chips. Yield: 8 servings.

Kris Griffith, Beta Alpha
Rockton, Illinois

VEGETARIAN TEX-MEX DIP

8 ounces cream cheese, softened
1/4 (2-ounce) envelope taco seasoning mix
1 (4-ounce) can chopped green chiles, drained
1 (15-ounce) can chili beans, well stirred
1 cup mild salsa (optional)
4 ounces (or more) sharp or extra-sharp Cheddar cheese, shredded
1 (12-ounce) package plain tortilla chips

Spread the cream cheese evenly in the bottom of an 8½×11-inch baking dish. Sprinkle with taco seasoning mix. Layer the green chiles, chili beans and salsa over the cream cheese layer. Sprinkle the Cheddar cheese over the top. Bake, uncovered, at 350 degrees for 25 to 30 minutes or until bubbly and cheese is melted. Serve warm with tortilla chips.
Yield: about 15 servings.

Freda I. Bush, Preceptor Gamma Kappa
Chesapeake, Virginia

SPICY JALAPENO DIP

Use green olives instead of black if you prefer; and add more jalapeños to make it extra-hot.

16 ounces cream cheese, at room temperature
1 envelope ranch salad dressing mix
1 (4-ounce) can chopped jalapeño peppers, drained
1 (4-ounce) can chopped black olives, drained
1 bunch green onions, chopped
1 (3-ounce) package chipped beef
1 (2-ounce) jar chopped pimentos (optional)

Combine the cream cheese, dry salad dressing mix, jalapeños, olives, green onions, chipped beef and pimentos in a bowl and mix well. Chill, covered, until serving time. Serve with crackers.
Yield: 3 to 4 cups.

Yvonne Salmon, Preceptor Lambda Gamma
Belton, Missouri

CHIPPED BEEF DIP

8 ounces cream cheese, softened
2 tablespoons milk
1/2 cup chopped green bell pepper
1/2 teaspoon black pepper
2 tablespoons minced onion
1 (5-ounce) package chipped beef
1/2 cup sour cream

Combine the cream cheese, milk, bell pepper, black pepper, onion, chipped beef and sour cream in a bowl and mix well. Spoon into a 1-quart baking dish. Bake, uncovered, at 350 degrees for 25 minutes. Serve hot with Triscuits. Yield: 2 to 3 cups.

Lally Jennings, Preceptor Rho
New Braunfels, Texas

MEXICAN SAUSAGE BEAN DIP

Chorizo is a highly seasoned pork sausage.

1 pound ground beef
1 pound chorizo
1 large onion, chopped
1 (15-ounce) can refried beans
1 (7-ounce) can sliced green chiles, drained
12 ounces shredded Cheddar cheese (3 cups)
Hot red pepper sauce to taste
2 cups sour cream
1/2 cup chopped green onions
3 ripe avocados, mashed
1 (4-ounce) can sliced black olives

Brown the ground beef with the chorizo and onion in a skillet, stirring until crumbly; drain. Spread the refried beans in the bottom of a large ovenproof bowl. Layer the beef mixture, green chiles and cheese over the bean layer. Drizzle with hot red pepper sauce. Bake, uncovered, at 400 degrees for 25 minutes. Let stand for a few minutes to cool slightly. Layer the sour cream, green onions, avocados and olives over the top. Serve with tortilla chips.
Yield: 12 to 15 cups.

Cheryl Krantz, Laureate Epsilon Pi
Crestview, Florida

EASY CHEESE FONDUE

1 (10-ounce) can Cheddar cheese soup
1 cup French onion dip
1 cup chopped Velveeta cheese
1/2 teaspoon dry mustard
2 dashes hot red pepper sauce
French bread cubes for dipping
Hot kielbasa slices for dipping

Combine the soup, onion dip, Velveeta cheese, dry mustard and hot pepper sauce in a saucepan over low heat. Heat until melted and uniform in texture. Pour into a small slow cooker or chafing dish. Serve with French bread and kielbasa. Yield: 4 cups.

Joyce Horvath, Preceptor Epsilon Lambda
Wellington, Ohio

SPICY FETA DIP

8 ounces cream cheese, softened
8 ounces feta cheese, crumbled
1/4 cup plain yogurt
4 to 6 garlic cloves, minced
1 teaspoon Worcestershire sauce
3 to 4 drops Tabasco sauce
1 tablespoon oregano
Salt and pepper to taste

Combine the ingredients in a small bowl and mix until smooth. Serve with toasted pitas or dipping vegetables. Yield: 2 cups.

Lesa Campbell, Xi Eta Tau
Windsor, Ontario, Canada

OLIVE CHEESE DIP

1 cup shredded mozzarella cheese
2 cups shredded Mexican-style cheese
2 cups mayonnaise
3 (4-ounce) cans chopped green chiles, drained
1 (10-ounce) jar green olives, drained

Mix the ingredients in a bowl. Spoon the cheese mixture into a 9×13-inch baking dish. Bake, uncovered, at 350 degrees for about 30 minutes or until bubbly. Serve with corn scoops or other heavy chips.
Yield: 4 to 5 cups.

Linda B. Freeney, Theta Master
Albany, Georgia

CHICKEN ARTICHOKE DIP

2 cups chopped cooked chicken
1 (14-ounce) can artichoke hearts, drained and chopped
1 cup freshly grated Parmesan cheese
1 cup mayonnaise
1 garlic clove, minced
Dash of cayenne pepper

Combine the chicken, artichokes, Parmesan cheese, mayonnaise and garlic in a bowl and mix well. Spoon into a 9-inch baking dish that has been sprayed with nonstick cooking spray. Sprinkle with cayenne pepper. Bake, uncovered, at 350 degrees for 25 minutes or until bubbly. Serve with crackers. Yield: 4 cups.

Carmella Lee, Delta Alpha
Lexington Park, Maryland

CHICKEN WING DIP

3 (10-ounce) cans chicken, well drained
1 (12-ounce) bottle Frank's RedHot Sauce
16 ounces cream cheese, softened
1 cup ranch salad dressing
1 to 2 cups shredded Cheddar cheese (or Monterey Jack cheese)

Combine the chicken and hot sauce in a skillet over medium heat and sauté for 5 minutes. Stir in the cream cheese and salad dressing and bring to a simmer. Spoon into a greased 9×13-inch glass baking dish. Sprinkle with Cheddar cheese. Bake at 350 degrees for 45 minutes. Serve with white corn chips or crackers. Yield: 30 to 40 servings.

Judy Ann Evans, Laureate Xi
Fairmont, West Virginia

✣ MEXICAN CHICKEN SCOOPS

5 cups chopped cooked chicken
2 cups (8 ounces) shredded sharp Cheddar cheese
1 (15-ounce) can kidney beans, drained
1 large red bell pepper, chopped
1/2 cup sliced black olives
3/4 cup chopped onion
1/2 cup sour cream
1/2 cup mayonnaise
3 (4-ounce) cans chopped green chiles, drained
1 envelope taco seasoning
Large sturdy corn chips for filling

Combine the first 10 ingredients in a bowl and mix well. Fill corn chips with chicken mixture and arrange on a baking sheet. Sprinkle with additional cheese. Broil until cheese melts. Yield: 40 to 50 servings.

Jane Humphrey, Preceptor Alpha Upsilon
Ventura, Iowa

---

*Kathryn Jensen, Beta Chi, Independence, Iowa, makes **Really Good Chicken Dip** by placing a mixture of three 10-ounce cans white chicken meat, 1 can cream of chicken soup, 8 ounces softened cream cheese, and 1/2 cup diced jalapeños in a 2-quart casserole and baking at 350 degrees for 30 minutes.*

SPICY CORN DIP

2 (11-ounce) cans Mexicorn, drained
1 (10-ounce) can tomatoes with green chiles, drained
1 (4-ounce) can chopped green chiles, drained
1/2 cup chopped green onions
1 cup sour cream
1 1/2 cups mayonnaise
2 cups shredded sharp Cheddar cheese
Hot red pepper sauce to taste (optional)

Combine the Mexicorn, tomatoes with green chiles, green chiles, green onions, sour cream, mayonnaise, Cheddar cheese and hot pepper sauce in a bowl and mix well. Serve with corn chip scoops.
Yield: 6 to 8 cups.

Sherry Murphy, Xi Epsilon Pi
Fayetteville, Georgia

CORN AND WALNUT DIP

16 ounces cream cheese, softened
1/4 cup vegetable oil
1/4 cup fresh lime juice
1 tablespoon red chili powder
1 tablespoon cumin
1/2 teaspoon salt
1/4 teaspoon pepper
1 (8-ounce) can whole kernel corn, drained
1 cup chopped walnuts
1/4 cup chopped red onion

Combine the cream cheese, vegetable oil, lime juice, chili powder, cumin, salt and pepper in a bowl and mix well. Stir in the corn, walnuts and red onion. Serve with corn chips, pita chips or shredded wheat crackers. Yield: 3 to 4 cups.

Mary Alice Moring, Preceptor Tau
Alexandria, Virginia

SWEET AUTUMN HARVEST DIP

This sweet dip makes a very nice presentation when served in a small pumpkin shell. Store the dip in an airtight container in the refrigerator.

8 ounces cream cheese, softened
2 cups confectioners' sugar
2 teaspoons cinnamon
1 teaspoon ginger
1 teaspoon pumpkin pie spice
1 (15-ounce) can pumpkin

Cream the cream cheese and confectioners' sugar in a mixing bowl until light and fluffy. Add the cinnamon, ginger, pumpkin pie spice and canned pumpkin; beat until smooth. Serve with ginger snaps or apple slices as dippers. Yield: 4 cups.

Donna Goodson, Preceptor Epsilon
Hot Springs, Arkansas

BRICKLE DIP

8 ounces cream cheese, softened
1/2 cup packed brown sugar
1/4 cup granulated sugar
1 teaspoon vanilla extract
2 cups toffee chips

Cream the cream cheese, sugars and vanilla in a mixing bowl until light and fluffy. Fold in the toffee chips. Chill, covered, until serving time. Serve with dippers such as sliced apples, fresh pineapple chunks, strawberries and banana chunks. To prevent apples from browning, dip in lemon-lime soda.
Yield: 1 1/2 cups.

Patricia Shaffer, Xi Beta Upsilon
Decatur, Alabama

HAM AND CHEESE DIP

1 loaf French bread
1/2 cup sour cream
8 ounces cream cheese, softened
1/2 cup chopped green onions
1 (4-ounce) can chopped green chiles, drained
1 1/2 to 2 cups shredded Cheddar cheese
1 cup chopped deli ham

Cut a 1-inch slice from the top of the bread. Scoop out the center of the loaf to leave a 3/4-inch-thick shell. Place bread shell on a baking sheet. Combine the sour cream, cream cheese, green onions, green chiles, Cheddar cheese and ham; mix well. Spoon the ham mixture into the bread shell. Wrap tightly in foil and bake at 375 degrees for 45 minutes. Serve with corn chip scoops. Yield: 15 to 20 servings.

Leigh Pirkle, Xi Lambda Zeta
Gonzales, Texas

SPICED HOAGIE DIP

1/4 pound boiled ham
1/4 pound beef bologna
1/4 pound provolone cheese
1/4 pound American cheese
1 medium onion
2 medium-size firm tomatoes
1/4 head lettuce
1/4 cup vegetable oil
2 teaspoons dry Italian dressing mix
1/2 to 1 teaspoon salt, to taste
1/2 to 1 teaspoon oregano, to taste
1/8 teaspoon garlic powder
1/8 teaspoon pepper

Finely chop the ham, bologna, provolone cheese, American cheese, onion, tomatoes and lettuce; combine in a large bowl and mix well. Combine the vegetable oil, dry salad dressing mix, salt, oregano, garlic powder and pepper in a small bowl and blend well. Stir the oregano mixture into the ham mixture. Chill, covered, for at least 3 hours to enhance flavors.

Serve with thinly sliced Italian or French bread. Yield: 4 to 5 cups.

Doris Furlong, Laureate Zeta Mu
Jenkintown, Pennsylvania

HOT HAM DIP

16 ounces cream cheese, softened
1 cup sour cream
3 (3-ounce) packages chipped ham
2 tablespoons dried minced onion
1½ teaspoons garlic salt
1 cup chopped pecans

Combine the cream cheese, sour cream, ham, onion and garlic salt in a bowl and mix well. Spoon into a square 1½-quart baking dish. Bake, uncovered, at 350 degrees for 20 minutes. Sauté the pecans in butter in a skillet for several minutes or until toasted and fragrant. Remove the dip from the oven and top with the pecans. Serve warm with large corn chips for dipping. Yield: 4 cups.

Kay Brown, Laureate Epsilon Theta
St. Petersburg, Florida

SWEET ONION DIP

3 cups finely chopped onions
2 cups sour cream
8 ounces cream cheese, softened
2 cups grated Parmesan cheese
1 tablespoon garlic powder
1½ teaspoons chopped parsley
1 cup finely chopped artichoke hearts
Salt and pepper to taste

Combine the ingredients in a bowl and mix well. Chill, covered, for 8 to 10 hours before serving. Serve with crackers or chips. Yield: 6 cups.

Lorraine Patterson, Laureate Gamma
Spencer, Iowa

VIDALIA ONION CHEESE DIP

3 large Vidalia onions, coarsely chopped
2 tablespoons butter or margarine, melted
1 cup mayonnaise
2 cups shredded sharp Cheddar cheese
½ teaspoon hot red pepper sauce
1 garlic clove, minced

Sauté the onions in the butter in a large skillet over medium-high heat for 5 minutes or until tender. Combine the sautéed onions, mayonnaise, Cheddar cheese, hot pepper sauce and garlic in a bowl and stir well. Spoon into a greased 1½-quart baking dish. Bake, uncovered, at 375 degrees for 20 to 25 minutes or until bubbly and golden. Serve with tortilla chips or assorted crackers. Yield: 4 cups.

Jean A. Housel, Preceptor Delta Epsilon
Independence, Kansas

JALAPENO PEPPER DIP

8 ounces cream cheese, softened
8 ounces purchased jalapeño pepper dip
1 green bell pepper, chopped
1 small onion, chopped
8 ounces Cheddar cheese, shredded

Combine the cream cheese and jalapeño pepper dip in a bowl and mix well. Spread the cheese mixture evenly over a serving plate. Layer the bell pepper, onion and Cheddar cheese over the cheese layer. Serve with taco chips. Yield: 3 cups.

Jeanette Upmeyer, Laureate Beta Gamma
Clinton, Iowa

ROASTED RED PEPPER DIP

3 roasted red peppers
4 ounces light cream cheese, softened
½ cup light mayonnaise
1½ teaspoons seasoned salt
¼ cup chopped fresh parsley, or 1 tablespoon dried
1 teaspoon oregano
¾ cup crumbled feta cheese

Purée the red peppers in a blender. Combine the puréed peppers, cream cheese, mayonnaise, seasoned salt, parsley and oregano in a bowl and mix until smooth. Stir in the feta cheese. Serve with raw vegetables, crackers or chips. Yield: 4 cups.

Rebecca Mossing, Xi Beta
Regina, Saskatchewan, Canada

SALSA

2 (15-ounce) cans diced tomatoes with garlic and onion
2 (15-ounce) cans black beans, rinsed and drained
1 (15-ounce) can yellow corn, drained
1 green bell pepper, chopped
1 red bell pepper, chopped
1 large bunch cilantro, chopped
2 jalapeño peppers, chopped
2 garlic cloves, minced
1 teaspoon cayenne pepper
2 teaspoons cumin
¼ cup olive oil
½ cup lime juice
1 red onion, chopped

Combine the tomatoes, black beans, corn, bell peppers, cilantro, jalapeño peppers, garlic, cayenne pepper, cumin, olive oil, lime juice and onion in a bowl and mix well. Chill, covered, until serving time. Yield: 8 cups.

Janet Munson, Epsilon Alpha
Canton, Illinois

HOT CRAB JALAPENO DIP

1 pound imitation lump crab meat
1 teaspoon chopped garlic
1/2 cup chopped pickled jalapeño peppers
4 ounces Monterey Jack cheese with jalapeños, shredded
1 teaspoon Worcestershire sauce
1 teaspoon hot red pepper sauce
1/2 teaspoon salt
1/2 cup mayonnaise
2 ounces Parmigiano-Reggiano, grated
Toasted Croutons

Combine the crab meat, garlic, jalapeños, Monterey Jack cheese, Worcestershire sauce, hot pepper sauce, salt and mayonnaise in a medium bowl; toss gently to mix. Spoon the crab mixture into a medium rectangular baking dish. Sprinkle the Parmigiano-Reggiano evenly over the top. Bake, uncovered, at 350 degrees for 25 minutes or until golden brown and bubbly. Remove from oven and let stand for 5 minutes. Serve with Toasted Croutons. Yield: 20 servings.

TOASTED CROUTONS

1 loaf French bread, ends trimmed
10 tablespoons olive oil
1/2 teaspoon salt
1/2 teaspoon freshly ground pepper

Cut the bread crosswise into 1/4-inch slices. Arrange the bread slices on a baking sheet that has been lined with parchment paper. Brush the bread slices with half the olive oil and sprinkle with half the salt and pepper. Turn the slices over and brush with the remaining olive oil and sprinkle with the remaining salt and pepper. Bake at 400 degrees for 6 minutes, turning the baking sheet to ensure even browning. Turn the bread slices. Bake for 6 minutes longer or until lightly browned. Remove from oven and let cool completely before serving with the dip.

LouAnn Rochford, Xi Alpha Sigma
No. Platte, Nebraska

HOT SEAFOOD DIP

This slow-cooker recipe may also be prepared in the microwave.

8 ounces cream cheese, softened
1 (10-ounce) can cream of shrimp soup
1 to 2 teaspoons Worcestershire sauce
1 teaspoon minced garlic
1 (4-ounce) can tiny shrimp, drained
1 (6-ounce) can crab meat, drained
Green onions or chives to taste

Combine the cream cheese and cream of shrimp soup in a small slow cooker. Heat on Low for 2 hours. Stir in the Worcestershire sauce, garlic, shrimp, crab meat and green onions. Keep hot in the slow cooker. Serve with homemade bread, crackers or corn chips. Yield: 12 to 14 servings.

Phyllis G. Moore, Xi Delta Tau
Jonesboro, Louisiana

ZESTY TOMATO DIP

2 (4-ounce) cans chopped black olives, drained
6 green onions, thinly sliced
2 (15-ounce) cans diced tomatoes
2 (4-ounce) cans chopped green chiles, drained
6 tablespoons olive oil
3 tablespoons white vinegar
1 tablespoon garlic salt

Combine the ingredients in a bowl and mix well. Chill, covered, for at least 2 hours before serving. Serve with scooping chips. Yield: 20 to 24 servings.

Sharon Palmer, Gamma Delta
Oskaloosa, Iowa

SUN-DRIED TOMATO HUMMUS

1 (15-ounce) can chick-peas, drained
6 or 7 slices soft sun-dried tomatoes, chopped
6 tablespoons olive oil
4 tablespoons lemon juice
1 or 2 garlic cloves
Salt and pepper to taste

Combine the chick-peas, sun-dried tomatoes, olive oil, lemon juice, 4 tablespoons water and garlic in a food processor or blender; process until smooth. Adjust seasonings to taste; increase amounts of oil, water and lemon juice for a softer texture. Serve with pita bread or chips. Yield: 6 servings.

Carol Rott, Preceptor Beta Omicron
Oshawa, Ontario, Canada

EGGPLANT ANTIPASTO

3 cups cubed peeled eggplant
1/3 cup chopped green bell pepper
1/2 cup green olives, halved
1 medium onion, chopped
3/4 cup (4 ounces) mushrooms, chopped
1 teaspoon minced garlic
1/3 cup vegetables oil
1 (6-ounce) can tomato paste
2 tablespoons wine vinegar
1 1/2 tablespoons sugar
1/4 teaspoon basil or oregano
1 teaspoon salt
1/8 teaspoon black pepper

Sauté the eggplant, bell pepper, olives, onion, mushrooms and garlic in hot vegetable oil in a skillet over medium-low heat for 10 minutes or until tender. Add the tomato paste, 1/4 cup water, vinegar, sugar, basil, salt and pepper; cook for 30 minutes longer, stirring frequently. Chill, covered, for 8 to 10 hours. May be frozen for future use. Serve with crackers or chips. Yield: 3 to 4 cups.

Christine Page, Preceptor Beta Sigma
Niagara Falls, New York

CARROT DIP

1/2 cup sour cream
4 ounces cream cheese, softened
1/4 cup mayonnaise
2 teaspoons soy sauce
1 1/2 teaspoons prepared horseradish
1/4 teaspoon salt
1/4 teaspoon freshly ground pepper
1 1/2 cups finely shredded carrots
1/3 cup chopped green onions

Combine the sour cream, cream cheese, mayonnaise, soy sauce, horseradish, salt and pepper in a mixing bowl; beat at medium speed until smooth. Stir in the carrots and green onions. Chill, covered, for at least 4 hours and no longer than 24 hours before serving. Stir and serve. Yield: 10 servings.

Nancy Wheaton, Xi Beta Xi
Paris, Missouri

HOT BROCCOLI CHEESE DIP

1 (10-ounce) package frozen chopped broccoli, thawed and drained
8 ounces cream cheese, softened
1 cup sour cream
1 envelope Italian salad dressing mix
1/2 cup minced onion
8 ounces Cheddar cheese, shredded

Chop the broccoli very fine. Combine the cream cheese, sour cream and dry salad dressing mix in a mixing bowl; beat at medium speed until smooth. Stir in the broccoli, onion and 3/4 of the Cheddar cheese. Spoon into an 8x8-inch baking dish. Bake, uncovered, at 350 degrees for 20 minutes. Sprinkle with the remaining Cheddar cheese and bake for 5 minutes longer. Yield: 6 to 8 servings.

Molly Todd, Xi Eta Xi
Merritt Island, Florida

SPINACH GOUDA DIP

1/2 cup mayonnaise or mayonnaise-type salad dressing
6 ounces ultra-light cream cheese, softened
1 tablespoon lemon juice
1 teaspoon minced garlic
Pinch of pepper
1/2 cup shredded Gouda cheese
1/4 cup canned chunky sun-dried tomatoes
1/4 cup (thawed and drained) frozen chopped spinach
4 or more pita bread rounds

Combine the mayonnaise, cream cheese, lemon juice, garlic, pepper, Gouda cheese, sun-dried tomatoes and spinach in a bowl and mix well. Spoon the spinach mixture into a pie plate. Bake at 350 degrees for 25 minutes. Cut each pita bread round into 8 wedges and lay them flat on a baking sheet. Bake at 400 degrees for 10 minutes, watching carefully to make sure they don't burn. Serve with the warm dip. Yield: 4 to 6 servings.

Krista Bouchard, Beta Zeta
Strathmore, Alberta, Canada

ASPARAGUS GUACAMOLE

4 cups (1 pound) fresh asparagus, trimmed and cut up
2 teaspoons fresh lime juice
1 (4-ounce) can chopped green chiles
1 garlic clove, minced
1/2 teaspoon salt
1/2 teaspoon cumin
2 tablespoons finely chopped onion
1/2 cup chopped seeded tomato

Cook the asparagus in a small amount of salted water in a saucepan over medium heat for 10 minutes or until tender. Drain well and let stand until cool. Combine the asparagus, lime juice, green chiles, garlic, salt and cumin in a food processor; process until smooth. Stir in the onion and tomato. Chill, covered, for at least 3 hours. Serve with tortilla chips or raw vegetables. Yield: 4 to 8 servings.

Beverly Coverley, Lambda Master
Reno, Nevada

AUTHENTIC MEXICAN GUACAMOLE

Do not substitute lemons for the limes. Avocados turn dark when exposed to air, so be sure to peel the avocados after all other ingredients are in the blender.

Juice of 2 limes
1 or 2 garlic cloves, minced
Tabasco sauce to taste
1/4 cup sour cream
1 tablespoon finely chopped scallion or white onion
Salt to taste
2 ripe avocados

Combine the first 6 ingredients in a blender. Peel the avocados, cut into chunks and place in the blender last. Blend immediately until very smooth. Taste to check the flavors of avocado, garlic, lime and salt; add more of whatever ingredient is needed. The garlic flavor will grow stronger as guacamole stands. Spoon the guacamole into a bowl. Cover the guacamole surface with plastic wrap; use another sheet of plastic wrap to cover the entire bowl. Chill until serving time. Serve with tortilla chips. Yield: 8 to 10 servings.

Diana Hunt, Xi Delta Alpha
Hamilton, Ontario, Canada

KENTUCKY CAVIAR

1 (15-ounce) can black-eyed peas, rinsed and drained
1 (11-ounce) can Shoe Peg corn, drained
1 (11-ounce) can tomatoes with green chiles, drained
1 green bell pepper, chopped
1 small onion, chopped
1 (8-ounce) bottle Italian salad dressing
1 teaspoon minced garlic
Salt and pepper to taste

Combine the black-eyed peas, Shoe Peg corn, tomatoes with green chiles, bell pepper, onion, salad dressing, garlic, salt and pepper; mix well. Serve with tortilla chips. Yield: 5 to 6 cups.

Norma Ferrell, Xi Alpha Omega
Paducah, Kentucky

TEXAS SALSA

1 (15-ounce) can black-eyed peas, rinsed and drained
3/4 cup each chopped red and green bell peppers
3 green onions, chopped, or 1/2 red onion, chopped
1/4 cup minced fresh parsley, or 1 tablespoon dried
1 medium onion, chopped
1 (2-ounce) jar chopped pimentos, drained
1 garlic clove, minced, or 1/2 teaspoon canned minced garlic
1 (8-ounce) bottle fat-free Italian salad dressing
1 (12-ounce) package tortilla chip scoops

Mix the black-eyed peas, bell peppers, green onions, parsley, onion, pimentos, garlic and Italian dressing in a large bowl. Chill, covered, for 24 hours. Spoon the salsa into tortilla scoops. Yield: 4 cups.

Dixie Elmes, Laureate Omicron
Westminster, Maryland

FRUIT SALSA AND CHIPS

4 (or more) flour tortillas to make chips
3/4 teaspoon cinnamon
1 tablespoon sugar
2 cups strawberries, hulled and chopped
1 banana, chopped
1 apple, peeled and chopped
1 kiwifruit, peeled and chopped
1/4 cup fresh lemon juice
1/4 cup sugar
1/4 teaspoon nutmeg
1/2 teaspoon cinnamon

Cut each tortilla into 8 wedges and arrange on a baking sheet. Spray the wedges with nonstick cooking spray and sprinkle with a mixture of the 3/4 teaspoon cinnamon and the 1 tablespoon sugar. Bake at 350 degrees for several minutes or until lightly browned. Place the strawberries, banana, apple and kiwifruit in a bowl with a mixture of the lemon juice, the 1/4 cup sugar, nutmeg and the 1/2 teaspoon cinnamon; toss lightly to combine. Serve with the cinnamon chips. Yield: 3 to 4 cups.

Lara Thompson, Alpha Kappa
Hot Springs, Arkansas

BLACK BEAN AND CORN SALSA

1 (15-ounce) can black beans, rinsed and drained
1 (15-ounce) can yellow corn, rinsed and drained
1 small red bell pepper, chopped
1/2 small purple onion, chopped
1/4 cup lime juice
3 tablespoons olive oil
1 garlic clove, minced
1 tablespoon roasted red pepper flakes

Place the black beans, corn, bell pepper and onion in a large bowl and toss gently to combine. Add the remaining ingredients; toss gently to coat. Serve with tortilla chips. Yield: 8 to 10 servings.

Michelle Jilek, Theta Rho
Hendersonville, Tennessee

PEACH SALSA

The peaches and cilantro give this salsa an amazingly fresh taste. Be careful when working with jalapeños; wear rubber gloves.

1 (16-ounce) can peaches, drained and chopped
6 to 9 Roma tomatoes, seeded and chopped
2 to 3 jalapeños, seeded and chopped
2 tablespoons chopped fresh cilantro
3 green onions, chopped
1 1/2 tablespoons vegetable oil
Juice of 2 small limes
1 tablespoon honey

Combine the peaches, tomatoes, jalapeños, cilantro, green onions, vegetable oil, lime juice and honey in a 1-quart bowl. Serve with tortilla chips. Yield: 4 cups.

Christi Bentley, Preceptor Beta Pi
Marshall, Missouri

BREAD BASKET PUMPKIN DIP

1 (8-inch) round loaf of bread
3 cups (12 ounces) shredded sharp Cheddar cheese
8 ounces cream cheese, softened
1 cup sour cream
3/4 cup canned pumpkin
1/2 cup sliced green onions
1/2 cup chopped parsley
1 (3-ounce) package sliced smoked beef, chopped
1 tablespoon Worcestershire sauce
Raw vegetable dippers

Cut a 1-inch slice from the top of the bread. Scoop out the center of the loaf to leave a 1/2-inch-thick shell.

Cut the scooped-out bread into cubes. Combine the Cheddar cheese, cream cheese and sour cream in a bowl and blend well. Add the pumpkin, green onions, parsley, smoked beef and Worcestershire sauce; mix well. Spoon the beef mixture into the hollow bread loaf. Wrap in foil and place on a baking sheet. Bake at 300 degrees for 2 hours. Serve with bread cubes and vegetable dippers. Yield: 5 cups.

Christina Davis, Preceptor Xi
Baxter Springs, Kansas

BRAUNSCHWEIGER BALL

8 ounces cream cheese, softened
1 tablespoon mayonnaise
Garlic salt (optional)
1 pound braunschweiger, cubed
1/2 cup chili sauce
2 teaspoons horseradish
5 or 6 dashes of Tabasco sauce

Combine the cream cheese, mayonnaise and garlic salt in a small bowl and whisk until smooth; chill, covered, until ready to use. Combine the braunschweiger cubes, chili sauce, horseradish and Tabasco sauce in a large mixing bowl and beat at medium speed until well mixed. Place on a sheet of foil or plastic wrap and shape into a ball with a small spatula. Chill, wrapped tightly, for about 2 hours. Remove ball from refrigerator and unwrap. Lay 2 or 3 waxed paper strips on a plate to keep the plate clean. Place the braunschweiger ball over the waxed paper and frost with the cream cheese mixture. Remove the waxed paper strips. Decorate with sliced stuffed green olives and finely chopped parsley if desired. Serve with assorted crackers.
Yield: 15 to 24 servings.

Zita Lomax, Laureate Omega
Beatrice, Nebraska

CHILI CHEESE BALLS

3 cups (12 ounces) shredded Monterey Jack cheese
1 cup (4 ounces) shredded fontina cheese
3 ounces cream cheese, softened
3 to 4 tablespoons prepared mustard
1 teaspoon Worcestershire sauce
1/2 teaspoon garlic powder
11/2 tablespoons chili powder

Combine the Monterey Jack cheese, fontina cheese, cream cheese, mustard, Worcestershire sauce and garlic powder in a bowl; mix well. Shape into 1-inch balls. Sprinkle the chili powder in a large bowl. Drop the cheese balls in the bowl and toss gently to coat with chili powder. Chill, covered, for at least 1 hour.
Yield: 31/2 dozen.

Shirley Goen, Delta Tau
Milner, Georgia

CHOCOLATE CHIP CHEESE BALL

Be sure to use real butter.

8 ounces cream cheese, softened
1/2 cup (1 stick) butter, softened
1/4 teaspoon vanilla extract
3/4 cup confectioners' sugar
2 tablespoons brown sugar
1 cup miniature chocolate chips
Chocolate graham crackers

Cream the cream cheese, butter, vanilla, confectioners' sugar and brown sugar in a mixing bowl until light and fluffy. Stir in 3/4 cup of the chocolate chips. Chill, covered, for 2 hours. Remove mixture from refrigerator and use plastic wrap to shape into a ball. Chill, wrapped in plastic wrap, for 8 to 10 hours. Just before serving, roll in the remaining 1/4 cup chocolate chips. Serve with chocolate graham crackers.
Yield: 15 to 20 servings.

Donna Barker, Xi Alpha Epsilon
Jeffersonville, Indiana

HOLIDAY BLEU CHEESE BALL

24 ounces cream cheese, softened
1/3 cup (or more, to taste) crumbled bleu cheese
1/3 cup minced onion
2 tablespoons Worcestershire sauce
1 tablespoon garlic powder
1 green bell pepper, diced
1 (4-ounce) can chopped pimentos, drained
2 cups chopped pecans

Combine the first 7 ingredients in a bowl; mix well. Shape into a ball or a log. Spread the pecans over a sheet of waxed paper. Roll the ball in the pecans to coat well. Wrap in plastic wrap. Chill for 8 to 10 hours. Serve with assorted crackers.
Yield: 25 to 30 servings.

Donna Myers, Xi Eta Kappa
Sterling, Kansas

---

*For her **Pumpkin Dip**, Karen Toth, Preceptor Zeta Zeta, Largo, Florida, combines 2 cups confectioners' sugar, 8 ounces softened cream cheese, 1 can of pumpkin, 1 teaspoon cinnamon, and 1/2 teaspoon ginger. Fold 4 ounces whipped topping into the mixture. Chill. Serve with gingersnaps and vanilla wafers.*

FRUIT CHEESE BALL

16 ounces cream cheese, softened
1 cup confectioners' sugar
1/2 cup candied pineapple
1/2 cup white raisins
1/2 cup chopped pecans
1/4 cup red candied cherries
1/4 cup green candied cherries
1/2 cup shredded coconut

Cream the cream cheese and confectioners' sugar in a mixing bowl until light and fluffy. Stir in the candied pineapple, raisins, pecans and red and green candied cherries. Shape into a ball and roll in the coconut to coat. Decorate with fruit pieces if desired. Chill in a sealed plastic bowl until serving time, or freeze for up to 3 months. Serve with crackers. Yield: 15 to 20 servings.

Louise Sledge, Delta Omicron
Lexington, South Carolina

SALMON BALL

1 (15-ounce) can red salmon, drained, bones removed
8 ounces cream cheese, softened
2 teaspoons grated onion
1 teaspoon horseradish
1 tablespoon lemon juice
1/4 teaspoon salt
3/4 cup finely chopped pecans
1/4 cup chopped fresh parsley

Combine the salmon, cream cheese, onion, horseradish, lemon juice and salt in a mixing bowl and beat at low speed until smooth. Wrap in plastic wrap and shape into a ball. Chill until very cold. Roll in pecans and parsley. Yield: 25 to 30 servings.

Mildred Sharp, Kappa Master
McClave, Colorado

SHRIMP MOLD

1 (10-ounce) can tomato soup
1 envelope unflavored gelatin, softened in 1/4 cup cold water
8 ounces cream cheese, softened
3/4 cup chopped onion
3/4 cup chopped celery
1 cup mayonnaise
2 (4-ounce) cans tiny shrimp (do not use fresh shrimp)
Salt and pepper to taste

Heat the soup in a medium saucepan over medium-high heat. Stir in the softened gelatin. Stir in the cream cheese, onion, celery and mayonnaise; stir in the shrimp last. Remove from heat. Season shrimp mixture to taste and pour into a greased bundt pan. Chill, covered, for 5 or more hours until firm. Serve with crackers. Yield: 25 to 30 servings.

Debbie Ducar, Alpha Zeta Theta
O'Fallon, Missouri

CURRIED CHICKEN LOG

To make 1 log, simply halve all ingredients.

16 ounces cream cheese, softened
1 tablespoon steak sauce
1/2 teaspoon curry powder
1/3 cup minced celery
1 (12-ounce) can chicken, or 1 1/2 cups shredded cooked chicken
1/4 cup slivered almonds
1/4 cup chopped parsley

Combine the cream cheese, steak sauce, curry powder, celery and chicken in a bowl and mix well. Shape into 2 logs. Wrap in plastic wrap and chill until firm. Roll the logs in almonds and parsley and serve with crackers. Yield: 2 logs.

Anna Hoge, Xi Zeta Epsilon
Kalamazoo, Michigan

SALMON MOUSSE

Use freshly poached salmon or canned salmon with bones and skin removed for this elegant, light mousse.

1 envelope unflavored gelatin
1/2 cup mayonnaise
2 tablespoons lemon juice
1 tablespoon grated onion
Dash of Tabasco sauce
1/2 teaspoon paprika
1 teaspoon salt
3 tablespoons finely chopped fresh dill weed
2 cups finely flaked salmon
1 cup whipping cream

Soften the gelatin in 1/4 cup cold water in a large bowl. Stir in 1/2 cup boiling water and whisk to dissolve. Cool to room temperature. Add the mayonnaise, lemon juice, onion, Tabasco sauce, paprika, salt and dill weed; whisk until smooth. Chill for 30 minutes or until mixture begins to thicken. Fold in the salmon. Whip the cream until soft peaks form. Fold into the salmon mixture. Spoon into a 6- or 8-cup decorative serving bowl. Chill, covered, for 4 to 10 hours. Serve with crackers or bread. Yield: 12 servings.

Charlotte Grarley, Laureate Alpha Gamma
Bella Vista, Arizona

SHRIMP MOUSSE

1 (10-ounce) can tomato soup
8 ounces cream cheese, softened
2 (6-ounce) cans shrimp, drained
1/2 cup finely chopped green bell pepper
1/2 cup minced celery
1 small onion, finely chopped
Salt and pepper to taste
1 envelope unflavored gelatin
1 cup mayonnaise or sour cream

Combine the soup and cream cheese in a saucepan over medium-low heat and heat until cream cheese is melted, stirring frequently. Stir in the shrimp, bell pepper, celery, onion, salt, pepper and gelatin. Remove from heat and cool slightly. Stir in the mayonnaise. Pour into a 4-cup mold. Chill, covered, for 8 to 10 hours. Serve with crackers.
Yield: 6 to 8 servings.

Elizabeth Ward, Laureate Beta Sigma
Sun City Center, Florida

BEEF AND VEAL PATE

2 eggs, slightly beaten
1 pound ground beef
1 pound ground veal
1 small onion, grated
1/2 teaspoon marjoram
1/4 teaspoon pepper
1/2 teaspoon salt
2 tablespoons flour
2 (10-ounce) cans beef broth
1 (2-crust) pie pastry
1 (16-ounce) jar sliced dill pickles
1 envelope unflavored gelatin

Measure 2 tablespoons of the beaten eggs into a cup and set aside to use as an egg wash. Combine the remaining eggs, ground beef, ground veal, onion, marjoram, pepper, salt, flour and 1/2 cup of the beef broth in a large bowl; mix well. Roll 2/3 of the pastry into a 10×15-inch rectangle on a lightly floured surface; fit into a 5×9-inch loaf pan. Spoon 1/3 of the beef mixture into an even layer in the bottom of the pan. Make a single layer of pickle slices over the beef layer. Repeat the layers and cover with the remaining beef mixture. Fold the pastry edges toward the center. Roll the remaining pastry into a rectangle; trim ends to make a 9×5-inch rectangle. Make 4 slits in the pastry to allow steam to escape. Fit the pastry over the meat loaf and pinch edges to seal. Brush with egg wash. Bake at 350 degrees for 1 hour and 45 minutes or until golden. Remove to a wire rack to cool. Soften the gelatin in 1/2 cup of the beef broth in a small saucepan. Heat over low heat to dissolve, stirring constantly. Stir in the remaining beef broth. Press a skewer or a thin knife through the slits in the top pastry, pushing carefully just to the bottom of the meat. Spoon in just enough gelatin mixture to fill the holes and let stand until gelatin mixture soaks into the meat. Repeat 2 or 3 more times with remaining gelatin mixture until no more will soak into meat. Chill, covered, for 3 to 10 hours. At serving time, loosen the edges with a knife and invert onto a serving plate. Cut in thick slices with a sharp knife.
Yield: 10 to 12 servings.

Nancy Parker, Lambda Master
North Bay, Ontario, Canada

SMOKED SALMON PATE

8 ounces cream cheese, softened
1 (15-ounce) can red salmon, drained, skin and bones removed
1 tablespoon grated onion
1 tablespoon prepared horseradish
1 tablespoon lemon juice
2 or 3 drops of liquid smoke
1/2 cup chopped fresh parsley
1/2 cup chopped pecans or almonds

Place the cream cheese in a large mixing bowl and beat at medium speed until creamy. Add the next 5 ingredients and mix well. Cover with plastic wrap and chill until firm. Combine the parsley and pecans on waxed paper. Shape the salmon mixture into 2 logs. Roll each log in parsley mixture. Serve with crackers, or wrap and freeze. Yield: 16 to 18 servings.

Rhoda Burkett, Alpha Xi Master
Delta, British Columbia, Canada

ARTICHOKE SPREAD

1 (14-ounce) can artichokes, drained and chopped
1/2 (8-ounce) jar roasted red peppers, drained, finely chopped
1/2 cup mayonnaise
2/3 cup grated Parmesan cheese
2 green onions, finely chopped
2 garlic cloves, minced

Combine the artichokes, red peppers, mayonnaise, Parmesan cheese, green onions and garlic in a bowl and mix well. Chill, covered, until baking time. Spoon into a 6- to 8-inch baking dish. Bake at 350 degrees for 10 to 12 minutes or until bubbly. Serve with crackers or bread. Yield: 20 to 24 servings.

Dorothy M. James, Laureate Alpha Zeta
Trenton, Ontario, Canada

CRAB SPREAD

8 ounces cream cheese, softened
1/2 cup sour cream
1/2 cup prepared horseradish sauce
1 1/2 teaspoons Worcestershire sauce
1/2 teaspoon Tabasco sauce
1/2 teaspoon dry mustard
4 ounces Cheddar, Swiss (or other) cheese, shredded
1/2 pound crab meat, shredded
1/2 cup chopped green onions

Combine the ingredients in a bowl and mix well. Chill, covered, for at least 2 hours. Serve with crackers or toasted bread squares. Yield: 3 to 4 cups.

Jill Walworth, Nu Epsilon
New Port Richey, Florida

HERB-MARINATED FETA AND OLIVES

1 tablespoon whole cumin seeds
2 teaspoons whole coriander seeds
1 teaspoon crushed red pepper
2 garlic cloves, minced
2 teaspoons grated orange zest
1 1/2 cups extra-virgin olive oil
10 ounces assorted brine-cured green and black olives
3 tablespoons minced fresh basil
2 tablespoons minced fresh cilantro
8 ounces feta cheese, cut into 1/2-inch cubes
1 baguette, sliced

Combine the first 3 ingredients in a small heavy skillet over medium-high heat. Cook for about 1 minute or until spices are fragrant, shaking the skillet gently. Remove from heat and place the spices in a medium bowl. Add the garlic, orange zest and olive oil; stir to combine. Mix in the olives, basil and cilantro. Stir in the feta gently. Chill, covered, for at least 24 hours and up to 1 week. Bring feta mixture to room temperature before serving. Place in a bowl on a platter. Surround with baguette slices and serve.
Yield: 6 servings.

Charlene Samsel, Xi Theta Eta
Nescopeck, Pennsylvania

SUN-DRIED TOMATO PATE

2 cups drained sun-dried tomatoes in oil
1/2 cup olive oil or oil drained from sun-dried tomatoes
1 cup grated Parmesan cheese
1/2 cup each packed fresh basil and parsley leaves
Garlic cloves to taste, crushed
Freshly ground pepper to taste

Combine the sun-dried tomatoes, olive oil, Parmesan cheese, basil, parsley, garlic and pepper in a food processor container and process until a thick paste is formed. Chill, covered, until serving time, for up to 1 month. Invert onto a platter and surround with thinly sliced Tuscan bread or baguettes, or cracked pepper crackers. Yield: 2 cups.

Joanne B. Derrico, Eta Master
Avondale Estates, Georgia

Carol Fielder, Laureate Kappa, Beatrice, Nebraska, makes ***Ham and Cheese Spread*** *by mixing 8 ounces softened cream cheese, 1 cup sour cream and 1/4 teaspoon garlic powder in a bowl. Stir in 5 ounces chopped deli ham and 2 to 3 thinly sliced green onions and spread on miniature bagels.*

✣ BASIL CHEESE TERRINE

16 ounces cream cheese, softened
4 ounces bleu cheese, crumbled
1 cup loosely packed spinach leaves
3/4 cup loosely packed Italian parsley
2 garlic cloves, minced
1/4 teaspoon salt
2 tablespoons olive oil
1/4 cup chopped pine nuts
1 cup freshly grated Parmesan cheese
1/2 cup drained sliced sun-dried tomatoes in oil

Process the cream cheese and bleu cheese in a food processor container until smooth. Spoon into a small bowl and set aside. Pulse the spinach and parsley with the garlic and salt in the food processor until evenly chopped. Add the olive oil in a fine stream, processing constantly until smooth. Spoon the spinach mixture into a bowl and stir in the pine nuts and Parmesan cheese. Line a 3×7-inch loaf pan with plastic wrap, allowing edges to hang over the outside of the pan. Spread half the cheese mixture in the pan. Layer half the sun-dried tomatoes over the cheese mixture. Layer the spinach mixture, the remaining sun-dried tomatoes and the remaining cheese mixture over the first layer of sun-dried tomatoes. Chill, covered with plastic wrap, for 24 hours. Let stand at room temperature for 30 minutes before serving and invert onto a serving platter. Garnish with fresh basil sprigs and cherry tomato wedges. Serve with crackers and breadsticks. Yield: 16 servings.

Catherine Ariemma, Beta Phi
Dahlonega, Georgia

CRANBERRY APRICOT SPREAD

1 cup sugar
1 (12-ounce) package fresh or frozen cranberries
1/2 cup apricot preserves
2 tablespoons lemon juice
1/3 cup slivered almonds, toasted
8 ounces cream cheese
Assorted crackers

Combine the sugar and 1 cup water in a saucepan over medium heat and bring to a boil without stirring; boil for 5 minutes. Add the cranberries and cook for about 10 minutes or until berries pop and sauce is thickened, stirring frequently. Remove from heat. Cut the apricots in the preserves into smaller pieces and add preserves to the cranberry mixture. Stir in the lemon juice. Let stand until cool. Stir in the almonds. Spoon the cranberry mixture over the block of cream cheese and serve with crackers. Store leftovers in the refrigerator. Yield: 3 cups.

Marlene Graves, Xi Delta Omicron
Muscatine, Iowa

CANDIED WALNUTS

1 cup sugar
1 rounded teaspoon cinnamon
2 tablespoons hot coffee
1 1/2 cups walnut halves

Combine the sugar, cinnamon and coffee in a small saucepan over medium-high heat and bring to a boil, stirring constantly. Remove from heat. Add the walnuts immediately, stirring to coat. Spread over waxed paper on a hard surface. Separate with a fork and let cool completely. Store in an airtight container. Yield: 1 1/2 cups.

Margaret Ellen Wallman, Preceptor Kappa Epsilon
Santa Rosa, California

GLAZED PECANS

2 egg whites
1/2 cup sugar
1/2 teaspoon cinnamon
1/4 teaspoon salt
1/4 teaspoon ground cloves
1 pound shelled pecans

Combine the egg whites and 2 teaspoons water in a mixing bowl and beat until frothy. Combine the sugar, cinnamon, salt and cloves in a separate bowl and blend. Add the cinnamon mixture to the egg whites and mix well. Add the pecans and stir to coat. Spread evenly over a baking sheet that has been lined with greased foil. Bake at 250 degrees for 1 hour and 15 minutes, stirring every 15 minutes. Cool. Store in an airtight container. Yield: 1 pound.

Tricia Roberts, Xi Kappa
Tulsa, Oklahoma

ALMOND BARK POPCORN

2 bags microwave popcorn, popped
1/2 (14-ounce) package each plain and peanut "M & M's" Chocolate Candies
1/2 to 1 cup raisins (optional)
1/2 to 1 cup pretzels (optional)
1/2 (12-ounce) package almond bark

Remove the seeds and "old maids" from the popcorn and discard. Mix with the "M & M's," raisins and pretzels in a large bowl. Melt the almond bark in a microwave oven. Drizzle over the popcorn mixture and stir. Spread on a waxed paper-lined baking sheet. Cool and break into pieces. Store in an airtight container. Yield: 20 to 24 servings.

Linda Thilges, Xi Eta Pi
West Bend, Iowa

BAKED CARAMEL CORN

1/2 cup butter or margarine
1 cup packed brown sugar
1/4 cup corn syrup
1/2 teaspoon salt
1/4 teaspoon baking soda
1/2 teaspoon vanilla extract
3 quarts popped popcorn

Melt the butter in a saucepan over medium heat; stir in the next 3 ingredients. Boil for 5 minutes, stirring constantly. Remove from heat. Stir in the baking soda and vanilla. Drizzle over the popcorn and stir to combine. Spread on a baking sheet. Bake at 300 degrees for 30 minutes, stirring at 15-minute intervals. Cool on the baking sheet. Break into pieces and store in an airtight container. Yield: 10 to 12 servings.

Judy Knight, Epsilon Alpha
Mesquite, Texas

MICROWAVE CARAMEL CORN

1/2 cup (1 stick) margarine
1 cup packed brown sugar
1/4 cup light corn syrup
1/2 teaspoon salt
1/2 teaspoon baking soda
4 quarts popped popcorn

Combine the margarine, brown sugar, corn syrup and salt in a microwave-safe bowl. Microwave on High for 2 minutes without stirring. Microwave on High for 2 minutes longer, stirring frequently. Add the baking soda and stir until foamy. Place the popcorn in a brown paper bag and add the brown sugar mixture. Fold down the top of the bag and microwave on High for 1 1/2 minutes. Remove bag from microwave oven and shake. Microwave for 1 1/2 minutes longer. Shake bag. Spread popcorn mixture evenly over a baking sheet. Cool. Yield: 4 to 6 servings.

Linda P. Tutwiler, Xi Gamma Nu
Alva, Oklahoma

FRUITED CHOCOLATE SNACK MIX

1 (9-ounce) package pretzel sticks
1 (16-ounce) package "M & M's" Chocolate Candies
24 ounces cocktail peanuts
6 ounces goldfish crackers
3 cups dried banana slices
1 (12-ounce) package Crispix
2 cups raisins
6 ounces craisins
6 ounces dried pineapple chunks

Combine the ingredients in a brown paper bag and fold down the top of the bag. Shake the bag from side to side and upside down to mix contents. Serve in several large bowls. Yield: 38 cups.

Dori Shackelford, Preceptor Sigma
Edgerton, Ohio

ALMOND BARK SNACK MIX

3 bags popped microwave popcorn
3 cups frosted toasted oats cereal
1 cup chopped pecans
1 (15-ounce) bag pretzels
2 (12-ounce) packages almond bark
3 tablespoons vegetable oil

Mix the popcorn, cereal, pecans and pretzels in a large pan such as a roasting pan. Combine the almond bark and vegetable oil in a large glass bowl. Microwave on High until melted, stirring once a minute. Pour the almond bark mixture over the popcorn mixture, stirring to coat. Spread on waxed paper to dry. Yield: 20 to 30 servings.

Barbara Wilson, Laureate Beta Xi
Dodge City, Kansas

SAVORY OYSTER CRACKERS

3/4 cup vegetable oil
1 envelope original ranch salad dressing mix
1/4 teaspoon lemon pepper
1/2 teaspoon dill weed
1/4 teaspoon garlic powder
12 to 16 ounces plain oyster crackers

Combine the vegetable oil, dry salad dressing mix, lemon pepper, dill weed and garlic powder in a bowl and whisk to blend. Pour over the oyster crackers in a large bowl; stir to coat. Spread over a baking sheet. Bake at 275 degrees for 15 to 20 minutes or until beginning to brown. Yield: 11 to 12 cups.

Barbara Selman, Xi Alpha Epsilon Pi
Houston, Texas

PUPPY CHOW

2 to 2 2/3 cups chocolate chips
1 1/2 cups peanut butter
1/2 cup (1 stick) margarine
1 (12-ounce) package Crispix
1 (1-pound) package confectioners' sugar

Melt the chocolate chips, peanut butter and margarine in the top of a double boiler over simmering water. Layer the Crispix, chocolate chip mixture and half the confectioners' sugar 1/4 at a time in a very large sealable bowl. Seal the bowl and shake vigorously. Add the remaining confectioners' sugar 1/2 cup at a time, shaking until all chocolate cereal is coated to look like puppy chow. Yield: 2 quarts.

Lorena Wilson, Xi Kappa Tau
Hardin, Missouri

BRANDY SLUSH

The grapefruit-flavor soda I use is called "Wink."

2 cups sugar
4 tea bags
1 (12-ounce) can frozen lemonade concentrate, thawed
2 cups (or more) brandy
Grapefuit-flavor soda

Combine the sugar and 7 cups of water in a saucepan over medium-high heat; bring to a boil. Remove from heat and let stand until cool. Steep the tea bags in 2 cups hot water; let stand until cool. Remove the tea bags and stir the tea into the sugar mixture. Stir in the lemonade and brandy and freeze. Serve as a slush with grapefruit-flavor soda poured over the slush.

Judy Ramer, Xi Beta Xi
North Little Rock, Arkansas

WATERMELON MIX

The mix may also be used to make Jello Shots. Dissolve a 3-ounce package of orange gelatin in 1 cup boiling water. Add 1 cup Watermelon Mix and fill disposable 1-ounce shot glasses. Chill until set. Jello Shots are served at mile marker 677 on the annual Missouri River Poker Run, making this poker stop one of the best.

4 1/4 cups (1 liter) vodka
4 cups strawberry liqueur
5 ounces sweet-and-sour mix
5 ounces Triple Sec
5 ounces Rose's lime juice
1/2 gallon orange juice

Combine the ingredients in the order listed in a 1-gallon jug. Pour into ice-filled glasses and serve.
Yield: about 1 gallon.

Jeanne Mudge, Xi Alpha Alpha
Council Bluffs, Iowa

PEACH BRANDY PUNCH

For a fresh substitute for the frozen peaches, combine 2 cups sliced fresh peaches and 1/2 cup sugar and let stand at room temperature for at least 1 hour.

1 (10-ounce) package frozen peaches, thawed
2 quarts white Rhine wine, chilled
1/2 cup brandy or Cognac
1 bottle good champagne, chilled
2 quarts ginger ale, chilled

Mix the peaches, wine and brandy in a bowl. Chill, covered, for at least 3 hours. Pour the peach mixture into a punch bowl at serving time; stir in the champagne and ginger ale. Yield: 30 (6-ounce) servings.

Verna Mae Dean, Iota Master
New Braunfels, Texas

COFFEE PUNCH

1/3 cup Maxwell House instant coffee granules
1 cup sugar
1 cup water
1/2 gallon chocolate ice cream
1/2 gallon vanilla ice cream
1/2 gallon 2% milk

Combine the coffee granules, sugar and water in a saucepan over medium-high heat and bring to a boil, stirring frequently. Remove from heat and chill, covered, until serving time. Remove the ice cream from the freezer and let stand at room temperature for about 1 hour before serving. Combine the ice cream, milk and coffee mixture in a punch bowl and serve. Yield: 2 gallons.

Carol Marshall, Laureate Zeta Eta
Leesburg, Florida

DRESS-UP CRANBERRY PUNCH

1 (12-ounce) can frozen pineapple juice concentrate
1 (12-ounce) can frozen orange juice concentrate
1 (48-ounce) bottle cranberry juice
1 cup amaretto (optional)
1 cup Malibu Rum (optional)
1/2 to 1 cup vodka (optional)
2 liters ginger ale

Prepare the pineapple and orange juices using the package directions. Combine the pineapple juice, orange juice, cranberry juice, amaretto, rum and vodka in a large bowl or pitcher and mix well. Freeze, covered, for 8 to 10 hours. At serving time, create a slush with an ice pick. Add the ginger ale and serve. Yield: 18 (8-ounce) servings.

Eva Snell, Preceptor Beta Kappa
Sierra Vista, Arizona

RAZZLE-DAZZLE RASPBERRY PUNCH

1 (3-ounce) package raspberry gelatin
1 (12-ounce) can frozen lemonade concentrate, thawed
2 cups cranberry juice
1 to 2 liters lemon-lime soda
1 pint raspberry sherbet

Dissolve the dry gelatin in 3 cups boiling water. Stir in 3 cups cold water. Stir in the lemonade and cranberry juice. Pour into a freezer bag and freeze. Thaw in a punch bowl until slushy. Stir in the lemon-lime soda and scoops of sherbet. Yield: 12 to 15 servings.

Jeanne K. Mahoney, Alpha Alpha Master
Battle Creek, Michigan

RHUBARB PUNCH

12 cups chopped raw rhubarb
3 cups sugar
1 (16-ounce) can frozen orange juice concentrate, thawed
1 (16-ounce) can frozen lemonade concentrate, thawed
4 liters ginger ale

Place the rhubarb in a saucepan over medium-high heat. Add enough water to cover. Simmer for 45 minutes or until rhubarb is very mushy; strain well and discard solids. Dissolve the sugar in 3 cups boiling water and stir into the rhubarb liquid. Add the orange juice and lemonade and mix well. Pour into a 2-liter plastic container and freeze until needed. To serve, thaw partially and add the ginger ale.
Yield: 40 servings.

Margaret Jennings, Laureate Alpha
Windsor, Ontario, Canada

SLUSHY CITRUS PUNCH

Use gelatin flavors of your choice—two peach gelatin packages with 1 pineapple gelatin is a very successful combination. Try substituting peach schnapps for half the ginger ale.

1 (12-ounce) can frozen orange juice concentrate, thawed
1 (6-ounce) can frozen lemonade concentrate, thawed
46 ounces pineapple juice concentrate
3 cups sugar
3 (3-ounce) packages any flavored gelatin
2 liters ginger ale

Combine the orange juice, lemonade and pineapple juice in a very large bowl; mix well and stir in the sugar. Dissolve the gelatin in 3 cups boiling water. Stir the gelatin mixture into the juice mixture. Add 1 gallon of water and freeze in 1-gallon freezer bags or plastic containers. Let stand at room temperature for 3 hours before serving. Stir in the ginger ale and serve. Yield: 50 servings.

Elaine McCulloch, Xi Zeta Rho
Lamar, Missouri

WEDDING SHERBET PUNCH

2½ cups pineapple juice
1 pint lime, lemon or raspberry sherbet
1 pint vanilla ice cream
12 ounces ginger ale or lemon-lime soda

Combine the pineapple juice, sherbet and half the ice cream in a large mixing bowl and beat until smooth. Stir in the ginger ale. Spoon the remaining ice cream over the top. Serve immediately.
Yield: 14 (½-cup) servings.

Chelsey Easter, Preceptor Epsilon Omega
Carl Junction, Missouri

LEMON GRAPE TEA

5 tea bags
1 (12-ounce) can frozen lemonade concentrate
2 cups white grape juice
1 cup sugar

Combine the tea bags and 1 quart water in a large kettle over medium-high heat; boil for 7 minutes. Remove from heat and stir in the lemonade, grape juice, sugar and 3 lemonade cans of water. Cool and serve over ice. Yield: about 2 quarts.

Missi Housman, Preceptor Epsilon
Madison, Tennessee

STRAWBERRY TEA

4 tea bags
6 cinnamon sticks, broken into pieces
1 teaspoon whole cloves
1 (6-ounce) can frozen orange juice concentrate, thawed
1 (6-ounce) can frozen lemonade concentrate, thawed
1 (46-ounce) can pineapple juice
1 (3-ounce) package strawberry gelatin

Pour 2 cups boiling water over the tea bags in a glass bowl or other container. Let stand, covered, for 12 minutes. Remove and discard the tea bags. Combine the cinnamon and cloves in a large tea ball or cheesecloth bag and place in a Dutch oven over medium-high heat. Add the tea, orange juice, lemonade, pineapple juice, dry gelatin mix and 2 cups water; bring to a boil. Reduce heat, cover and simmer for 45 minutes. Remove spice ball and serve hot.
Yield: 10 cups.

Hazel Irene Ivey, Beta Epsilon Omicron
Brackettville, Texas

FRUIT SHAKE

1 frozen banana, cut up
1½ cups vanilla or regular soy milk
2 tablespoons soy powder
2 tablespoons flaxmeal
½ cup frozen blueberries, strawberries or raspberries

Combine the banana, soy milk, soy powder and flaxmeal in a blender container and process until smooth. Add the berries and process at high speed until smooth. Yield: 2 servings.

Darlene A. Ruedy, Laureate Omega
Carson City, Nevada

WASSAIL

2 quarts apple cider
½ cup granulated sugar
¼ cup firmly packed brown sugar
2 (3-inch) cinnamon sticks
12 whole cloves, tied in cheesecloth bag
4 cups grapefruit juice
4 cups orange juice
1 cup pineapple juice

Combine the apple cider, granulated sugar, brown sugar, cinnamon sticks and clove ball in a Dutch oven over high heat. Bring to a boil; boil until sugar is dissolved. Reduce heat and simmer, uncovered, for 5 minutes. Add the grapefruit juice, orange juice and pineapple juice and heat until hot; do not boil. Strain; discard the spices. Serve hot. Yield: 4½ quarts.

Elizabeth Donn Beeler, Alpha Master
Nicholasville, Kentucky

APPLE CRUNCH SALAD

2 (3-ounce) packages strawberry gelatin
1½ cups cold water or apple juice
¼ teaspoon cinnamon
1 cup diced peeled apple
½ cup diced celery
¼ cup chopped walnuts or pecans

Dissolve the gelatin in 2 cups boiling water. Add the cold water and cinnamon. Chill until thickened. Fold in the apple, celery and walnuts. Spoon into a 4×8-inch loaf pan. Chill until firm, for about 4 hours. Unmold onto a serving plate. Yield: 8 servings.

Kathy Etter, Preceptor Delta Gamma
Indianapolis, Indiana

TAFFY APPLE SALAD

1 (20-ounce) can pineapple chunks, drained, juice reserved
1 tablespoon flour
½ cup sugar
1 egg, well beaten
½ teaspoon vinegar
2 cups miniature marshmallows
8 ounces whipped topping
2 cups diced peeled apples
1½ cups peanuts

Whisk the pineapple juice, flour, sugar, egg and vinegar in a saucepan over medium-low heat until smooth. Cook until thickened, stirring constantly. Pour into a bowl. Mix the pineapple chunks and marshmallows in a bowl. Chill both mixtures, covered, for 8 to 10 hours. Combine the marshmallow mixture, sugar mixture, whipped topping, apples and peanuts and mix well. Chill, covered, until serving time. Yield: 8 cups.

Chris Threlkeld, Xi Beta Xi
Paris, Missouri

CARAMEL APPLE SALAD

1 cup miniature marshmallows
1 cup crushed pineapple
3 cups diced unpeeled apples
1 (3-ounce) package butterscotch instant pudding mix
1 cup peanuts
8 ounces whipped topping

Combine the marshmallows, pineapple, apples, butterscotch pudding mix, peanuts and whipped topping in a bowl and mix well. Serve as a salad or a dessert. Yield: 10 servings.

Florence Helle, Laureate Xi
Luverne, Minnesota

BANANA APPLE PEANUT SALAD

⅓ cup honey
½ teaspoon grated lemon zest
3 tablespoons lemon juice
¼ teaspoon salt
¼ teaspoon ginger
¼ teaspoon nutmeg
1 pound bananas, cut into ¼- to ½-inch slices
1 pound apples, cut into ¼- to ½-inch chunks
⅔ cup dry-roasted peanuts, coarsely chopped

Combine the honey, lemon zest, lemon juice, salt, ginger and nutmeg in a large bowl and whisk until smooth. Add the sliced bananas and chopped apples; toss until coated. Chill until serving time. Add the peanuts and mix lightly. Spoon into a serving bowl. Yield: 4 servings.

Wilberta Tivis, Sigma Master
Eunice, New Mexico

CRANBERRY GELATIN SALAD

You can use frozen cranberries if you reduce the amount of boiling water to 2½ cups.

10 ounces fresh cranberries
2¼ cups sugar
1 (20-ounce) can crushed pineapple, drained, juice reserved
1 cup chopped walnuts or pecans
2 (3-ounce) packages strawberry or cherry gelatin
2 tablespoons flour
1 egg, beaten
2 tablespoons margarine
1 envelope whipped topping mix, whipped, or 1 cup whipped cream

Put the cranberries through a food mill. Combine the ground cranberries, 1¾ cups of the sugar, pineapple and walnuts in a bowl and mix well. Dissolve the gelatin in 3 cups boiling water in a separate large bowl; stir in the cranberry mixture. Pour into a 9×13-inch baking dish. Chill until firm. Combine the remaining ½ cup sugar and flour in a saucepan over medium heat. Add the egg, margarine, and 1 cup of the reserved pineapple juice. Cook until thickened, stirring constantly. Remove from heat. Fold in the whipped topping. Spread the whipped topping mixture over the chilled cranberry layer.
Yield: 12 to 15 servings.

Louise A. Springer, Laureate Alpha Upsilon
Marshalltown, Iowa

CRANBERRY SALAD

1 (3-ounce) package cherry gelatin
1 (3-ounce) package lemon gelatin
1 (8-ounce) can crushed pineapple in juice, drained
1 (16-ounce) can whole cranberries, drained
½ apple, peeled and chopped
½ orange, peeled and chopped
½ cup chopped walnuts

Dissolve the cherry gelatin and lemon gelatin in 2 cups hot water in a glass bowl. Stir in 1½ cups cold water. Chill, covered, until cold but not firm. Stir in the pineapple, cranberries, apple, orange and walnuts. Chill until firm. Yield: 10 to 12 servings.

Jeanne Beltz, Alpha Alpha Iota
Hudson, Florida

Georgia M. Cuneo, Gamma Master, Winston Salem, North Carolina, makes ***Cranberry Orange Salad*** *by combining 1 can whole cranberries, 1 cup mandarin oranges and 1 cup chopped nuts. Chill several hours. Serve on a bed of lettuce.*

CREAMY CRANBERRY SALAD

4 cups fresh cranberries, washed
2 cups sugar
2 cups red grapes, halved and seeded
½ to 1 cup chopped walnuts or pecans
1 cup heavy cream
½ cup confectioners' sugar

Put the cranberries through a food mill, or place them in a food processor container and process until very finely chopped. Combine the cranberries and sugar in a bowl and mix well. Place the cranberry mixture in a colander over a bowl; let stand in the refrigerator to drain for 8 to 10 hours. Combine the cranberry mixture, grapes and walnuts in a large bowl and mix well. Whip the cream and confectioners' sugar with chilled beaters until stiff peaks form. Fold the whipped cream mixture into the cranberry mixture; mix well. Serve on lettuce leaves. The salad may chill for a short time before serving.
Yield: 8 servings.

Judith Anne Porter, Delta Master
Pueblo, Colorado

GRAPE SALAD

This make-ahead dish may be prepared 3 to 4 days before serving.

3 pounds green grapes
3 pounds red grapes
1 cup sour cream
8 ounces cream cheese, softened
½ cup granulated sugar
1 cup packed light brown sugar
1 cup finely chopped pecans

Separate the green and red grapes from their stems; do not cut the grapes. Wash them and dry well. Combine the sour cream, cream cheese and granulated sugar in a mixing bowl and beat at high speed until creamy. Spoon into a bowl. Chill, covered, until serving time. Just before serving, sprinkle a mixture of brown sugar and pecans evenly over the top.
Yield: 8 to 10 servings.

Janetta Kunkel, Laureate Eta
Warner Robins, Georgia

ORANGE GELATIN SALAD

1 (6-ounce) package orange gelatin
1 (11-ounce) can mandarin oranges, drained, liquid reserved
1 (14-ounce) can crushed pineapple, drained
1 envelope whipped topping mix
1 (4-ounce) package lemon instant pudding mix
1 cup milk
2 tablespoons chopped walnuts or pecans or sliced almonds

Prepare the orange gelatin using the package directions, substituting mandarin orange liquid for part of the water. Pour into a 9×13-inch baking dish. Chill until beginning to thicken. Stir in the mandarin oranges and pineapple. Chill until firm. Prepare the whipped topping using the package directions. Combine the instant pudding mix and 1 cup milk in a mixing bowl; beat at high speed until smooth. Fold the whipped topping into the pudding mixture and spread over the gelatin layer. Sprinkle with walnuts. Chill until firm. Yield: 8 to 10 servings.

Gail Kunsman, Xi Sigma Omicron
Yuba City, California

MANDARIN ORANGE SALAD

10 ounces orange soda
1 (3-ounce) package lemon gelatin
4 ounces whipped topping
1 (15-ounce) can mandarin oranges, drained

Place the orange soda in a saucepan over medium heat and heat until steaming hot. Pour into a medium bowl. Stir the dry gelatin mix into the hot soda. Freeze until almost set. Remove from freezer and fold in whipped topping and oranges. Chill, covered, until firm. Yield: 6 to 8 servings.

Nancy Taylor, Alpha Pi Master
Decatur, Illinois

LIME AND PINEAPPLE SALAD

This salad, a favorite for Saint Patrick's Day, is a good potluck dish. Serve with corned beef.

1 (6-ounce) package lime gelatin
3 ounces cream cheese
1 cup miniature marshmallows
Sour cream to taste
1 (8-ounce) can crushed pineapple, drained
1 cup finely chopped celery
1/2 cup crushed walnuts or pecans (optional)

Dissolve the gelatin in 3 cups boiling water. Cut up the cream cheese and stir into the hot gelatin mixture. Add the marshmallows; stir to dissolve. Stir in enough sour cream to make a creamy mixture. Stir in the pineapple, celery and walnuts. Chill until firm. Yield: 8 to 10 servings.

Mary Ellen Bradley, Preceptor Kappa
Landisville, Pennsylvania

PINEAPPLE PUDDING SALAD

This recipe can be changed to fit the occasion. For Saint Patrick's Day, use pistachio pudding and green food coloring and omit the cherries. Use yellow or pink food coloring for Easter, orange food coloring for Halloween or Thanksgiving, red or green for Christmas, and red food coloring for Valentine's Day.

1 (20-ounce) can crushed pineapple in juice
Food coloring of choice
1 small package sugar-free vanilla instant pudding mix
1 cup fat-free small curd cottage cheese
1/2 to 1 cup chopped pecans or walnuts
2 cups fat-free whipped topping
10 to 12 maraschino cherries, rinsed, drained, chopped

Combine the undrained pineapple and food coloring in a large bowl and stir well. Stir in the dry pudding mix, cottage cheese and pecans. Add the whipped topping, stirring gently to blend. Garnish with cherries. Chill, covered, for 1 to 2 hours or until serving time. Yield: 6 to 8 servings.

Eveline K. Frow, Theta Chi
Steinhatchee, Florida

RED AND GREEN LAYER SALAD

1 (3-ounce) package green gelatin
1 (3-ounce) package lemon gelatin
12 large marshmallows
3 ounces cream cheese, softened
1 (8-ounce) can crushed pineapple, drained
1 cup mayonnaise-type salad dressing
1 cup whipped topping
1 (3-ounce) package red gelatin

Pour a mixture of the green gelatin mix and 2 cups hot water into a 9×13-inch baking dish. Chill until firm. Combine another 2 cups hot water, the lemon gelatin mix, marshmallows and cream cheese in a bowl; stir until gelatin is dissolved and marshmallows and cream cheese are melted and mixture is smooth. Set aside to cool. Add the pineapple, mayonnaise-type salad dressing and whipped topping to the cooled marshmallow mixture; mix well. Pour the pineapple mixture evenly over the green gelatin layer. Chill until firm. Dissolve the red gelatin in 2 cups hot water; cool. Pour the red gelatin mixture evenly over the pineapple layer. Chill until firm. Yield: about 10 servings.

Judy A. Smith, Xi Delta Omicron
Muscatine, Indiana

SPARKLING SALAD

2 (3-ounce) packages lemon gelatin
2 cups lemon-lime soda
1 (20-ounce) can crushed pineapple, drained, juice reserved
2 bananas, sliced
1½ cups miniature marshmallows
½ cup sugar
2 tablespoons cornstarch
1 egg, lightly beaten
1 cup whipped cream

Dissolve the lemon gelatin in 2 cups boiling water in a large bowl. Stir in the Seven Up. Cool until beginning to thicken. Stir in the pineapple, bananas and marshmallows. Chill until firm. Combine the sugar and cornstarch in a saucepan. Whisk in the egg. Stir in ½ cup of the reserved pineapple juice. Cook over medium heat until thickened, stirring constantly. Cool. Stir in the whipped cream. Spread the whipped cream mixture evenly over the marshmallow layer. Sprinkle with a little grated cheese if desired. Chill until serving time. Yield: 8 servings.

Alice Selzler, Laureate Beta Omicron
Quesnel, British Columbia, Canada

RIBBON GELATIN SALAD

When I married into my husband's family, this recipe was given to me to prepare for my new sister-in-law's baby shower. Since then it has become a refreshing favorite—for special occasions only, because it is time-consuming.

2 envelopes unflavored gelatin
1 (3-ounce) package lemon gelatin
1 (3-ounce) package lime gelatin
1 (3-ounce) package orange gelatin
1 (3-ounce) package any flavor red gelatin
2 cups milk
1 cup sugar
2 teaspoons vanilla extract
2 cups sour cream

Soften the unflavored gelatin in ½ cup cold water. Dissolve each (3-ounce) package of gelatin in 1 cup boiling water; stir ½ cup cold water into each bowl of dissolved flavored gelatin. Let stand at room temperature. Pour one of the flavored gelatin mixtures into a 9×13-inch baking dish; let stand in the refrigerator for 30 minutes or until set. Bring the milk to a boil in a saucepan over medium-high heat. Remove from heat. Add the sugar and stir until dissolved; stir in the vanilla and the unflavored gelatin mixture. Place the sour cream in a large mixing bowl. Add the milk mixture gradually, beating at medium speed; beat for a total of 5 minutes. Divide into 3 equal portions and set aside. Pour 1 portion over the first (set) gelatin layer. Chill until set. Layer a second flavored gelatin mixture over the sour cream layer; chill until set. Layer a second portion of sour cream mixture over the second gelatin layer; chill until set. Repeat the layers, ending with a flavored gelatin layer and allowing 30 to 45 minutes in the refrigerator for each layer to become firm. Yield: 24 to 32 servings.

Jennifer Lenart, Tau Omega
Olmsted Falls, Ohio

TWENTY-FOUR-HOUR FRUIT SALAD

1 egg
2 tablespoons fresh lemon juice
2 tablespoons sugar
Pinch of salt
1 cup chopped orange
1 cup whipping cream, whipped
2 cups miniature marshmallows
1 cup drained pineapple chunks
1 cup seedless green grapes, halved
1 cup diced bananas

Beat the egg with a fork. Combine the egg, lemon juice, sugar and salt in the top of a double boiler and cook over simmering water until thickened, stirring constantly. Remove from heat and let stand until cool. Fold in the remaining ingredients. Spoon into a serving dish. Chill, covered, for 8 to 10 hours.
Yield: 6 servings.

Brenda Hall, Preceptor Alpha Eta
Abbotsford, British Columbia, Canada

COCONUT AMBROSIA

1 (20-ounce) can pineapple chunks, drained
1 (11-ounce) can mandarin oranges, drained
1½ cups seedless green grapes
1 cup miniature marshmallows
1 cup flaked coconut
½ cup pecan halves
¾ cup sour cream or vanilla yogurt
1 tablespoon sugar

Combine the first 6 ingredients in a bowl. Stir in a mixture of the sour cream and sugar. Chill, covered, until serving time. Yield: 4 to 6 servings.

Jayne Hornsby, Xi Alpha Xi
Hueytown, Alabama

STRAWBERRY BANANA MARBLE SALAD

1 (3-ounce) package strawberry gelatin
4 ounces whipped topping
1 banana, sliced
½ cup sliced fresh strawberries (optional)

Dissolve the gelatin in 1 cup boiling water. Stir in 7 to 10 ice cubes (2 cups) to thicken. Remove the unmelted ice and pour half the gelatin mixture into another bowl. Add the whipped topping, banana and strawberries to 1 of the halves; stir well. Add the remaining gelatin mixture to the fruited mixture; use a spatula to marbleize the 2 mixtures. Chill until firm. Yield: 4 to 6 servings.

Rita Hart, Xi Iota
Sidney, Nebraska

FRUIT GELATIN SALAD

1 (6-ounce) package lemon gelatin
1 (8-ounce) can crushed pineapple, drained, juice reserved
2 large bananas
1/2 to 3/4 cup miniature marshmallows
1 egg, beaten
2 tablespoons flour
1/2 cup sugar
2 tablespoons lemon juice
2 teaspoons butter
1 cup whipped topping
2 cups (8 ounces) shredded Cheddar cheese

Dissolve the lemon gelatin in 2 cups hot water; let stand until beginning to thicken. Stir in the pineapple, bananas and marshmallows. Chill until firm. Mix the reserved pineapple juice with enough water to make 1 cup liquid. Combine the pineapple juice mixture, egg, flour, sugar and lemon juice in a saucepan over medium-low heat. Cook until thickened, stirring constantly. Stir in the butter. Remove from heat and let stand until cool. Blend in the whipped topping. Spread the whipped topping mixture over the gelatin layer. Layer the cheese over the whipped topping layer. Chill, covered, until serving time. Yield: 12 to 15 servings.

Lydia Johnson, Laureate Iota Mu
Soquel, California

SALON GELATIN SALAD

This recipe was given to me by a dear customer at the beauty salon where I work.

1 (6-ounce) package flavored gelatin
1 (21-ounce) can pie filling
2 (8-ounce) cans crushed pineapple, drained
1 cup chopped pecans
1/2 cup sugar
8 ounces cream cheese, softened
1 cup sour cream

Combine the gelatin, pie filling, pineapple, pecans and 1 cup boiling water in a large bowl; stir until well mixed and gelatin is dissolved. Add 1 scant cup cold water and mix well. Pour into a 9×13-inch baking dish. Chill until firm. Drizzle a mixture of the sugar, cream cheese and sour cream over the gelatin layer. Chill until serving time. Yield: 10 to 12 servings.

Susan Parsley, Xi Eta Delta
Savannah, Georgia

FROSTED FRUIT SALAD

2 (3-ounce) packages lemon gelatin
2 cups ginger ale
1 (20-ounce) can apricots, drained
1 (20-ounce) can crushed pineapple, drained
2 large bananas, cut into small pieces
1/2 cup sugar
1 tablespoon flour
1 cup pineapple juice
1 egg, beaten
2 tablespoons butter
1 cup whipped cream
1/4 cup shredded American cheese

Dissolve the lemon gelatin in 2 cups boiling water. Stir in the ginger ale; cool until partially set. Stir in the apricots, pineapple and bananas. Combine the sugar and flour in a saucepan. Mix in the pineapple juice and egg. Cook over low heat until thickened, stirring constantly. Remove from heat and stir in the butter. Let cool. Chill for about 1 hour. Fold in the whipped cream. Spread the whipped cream mixture over the fruited gelatin. Chill, covered, for 8 to 24 hours. Sprinkle the cheese over the top and serve. Yield: 12 to 15 servings.

Elaine Laws Muse, Xi Kappa
Huber Heights, Ohio

WINE AMBROSIA MOLD

2 (3-ounce) packages apricot gelatin
1 cup white wine or rosé, chilled
1 (8-ounce) can crushed pineapple in juice
1 (10-ounce) package frozen sliced strawberries, thawed
2 bananas, peeled and sliced

Dissolve the apricot gelatin in 1 1/2 cups boiling water. Stir in the wine and 3/4 cup cold water. Chill until the consistency of unbeaten egg whites. Fold in the undrained pineapple, undrained strawberries and bananas. Pour the mixture into a 6 1/2-cup mold or 12 individual 1/2-cup molds. Chill until firm. Garnish with whipped cream if desired, and serve.
Yield: 12 servings.

Juanita W. Gray, Xi Omicron
Bluefield, West Virginia

Judy Silver, Xi Rho Chi, Roseville, California, prepares ***Dried Fruit and Fresh Apple Salad*** *by combining 1 cup sliced dried apricots, 1 cup chopped dried figs, 1/2 cup chopped pecan halves, 1 1/2 teaspoons grated orange zest, and 1/2 cup thawed orange juice concentrate. Chill, covered, for 8 to 10 hours. Peel and dice 1 medium tart apple and 1 medium sweet apple. Stir the apples into the fruit mixture just before serving.*

Vegetable Salads

COUNTRY COLESLAW

1 small head cabbage, finely sliced or chopped
1/2 cup white vinegar
1/2 cup sugar
2 tablespoons mustard
Milk or buttermilk as needed
Salt and pepper to taste
1/2 cup finely chopped peanuts

Place the cabbage in a bowl. Pour a mixture of the vinegar and sugar over the cabbage and mix well. Let stand, covered, in the refrigerator for 2 to 10 hours; a longer time is better. Mix in the mustard and enough milk to make a creamy mixture. Add the salt, pepper and peanuts just before serving; mix well and serve. Yield: 6 servings.

Gina Rollins, Preceptor Alpha Kappa
Glendale, Arizona

CRISP COLESLAW

This slaw will keep for several days and gets better the longer it stands.

3 pounds (3 heads) cabbage
1 yellow bell pepper
1 green bell pepper
1 red bell pepper
2 medium onions, finely chopped
3 to 4 cups sugar
1 1/4 cups white vinegar
1 cup vegetable oil
1 tablespoon salt
2 teaspoons celery seed
2 (2-ounce) jars chopped pimentos, drained

Finely shred the cabbage and bell peppers. Combine the cabbage, bell peppers, onions and sugar in a large bowl and mix well. Let stand, covered, in the refrigerator for 1 hour. Combine the vinegar, vegetable oil, salt and celery seed in a saucepan over medium-high heat; bring to a boil. Pour the vinegar mixture over the cabbage mixture and stir well. Add the pimentos. Chill, covered, until very cold.
Yield: 18 to 20 servings.

Frances Patton, Xi Theta Theta
Brownfield, Texas

CRANBERRY BACON COLESLAW

1 cup golden raisins
4 cups shredded cabbage
2 cups small fresh broccoli florets
1 1/4 cups dried cranberries
1 small onion, chopped
1 cup walnuts, chopped
8 slices bacon, crisp-cooked, crumbled
1 cup mayonnaise
1/3 cup sugar
2 tablespoons apple cider vinegar

Soak the raisins in hot water for 10 minutes; drain. Combine the raisins, cabbage, broccoli, dried cranberries, onion, walnuts and bacon in a large sealable container. Combine the mayonnaise, sugar and vinegar in a small bowl; whisk until smooth. Pour the mayonnaise mixture over the cabbage mixture; mix well. Let stand, covered, in the refrigerator for 24 hours before serving. Yield: 10 servings.

Janice Fern, Master Iota
Kearney, Nebraska

SAUERKRAUT SALAD

1 (15-ounce) can sauerkraut, drained
1/4 cup chopped onion
1/2 cup chopped green bell pepper
3/4 cup chopped celery
1 (2-ounce) jar chopped pimentos, drained
Salt to taste
1/4 cup white vinegar
1 cup sugar

Combine the sauerkraut, onion, bell pepper, celery, pimentos and salt in a bowl and mix well. Combine the vinegar and sugar in a small saucepan and bring to a boil. Pour the vinegar mixture immediately over the sauerkraut mixture. Chill, covered, for 8 to 10 hours. Yield: 6 to 8 servings.

Betty L. Crepps, Pi Master
Bethalto, Illinois

ORIENTAL CABBAGE SALAD

2 (3-ounce) packages chicken-flavored ramen noodles
1 pound coleslaw mix
8 green onions, sliced (about 1/2 cup)
1/4 cup sesame seeds
6 tablespoons white vinegar
1/4 cup sugar
1/4 cup vegetable oil
1 teaspoon white pepper
1/2 teaspoon salt
1 cup slivered almonds

Crush the noodles slightly and place in a colander. Pour boiling water over the noodles to soften; drain well. Combine the noodles, coleslaw mix, green onions and sesame seeds in a large bowl. Place the seasoning packets from the ramen noodles, vinegar, sugar, vegetable oil, white pepper and salt in a jar and shake vigorously to combine. Pour over the cabbage mixture and toss. Chill, covered, for 3 to 10 hours. Stir in the almonds just before serving. Yield: 6 to 8 servings.

Dorothy Rigaud, Preceptor Beta Delta
Sayville, New York

CRANBERRY AND APPLE SLAW

5 cups (about) thinly sliced red cabbage
1/2 cup dried cranberries
1/3 cup rice vinegar
1/3 cup sugar
2 tablespoons white wine vinegar
2 teaspoons olive oil
3/4 teaspoon salt
1/2 teaspoon freshly ground pepper
2 1/4 cups thinly sliced Granny Smith apples
1/4 cup chopped pecans, toasted

Combine the cabbage and cranberries in a large bowl; mix well. Combine the rice vinegar, sugar, white wine vinegar, olive oil, salt and pepper in a small bowl; whisk to blend. Drizzle the vinegar mixture over the cabbage mixture, tossing gently to coat. Chill, covered, for 2 hours. Add the apples; toss well to combine. Sprinkle with pecans and serve. Yield: 8 servings.

Myrna Zielinski, Xi Gamma Eta
Grand Rapids, Michigan

SWEET-AND-SOUR COLESLAW

1 pound angel hair coleslaw mix, or 1 head cabbage, shredded
1 apple, peeled and chopped
3/4 cup raisins
1 cup toasted chopped pecans
1 cup mayonnaise
1/2 cup sugar
1/4 cup white vinegar

Combine the coleslaw mix, apple and raisins in a large bowl; mix well. Stir in the pecans. Blend the mayonnaise, sugar and vinegar in a small bowl. Pour the mayonnaise mixture over the coleslaw and toss gently. Chill, covered, for at least 2 hours before serving. Yield: 8 to 10 servings.

Martha S. Shelton, Xi Tau
Northport, Alabama

TEXAS TWO-STEP COLESLAW

4 cups shredded green cabbage
1 cup shredded red cabbage
1/4 cup chopped red onion
2 jalapeños, seeded, finely chopped
2 tablespoons chopped fresh cilantro
1 (11-ounce) can Mexicorn, drained
4 ounces shredded Cheddar cheese (1 cup)
3/4 cup prepared ranch salad dressing
1 teaspoon cumin
1 tablespoon fresh lime juice

Toss the first 7 ingredients in large bowl. Combine the ranch dressing, cumin and lime juice in a small bowl; whisk well to blend. Pour over the cabbage mixture and toss to coat. Refrigerate until serving time. Garnish with cilantro leaves. Yield: 8 servings.

Joyce Ann Trojan, Laureate Theta Eta
Moscow, Texas

TOMATO AND CABBAGE SALAD

6 sweet pickles, drained, liquid reserved
4 cups shredded cabbage
1 small onion, minced
1 cup diced fresh tomatoes or chopped canned tomatoes
1 cup tomato juice
2 tablespoons white vinegar or pickle liquid
2 tablespoons sugar
Salt and pepper to taste

Chop the pickles. Place the cabbage, pickles, onion and tomatoes in a large bowl and toss to combine. Place the tomato juice, vinegar, sugar, salt and pepper in a jar and shake vigorously. Drizzle desired amount of dressing over the cabbage mixture and toss gently to coat. Chill, covered, for 8 to 10 hours. Yield: 8 to 10 servings.

Dorothy McIntosh, Beta Beta
Bethany, Missouri

ANTIPASTO SALAD

2 teaspoons Dijon mustard
2 teaspoons red wine vinegar
1 teaspoon Italian seasoning
1/2 teaspoon salt
1/4 teaspoon pepper
1/2 cup olive oil
4 ounces salami or pepperoni, cut into 1/2-inch cubes
1 head romaine, torn into bite-size pieces
4 ounces provolone cheese, cut into 1/2-inch cubes
1/2 (12-ounce) jar pepperoncini peppers
1 (4-ounce) jar sliced pimentos, drained
1 medium red onion, thinly sliced and separated into rings

Combine the Dijon mustard, vinegar, Italian seasoning, salt and pepper in a small bowl and whisk to blend. Add the olive oil slowly, whisking until blended and thick. Cover and set aside. Combine the salami, romaine, provolone cheese, pepperoncini and onion in a salad bowl. Drizzle the dressing over the salad just before serving. Toss and serve.
Yield: 8 to 12 servings.

Cecelia M. Grossman, Laureate Alpha
Albuquerque, New Mexico

✣ CRAISIN SALAD

This wonderful recipe may be halved.

1 head red leaf lettuce
1 head romaine
1 head iceberg lettuce
8 ounces mozzarella cheese, shredded (2 cups)
6 ounces Parmesan cheese, shredded
1 cup dried cranberries
1 pound bacon, crisp-cooked, crumbled
1/2 cup sliced almonds
6 chicken breasts, cooked and diced
1/2 cup chopped sweet onion
1 cup sugar
2 teaspoons dry mustard
1/2 cup red wine vinegar
1 cup canola oil

Wash the red leaf lettuce, romaine and iceberg lettuce and tear into bite-size pieces; place in a large bowl. Add the mozzarella cheese, Parmesan cheese, cranberries, bacon, almonds and chicken and toss gently. Combine the onion, sugar, dry mustard and vinegar in a blender container and pulse to blend. Add the canola oil in a fine stream, processing constantly at high speed until smooth. Pour the dressing over the salad and toss, or serve the dressing on the side.
Yield: 18 servings.

Fawn Wright, Laureate Omicron
Clear Lake, Minnesota

CRUNCHY LETTUCE SALAD

6 ounces sliced almonds
1/4 cup sesame seeds
1 cup chow mein noodles
1 head lettuce, torn into bite-size pieces
5 to 6 slices bacon, crisp-cooked, cut into pieces
1/4 cup sugar
1 1/2 teaspoons salt
6 tablespoons white vinegar
1/2 cup vegetable oil

Spread the almonds, sesame seeds and chow mein noodles on a baking sheet. Bake at 350 degrees for 15 minutes, stirring occasionally. Combine the lettuce and bacon in a salad bowl and toss gently. Place the sugar, salt, vinegar and vegetable oil in a jar and shake vigorously to combine. At serving time, add the toasted almond mixture and dressing to the lettuce mixture; toss and serve. Yield: 8 servings.

Audrey Hill, Beta Chi
Independence, Iowa

✣ MANDARIN SALAD

1/2 cup orange juice
1/3 cup vegetable oil
1/3 cup apple cider vinegar
1/4 cup sugar
6 cups torn salad greens
1 (11-ounce) can mandarin oranges, drained
1 small onion, sliced
4 radishes, thinly sliced
4 green onions, thinly sliced
1/3 cup dried cranberries
1/3 cup sunflower seeds
3/4 cup crumbled feta cheese or bleu cheese
3/4 cup halved cherry tomatoes

Place the orange juice, vegetable oil, vinegar and sugar in a jar and shake vigorously to combine; chill for at least 1 hour. Combine the salad greens, mandarin oranges, onion, radishes, green onions, dried cranberries, sunflower seeds, feta cheese and tomatoes in a salad bowl; chill for at least 1 hour. Just before serving, add the dressing to the salad. Toss and serve. Yield: 6 servings.

Lina Steel, Xi Master
Sudbury, Ontario, Canada

FRUITED VEGETABLE SALAD

1 pound assorted lettuce, torn into bite-size pieces
1 pound fresh spinach, torn into bite-size pieces
2 medium avocados, peeled and sliced
1 pint strawberries, halved
1 cantaloupe, scooped into balls
1 pint cherry tomatoes, halved
2 cucumbers, peeled and sliced
8 ounces fresh mushrooms, sliced
Poppy Seed Dressing

Combine the lettuce, spinach, avocados, strawberries, cantaloupe, cherry tomatoes, cucumbers and mushrooms in a salad bowl. Just before serving, add the Poppy Seed Dressing. Toss and serve.
Yield: 20 servings.

POPPY SEED DRESSING

1 cup vegetable oil
1/2 cup tarragon vinegar
1/2 cup sugar
1 tablespoon poppy seeds
1 teaspoon salt
1 teaspoon dry mustard
1 teaspoon grated onion
3/4 teaspoon onion salt

Place the vegetable oil, vinegar, sugar, poppy seeds, salt, dry mustard, onion and onion salt in a jar and shake vigorously to combine.

Carolyn Waters, Xi Psi
Crestview, Florida

FALL SALAD WITH CRANBERRY DRESSING

10 ounces romaine or field greens, torn into bite-size pieces
1/3 purple onion, sliced
1/3 cup crumbled bleu cheese
2 cups sliced apples
2 tablespoons orange juice
2 tablespoons toasted chopped walnuts
1/3 cup canned whole cranberry sauce
1/4 cup orange juice
1 tablespoon olive oil
2 tablespoons balsamic vinegar
1 teaspoon sugar
1 teaspoon minced peeled fresh gingerroot
1/4 teaspoon salt

Place the romaine, onion and bleu cheese in a salad bowl. Toss the apple slices with the 2 tablespoons orange juice and add to the salad. Add the walnuts and toss. Combine the cranberry sauce, the 1/4 cup orange juice, olive oil, balsamic vinegar, sugar, ginger and salt in a bowl and mix well. Add the cranberry mixture to the salad just before serving. Toss and serve. Yield: 5 servings.

Leigh O'Brien, Beta Tau
Newport News, Virginia

PEAR AND GORGONZOLA CHEESE SALAD

8 cups bite-size pieces romaine
2 red pears, thinly sliced
1/2 cup crumbled Gorgonzola cheese
1/2 cup coarsely chopped walnuts, toasted
Dijon Dressing

Combine the romaine, pears, cheese and walnuts in a salad bowl. Add the Dijon Dressing just before serving. Toss and serve. Yield: 8 servings.

DIJON DRESSING

1/2 cup olive oil or vegetable oil
2 tablespoons apple cider vinegar
1 teaspoon Dijon mustard
1/4 teaspoon salt
1/4 teaspoon pepper

Place the olive oil, vinegar, Dijon mustard, salt and pepper in a jar and shake vigorously to combine.

Shirley MacMullen, Laureate Delta Phi
St. Augustine, Florida

SEVEN-LAYER SALAD

1 head lettuce, chopped
1/2 cup finely chopped green bell pepper
1/2 cup chopped broccoli or cauliflower or both
1/2 cup minced celery
1/2 small onion, minced
Sliced fresh mushrooms, enough for 1 layer
1 (10-ounce) package frozen peas, thawed, well drained
1 1/2 cups sour cream
1/2 cup mayonnaise
1 teaspoon sugar
10 ounces Cheddar cheese, shredded
Bacon bits to taste

Layer the lettuce, bell pepper, broccoli, celery, onion, mushrooms and peas in a 9×13-inch baking dish. Spread a mixture of the sour cream and mayonnaise over the top, sealing to the edge. Sprinkle with the sugar, cheese and bacon bits. Chill, tightly covered, for up to 12 hours before serving. Spoon through all the layers when serving. Yield: 12 to 14 servings.

Barbara Johns, Xi Theta
Bartlesville, Oklahoma

TROPICAL GREEN SALAD WITH PINEAPPLE VINAIGRETTE

6 slices bacon, crisp-cooked, crumbled
10 ounces romaine, cut into bite-size pieces
1 cup drained pineapple chunks
1/2 cup chopped macadamia nuts
3 green onions, chopped
1/4 cup pineapple juice
3 tablespoons red wine vinegar
1/4 cup light olive oil
Salt and pepper to taste
1/4 cup flaked coconut, toasted

Combine the bacon, romaine, pineapple, macadamia nuts and green onions in a salad bowl. Place the pineapple juice, vinegar, olive oil, salt and pepper in a jar and shake vigorously. Add the dressing to the salad just before serving and toss well. Divide among 6 salad bowls and garnish each serving with toasted coconut. Serve immediately. Yield: 6 servings.

Rose Ann Abernathy, Preceptor Delta
Centralia, Illinois

GREEN SALAD WITH WINTER FRUIT

1/2 cup sugar
1/2 cup lemon juice
1 teaspoon Dijon mustard
1/2 teaspoon salt
2/3 cup vegetable oil
1 tablespoon poppy seeds
1 head romaine, torn into bite-size pieces
4 ounces Swiss cheese, shredded (1/2 cup)
1 cup cashews
1/4 cup dried cranberries
1 fresh apple, peeled and diced
1 fresh pear, peeled and diced

Combine the sugar, lemon juice, Dijon mustard and salt in a blender container and process until smooth. Add the vegetable oil in a fine stream, processing constantly at high speed until smooth and thickened. Add the poppy seeds and process briefly to mix. Chill, covered, until ready to use. Combine the romaine, cheese, cashews, cranberries, apple and pear in a salad bowl. Add desired amount of dressing at serving time. Toss and serve. Yield: 8 servings.

Betty Teston, Alpha Gamma Omega
San Angelo, Texas

MANDARIN SPINACH SALAD

10 ounces fresh spinach, cleaned, stems removed
1/2 cup sliced celery
1 pound sliced bacon, crisp-cooked, crumbled
4 hard-cooked eggs, peeled and sliced
8 ounces fresh mushrooms
1 small red onion, sliced
1/2 cup raisins
2 (11-ounce) cans mandarin oranges, drained
1/2 cup chopped pecans
1 (6-ounce) package seasoned croutons
1 (8-ounce) bottle Italian dressing
1 (6-ounce) can frozen orange juice, thawed

Combine the spinach and celery in a large bowl. Add the bacon, eggs, mushrooms, onion, raisins, mandarin oranges, pecans and croutons; toss gently. Combine the Italian dressing and orange juice in a small bowl and mix until smooth; serve with the spinach salad. Yield: about 20 servings.

Mary Ann O'Sullivan, Preceptor Alpha Beta
Terrytown, Louisiana

*For **Sweet-and-Spicy Salad Dressing**, Lila Couch, Preceptor Alpha Phi, Toccoa, Georgia, combines 1 grated medium onion, 1 tablespoon each salt and Worcestershire sauce, 1 cup sugar, 2/3 cup white vinegar, 1/2 cup ketchup, and 1/2 cup vegetable oil in a jar. Shake to mix.*

ORANGE SPINACH SALAD WITH HONEY SESAME DRESSING

1 medium garlic clove, minced
2 tablespoons honey
2 tablespoons Dijon mustard
2 tablespoons orange juice
3 tablespoons white wine vinegar
1/8 teaspoon salt
Pepper to taste
1/3 cup olive oil
1 tablespoon sesame seeds
2 oranges
10 ounces fresh spinach, torn into bite-size pieces
4 green onions, thinly sliced
4 slices bacon, crisp-cooked, crumbled

Combine the first 7 ingredients in a blender container. Add the olive oil in a fine stream, processing constantly at high speed until emulsified. Pour the dressing into a jar and stir in the sesame seeds. Chill until 30 minutes before serving time. Cut a 1/2-inch slice from the tops and bottoms of the oranges. Cut away the zest and white pith with a small sharp knife. Cut between the membranes to remove the sections. Chill the orange sections, wrapped in plastic wrap, until serving time. Just before serving, combine the spinach, green onions, bacon, orange sections and dressing in a salad bowl. Toss and serve. Yield: 4 to 6 servings.

Paula J. Palmer, Preceptor Iota Gamma
San Diego, California

SPINACH SALAD WITH MAPLE DIJON VINAIGRETTE

1/4 cup maple syrup
1/4 cup white balsamic vinegar
2 tablespoons vegetable oil
1 tablespoon Dijon mustard
1 garlic clove, minced
Dash of salt
6 slices bacon, cut into 1/2-inch pieces
1/2 cup chopped walnuts or pecans
1/8 teaspoon coarse black pepper
10 cups torn baby spinach
1/2 cup slivered red onion
1 red bell pepper, cut into strips
1/2 cup crumbled feta cheese

Place the first 6 ingredients in a jar and shake vigorously. Chill. Cook the bacon pieces in a medium skillet until nearly crisp. Add the walnuts and cook until bacon is crisp; sprinkle with pepper; drain on paper towels. Toss the spinach, onion and bell pepper in a large salad bowl. Drizzle with dressing. Top servings with bacon mixture and feta cheese.
Yield: 8 servings.

Glenna Lawson, Preceptor Pi
Columbia, Missouri

CALICO CORN SALAD

2 (14-ounce) cans yellow corn, drained
2 (14-ounce) cans white corn, drained
2 bunches green onions, chopped
1 large cucumber, peeled and chopped
1 green bell pepper, chopped
12 ounces sour cream
Salt and pepper to taste

Combine the yellow corn, white corn, green onions, cucumber and bell pepper in a large bowl and mix well. Add the sour cream and mix well. Season with salt and pepper. Chill, covered, for 8 to 10 hours. Yield: 6 servings.

Sara Rouner, Beta Kappa Sigma
Hilltop Lakes, Texas

PILGRIM CORN SALAD

You can't have a chapter Thanksgiving dinner without it!

2 (11-ounce) cans white Shoe Peg corn, drained
3/4 cup dried cranberries
1/4 cup chopped pecans
2 tablespoons balsamic vinegar
2 tablespoons olive oil
1 tablespoon apricot preserves
1 teaspoon Dijon mustard
1 teaspoon Worcestershire sauce
2 tablespoons finely chopped fresh basil

Combine the corn, dried cranberries and pecans; toss to mix. Combine the vinegar, olive oil, apricot preserves, Dijon mustard and Worcestershire sauce in a small bowl and whisk until smooth. Add the vinegar mixture and basil to the corn mixture; toss to coat well. Let stand for 10 minutes. Stir gently. Garnish with basil sprigs and serve. Yield: 8 (1/2 cup) servings.

Margaret Wilburn, Laureate Theta Phi
Houston, Texas

SUMMER CORN SALAD

3 cups fresh corn kernels or thawed frozen corn
1 large onion, chopped
2 medium zucchini, peeled and diced
1 bunch green onions, chopped
1/4 cup minced parsley
1 garlic clove, minced
2 teaspoons sugar
2 teaspoons Dijon mustard
1/2 teaspoon hot red pepper sauce
2/3 cup vegetable oil
1/3 cup white vinegar
1/4 teaspoon salt
1/4 teaspoon pepper

Cook the corn in a small amount of water in a saucepan for 5 minutes. Drain and cool. Combine the corn, onion, zucchini, green onions, parsley and garlic in a bowl and mix gently. Combine the sugar, Dijon mustard, hot pepper sauce, vegetable oil, vinegar, salt and pepper in a small bowl and whisk to blend. Add the mustard mixture to the corn mixture and toss gently to combine. Chill, covered, for 8 hours to marry the flavors. Yield: 6 servings.

Marcia Carter, Theta
Vincennes, Indiana

CORN BREAD SALAD

1 (8-ounce) package quick corn bread mix
1 cup mayonnaise-type salad dressing
1/2 cup sweet pickle relish, drained, juice reserved
4 medium tomatoes, peeled and chopped
1 green bell pepper, chopped
1 medium onion, chopped
1/3 cup bacon bits

Prepare and bake the corn bread using the package directions; cut or tear into small pieces. Combine the mayonnaise-type salad dressing and 1/4 cup of the reserved pickle juice in a small bowl; whisk until smooth. Layer the corn bread, tomatoes, bell pepper, onion, pickle relish, bacon bits and mayonnaise-type salad dressing mixture 1/2 at a time in a large salad bowl. Chill, tightly covered, for 2 to 10 hours.
Yield: 12 to 14 servings.

Clair S. Ledger, Preceptor Kappa
Montrose, Colorado

CRACKER EGG SALAD

8 ounces saltines, crushed or ground
1 cup chopped onions
1 cup chopped sweet pickles
1 cup chopped green bell peppers
1 (2-ounce) jar chopped pimentos, drained
5 hard-cooked eggs, peeled and chopped
2 cups mayonnaise
1/2 cup finely chopped celery (optional)

Combine the crushed saltines, onions, pickles, bell pepper, pimentos, eggs, mayonnaise and celery in a bowl; mix well. Chill, covered, for at least 3 hours.
Yield: 8 servings.

Bobbi Shannon, Laureate Lambda
Port St. Lucie, Florida

---

*Ruth Edwards, Preceptor Beta Tau, King City, Oregon, makes **Bleu Cheese Dressing** by whisking 2 ounces crumbled bleu cheese, 2 tablespoons lemon juice, 1 1/2 tablespoons prepared horseradish, 1/4 teaspoon garlic powder, 1/2 teaspoon Worcestershire sauce, 1/4 cup milk, and 2 cups mayonnaise until blended.*

CRUNCHY PEA SALAD

1 cup sliced celery
4 green onions, chopped
1/2 (9-ounce) jar Major Grey chutney
1/4 cup mayonnaise
1/4 cup sour cream
1 tablespoon curry powder
1 teaspoon garlic powder
1 tablespoon lemon juice
1 (5-ounce) can chow mein noodles
1 (16-ounce) package frozen English peas
1 cup cashews
10 slices bacon, crisp-cooked, cut into pieces

Combine the celery, green onions, chutney, mayonnaise, sour cream, curry powder, garlic powder, lemon juice and a sprinkle of salt in a bowl and mix well. Stir in the chow mein noodles, peas, cashews and bacon no more than 10 minutes before serving. Yield: 10 to 12 servings.

Jody E. King, Alpha Psi Beta
Lockhart, Texas

PEA SALAD

1 (16-ounce) package frozen peas
1 cup cubed Cheddar or Colby cheese
8 hard-cooked eggs, peeled and chopped
1 cup mayonnaise-type salad dressing
1/4 cup sweet pickle relish
1 tablespoon prepared mustard

Place the frozen peas in a saucepan. Add enough water to cover. Bring to a boil over medium heat; cook for 1 minute. Drain. Rinse with cold water to cool; drain well. Combine the peas, cheese and eggs in a large bowl and mix gently. Combine the mayonnaise-type salad dressing, pickle relish and mustard in a small bowl and mix well. Add the relish mixture to the peas mixture; mix well. Chill, covered, until serving time. Yield: 15 servings.

Darlene Lannholm, Preceptor Mu Tau
Galesburg, Illinois

GERMAN POTATO SALAD

5 pounds red potatoes
1/2 pound sliced bacon
2 bunches green onions, chopped
Salt and pepper to taste
1 cup white vinegar
1 cup sugar
3 tablespoons cornstarch

Cook the potatoes in their skins until tender; peel. Cook the bacon until crisp, reserving the drippings. Crumble the bacon. Combine the potatoes, bacon, green onions, salt and pepper in a bowl; mix gently. Combine the vinegar, 1 1/2 cups water, sugar, cornstarch and 4 tablespoons of the reserved bacon drippings in a medium saucepan or in the skillet used to cook the bacon. Cook over medium heat until thickened, stirring constantly. Pour the vinegar mixture over the potato mixture; mix gently. Serve at room temperature or chilled. Yield: 10 to 12 servings.

Renée Hesselrode, Xi Nu Phi
Jackson, Missouri

HOT GERMAN POTATO SALAD

This recipe has been in my family for years, and I have now passed it on to my children. It is a great salad for summer picnics, as it does not have mayonnaise. It can be placed in a slow cooker to keep warm.

8 to 10 medium potatoes
1 1/2 teaspoons celery seed
2 teaspoons salt
1/4 teaspoon black pepper
4 or 5 slices bacon, chopped
2 ribs celery, chopped
1 cup chopped onion
1/4 cup chopped green bell pepper
2 tablespoons flour
2/3 cup apple cider vinegar
4 to 5 tablespoons sugar
4 hard-cooked eggs, diced
2 hard-cooked eggs, sliced

Place the potatoes in a saucepan. Add enough water to cover and bring to a simmer. Simmer for 20 minutes or until potatoes are tender; drain. When the potatoes are almost cool, peel them and cut into bite-size pieces (1-inch cubes). Place in a large bowl. Add the celery seed, 1 teaspoon salt and black pepper and mix gently. Cook the bacon slowly in a skillet over medium heat just until crisp. Before the pieces become very crisp, add the celery, onion and bell pepper. Sauté until vegetables are tender. Stir in the flour and cook for a few minutes; do not brown. Add the vinegar, 2/3 cup water and sugar; cook until smooth and slightly thickened, stirring constantly. Add the remaining 1 teaspoon salt and the 4 diced hard-cooked eggs to the potato mixture; mix gently. Pour the hot vinegar mixture over the potato mixture, gently lifting and blending. Taste for seasoning, adding salt and pepper if needed. Spoon into a serving bowl. Garnish with the 2 sliced eggs and parsley flakes. Serve warm. Yield: 6 to 8 servings.

Joyce Fred, Alpha Iota Master
Springfield, Illinois

La Dana W. Singleton, Xi Alpha Sigma, Ocean Springs, Mississippi, makes ***Balsamic Vinegar Salad Dressing*** *by whisking 1/4 cup each balsamic vinegar and extra-virgin olive oil, 2 tablespoons fresh lemon juice, 2 teaspoons soy sauce, 1 teaspoon sugar and freshly ground pepper to taste with a combination of 3 or 4 mashed garlic cloves and 1/2 teaspoon coarse salt.*

LAYERED POTATO SALAD

6 to 8 medium potatoes, peeled
1 onion, cut into narrow rings
6 hard-cooked eggs, peeled and sliced
24 ounces cottage cheese
2 cups real mayonnaise
3 tablespoons vegetable oil
Seasoned salt to taste

Place the potatoes in a saucepan. Add enough water to cover and bring to a simmer. Simmer for 20 minutes or until potatoes are tender; drain. Cool and slice. Layer the potatoes, onion, hard-cooked eggs and cottage cheese 1/3 at a time in a 9×13-inch baking dish, spreading mayonnaise between layers and drizzling layers with vegetable oil and sprinkling with seasoned salt. Chill, covered, for 24 hours. Let stand at room temperature for 30 minutes before serving. Yield: 10 to 12 servings.

Tammie Schmidt, Xi Epsilon Gamma
Clinton, Oklahoma

PICNIC POTATO SALAD

3 medium potatoes
1 large rib celery, diced
1/2 medium sweet onion, diced
5 hard-cooked eggs, peeled and sliced
1 cup mayonnaise
1 teaspoon prepared mustard
1 tablespoon white vinegar
Salt and pepper to taste

Place the unpeeled potatoes in a saucepan. Add enough water to cover and bring to a simmer. Simmer for 20 minutes or until potatoes are tender; drain. When the potatoes are almost cool, peel them and cut into 1/2-inch cubes. Combine the potatoes, celery, onion and eggs in a large bowl and toss gently. Combine the mayonnaise, mustard, vinegar, salt and pepper in a small bowl and blend until smooth, thinning with milk if necessary. Add the mayonnaise mixture to the potato mixture and toss gently. Chill, covered, until serving time. Yield: 4 to 5 servings.

Mae Ann Schoenborn, Laureate Zeta Eta
Lake Panasoffkee, Florida

SWEET POTATO SALAD WITH PINEAPPLE AND RED PEPPERS

4 orange-fleshed sweet potatoes
1 small red bell pepper
1/4 cup mayonnaise
2 tablespoons Dijon mustard
4 ribs celery, cut into 1/4-inch slices
1 (8-ounce) can pineapple chunks, drained
2 scallions, minced
Salt and freshly ground black pepper to taste
1/2 cup (2 ounces) coarsely chopped pecans, toasted

Wrap the sweet potatoes individually in foil. Bake at 400 degrees for 1 hour or until tender. Cool until easy to handle. Peel the sweet potatoes, then cut into 3/4-inch chunks. Remove seeds from the bell pepper and cut into 1/4-inch dice. Combine the mayonnaise and Dijon mustard in a large bowl and whisk until smooth. Add the sweet potatoes, celery, bell pepper, pineapple and scallions; toss gently, seasoning with salt and black pepper. Chill, covered, for 1 to 10 hours. Just before serving, adjust the seasoning, fold in the pecans and sprinkle with chopped fresh chives. Serve cold. Yield: 6 servings.

Shirley Gabrielli, Xi Xi Psi
Dublin, California

BACON AND TOMATO SALAD

Try including cauliflower and at least 1 green vegetable in your vegetable selection. You can use a larger amount of any vegetable you prefer.

2 pints grape tomatoes, halved
4 green onions, chopped
1/4 cup crisp-cooked crumbled bacon
1/2 cup chopped raw asparagus (optional)
1/2 cup chopped raw green beans (optional)
3/4 cup chopped raw cauliflower (optional)
1/2 cup chopped raw red bell pepper (optional)
Purchased bacon and tomato salad dressing to taste

Combine the tomatoes, green onions, bacon and a selection of the optional vegetables in a bowl. Add the salad dressing. Toss and serve.
Yield: 8 to 12 servings.

Susan Maxey, Xi Mu Lambda
Caulfield, Missouri

TANGY TOMATO SALAD

1 (14-ounce) can stewed tomatoes
1 (3-ounce) package lemon gelatin
Dash of Tabasco sauce or Louisiana hot sauce
Sour cream to taste

Pour the undrained tomatoes into a bowl. Cut larger tomato pieces into smaller pieces. Let stand in the refrigerator, covered, until chilled. Prepare the lemon gelatin in a medium bowl using the package directions; chill until it begins to thicken. Stir the Tabasco sauce into the tomatoes. Add the tomato mixture to the partially set gelatin mixture and mix well. Spoon into an 8- or 9-inch serving dish. Chill until firm. Top each serving with a dollop of sour cream.
Yield: 6 to 8 servings.

Emily Anne Williamson, Laureate Epsilon Phi
Dover, Florida

HEARTY REUBEN SALAD

4 cups torn iceberg lettuce
1 (16-ounce) can sauerkraut, rinsed and drained
5 to 6 ounces sliced or canned corned beef, chopped
1 cup cubed Swiss cheese
2 tablespoons chopped fresh parsley
1/4 to 1/2 cup Thousand Island salad dressing
1/2 cup rye croutons
4 hard-cooked eggs, quartered

Place the lettuce, sauerkraut, corned beef, cheese and parsley in a large bowl and toss to combine. Drizzle with salad dressing. Garnish with croutons and eggs. Yield: 4 or 5 servings.

Florence Heintschel, Alpha Eta Master
Curtice, Ohio

HAM AND LEEK SALAD

2 leeks, thinly sliced
1 (16-ounce) can pineapple tidbits, drained, juice reserved
1 (16-ounce) can corn, drained
1 large apple, peeled and diced
12 ounces ham, thinly sliced
12 ounces shredded mozzarella cheese (3 cups)
5 hard-cooked eggs, thinly sliced
Curry powder to taste
1 cup mayonnaise
1 cup sour cream

Layer the leeks, pineapple, corn, apple, ham, cheese and eggs in a trifle bowl, sprinkling some of the layers with curry powder. Combine the mayonnaise, sour cream and reserved pineapple juice in a small bowl and whisk until smooth. Pour the mayonnaise mixture evenly over the top of the salad. Marinate, covered, in the refrigerator for 24 hours before serving. Yield: 15 servings.

Janice Nepita, Xi Beta Kappa
Columbia, South Carolina

TURKEY HAM SALAMI SALAD

1/4 pound shaved cooked turkey
1/4 pound shaved cooked ham
1/4 pound shaved salami
4 ounces (1 cup) shredded Swiss cheese
1 head lettuce, torn into bite-size pieces
2 small tomatoes, chopped
1 small onion, chopped
3/4 cup vegetable oil
1/4 cup tarragon vinegar
Oregano to taste
Garlic salt to taste
1 small loaf French bread, cubed

Place the turkey, ham, salami, cheese, lettuce, tomatoes and onion in a salad bowl and toss to combine. Place the vegetable oil, vinegar, oregano and garlic in a jar and shake vigorously to combine. Toss the dressing and bread cubes into the turkey mixture just before serving. Yield: 8 to 10 servings.

Julie Eilers, Delta Phi
Kansas City, Missouri

Mary Darby, Laureate Beta Omicron, North Fort Myers, Florida, makes ***Pappy Mac's Meat Slaw*** *by combining 16 ounces cole slaw mix, a 10-ounce can of lean ham, 8 ounces diced hard salami, 1 chopped medium onion, 8 ounces cubed cheese, 4 ounces sliced and quartered pepperoni, 1 diced large tomato, 1 bottle Italian salad dressing, 1/2 drained (6-ounce) jar of green olives, and 1 jar bacon bits. Refrigerate, covered, for 8 to 10 hours.*

BEST CHICKEN SALAD

5 or 6 cooked chicken breasts, chopped
4 ribs celery, finely chopped
1/4 medium onion, finely chopped
2 tablespoons dill pickle relish
2 tablespoons sweet pickle relish
1 tablespoon apple cider vinegar
1 teaspoon prepared mustard
1 teaspoon sugar
Mayonnaise-type salad dressing to taste
Salt and pepper to taste

Combine the chicken, celery, onion, dill pickle relish, sweet pickle relish, vinegar, mustard, sugar, mayonnaise-type salad dressing, salt and pepper in a bowl and mix well. Chill, covered, until ready to serve. Yield: 8 to 12 servings.

Rose Albert, Laureate Alpha
Madison, Alabama

CALIFORNIA CHICKEN SALAD

1/2 cup butter
2 cups mayonnaise
1/4 cup minced parsley
1/2 teaspoon curry powder
1/4 teaspoon minced garlic
Pinch of marjoram
Salt and pepper to taste
4 cups shredded cooked chicken
2 cups seedless green grapes, sliced
1/2 cup toasted slivered almonds

Melt the butter in a saucepan and cool to room temperature. Combine the mayonnaise, parsley, curry powder, garlic, marjoram, salt and pepper in a small bowl and mix well. Stir the cooled butter gently into the mayonnaise mixture. Combine the chicken, grapes and almonds in a large bowl and mix gently. Mound the chicken mixture on lettuce leaves. Spoon the curry dressing over the chicken and sprinkle with paprika. Yield: 4 servings.

Margie F. Shanafelt, Nu Master
Centralia, Illinois

GRAPE ALMOND CHICKEN SALAD

8 chicken breast halves, cooked
3 cups diced celery
1/2 cup finely diced onion
1 (8-ounce) can sliced water chestnuts, drained
3 cups red or green seedless grapes, halved
3/4 cup slivered almonds
10 ounces pasta shells, cooked and drained
1 (16-ounce) bottle buttermilk ranch salad dressing
3 tablespoons milk
1/2 cup mayonnaise
2 teaspoons Beau Monde seasoning
1 teaspoon salt
1/2 teaspoon pepper

Remove the skin and bones from the chicken and cut the chicken into 1/2-inch chunks. Combine the chicken, celery, onion, water chestnuts, grapes, almonds and pasta in a large bowl and mix gently. Place the salad dressing, milk, mayonnaise, Beau Monde seasoning, salt and pepper in a jar and shake vigorously to combine. Pour the dressing over the salad and mix well. Chill, covered, for 8 to 10 hours to marry the flavors. Yield: 12 to 16 or more servings.

Carol Julian, Laureate Gamma Kappa
Columbia, Missouri

ORANGE CHICKEN PASTA SALAD

2 cups diced cooked chicken
2 cups bow tie pasta, cooked and drained
1 (8-ounce) can mandarin oranges, drained
1/2 cup diced red bell pepper
1/2 cup diced celery
1/2 cup frozen green peas, cooked and drained
1/2 cup wine vinegar
1 cup sugar
1 teaspoon salt
1 teaspoon dry mustard
1 cup vegetable oil
1/2 cup cashews

Combine the chicken, pasta, mandarin oranges, bell pepper, celery and peas in a large bowl and toss. Combine the vinegar, sugar, salt and dry mustard in a blender container. Add the vegetable oil in a fine stream, processing constantly at high speed until emulsified. Add the dressing to the chicken mixture and toss gently. Toss in the cashews just before serving. Yield: 8 servings.

Ruth Ann Carlisle, Preceptor Zeta Upsilon
Richardson, Texas

APPLE CHICKEN SALAD

1 1/2 cups diced unpeeled red apples
1 1/4 teaspoons lemon juice
1 1/2 cups cubed cooked chicken
1/2 cup diced celery
1 tablespoon chopped green onion tops
1/2 cup chopped walnuts
3 tablespoons mayonnaise, regular or light
1 tablespoon Dijon mustard
1/2 teaspoon salt
1/8 teaspoon cracked pepper

Toss the apples with the lemon juice and set aside. Combine the chicken, celery, green onion, walnuts, mayonnaise, Dijon mustard, salt and pepper in a bowl and stir gently. Add the undrained apples; mix well. Serve on a bed of lettuce surrounded with thin slices of cantaloupe or other fruit. Garnish with chopped walnuts. Yield: 4 to 6 servings.

Donna de Zayas, Preceptor Xi
Pawleys Island, South Carolina

COLD CHINESE NOODLES

1 boneless skinless chicken breast, poached, cooled, julienned
5 ounces ham, julienned
1 bunch scallions, julienned
1/2 cup coarsely chopped walnuts
16 ounces vermicelli or angel hair pasta, cooked al dente, chilled
1 cup vegetable oil
2 1/2 tablespoons dark sesame oil
2 tablespoons sesame seeds
3 tablespoons ground coriander seeds
3/4 cup soy sauce
1 scant teaspoon hot chile oil
1/2 cup chopped pecans, toasted

Combine the chicken, ham, scallions and walnuts in a large bowl; mix gently. Stir in the pasta. Combine the vegetable oil, sesame oil and sesame seeds in a small saucepan over medium heat and cook until seeds turn light brown. Remove from heat. Stir in the coriander and soy sauce, being careful to stand back, as the mixture will sizzle. Stir in the chile oil. Pour the hot dressing over the pasta mixture and toss to coat evenly. Chill, covered, for 3 to 10 hours. Garnish with toasted pecans and serve. Yield: 6 to 8 servings.

Martha Smith, Preceptor Beta Delta
Niles, Michigan

RASPBERRY CHICKEN SALAD

This chicken salad is a favorite at my daughter's bakery and deli, where she sells it in sandwiches and salads. She got the recipe from me.

8 chicken breast halves
2 chicken bouillon cubes
4 ribs celery, finely chopped
1 tablespoon lemon juice
1/4 cup raspberry salad dressing
1/2 cup toasted slivered or sliced almonds
1/2 cup red grapes, halved
1 cup mayonnaise
1 teaspoon Cavender's Greek Seasoning
Salt and pepper to taste

Combine the chicken and bouillon cubes in a saucepan. Add enough water to cover and bring to a simmer. Simmer for about 30 minutes or until chicken is cooked through. Drain and cool to room temperature. Chop the chicken into small bite-size pieces. Combine the chicken, celery, lemon juice and salad dressing in a bowl and mix well. Stir in the almonds, grapes and mayonnaise. If mixture is too dry or thick, stir in more salad dressing. Season with the Cavender's, salt and pepper. Yield: 8 to 10 servings.

Alfreda Bruen, Zeta Sigma
Fairfield Bay, Arkansas

TROPICAL CHICKEN SALAD

2 cups cubed cooked chicken
1 cup chopped celery
1 cup mayonnaise
1/2 to 1 teaspoon curry powder
1 (20-ounce) can pineapple chunks, drained
2 large, firm bananas, sliced
1 (11-ounce) can mandarin oranges, drained
1/2 cup flaked coconut
3/4 cup salted peanuts or cashew halves

Combine the chicken, celery and a mixture of the mayonnaise and curry powder in a large bowl; mix well. Chill, covered, for at least 30 minutes. Add the pineapple, bananas, oranges and coconut just before serving; toss gently. Sprinkle with peanuts and serve over salad greens if desired. Yield: 4 to 6 servings.

Tish Fitzsimmons, Laureate Beta Beta
Glenwood, Iowa

SHRIMP AND AVOCADO SALAD

1 pound frozen cooked popcorn shrimp, thawed
1 cup thinly sliced celery
2 tablespoons Italian dressing
4 tablespoons mayonnaise
Salt and pepper to taste
1 avocado
2 teaspoons lemon juice

Combine the shrimp, celery, Italian dressing and mayonnaise in a bowl and mix well. Season with salt and pepper. Chill, covered, until serving time. Peel and dice the avocado and toss it with the lemon juice to prevent darkening. Add the avocado to the shrimp mixture and mix gently. Yield: 6 servings.

Nancy K. Corn, Laureate Delta Omicron
San Antonio, Texas

SUPER SHRIMP PASTA SALAD

1/2 cup French salad dressing
1 cup mayonnaise
1/2 cup chili sauce
1/2 teaspoon pepper
4 cups cooked small pasta shells
2 cups raw cauliflower pieces
1 cup sliced black olives
1 cup sliced scallions
2 cups cooked small shrimp

Combine the French dressing, mayonnaise, chili sauce and pepper in a large bowl and whisk until smooth. Add the pasta and toss to coat. Fold in the cauliflower, olives, scallions and shrimp so that all are lightly coated with dressing. Chill, covered, for 1 hour before serving. Yield: 4 servings.

Toni V. Sweeney, Preceptor Omicron Alpha
Rancho Santa Margarita, California

SALADE NICOISE

5 ounces fresh baby spinach leaves
2 (6-ounce) cans albacore white tuna, drained
1 medium red onion, chopped
3/4 pound small red potatoes, cooked and quartered
1 (10-ounce) package frozen green beans, cooked and drained
8 tablespoons olive oil
2 teaspoons Dijon mustard
2 crushed garlic cloves
3/4 teaspoon salt
3 tablespoons balsamic vinegar
1 1/2 cups grape tomatoes, halved
16 small black olives
1/3 cup crumbled feta cheese
Freshly ground black pepper to taste

Spread the spinach leaves over the bottom of a large shallow salad bowl. Combine the next 4 ingredients in a separate bowl and toss. Place the olive oil, Dijon mustard, garlic, salt and vinegar in a jar and shake to combine. Pour the dressing over the tuna mixture and toss to combine. Spoon the tuna mixture over the spinach leaves. Garnish with tomatoes, olives and feta cheese. Sprinkle pepper over the top and serve. Yield: 25 to 30 servings.

Jane Johnson, Xi Zeta Phi
Charleston, Illinois

TUNA POTATO SALAD

1 (6-ounce) can tuna, drained and flaked
3 or 4 white potatoes, peeled, cooked, sliced
1 apple, peeled and chopped
1/2 cup frozen peas, cooked and drained
1/4 cup sliced green olives
3 hard-cooked eggs, sliced
1/4 cup minced onion
1 (2-ounce) jar chopped pimentos, drained
3/4 cup mayonnaise or salad dressing
1/2 teaspoon prepared mustard
Salt and pepper to taste

Combine the tuna, potatoes, apple, peas, olives, eggs, onion, pimentos, mayonnaise, mustard, salt and pepper in a large bowl; mix well. Chill, covered, until serving time. Garnish with additional hard-cooked egg slices if desired. Sprinkle with paprika and serve. Yield: 6 servings.

Patricia Roberson, Alpha Beta Master
Plantation, Florida

June B. Badgett, Zeta Pi, Burleson, Texas, makes ***Vegetable Salad*** *by tossing 2 diced peeled cucumbers, 2 diced zucchini, 3/4 cup shredded carrots, 1/2 cup ranch salad dressing, and black pepper to taste together in a large bowl.*

TOMATO TUNA SALAD

1/2 head iceberg lettuce, shredded
1 bunch romaine or leaf lettuce, torn
1 large carrot, shredded
2 ribs celery, chopped
1/4 small head red cabbage, shredded
1 cup cherry tomatoes, halved
2 (6-ounce) cans tuna in water, drained and flaked
1 (3-ounce) package ramen noodles

Place the first 7 ingredients in a large bowl; toss to combine. Set aside until serving time. Crush the dry ramen noodles. Save the flavor packet for another use. Add the crushed noodles to the lettuce mixture and toss. Serve with salad dressing. Yield: 6 servings.

Gloria R-Feist, Tau Master
Tacoma, Washington

HONEY MUSTARD ZITI SALAD

8 ounces ziti, cooked and drained
2 to 3 ounces (2 cups) torn fresh spinach
11 ounces (2 cups) cherry tomatoes, halved
11 to 12 ounces (1 1/2 cups) fresh peas or thawed frozen peas
1/2 to 3/4 cup pistachios
2 tablespoons honey
2 1/2 tablespoons Dijon mustard
1 1/2 teaspoons oregano
1/2 teaspoon garlic powder
3 tablespoons red wine vinegar

Combine the pasta, spinach, cherry tomatoes, peas and pistachios in a large bowl. Combine the remaining ingredients in a small bowl and whisk until smooth. Drizzle over the pasta mixture. Toss and serve. Yield: 4 servings.

Joanne Farmer, Preceptor Delta Sigma
Bedford, Texas

GARDEN ROTINI SALAD

16 ounces garden rotini
2 ribs celery, chopped
1 green bell pepper, chopped
1 medium onion, chopped
4 carrots, shredded
1 cup sugar
1/2 cup apple cider vinegar
1 (14-ounce) can sweetened condensed milk
2 cups mayonnaise

Cook the rotini using the package directions; drain and cool. Mix the rotini, celery, bell pepper, onion and carrots in a large bowl. Whisk the remaining ingredients in a small bowl until smooth. Pour over the rotini mixture and mix well. Chill, covered, for 4 to 10 hours. Yield: 10 to 12 servings.

Dorothy Eyberg, Laureate Tau
Arispe, Iowa

SWEET NOODLE VEGETABLE SALAD

2 (3-ounce) packages ramen noodles
3 cups chopped broccoli
1/2 cup chopped cauliflower
1 cup shredded carrots
1 cup sliced celery
1 cup chopped red onion
1/2 cup sugar
1/2 cup light canola oil
1/2 cup apple cider vinegar
1/3 cup sunflower seeds
1/4 cup chopped almonds

Crush the dry ramen noodles; save the flavor packets for another use. Combine the broccoli, cauliflower, carrots, celery, onion and ramen noodles in a large bowl and mix well. Place the sugar, canola oil, vinegar and 2 tablespoons water in a jar and shake vigorously to combine. Add the dressing to the vegetable mixture and toss. Chill, covered, for 8 to 10 hours. Toss in the sunflower seeds and almonds just before serving. Yield: 4 to 6 servings.

Sheila Woodard, Xi Gamma
Lewiston, Maine

ORZO SALAD

Orzo is a pasta shaped like pearls of barley. This is a great side dish for grilled fish or chicken.

16 ounces orzo
1/4 cup fresh lemon juice
6 teaspoons finely chopped fresh marjoram
4 teaspoons Dijon mustard
1 teaspoon grated lemon zest
1/2 cup olive oil
1 1/2 cups crumbled feta cheese
3 green onions, thinly sliced
1 cup pitted kalamata olives, quartered
24 cherry tomatoes, halved

Cook the orzo in boiling salted water just until tender but still firm to bite, stirring occasionally; drain. Rinse under cold water. Drain well and place in a large bowl. Combine the lemon juice, 5 teaspoons of the marjoram, Dijon mustard and lemon zest in a small bowl and whisk to blend. Whisk in the olive oil to make the vinaigrette. Set aside 2 tablespoons of the vinaigrette. Add the remaining vinaigrette, cheese, green onions and olives to the orzo and toss to coat. Season to taste with salt and pepper. Let stand, covered, at room temperature for 2 hours. Combine the reserved 2 tablespoons vinaigrette and tomatoes in a medium bowl and toss to coat. Season to taste with salt and pepper. Stir the tomato mixture into the orzo mixture. Sprinkle with the remaining 1 teaspoon marjoram and serve. Yield: 8 servings.

Catherine McNamara, Preceptor Eta Sigma
Jefferson City, Missouri

SOUTHWESTERN BLACK BEAN AND PASTA SALAD

16 ounces penne
2 teaspoons olive oil
1 teaspoon cumin
1 (15-ounce) can black beans, drained
1 (8-ounce) can whole kernel corn, drained
1/2 red bell pepper, chopped
1/2 green bell pepper, chopped
3 green onions, chopped
1 (4-ounce) can sliced black olives, drained
1/2 teaspoon McCormick's Santa Fe Spice
1 cup sour cream
1/2 cup mayonnaise
1/4 cup salsa
1/4 cup chopped fresh cilantro
3 or 4 cherry tomatoes, halved

Cook the pasta using the package directions; drain and rinse under ice water. Drain well and place in a large bowl with the olive oil; toss to coat. Sprinkle with 1/2 teaspoon of the cumin. Add the beans, corn, bell peppers, green onions and olives and toss. Sprinkle with Santa Fe Spice. Combine the sour cream, mayonnaise, salsa, remaining 1/2 teaspoon cumin and cilantro in a small bowl; mix well. Add to the pasta mixture and stir well. Chill for 1 to 2 hours before serving. Garnish with tomatoes and additional cilantro and serve. Yield: 8 to 10 servings.

Sharon Robinson, Zeta Sigma
Fairfield Bay, Arkansas

SPICY SESAME NOODLES

16 ounces lo mein noodles or thin linguini, cooked, drained
6 tablespoons peanut oil
2 tablespoons sesame oil
2/3 cup soy sauce
2 tablespoons lemon juice
3/4 cup hoisin sauce
1/4 cup brown sugar
3 dashes of Tabasco sauce
1 teaspoon cayenne pepper
1/4 cup white wine
1 tablespoon minced garlic
1/4 cup sesame seeds
Snow peas, red bell pepper strips and julienned carrots in desired amounts

Place the noodles in a glass dish. Combine the peanut oil, sesame oil, soy sauce, lemon juice, hoisin sauce, brown sugar, Tabasco sauce, cayenne pepper, wine and garlic in a blender and process until smooth. Pour the soy sauce mixture over the noodles. Toss in the sesame seeds, snow peas, bell pepper and carrots. Marinate, covered, in the refrigerator for at least 2 hours. Yield: 6 to 8 servings.

Val Knickerbocker, Delta Gamma
Severna Park, Maryland

TORTELLINI SALAD

Tortellini is a small ring-shaped stuffed pasta available in grocery stores. This makes a large salad—if it seems too dry, add more salad dressing.

3 tablespoons olive oil
2/3 cup tomato salad dressing
2 (7-ounce) packages tortellini, cooked, drained
6 radishes, sliced
2 ribs celery, chopped
1 cup chopped carrots
2 Roma tomatoes, chopped
1 1/2 cups chopped broccoli
1/2 cup chopped red bell pepper
1/4 cup chopped red onion
1/2 cup chopped cucumber
1 (6-ounce) can sliced black olives, drained
1 cup julienned summer sausage
1/2 cup grated Parmesan cheese
1 teaspoon salt
1 teaspoon pepper

Combine the olive oil and 1/3 cup of the salad dressing in a large glass dish and whisk to blend. Stir in the tortellini and marinate, covered, in the refrigerator for 8 to 10 hours. Add the radishes, celery, carrots, tomatoes, broccoli, bell pepper, onion, cucumber, olives, summer sausage, Parmesan cheese, salt and pepper and toss to combine. Add the remaining salad dressing; toss and serve. Yield: 20 servings.

Kathleen L. Goetzinger, Xi Chi
Sioux Falls, South Dakota

JALAPENO PASTA SALAD

A food processor is great for chopping the jalapeños, onion, and tomato.

2 cups sour cream
2 cups mayonnaise
12 ounces rotini
1/2 cup chopped onion
2 or 3 jalapeño peppers, chopped
1 tomato, chopped
1 tablespoon garlic powder
16 ounces shredded Cheddar cheese (or other cheese) (4 cups)

Combine the sour cream and mayonnaise in a large bowl and whisk to blend. Cook the rotini according to package directions. Drain, rinse under cold running water and drain well. Stir the rotini into the sour cream mixture gently. Add the onion, jalapeños, tomato, garlic powder and half the cheese and toss gently until well mixed. Layer the remaining cheese over the top. Chill, covered, for 8 to 10 hours.
Yield: 6 to 10 servings.

Theresa Lackey, Beta
Lincoln, Nebraska

RICE ARTICHOKE SALAD

1 (7-ounce) package Rice-A-Roni
2 green onions, chopped
1/2 green bell pepper, chopped
8 stuffed green olives, chopped
2 (6-ounce) jars marinated artichokes, drained, juice reserved
1/3 cup mayonnaise
1/4 teaspoon curry powder

Prepare and cook the Rice-A-Roni using the package directions, omitting the butter. Remove from heat and place in a bowl to cool. Add the green onions, bell pepper and olives to the rice mixture. Chop the artichokes and add to the rice mixture; mix well. Combine the reserved artichoke juice, mayonnaise and curry powder in another bowl and whisk to blend. Stir the curry mixture into the rice mixture; mix well. Chill, covered, for 8 to 10 hours.
Yield: 8 to 10 servings.

Jody Carder, Xi Alpha Chi
Maple Valley, Washington

RICE SALAD RING

1 1/2 cups uncooked rice
2 or 3 chicken bouillon cubes
1/4 cup vegetable oil
2 tablespoons white vinegar
1/4 cup (about) mayonnaise
1 teaspoon curry powder
Salt to taste
Pinch of pepper
1 cup finely chopped celery
1/2 cup chopped green onions
1/2 cup chopped green bell pepper
1/4 cup chopped parsley

Cook the rice with the bouillon cubes in water for 16 minutes or until tender and fluffy. Place the rice in a bowl and toss lightly with the vegetable oil and vinegar. Stir in enough mayonnaise to moisten. Season with curry powder, salt and pepper. Add the celery, green onions, bell pepper and parsley, tossing to mix. Press lightly into an oiled 6-cup ring mold. Chill if desired. Unmold the rice ring and fill the center with shrimp, tomatoes or mixed vegetables.
Yield: 8 to 10 servings.

Barbara Laluk, Laureate Epsilon
Brandon, Manitoba, Canada

---

*For **Chef's Salad Dressing,** Mary S. Mentz, Alpha Zeta, Walden, New York, combines a 10-ounce can of tomato soup, 3/4 cup sugar, 1/2 cup olive oil, 3/4 cup vinegar, 1 finely chopped green bell pepper, 1 finely chopped large onion, 1 teaspoon salt, 1/4 teaspoon black pepper, 2 tablespoons Worcestershire sauce, 1/2 teaspoon dry mustard and 1/2 teaspoon paprika in a jar. Shake to mix. Use immediately.*

Soups

JAILHOUSE CHILI

When I was a child, my granddaddy was sheriff of Coosa County, Alabama. He led an exciting life!

1/4 cup vegetable oil
3 pounds lean stew beef, cubed
8 chile peppers, chopped, or 6 tablespoons chili powder
1 tablespoon salt
5 garlic cloves, minced
1 teaspoon cumin
1 teaspoon marjoram
1 teaspoon cayenne pepper
1 tablespoon sugar
3 tablespoons paprika
3 tablespoons flour
6 tablespoons white cornmeal

Heat the vegetable oil in a Dutch oven or large kettle over high heat; add the beef and cook until meat is gray but not browned, stirring constantly. Add 1 quart water and bring to a boil. Reduce heat and simmer, covered, for 1 1/2 to 2 hours. Add the next 8 ingredients; simmer, covered, for 30 minutes longer. Combine the flour, cornmeal and 1 cup water in a small bowl; blend until smooth. Stir the flour mixture into the chili and simmer, uncovered, for 5 minutes, stirring constantly and adding more water if too thick. Yield: 10 to 12 servings.

Glenda Cardwell, Xi Beta Chi
Rockford, Alabama

CORNED BEEF AND CABBAGE SOUP

2 to 3 pounds corned beef
1 beef bouillon cube
1/2 cup chopped onion
2 garlic cloves, sliced
2 whole cloves
1 bay leaf
1 teaspoon peppercorns
6 new potatoes
3 carrots, julienned
6 cups chopped cabbage

Combine the corned beef and 7 cups water in a kettle or Dutch oven over medium-high heat and bring to a simmer. Simmer for 15 minutes; skim. Add the bouillon cube, onion, garlic, cloves, bay leaf and peppercorns. Simmer, covered, for 3 to 4 hours. Remove the corned beef from the broth and allow both broth and corned beef to cool. Cut the corned beef into bite-size pieces. Return the meat to the broth; add the potatoes and carrots; simmer, covered, for 15 minutes. Stir in the cabbage and simmer, covered, for 15 minutes longer. Remove the cloves, bay leaf and peppercorns. Yield: 4 to 6 servings.

Dianne Cihal, Preceptor Beta
Kearney, Nebraska

CABBAGE SOUP

1 pound lean ground beef
1/2 teaspoon garlic salt
1/4 teaspoon garlic powder
1/4 teaspoon pepper
1 (16-ounce) can kidney beans
2 ribs celery, chopped
1/2 medium head cabbage, chopped
1 (28-ounce) can tomatoes, drained and chopped
4 beef bouillon cubes

Brown the ground beef in a skillet, stirring until crumbly; drain. Finely chop the browned ground beef and return to the skillet. Add the garlic salt, garlic powder, pepper, undrained kidney beans, celery, cabbage, tomatoes, bouillon cubes and a 28-ounce can of water; bring to a boil. Reduce heat and simmer, partially covered, for 1 hour. Garnish with chopped fresh parsley and serve. Yield: 6 servings.

Wanda E. Dudley, Upsilon Master
Albuquerque, New Mexico

HERBED CHEESEBURGER SOUP

1 pound ground beef
4 tablespoons butter
1 medium onion, chopped
3/4 cup shredded carrots
3/4 cup chopped celery
1 teaspoon basil
1 teaspoon dried parsley
4 cups diced peeled potatoes
3 cups chicken broth
1/4 cup flour
8 ounces Velveeta cheese, cubed
1 1/2 cups milk
3/4 teaspoon salt
1/2 teaspoon pepper
3 to 4 tablespoons sour cream

Brown the ground beef in a large Dutch oven, stirring until crumbly. Remove the beef from the Dutch oven and drain; set beef aside. Melt 1 tablespoon of the butter in the Dutch oven. Sauté the onion, carrots, celery, basil and parsley in the butter for 5 to 10 minutes or until vegetables are tender. Return the beef to the Dutch oven. Add the potatoes and chicken broth; bring to a boil. Reduce heat and simmer, covered, for 10 to 12 minutes or until potatoes are tender. Melt the remaining 3 tablespoons butter in a small skillet over medium heat. Whisk in the flour; cook until bubbly, stirring constantly. Add the flour mixture to the soup; bring to a boil. Boil gently for 2 minutes, stirring constantly. Reduce heat and stir in the Velveeta cheese, milk, salt and pepper. Cook until cheese is melted, stirring constantly. Remove from heat. Stir in sour cream before serving. Serve in bread bowls if desired. The soup reheats nicely. Yield: 10 servings.

Linda Staiger, Preceptor Gamma Omicron
Liberal, Kansas

BACK PORCH BEAN SOUP

1 pound ground beef or turkey
1 onion, chopped
3 garlic cloves, chopped
1 (10-ounce) can tomatoes with green chiles (mild)
1 (14-ounce) can white hominy
1 (15-ounce) can black beans
1 (16-ounce) can kidney beans
2 (16-ounce) cans pinto beans
2 envelopes taco seasoning mix
1 envelope ranch salad dressing mix
1 (15-ounce) can whole kernel corn

Brown the ground beef with the onion and garlic in a skillet, stirring until crumbly; drain. Add remaining ingredients; do not drain the canned ingredients. Simmer, partially covered, for 30 minutes to 2 hours, stirring occasionally. Serve with corn chips and shredded cheese. Yield: 18 to 20 servings.

Gayle Marcks, Nu
Little Rock, Arkansas

EASY CHILI

Use an assortment of beans for this chili: pork and beans, chili beans, navy beans, lima beans, garbanzo beans or black-eyed peas, any kind you like, from 4 to 6 different cans of beans.

2 pounds ground beef
1 large onion, chopped
4 to 6 cans beans (kidney, pinto, red, others)
1/2 cup ketchup
1/3 cup brown sugar
1 tablespoon white vinegar
1 tablespoon prepared mustard
Salt and pepper to taste
Dash of chili powder, or to taste

Brown the ground beef with the onion in a skillet, stirring until crumbly. Drain the plain canned beans. Combine the beef, onion, beans, ketchup, brown sugar, vinegar, mustard, salt, pepper and chili powder in a large kettle over medium heat and stir well. Bring to a simmer. Simmer, covered, for at least 30 minutes. Yield: variable.

Carmel V. Payton, Nu Master
Pacifica, California

RED WINE CHILI

1 cup finely chopped onion
1 cup finely chopped green bell pepper
2 garlic cloves, finely chopped
1 cup dry red wine
1/4 cup Worcestershire sauce
2 pounds ground beef
1 tablespoon chili powder
1 teaspoon celery seed
1 teaspoon black pepper
1/2 teaspoon salt
1/2 teaspoon cumin
2 (16-ounce) cans tomatoes
2 (16-ounce) cans kidney beans

Combine the onion, bell pepper and garlic in a large kettle over low heat and cook for 3 minutes, stirring constantly. Stir in the wine and Worcestershire sauce; bring to a boil. Reduce heat and simmer, uncovered, for 10 minutes, stirring occasionally. Brown the ground beef in a skillet, stirring until crumbly; drain. Stir the chili powder, celery seed, black pepper, salt and cumin into the onion mixture. Simmer, uncovered, for 10 minutes, stirring occasionally. Stir in the undrained tomatoes and ground beef, breaking up the tomatoes with a fork. Bring to a boil. Reduce heat and simmer, covered, for 30 minutes. Stir in the undrained kidney beans; bring to a boil. Reduce heat and simmer, covered, for 30 minutes. Simmer, uncovered, for 30 minutes longer, stirring occasionally. Yield: 10 servings.

Kathy Carle, Xi Beta Delta
Midlothian, Virginia

ITALIAN WEDDING SOUP

The key ingredient is Mrs. Dash seasoning.

2 (32-ounce) cartons 99% fat-free chicken broth
1 cooked chicken breast, coarsely chopped
Chopped celery and carrots to taste
Chopped raw escarole or spinach to taste
2 bay leaves
Garlic powder to taste
Mrs. Dash seasoning to taste
1/3 to 1 cup uncooked very small round or star-shaped pastini or tiny macaroni
Italian Meatballs

Combine the chicken broth, chicken, celery, carrots, escarole, bay leaves, garlic powder and Mrs. Dash seasoning in a large kettle and bring to a boil. Reduce heat and simmer, covered, for 30 minutes or until vegetables are tender. Stir in the pastini and simmer for 5 minutes or until tender. Stir in the Italian Meatballs and heat through. Serve hot with a mountain of grated Romano cheese on top and accompanied by a salad, hot Italian bread and wine. Yield: 15 to 20 servings.

ITALIAN MEATBALLS

1 pound ground beef, or 1/2 pound ground beef mixed with 1/2 pound ground veal
1 large egg, slightly beaten
Parsley flakes to taste
1/4 cup Italian bread crumbs
Oregano to taste
Salt and pepper to taste
1/2 cup shredded provolone cheese

Combine the ground beef, egg, parsley, bread crumbs, oregano, salt, pepper and provolone in a bowl and mix well. Shape into small balls and arrange on a baking sheet that has been sprayed with nonstick cooking spray. Bake at 350 degrees for 25 to 30 minutes or until meatballs are lightly browned but still tender, not crisp. Drain on paper towels. Use immediately in the soup; or arrange in a single layer on a plate, freeze until hard, place in a plastic bag and store in the freezer for future use. Yield: 2 dozen.

Sharon Spence, Alpha Beta Eta
Lees Summit, Missouri

---

*Phyllis Moore, Pi Master, Longview, Washington, prepares **Easy Bake Stew** by layering 1 pound of bite-size pieces of beef chuck, 1 coarsely chopped onion, 4 sliced medium potatoes, 4 sliced medium carrots, one 15-ounce can of beans, one 15-ounce can of whole corn, a can of tomato soup, 1/2 cup water, salt and pepper in a 6-quart baking dish. Bake, covered, at 250 degrees for 5 to 6 hours.*

SPAETZLE SOUP

1/2 cup chopped onion
1/2 to 1 cup sliced fresh mushrooms
1 (15-ounce) can beef broth
1/2 to 1 tablespoon beef bouillon granules
1/2 cup sour cream
1 cup thawed frozen peas
1 pound pork, cooked and cubed
2 cups Spaetzle

Sauté the onion and mushrooms in a small amount of the beef broth in a skillet. Add the remaining broth, 1 1/2 cups water and bouillon to the onion mixture. Stir in the sour cream, peas and pork. Stir in the Spaetzle 10 to 15 minutes before serving. Simmer for 10 to 15 minutes and serve. Yield: 4 to 6 servings.

SPAETZLE

2 cups flour
2 eggs
1 teaspoon vegetable oil
1/4 teaspoon white pepper
1/4 teaspoon salt
Milk as needed
2 tablespoons chopped parsley

Combine the flour, eggs, vegetable oil, white pepper and salt in a bowl and mix with a wooden spoon to make a stiff dough; stir in enough milk to make a stiff batter. Mix in the parsley. Pour the batter into a colander; you will know the batter is the right consistency if it remains in the colander but can be pressed through the holes with ease with the heel of the hand. Press it through the holes of the colander into 3 quarts of boiling salted water, taking care to keep the droplets of batter fairly separated. Boil the Spaetzle until they are a uniform light brown color. Use a strainer or slotted spoon to remove Spaetzle to a bowl of ice water; drain well. Serve immediately or reheat by sautéing in butter. If reheating, add a small amount of breadcrumbs to soak up the excess butter.

Sarah Nowack, Pi Gamma
Fort Atkinson, Iowa

BLACK-EYED PEA SOUP

If you like spicy food, use the tomatoes with green chiles instead of the tomato sauce.

1 pound dried black-eyed peas
1 pound cooked ham, chopped
3 ribs celery, chopped
3 medium onions, chopped
3 carrots, grated
1 (15-ounce) can tomato sauce, or 1 (10-ounce) can tomatoes with green chiles
2 quarts chicken broth
Salt and pepper to taste

Fill a teakettle with water and heat until very hot. Sort and rinse the black-eyed peas. Place in a saucepan and add enough cold water to barely cover. Bring to a full boil; boil for 3 minutes. Drain the peas in a colander. Return the peas to the kettle and add enough teakettle water to cover. Add the ham, celery, onions, carrots, tomato sauce and chicken broth; bring to a boil. Reduce heat and simmer for 20 minutes or until peas and vegetables are tender. Season with salt and pepper. Serve hot. Yield: 6 to 8 servings.

Debbie Ciaccio, Alpha Pi
Natchitoches, Louisiana

HAM AND LIMA BEAN CHILI

1 medium onion, chopped
1 garlic clove, minced
1 tablespoon butter or margarine
2 cups diced cooked ham
2 (10-ounce) packages frozen lima beans, or 2 (15-ounce) cans lima beans
1 (15-ounce) can tomato sauce
1 tablespoon prepared mustard
1½ teaspoons brown sugar
1 envelope chili seasoning mix
1 (16-ounce) can red or kidney beans

Sauté the onion and garlic in the butter in a skillet over medium-low heat for 5 to 10 minutes or until tender. Add the ham, lima beans, tomato sauce, 1 cup water, mustard, brown sugar, chili seasoning mix and undrained red beans; bring to a boil. Reduce heat and simmer, covered, for 10 minutes, or longer if using frozen lima beans. Top with sour cream, Cheddar cheese or chopped onion and serve.
Yield: 4 to 6 servings.

Patricia J. McMahon, Iota Master
Amherst, Nebraska

OLD-FASHIONED PEA SOUP

2 cups dried yellow soup peas or split peas
1 hambone, or desired amount of chopped cooked ham
5 onions, chopped
3 carrots, chopped
2 ribs celery with leaves, chopped
1 teaspoon summer savory
1 bay leaf
Dash of salt
Dash of pepper

Sort and rinse the peas. Combine the peas, hambone, onions, carrots, celery, summer savory, bay leaf and 10 cups water in a large kettle. Bring to a boil; skim. Reduce heat and simmer, covered, for 3 hours or until peas are soft and soup is thin. Simmer, uncovered, for 30 minutes longer or until desired thickness. Season with salt and pepper. Discard bay leaf and hambone. Yield: 6 to 8 servings.

Liz Winters, Xi Delta Upsilon
Golden, British Columbia, Canada

HAM AND POTATO SOUP

½ cup chopped onion
2 tablespoons butter or margarine
1 (10-ounce) can cream of potato soup
1 soup can milk
1 cup diced cooked ham
1 cup frozen cut green beans or canned green beans
¼ teaspoon hot red pepper sauce
⅓ cup grated Parmesan cheese

Sauté the onion in the butter in a saucepan over medium-low heat for 5 to 10 minutes or until tender. Add the next 5 ingredients; bring to a boil. Reduce heat and simmer, covered, for 10 minutes. Add the Parmesan cheese. Heat until cheese is melted, stirring frequently. Yield: about 4 cups.

Ramona Wilkinson, Xi Eta Xi
Rushville, Indiana

SAUSAGE BEAN CHOWDER

2 pounds bulk pork sausage
2 (16-ounce) cans kidney beans
2 (16-ounce) cans diced tomatoes
2 medium onions, chopped
10 to 12 medium potatoes, peeled and cubed
1 small green bell pepper, chopped
2 large bay leaves
½ teaspoon salt
½ teaspoon dried whole thyme
¼ teaspoon garlic powder
¼ teaspoon black pepper

Brown the sausage in a skillet, stirring until crumbly; drain. Combine the sausage, 4 cups of water, undrained kidney beans, undrained tomatoes, onions, potatoes, bell pepper, bay leaves, salt, thyme, garlic powder and black pepper in a large kettle; bring to a boil. Reduce heat and simmer, covered, for 1 hour. Remove bay leaves. Yield: 15 servings.

Carol Jarman, Xi Delta Tau
New Bern, North Carolina

Linda Terry, Preceptor Kappa, Charlottesville, Virginia, makes ***Mixed Vegetable Soup*** *by combining 1 chopped head of cabbage, ½ sliced bunch of celery, one 16-ounce package frozen sliced carrots, one 16-ounce package frozen chopped onions, one 15-ounce can French-cut green beans, one 28-ounce can diced tomatoes, one 16-ounce package frozen okra, one 16-ounce package frozen broccoli and cauliflower, 1 quart tomato juice, and 2 tablespoons each beef bouillon granules and chicken bouillon granules in a large stockpot. Add water to cover and simmer for 20 to 30 minues. Season with salt and pepper.*

SAUSAGE POTATO SOUP

6 cups chicken stock or canned chicken broth
1 pound smoked summer sausage, diced
1 pound red potatoes, peeled and diced
1 (16-ounce) can red kidney beans, drained
1 (15-ounce) can diced tomatoes
1/2 medium head green cabbage, chopped
1 medium onion, chopped
1 large carrot, diced
1/2 green bell pepper, diced
3 garlic cloves, minced
Black pepper to taste

Combine all the ingredients except the black pepper in a large kettle; bring to a boil, stirring occasionally. Reduce heat and simmer, uncovered, for about 2 hours or until desired thickness, stirring occasionally. Season with black pepper. Yield: 3 quarts.

Jeannette Schuh, Preceptor Omega
Dow, Illinois

SMOKED SAUSAGE BEAN SOUP

8 ounces smoked sausage
1 cup chopped onion
1 cup minced celery
2 teaspoons minced garlic
1 tablespoon vegetable oil
6 cups chicken broth
1 (15-ounce) can diced potatoes, drained
1 (15-ounce) can sweet potatoes, drained
1 (15-ounce) can navy beans, rinsed and drained
1 (15-ounce) can pinto beans, rinsed and drained
1 (15-ounce) can black beans, rinsed and drained
3/4 teaspoon thyme
1 bay leaf
1 1/2 teaspoons salt
1/2 teaspoon pepper

Cut the sausage into 1/4-inch slices. Sauté the sausage, onion, celery and garlic in the oil in a heavy kettle over medium heat for 10 minutes or until vegetables are tender. Stir in the remaining ingredients; bring to a boil. Reduce heat and simmer, partially covered, for 15 minutes. Yield: 6 to 8 servings.

Janet Hamilton, Preceptor Alpha Beta
Kalamazoo, Michigan

Debra Carey, Mu Gamma, Fairview, Oklahoma, makes ***Santa Fe Soup*** *by browning 1 pound ground beef with 1/2 chopped onion; drain. Add 1 envelope taco seasoning mix and 1 can diced stewed tomatoes. Bring to a boil. Pour into a slow cooker and add 1 can kidney beans, 1 can whole kernel corn, 1 can tomatoes with green chiles, 8 ounces Velveeta cheese, and salt and pepper to taste. Cook on High for 3 hours.*

CREAMY BRATWURST AND POTATOES

This recipe can be easily doubled or tripled.

1/2 cup chopped onion
1/2 cup shredded or julienned carrots
1 tablespoon butter or margarine, melted
1 (15-ounce) can chicken broth
2 cups diced peeled potatoes
1 cup milk
2 tablespoons flour
12 ounces reduced-fat bratwurst, summer sausage or Polish sausage, cut into bite-size pieces
1/4 to 1/2 pound light Velveeta cheese
1/2 cup frozen peas
Dash of hot red pepper sauce

Sauté the onion and carrots in the butter in a stockpot or 3-quart saucepan over medium-low heat for 5 minutes or until the onion is tender. Add the chicken broth and potatoes; bring to a boil. Reduce the heat and simmer, covered, for 20 minutes or until the potatoes are tender. Combine the milk and flour in a small bowl and whisk to blend. Stir the flour mixture into the potato mixture. Add the bratwurst, cheese, peas and hot pepper sauce and mix well. Cook until bubbly, stirring frequently. Yield: 4 to 6 servings.

Gwen Davenport, Tau Epsilon
Grain Valley, Missouri

KIELBASA CHEESE SOUP

1/2 onion, chopped
1 cup chopped celery
1/4 cup butter, melted
1/4 cup flour
2 teaspoons Worcestershire sauce
3/4 teaspoon dry mustard
1 (15-ounce) can chicken broth
3 cups cubed peeled potatoes
1 cup chopped carrots
8 ounces kielbasa, thinly sliced
3 1/4 cups milk
3 cups shredded Velveeta cheese

Sauté the onion and celery in the butter in a large kettle over medium-low heat for 5 minutes or until tender. Stir in the flour, Worcestershire sauce and mustard. Carefully stir in the chicken broth. Add the potatoes, carrots and kielbasa; bring to a boil. Reduce heat and simmer, covered, for 20 to 30 minutes until vegetables are tender, stirring frequently. Stir in the milk and cheese. Cook until cheese is melted, stirring frequently. Yield: 6 to 8 servings.

Holly Crowell, Zeta Kappa
Red Oak, Iowa

KIELBASA CABBAGE SOUP

6 cups coleslaw mix
2 medium carrots, chopped
1/2 cup chopped onion
2 tablespoons butter or margarine, melted
1 teaspoon celery salt
1 pound kielbasa
4 medium unpeeled apples, chopped
3 medium unpeeled potatoes, chopped
2 teaspoons garlic powder
4 (14-ounce) cans roasted garlic chicken broth
Salt to taste

Sauté the coleslaw mix, carrots and onion in the butter in a large saucepan over medium-low heat for 5 to 8 minutes or until vegetables are tender. Stir in the celery salt, kielbasa, apples, potatoes, garlic powder, chicken broth, 2 soup cans of water and salt. Simmer, uncovered, for 30 minutes or until potatoes are tender. Yield: 8 servings.

Sally Shuck, Iota Iota
Blairsville, Georgia

SPICY SAUSAGE AND POTATO SOUP

1 pound hot Italian sausage links, casings removed
3/4 cup chopped onion
6 slices bacon
1 1/2 teaspoons minced garlic
2 tablespoons chicken soup base
2 large potatoes, peeled, cubed
2 cups shredded washed-and-dried kale or spinach
1/3 cup heavy cream

Arrange the sausage links on a nonstick baking sheet and bake at 300 degrees for 25 minutes or until well browned. Cut into 1/2-inch diagonal slices. Combine the onion and bacon in a large saucepan over medium heat and cook until onion is translucent, stirring frequently. Remove and crumble the bacon; set aside. Add the garlic to the onion and cook for 1 minute longer. Add 1 quart water, chicken soup base and potatoes; bring to a simmer. Simmer for 15 minutes. Stir in the bacon, sausage, kale and cream. Simmer for 4 minutes and serve. Yield: 6 servings.

Natasha Kellerman, Beta Gamma
Batesville, Indiana

---

*For **Ten Can Soup,** Phyllis Walker, Kappa Master, Clovis, New Mexico, browns 1 1/2 pounds ground beef with 1 chopped large onion. Add 3 cans minestrone, 2 cans tomatoes with green chiles, 2 cans ranch-style beans, and 1 can each green beans, black-eyed peas, corn or hominy, and spicy tomato juice. Cook over low heat.*

TUSCAN SAUSAGE SOUP

Try using Italian sausage of medium spiciness.

3 Italian sausage links, casings removed
1 (49-ounce) can chicken broth
1 tablespoon chopped fresh basil
1 tablespoon chopped fresh parsley
4 bay leaves
Salt and pepper to taste
Garlic powder to taste
4 slices bacon, crisp-cooked, crumbled
2 large unpeeled baking potatoes, thinly sliced
1/2 small onion, chopped
1 tablespoon butter
2 cups shredded endive
1 cup half-and-half

Brown the sausage in a skillet, breaking into bite-size pieces; drain. Pour the chicken broth into a kettle over medium-low heat. Add the sausage, basil, parsley, bay leaves, salt, pepper and garlic powder. Cook the bacon in the skillet until crisp; drain. Crumble bacon and set aside. Cut the potato slices into quarters. Combine the potatoes, onion and butter in a microwave-safe bowl. Microwave on High for 4 minutes or until potatoes are about 3/4 cooked. Add the potato mixture and bacon to the sausage mixture. Simmer for 8 minutes or until potatoes are fully cooked. Stir in the endive and simmer for 2 minutes longer. Remove the bay leaves. Stir in the half-and-half and serve with grated Parmesan cheese.
Yield: 6 servings.

Carolyn J. Hall, Beta Tau
Newport News, Virginia

CORN AND SAUSAGE CHOWDER

1 (20-ounce) package frozen hash brown potatoes, thawed
1 (15-ounce) can chicken broth
1 (10-ounce) package frozen corn, thawed
2 cups milk
12 ounces Polish sausage, halved lengthwise, sliced crosswise
1/3 cup sliced green onions
1/4 teaspoon pepper

Combine the potatoes, chicken broth and corn in a Dutch oven; bring to a boil. Reduce heat and simmer, covered, for 10 minutes. Mash the potato mixture slightly with a potato masher. Stir in the milk, sausage, green onions and pepper. Cook over medium-low heat until heated through. Season to taste with salt and pepper, cilantro sprigs and bottled green or red hot pepper sauce if desired.
Yield: 5 servings.

Kaye Clay, Laureate Alpha
Guthrie, Oklahoma

CHEESY TORTILLA SOUP

1 small onion, finely chopped
6 cups chicken broth
2 (14-ounce) cans diced tomatoes
1 (4-ounce) can chopped green chilies
1 jalapeño pepper, chopped (optional)
Salt and pepper to taste
1 teaspoon sugar
Juice of 1 lime
1 cup chopped cooked chicken
1 cup shredded Monterey Jack cheese

Combine the onion and chicken broth in a 6-quart kettle over high heat and bring to a boil. Reduce heat and simmer, uncovered, for 10 minutes. Stir in the undrained tomatoes, undrained green chiles, jalapeño pepper, salt, pepper, sugar, lime juice and chicken. Simmer, covered, for 30 minutes, adding water if soup becomes too thick. At serving time, place a handful of tortilla chips and a rounded tablespoon of shredded cheese in each soup bowl and fill with very hot soup. Garnish with cilantro and serve immediately. Yield: 6 to 8 servings.

Jeanette Hollowell, Laureate Beta Theta
Yorktown, Virginia

TURKEY TORTILLA SOUP

Precook the carrots in the microwave to save time, and add the zucchini last to avoid overcooking.

1 pound ground turkey or chicken
1 onion, chopped
1 or 2 garlic cloves, minced
Dash of pepper
4 (15-ounce) cans chicken broth
1 (24-ounce) jar salsa
1 (15-ounce) can hominy or corn
1 (15-ounce) can pinto beans
2 carrots, sliced
2 medium zucchini, sliced
8 ounces (2 cups) shredded Mexican cheeses

Brown the ground turkey with the onion, garlic and pepper in a skillet, stirring until crumbly; drain. Combine the turkey mixture, chicken broth, salsa, hominy, undrained pinto beans, carrots and zucchini in a 6-quart kettle over medium-high heat. Simmer for 20 to 30 minutes or until cooked through. Serve over broken tortilla chips in soup bowls. Garnish with shredded cheese and chopped cilantro.
Yield: 10 servings.

Linda Pfeifer, Preceptor Mu Omicron
Fullerton, California

CHICKEN ENCHILADA SOUP

4 (10-ounce) cans cream of chicken soup
1 (10-ounce) can tomatoes with green chiles
2 cups heavy cream
1 cup milk
3 or 4 chicken breasts, cooked and cubed
16 ounces Mexican Velveeta cheese, cut into small pieces
Chili powder to taste

Combine the soup, tomatoes, cream, milk, chicken, cheese and chili powder in a slow cooker. Cook on High for 1 hour or until cheese is melted. Reduce heat to Low and cook for 2 to 3 hours, stirring occasionally. Serve topped with crushed white corn chips and sour cream. Yield: 10 to 12 servings.

Crista Eberle, Xi Zeta Nu
West Chester, Ohio

✣ CREAMY WHITE CHILI

1 pound boneless skinless chicken, cut into 1/2-inch cubes
1 onion, chopped
1 1/2 teaspoons garlic powder
1 tablespoon vegetable oil
2 (15-ounce) cans Great Northern beans, rinsed and drained
1 (15-ounce) can chicken broth
2 (4-ounce) cans chopped green chiles, drained
1 teaspoon salt
1 teaspoon cumin
1 teaspoon oregano
1/2 teaspoon black pepper
1/4 teaspoon cayenne pepper
1 cup sour cream
1/2 cup heavy cream

Sauté the chicken, onion and garlic powder in hot oil in a large saucepan over medium heat for 5 to 10 minutes or until chicken is no longer pink. Stir in the next 8 ingredients; bring to a boil. Reduce heat and simmer, uncovered, for 30 minutes. Remove from heat. Stir in the sour cream and heavy cream and serve immediately. Yield: 4 to 6 servings

Debra Pellett, Xi Beta Phi
Atlantic, Iowa

Brenda Kimberly, Xi Zeta Zeta, Colby, Kansas, makes a quick version of ***Chicken Chili*** *by combining 4 chopped cooked chicken breasts, 4 cups chicken broth, 2 cans Great Northern beans, 2 drained cans white corn, two 4-ounce cans diced chiles, 2 tablespoons lime juice, 2 teaspoons cumin, and 1 teaspoon lemon pepper in a stockpot and simmering for 30 minutes. Top individual servings with shredded Monterey Jack cheese. Serve with warm tortillas.*

WHITE CHILI

1 medium onion, chopped
2 (10-ounce) cans tomatoes with green chiles, drained
1 tablespoon minced garlic
2 teaspoons cumin
2 teaspoons cayenne pepper
2 (15-ounce) cans Great Northern beans, partially drained
2 pounds chicken breasts, cooked, skin and bones removed, shredded
3 cups chicken broth
2 cups sour cream
3 cups shredded Monterey Jack or Cheddar cheese

Sauté the onion, tomatoes with green chiles, garlic, cumin and cayenne pepper in hot oil in a skillet over medium heat for 8 to 10 minutes or until onion is tender. Combine the onion mixture, beans, chicken and chicken broth in a large kettle over medium heat; simmer for 1 hour. Stir in the sour cream and cheese and cook until heated through.
Yield: 8 to 12 servings.

Julie Meeker, Xi Psi
Sioux Falls, South Dakota

CHICKEN AND SAUSAGE GUMBO

You may use 10 chicken bouillon cubes in water instead of the chicken stock.

1/2 cup flour
1/2 cup vegetable oil
1 cup chopped onions
1 cup chopped celery
1 cup chopped green bell pepper
2 garlic cloves, minced
5 pounds chicken, cut into pieces
1 pound smoked sausage, cut into pieces
4 quarts chicken stock
1 cup chopped fresh parsley
Salt and black pepper to taste
2 teaspoons gumbo filé

Cook the flour in hot oil in an 8-quart kettle over medium heat for 5 minutes or until flour is the color of chestnuts, stirring constantly. Stir in the onions, celery and bell pepper. Sauté for 8 minutes or until vegetables are tender. Add the garlic, chicken, sausage, and chicken stock; simmer for 30 minutes or until chicken is cooked through. Stir in the parsley, salt, black pepper and gumbo filé. Serve over rice.
Yield: 8 servings.

Monafae Meyers, Laureate Rho
Marrero, Louisiana

CHICKEN FLORENTINE SOUP

3/4 cup chopped onion
2 tablespoons butter or margarine
1/3 cup flour
1 teaspoon salt
1/4 teaspoon garlic powder
2 1/2 cups milk
1 cup chicken broth
1 cup cubed American cheese
1 (10-ounce) package frozen chopped spinach, thawed and drained
1 to 2 cups chopped cooked chicken

Sauté the onion in butter in a 2-quart saucepan over medium-low heat for 5 to 8 minutes or until translucent. Add the flour, salt and garlic powder, stirring until smooth. Add the milk and chicken broth gradually, whisking until smooth. Add the cheese and cook until cheese is melted and soup is thickened, stirring constantly. Stir in the spinach and chicken. Simmer, covered, until heated through. Yield: 4 to 6 servings.

Linda Burgan, Preceptor Gamma Epsilon
Kalamazoo, Michigan

CHUNKY CHICKEN VEGETABLE SOUP

1/2 pound boneless skinless chicken breasts, cubed
1 teaspoon vegetable oil
1 (15-ounce) can chicken broth
2 cups shredded carrots
2 cups chopped onion
2 cups thinly sliced celery
1 envelope Italian salad dressing mix
1/2 cup uncooked quick-cooking rice
2 tablespoons chopped fresh parsley

Brown the chicken in hot oil in a large saucepan. Add the chicken broth, 1 1/2 cups water, carrots, onion, celery and salad dressing mix; bring to a boil. Reduce heat and simmer, covered, for 15 minutes. Stir in the rice and parsley. Cover and remove from heat. Let stand for 5 to 10 minutes or until rice is cooked.
Yield: 5 cups.

Elaine Wilson, Xi Beta Alpha
Artesia, New Mexico

---

*Miriam Blazewick, Preceptor Zeta Delta, Lodi, Ohio, makes **Veggie Cheese Soup** by combining three 15-ounce cans of chicken broth, two 16-ounce packages of frozen mixed vegetables, and 2 cans of garlic and onion diced tomatoes. Cook until the vegetables are tender. Stir in 10 ounces chopped Velveeta cheese. Cook until the cheese melts. Season with hot sauce, basil, or oregano, if desired.*

COCONUT CURRIED CHICKEN SOUP

To toast the curry powder, place it in a heated skillet and cook until the aroma begins to fill the air, stirring constantly.

1 whole chicken, cut into 8 pieces
Salt and pepper to taste
3 tablespoons curry powder, toasted
6 tablespoons butter
1 scant cup flour
4 cups chicken stock
1 cup coconut milk
1 cup chopped onion
1 cup coarsely chopped red bell pepper
1 jalapeño pepper, seeds removed, sliced
1 cup coarsely chopped potato
1 cup honey
Cayenne pepper to taste
1/2 cup chopped cilantro

Sprinkle the chicken with salt and pepper and 1 tablespoon of the curry powder. Sear the chicken in a heavy skillet over medium-high heat until golden brown and 3/4 cooked. Set aside. Melt the butter in a small saucepan and whisk in the flour to make a roux. Combine the chicken stock, the remaining curry powder, coconut milk and roux in a large saucepan over medium-low heat. Simmer until thickened, stirring constantly. Add the chicken, onion, bell pepper, jalapeño pepper and potato. Simmer until chicken is cooked through, stirring occasionally. Stir in the honey and cayenne pepper. Adjust the seasoning. Sprinkle with cilantro and serve.
Yield: 4 large servings.

Barbara Hall, Preceptor Xi
Baxter Springs, Kansas

CLAM CHOWDER

1 small onion, chopped
4 slices bacon, chopped
2 (8-ounce) cans minced clams
1 (15-ounce) can chicken broth
4 medium potatoes, finely diced
1 1/2 teaspoons salt
1/4 teaspoon pepper
2 tablespoons cornstarch
4 cups half-and-half
2 tablespoons butter or margarine

Cook the onion and bacon in a large heavy kettle over medium heat until slightly browned. Stir in the undrained clams, chicken broth, potatoes, salt and pepper. Simmer, covered, for 20 minutes or until potatoes are tender. Dissolve the cornstarch in a small amount of the half-and-half and add to the clam mixture. Add the butter and the remaining half-and-half. Cook over medium heat until thickened, stirring constantly; do not boil. Serve with oyster crackers. Yield: 8 to 10 servings.

Patricia A. Siron, Laureate Gamma Mu
Mexico, Missouri

CREAMY CRAB SOUP

4 tablespoons butter or margarine
4 tablespoons flour
1 teaspoon salt
1/8 teaspoon pepper
1 teaspoon seafood seasoning
3 cups hot milk
1 teaspoon grated onion
8 ounces fresh crab meat, shredded
2 teaspoons chopped parsley

Melt the butter in a saucepan over medium heat. Whisk in the flour, salt, pepper and seafood seasoning. Remove from heat and whisk in the milk and onion gradually. Bring to a boil; boil for 1 minute, stirring constantly. Stir in the crab meat and heat for 1 minute. Sprinkle with parsley and serve. Yield: 6 servings.

Debbie Howard, Xi Beta Mu
Fredericksburg, Virginia

CIOPPINO

3/4 cup (1 1/2 sticks) butter
2 onions, chopped
2 garlic cloves, minced
1 bunch fresh parsley, chopped
2 (15-ounce) cans stewed tomatoes
2 (15-ounce) cans chicken broth
2 bay leaves
1 tablespoon basil
1/2 teaspoon thyme
1/2 teaspoon oregano
1 1/2 cups white wine
1 1/2 pounds large shrimp, peeled and deveined
1 1/2 pounds bay scallops
18 small clams
18 mussels, cleaned and debearded
1 1/2 cups crab meat
1 1/2 pounds catfish or cod, chopped

Melt the butter in a large stockpot over medium-low heat. Stir in the onions, garlic and parsley. Cook slowly for 10 minutes or until onions are tender, stirring occasionally. Add the tomatoes and break them into chunks. Mix in the chicken broth, bay leaves, basil, thyme, oregano, wine and 1 cup water. Simmer, covered, for 30 minutes. Stir in the next 5 ingredients. Stir in the catfish and bring to a boil. Simmer, covered, for 5 to 7 minutes or until clams open. Serve with warm crusty bread. Yield: 12 to 14 servings.

Marie Umbriac, Preceptor Alpha Upsilon
Tamaqua, Pennsylvania

Dorothy Heaton, Metairie, Louisiana, prepares ***Corn and Crab Meat Bisque*** *by combining 1 pound crab meat, 2 cans cream-style corn, 1 can cream of chicken soup, 2 cups milk, 2 cups heavy cream, 1/2 cup butter or margarine, 1 cup white gravy mix, 2 tablespoons chopped green onions, and 1 tablespoon Tony Chachere's seasoning in a large stockpot. Cook until thickened.*

CREAMY FISH CHOWDER

8 to 10 green onions, thinly sliced
2 garlic cloves, minced
2 tablespoons butter
4 (10-ounce) cans cream of potato soup
2 (10-ounce) cans cream of mushroom soup
16 ounces cream cheese, cubed
4 cups milk
1 1/2 pounds halibut, salmon or whitefish
1 1/2 cups frozen sliced carrots, thawed
1 1/2 cups frozen corn, thawed
1/8 to 1/4 teaspoon cayenne pepper

Sauté the green onions and garlic in the butter in a Dutch oven or kettle over medium-low heat for 5 to 8 minutes or until tender. Add the soups, cream cheese and milk. Cook until cheese melts, stirring constantly. Bring to a boil. Stir in the halibut, carrots and corn. Reduce heat and simmer, uncovered, for 5 to 10 minutes or until fish flakes easily and all vegetables are tender. Add cayenne pepper. Serve hot. Yield: 16 servings.

Olga Lankford, Laureate Delta Zeta
Houston, Texas

VEGETARIAN BORSCHT

3 medium onions, chopped
1 large carrot, chopped
1 tablespoon vegetable oil
1 to 2 ribs celery, sliced
1 or 2 bay leaves
10 peppercorns
1 or 2 hot chile peppers, chopped
1 teaspoon salt
5 to 6 tomatoes, chopped
6 or 7 beets, julienned
6 cups water or vegetable stock
1 small potato, peeled and chopped

Sauté the onions and carrot in hot oil in a large cast-iron skillet over medium-low heat for 10 minutes or until tender. Add the celery, bay leaves, peppercorns, chile peppers, salt, tomatoes, beets and water; bring to a boil. Reduce heat and simmer, covered, for 2 hours. Serve with sour cream. Yield: 8 to 10 servings.

Marie Melnichuk, Xi Epsilon Gamma
Collingwood, Ontario, Canada

Louisa Adelung, Xi Alpha Alpha Lambda, Sugar Land, Texas, makes ***Zucchini Soup*** *by boiling a combination of one 49-ounce can chicken stock, 6 thinly sliced medium zucchini, 2 shredded carrots, and 1 diced onion in a large stockpot. Simmer, covered, for 30 minutes. Purée soup with 8 ounces softened chive-and-onion cream cheese. Season with salt, pepper, and Cajun seasoning. Serve hot or cold.*

VEGETARIAN BLACK BEAN SOUP

1 large onion, chopped
1 rib celery, chopped
2 carrots, chopped
1 teaspoon minced garlic
2 tablespoons chili powder
1/2 teaspoon black pepper
2 cups vegetable broth
3 (15-ounce) cans black beans, partially drained
1 (11-ounce) can Mexicorn
1 (15-ounce) can diced tomatoes with jalapeño peppers

Place the onion, celery, carrots and garlic in a 4-quart kettle that has been sprayed with nonstick cooking spray. Sauté the vegetables over medium-high heat for 10 minutes. Season with chili powder and black pepper and cook for 5 minutes longer. Stir in the vegetable broth, 2 cans of the black beans, Mexicorn and undrained tomatoes; bring to a boil. Reduce heat to medium. Place the remaining can of beans in a food processor or blender and process until smooth. Stir the puréed beans into the soup and simmer for 15 minutes. Serve with tortilla chips.
Yield: 6 servings.

Betty Hilgadiack, Preceptor Sigma
Gallatin, Tennessee

CARROT SOUP

Pearl rice, often used in Asian cooking, can be found in the packaged-rice section of grocery, health food, or specialty stores.

1 onion, sliced
1/4 cup butter
2 small garlic cloves, peeled
2 1/2 cups sliced carrots
1/4 cup uncooked pearl rice
1 tablespoon beef bouillon granules
Salt and pepper to taste
1 teaspoon chopped fresh parsley

Sauté the onion in the butter in a skillet over medium-low heat for 10 minutes. Combine the sautéed onion, garlic, carrots, pearl rice, bouillon and 5 cups water in a kettle over medium-high heat; bring to a boil. Reduce heat and simmer, covered, for 30 minutes or until vegetables and rice are tender, stirring occasionally. Pour soup into a blender and process until smooth. Return the soup to the kettle and stir in the salt, pepper and parsley. Cook over low heat for about 15 minutes. Yield: 4 servings.

Nancy Bobick, Laureate Delta
Saskatoon, Saskatchewan, Canada

CHEESY MIXED VEGETABLE SOUP

2½ cups chopped peeled potatoes
1½ cups chopped celery
1 cup chopped onion
4 chicken bouillon cubes
1 (18- to 20-ounce) package frozen mixed vegetables (carrots, cauliflower, broccoli)
2 (10-ounce) cans cream of celery, cream of mushroom or cream of broccoli soup
16 ounces Velveeta cheese, cubed

Combine the potatoes, celery, onion, bouillon cubes and 6 cups hot water in a large kettle; bring to a boil. Simmer, covered, for 20 minutes. Add the frozen mixed vegetables and simmer for 10 minutes longer. Add the soup and whisk until smooth. Add the cheese 10 minutes before serving and heat until melted, stirring constantly. Yield: about 20 servings.

Pam Niederhauser, Preceptor Pi
Columbia, Missouri

CHEDDAR CHEESE SOUP

1 onion, finely chopped
16 ounces mini carrots
1 bunch celery, no leaves, finely chopped
½ cup (1 stick) butter
¼ cup flour
1½ tablespoons cornstarch
4 (15-ounce) cans chicken broth
4 cups half-and-half
⅛ teaspoon baking soda
16 ounces Velveeta cheese, cut into small pieces
16 ounces sharp Cheddar cheese, shredded (4 cups)
1 teaspoon salt
1 teaspoon pepper

Sauté the onion, carrots and celery in the butter in a large kettle over medium-low heat for 10 to 15 minutes or until very soft. Stir in the flour and cornstarch and cook until bubbly, stirring constantly. Stir in the chicken broth and half-and-half. Cook until hot. Add the baking soda, Velveeta cheese, Cheddar cheese, salt and pepper. Cook over medium-low heat for 20 to 30 minutes or until hot and smooth, stirring frequently. Yield: 30 to 40 servings.

Billie Fitts, Xi Alpha Gamma Lambda
Palestine, Texas

Jean Kuhn, Preceptor Beta Gamma, Wyoming, Michigan, prepares ***Old-Fashioned Cream of Tomato Soup*** *by combining one 32-ounce can diced tomatoes, one 9-ounce can condensed chicken broth, 2 tablespoons each butter and sugar, 1 tablespoon chopped onion, and a pinch of baking soda in a large kettle. Simmer for 1 hour. Heat 2 cups heavy cream in a double boiler or microwave. Stir into the soup.*

MEATLESS CHILI

½ cup frozen chopped onions, thawed
1 (12-ounce) package frozen ground beef substitute (Boca Crumbles), thawed
1 (15-ounce) can diced tomatoes
1 (16-ounce) can kidney beans, drained
1 (8-ounce) can tomato sauce
1 tablespoon chili powder
⅛ teaspoon cumin
1 teaspoon sugar (optional)
Salt and pepper to taste

Brown the onions and beef substitute in a large skillet that has been sprayed with nonstick cooking spray. Add the undrained tomatoes, beans, tomato sauce, chili powder, cumin, sugar, salt and pepper and simmer for 30 to 45 minutes or until thickened to taste. Serve alone or over pasta with shredded cheese. Yield: 4 cups.

Lodema L. Erbacher, Preceptor Zeta
Williamsville, New York

VEGETABLE CHILI

2 tablespoons vegetable oil
2 ribs celery, chopped
1 onion, chopped
1 green bell pepper, chopped
1 (28-ounce) can tomatoes, cut up
1 (16-ounce) can kidney beans, partially drained
1 (16-ounce) can pinto beans, partially drained
2 small zucchini, chopped
1 large carrot, chopped
½ teaspoon oregano
½ teaspoon salt
1 teaspoon chili powder
½ teaspoon cayenne pepper (optional)

Heat the vegetable oil in a Dutch oven over medium-high heat. Cook the celery, onion and bell pepper in the oil for 5 to 8 minutes or until tender, stirring occasionally. Add the undrained tomatoes, kidney beans, pinto beans, zucchini, carrot, oregano, salt, chili powder and cayenne pepper and bring to a simmer. Simmer, covered, for 20 minutes, stirring occasionally. Top each serving with shredded cheese and a dollop of sour cream if desired. Yield: 5 large servings.

Dorothy Baker, Laureate Alpha Chi
Pittsburg, Kansas

Carolyn Sharp, Omicron Master, Maryville, Missouri, makes ***Patty's Cheese Soup*** *by combining 2 pounds frozen California-blend vegetables, 3 cans chicken broth, and 1 can tomatoes with green chiles. Simmer for 45 minutes. Add 10 ounces light Velveeta cheese. Cook and stir until melted.*

COUNTRY BARLEY SOUP

1/2 cup barley
1/2 cup split peas
1/2 cup uncooked rice
1/2 cup lentils
2 tablespoons dried minced onion
2 tablespoons dried minced parsley
2 tablespoons beef bouillon granules
1/2 cup uncooked small pasta
1 cup uncooked pasta twists
2 ribs celery, chopped
2 carrots, sliced
2 cups diced tomatoes, or 1 (19-ounce) can tomatoes

Combine the barley, split peas, rice, lentils, onion, parsley, beef bouillon, small pasta, pasta twists, celery, carrots, tomatoes and 3 quarts water in a large kettle. Bring to a boil. Reduce heat and simmer for about 1 hour or until vegetables are tender.
Yield: 12 servings.

Joan Petainen, Laureate Delta Eta
Sault Ste. Marie, Ontario, Canada

CURRIED EGGPLANT SOUP

1 large eggplant, peeled and sliced
1 tablespoon salt
1 large onion, chopped
2 garlic cloves, minced
1 tablespoon extra-virgin olive oil
6 cups vegetable broth
1 large baking potato, peeled and shredded
1 cup (4 ounces) shredded Swiss cheese
1 tablespoon curry powder, or to taste
2 cups low-fat sour cream
Croutons (optional)

Sprinkle the eggplant slices with salt and place on a tilted cutting board. Let stand for about 10 minutes or until eggplant "sweats." Wipe off the liquid. Arrange the slices on a baking sheet and broil 6 inches from the heat source for 10 minutes, turning once. Sauté the onion and garlic in hot olive oil in a large skillet for 5 to 10 minutes or until onion is translucent. Add the vegetable broth, eggplant and potato; bring to a boil. Reduce heat and simmer for 15 minutes, stirring frequently, adding water if sticking occurs. Remove from heat; let stand until cool. Pour the eggplant mixture in batches into a food processor fitted with a steel blade and process until smooth. Return to the skillet. Heat gently over low heat, adding water if too thick. Add the cheese and heat until melted, stirring constantly. Stir in the curry powder and sour cream and heat through, stirring constantly so the sour cream will not curdle. Garnish with croutons and serve. Yield: 4 to 6 servings.

Betsy Heilman, Xi Zeta Lambda
Reston, Virginia

CURRIED GREEN PEA SOUP

We serve this soup warm as a nice alternative to salad when we have company. Chicken meat may be added to make a main-dish soup.

1 onion, finely chopped
1 garlic clove, minced
2 tablespoons butter
1 tablespoon vegetable oil
1 cup frozen peas
1/4 teaspoon salt
2 teaspoons mild curry powder
2 tablespoons flour
2 cups chicken broth
3/4 cup light cream

Sauté the onion and garlic in the butter and oil in a large saucepan over medium-low heat for 5 minutes. Stir in the peas, salt and curry powder and bring to a simmer. Simmer for 10 minutes or until peas are tender. Remove from heat. Stir in the flour. Stir in the chicken broth. Return to heat and bring to a boil. Purée in a blender or rub through a sieve. Freeze at this point if desired. Stir in the cream. Reheat, or chill to serve cold. Garnish with chives or minced green onion and serve. Yield: 4 servings.

Lori Kester, Alpha
Cheyenne, Wyoming

CHEESY CORN CHOWDER

You may substitute 1 cup evaporated milk and 1 cup water for the 2 cups milk.

4 slices bacon, cut up
2 tablespoons sliced green onions
1/2 cup chopped celery
1/2 cup thinly sliced carrots
2 cups prepared instant mashed potatoes (4 servings)
1 teaspoon salt
1 (17-ounce) can golden cream-style corn
1/2 cup peas, fresh or frozen
2 cups milk
4 ounces shredded Cheddar cheese (1 cup)
1 large tomato, peeled, thinly sliced
Bacon bits to taste
Seasoned pepper to taste

Cook the bacon in a kettle or saucepan over medium heat until crisp; remove the bacon pieces with a slotted spoon and set aside. Drain the kettle of all but 1 tablespoon bacon drippings. Sauté the green onions, celery and carrots in the bacon drippings over medium-low heat for 5 to 8 minutes. Add the mashed potatoes, salt, corn, peas, milk and cheese; heat until cheese is melted, stirring occasionally. Top each serving with a tomato slice. Sprinkle with bacon bits and seasoned pepper and serve.
Yield: 6 servings.

Linda J. Miller, Xi Gamma Alpha
Clarkston, Michigan

ONION MUSHROOM SOUP

2 tablespoons butter
2 medium onions, sliced
16 ounces mushrooms, sliced
3 cups beef or chicken broth or bouillon
3 tablespoons tomato paste
1/4 teaspoon pepper
1 garlic clove, crushed
1/3 cup minced fresh parsley
1/2 cup dry white wine
8 slices caraway rye bread
1 cup each Jarlsberg, Parmesan and Cheddar cheese, mixed

Melt the butter in a large saucepan over medium heat. Sauté the onions in the butter until translucent. Add the mushrooms and sauté briefly. Stir in the beef broth, tomato paste, pepper, garlic and parsley; bring to a boil. Stir in the wine. Reduce heat and simmer for 5 minutes. Place a bread slice in the bottom of each soup bowl; cover each slice with 6 tablespoons mixed cheese. Ladle hot soup over the cheese and serve immediately. Yield: 8 servings.

Clara E. Fruchtl, Alpha Master
Lancaster, Pennsylvania

ASPARAGUS POTATO SOUP

2 cups diced peeled potatoes
8 ounces fresh asparagus, chopped
1/2 to 1 cup chopped onion
2 ribs celery, chopped
1 tablespoon chicken bouillon granules
1/4 cup margarine
1/2 cup flour
1 cup heavy cream
1/2 cup milk
1/2 teaspoon salt
Dash of pepper
12 slices bacon, crisp-cooked, crumbled
3/4 cup shredded Cheddar cheese

Combine the potatoes, asparagus, onion, celery, bouillon and 4 cups water in a large kettle; bring to a boil. Simmer, covered, for 15 minutes or until vegetables are tender. Stir in the margarine. Combine the flour, cream, milk, salt and pepper in a bowl and whisk until smooth. Add the flour mixture to the vegetable mixture; bring to a boil. Cook for 2 minutes or until thickened, stirring constantly. Garnish with bacon and cheese and serve. Yield: 6 or 7 servings.

Dorothy Armstrong, Xi Gamma
Miles City, Montana

---

*Louise Salerno, Xi Beta Eta, Glen Head, New York, prepares **Pumpkin Soup** by browning 1 chopped onion in 2 tablespoons butter and adding three 8-ounce cans chicken broth and 1 large can pumpkin purée. Simmer for 10 minutes. Add 1 cup heavy cream and 8 cooked and crumbled slices of bacon.*

BAKED POTATO SOUP

4 large baking potatoes
2/3 cup butter or margarine
2/3 cup flour
6 cups milk
3/4 teaspoon salt
1/2 teaspoon pepper
6 ounces (1 1/2 cups) shredded Cheddar cheese
12 slices bacon, crisp-cooked, crumbled
4 green onions, chopped
1 cup sour cream

Wash the potatoes and prick with a fork. Bake at 400 degrees for 1 hour or until done; cool. Cut potatoes in half lengthwise; scoop out the pulp and reserve. Discard the potato peels. Melt the butter in a Dutch oven over low heat. Add the flour, stirring until smooth; cook for 5 minutes, stirring constantly. Add the milk gradually; cook over medium heat until thickened and bubbly, stirring constantly. Stir in the potato pulp, salt, pepper and 1 cup of the cheese. Add half the bacon and half the green onions. Stir in the sour cream and cook briefly until hot. Ladle the soup into serving bowls and top with the remaining cheese, bacon and green onions. Yield: 10 cups.

Wanda Holman, Xi Beta Chi
Alexander City, Alabama

CABBAGE POTATO LEEK SOUP

2 (15-ounce) cans chicken broth
2 cups shredded cabbage
2 cups diced peeled potatoes
2 tablespoons butter
1 cup chopped leeks
3 tablespoons flour
4 cups half-and-half
2 teaspoons Dijon mustard
3/4 teaspoon Worcestershire sauce
1/4 teaspoon pepper
1/8 teaspoon salt
1 to 3 drops of Tabasco sauce

Heat the chicken broth in a large kettle over medium heat. Add the cabbage and potatoes; simmer, covered, for 10 minutes or until potatoes are tender. Melt the butter in a skillet over medium-high heat. Sauté the leeks in the butter for 5 to 8 minutes or until tender. Stir in the flour and cook for 2 to 3 minutes, stirring constantly. Add the sautéed leeks, 2 cups of the half-and-half, Dijon mustard, Worcestershire sauce, pepper, salt and Tabasco sauce to the potato mixture. Stir in the remaining 2 cups half-and-half. Cook over low heat for 10 to 15 minutes.
Yield: 8 servings.

Michelle Hocraffer, Omicron Phi
Cedar Rapids, Iowa

GOLDEN POTATO SOUP

8 to 10 diced peeled potatoes
1 (26-ounce) can cream of celery soup
1 (26-ounce) can cream of chicken soup
1 (10-ounce) package chopped cooked ham
2 (12-ounce) cans evaporated milk
Milk as desired
Garlic powder to taste
Salt to taste
Pepper to taste
1 onion, chopped
1/2 carrot, shredded

Combine the potatoes, soups, ham, evaporated milk, milk, garlic powder, salt, pepper, onion and carrot in a large slow cooker. Cook on High for at least 2 hours or until potatoes are tender, stirring occasionally. Garnish with shredded cheese and serve.
Yield: 15 to 20 servings.

Nancy Veach, Laureate Zeta
Lafayette, Indiana

CREAMY POTATO SOUP

2 cups finely chopped peeled potatoes
1/2 cup minced onion
2 ribs celery, finely chopped
2 1/2 cups chicken broth
4 tablespoons butter
3 1/2 tablespoons flour
1 1/2 teaspoons salt
1/2 teaspoon pepper
2 cups milk, scalded and cooled
1 teaspoon dried parsley flakes

Combine the potatoes, onion, celery and chicken broth in a kettle over medium-low heat; simmer, covered, for 15 minutes or until potatoes are tender. Melt the butter in a saucepan over medium-low heat. Whisk in the flour, salt and pepper. Slowly whisk in the milk. Cook until smooth and thickened, stirring constantly. Add the flour mixture to the vegetable mixture. Stir in the parsley flakes. Yield: 6 servings.

Lisa Williams, Xi Gamma Psi
Princeton, Indiana

CELERY POTATO SOUP

6 medium potatoes, peeled and diced
2 carrots, diced
6 ribs celery, diced
1 medium onion, chopped
6 tablespoons butter
1/4 cup chicken base
6 tablespoons flour
1 1/2 cups milk
1 teaspoon salt
1/2 teaspoon pepper
1 tablespoon chopped parsley (optional)

Combine the potatoes, carrots, celery, onion, butter and 2 quarts of water in a stockpot over medium heat. Simmer, covered, for about 20 minutes or until vegetables are tender. Stir in the chicken base. Whisk the flour and milk together in a small bowl and add to the soup. Add salt, pepper and additional chicken base if desired. Mash some of the potatoes and other vegetables to make a thicker soup. Stir in the parsley.
Yield: 10 to 12 servings.

Jennifer Havens, Xi Lambda Lambda
Uniontown, Ohio

ROASTED RED PEPPER SOUP

3 cups chicken broth
2 (7-ounce) jars sweet roasted red peppers, rinsed and drained
1 large onion, chopped
1 medium carrot, sliced
1/4 teaspoon sugar
1 rib celery, thinly sliced
1/4 teaspoon salt
1 1/4 cups half-and-half, light cream or milk

Combine the chicken broth, roasted peppers, onion, carrot, sugar, celery and salt in a kettle; bring to a boil. Reduce heat and simmer, uncovered, for 15 minutes or until carrots are tender. Cool slightly. Purée the roasted pepper mixture 1/2 at a time in a blender or food processor. Return to the saucepan over medium heat. Stir in the half-and-half and cook until piping hot, stirring frequently.
Yield: 4 generous servings.

Lois Broman, Xi Beta Lambda
Gold Canyon, Arizona

GOURMET SPINACH SOUP

4 ounces fresh mushrooms, diced
1 onion, chopped
5 tablespoons unsalted butter
5 tablespoons flour
2 cups chicken broth
2 cups milk
1/2 teaspoon salt
Pepper to taste
4 ounces cream cheese, cubed
4 ounces (1 cup) shredded Swiss cheese
12 ounces fresh spinach, chopped and cooked

Sauté the mushrooms and onion in the butter in a large skillet over medium-low heat for 5 to 8 minutes or until tender. Add the flour and cook for 2 or 3 minutes, stirring constantly. Whisk in the chicken broth and milk; cook until thickened, stirring constantly. Add the salt, pepper, cream cheese and Swiss cheese; heat until the cheese is melted, stirring constantly. Add the spinach and stir gently. Serve hot.
Yield: 4 to 6 servings.

Patty Shannon, Laureate Delta Tau
St. Charles, Missouri

Meats

BEEF BRISKET

1 (4- to 6-pound) beef brisket, trimmed
Liquid smoke to taste
MSG to taste
1 cup ketchup
1/4 cup apple cider vinegar
1/4 cup firmly packed light brown sugar
1/4 cup strong coffee
1 tablespoon Worcestershire sauce
1 tablespoon fresh lemon juice
1 teaspoon kosher salt
1 large garlic clove, crushed

Rub the brisket with liquid smoke and MSG. Place in an 11×15-inch glass baking dish, or a 9×13-inch dish for a larger brisket. Combine the remaining ingredients in a small bowl and mix until smooth. Pour the coffee mixture over the brisket. Seal tightly with heavy-duty foil. Bake at 325 degrees for 3 1/2 to 4 hours or until tender. Serve with buns or crescent rolls. Yield: variable.

Doris McKinney, Preceptor Chi
Murrells Inlet, South Carolina

SLOW-COOKER BEEF

1 (3- to 4-pound) rump roast, chuck roast or arm roast
1 garlic clove, minced
1 1/2 teaspoons oregano
3/4 teaspoon rosemary
2 1/2 teaspoons seasoned salt

Place the roast in a slow cooker and add 2 cups of water; slow cooker should be about half full. Add the garlic, oregano, rosemary and seasoned salt. Cook on Low for 8 to 12 hours. Remove the roast and pull apart the meat. Return to its juice. Serve over buns. Yield: 4 servings per pound.

Audrey Henderson, Gamma Zeta
Mobridge, South Dakota

SLOW-COOKER ITALIAN BEEF

1 (3- to 4-pound) rump roast
1 (8-ounce) can tomato sauce
1 teaspoon salt
1 teaspoon pepper
1 teaspoon parsley flakes
1 teaspoon garlic powder
1 teaspoon basil
1 teaspoon oregano
Dash of Worcestershire sauce
Dash of soy sauce
1 envelope Italian salad dressing mix

Place the roast in a slow cooker. Combine the tomato sauce, 2 1/2 cups water, salt, pepper, parsley, garlic powder, basil, oregano, Worcestershire sauce, soy sauce and salad dressing mix in a saucepan over medium-high heat; bring to a boil. Pour the tomato mixture over the roast. Cook on Low for 8 to 10 hours. About 1 1/2 hours before serving, remove the meat from the slow cooker and pull apart to shred. Return the meat to the slow cooker and cook for 1 1/2 hours longer. Yield: variable.

Kelli Cole, Beta Omicron
Pocola, Oklahoma

BEEF TENDERLOIN WITH POTATOES

1 1/2 cups ketchup
3 envelopes Italian salad dressing mix
3/4 teaspoon Worcestershire sauce
1 (3- to 4-pound) beef tenderloin, trimmed
10 medium potatoes, peeled and quartered
1/2 cup (1 stick) butter or margarine, melted
1/2 teaspoon salt
1/4 teaspoon pepper

Combine the ketchup, salad dressing mix, Worcestershire sauce and 2 1/4 cups water in a large sealable

plastic bag. Pierce the tenderloin in several places with a skewer or fork; place in the plastic bag and turn to coat. Chill, sealed, for 8 to 10 hours. Place the potatoes in a large saucepan and add enough water to cover. Bring to a boil. Reduce heat and simmer, covered, for 10 to 15 minutes or until tender; drain. Toss with the butter, salt and pepper. Remove the tenderloin from the plastic bag and place on a rack in a roasting pan. Pour the marinade into a saucepan and bring to a rolling boil. Boil for 1 minute and pour over the tenderloin. Arrange the potatoes around the tenderloin. Bake, uncovered, at 375 degrees for 60 to 75 minutes or to 140 on a meat thermometer for rare, 160 for medium, 170 for well done. Slice the beef and serve with pan juices and potatoes.
Yield: 8 to 10 servings.

Cindy Kruckenberg, Xi Theta Zeta
Gilbert, Iowa

BEEF WELLINGTON

1 (3-pound) beef fillet
1 tablespoon vegetable oil
3 tablespoons butter
1 (8-ounce) can sliced mushrooms, drained
6 ounces smooth liver paté
1 (13-ounce) package puff pastry
1 egg, beaten

Trim the fillet and tie it at intervals with fine string so it will retain its shape. Heat the vegetable oil and 1 tablespoon of the butter in a large skillet over medium heat. Fry the fillet in the butter mixture briskly on all sides, pressing with a wooden spoon while cooking to seal well. Place the fillet in a roasting pan. Roast, uncovered, in a preheated 425-degree oven for 20 minutes. Let cool and remove the string. Sauté the mushrooms in the remaining 2 tablespoons butter in a skillet over medium heat for about 5 minutes; cool. Combine the mushrooms and paté in a small bowl and mix well. Roll the pastry into a 1/4-inch-thick 11×13-inch rectangle on a lightly floured surface. Spread the paté mixture down the center. Place the meat over the paté mixture. Brush the edges of the pastry with the egg and fold lengthwise to enclose the fillet. Place seam side down on a baking sheet and tuck the ends under the fillet. Decorate with leaves cut from the pastry trimmings and brush with egg. Bake, uncovered, at 425 degrees for 50 to 60 minutes or until done to taste, covering with foil after 25 minutes of baking. Let stand at room temperature for 10 minutes before serving. Yield: 8 servings.

Patricia M. Crum, Preceptor Gamma Zeta
Ankeny, Iowa

SPICY MARINATED ROAST BEEF

Use any beef roast you like; I like sirloin tip.

1 cup white vinegar
1 cup dry red wine
1/4 cup Worcestershire sauce
1 large onion, cut into 1-inch squares
1 garlic clove, minced or crushed
3/4 cup firmly packed brown sugar
1/2 teaspoons crushed bay leaf
1 cup extra-virgin olive oil
1/4 cup soy sauce
2 teaspoons salt
1/2 teaspoon crushed red pepper
1/2 teaspoon mace
1/2 teaspoon ginger
1/4 teaspoon cardamom
1 (4-pound) boneless beef roast

Combine the vinegar, wine, Worcestershire sauce, onion, garlic, brown sugar, bay leaf, olive oil, soy sauce, salt, crushed red pepper, mace, ginger and cardamom in a large saucepan over medium-high heat; bring to a boil. Rinse the beef roast and puncture it deeply on all sides with a long-tined meat fork. Place it in a large oven-cooking bag in a roasting pan or Dutch oven. Pour the boiling marinade carefully over the beef roast in the oven-cooking bag; let stand until cool. Seal the bag. Marinate in the refrigerator for 3 to 6 days, turning the sealed bag with the roast and marinade over 2 to 4 times a day. The longer it's marinated, the spicier it will become. Three days is perfect for mild to medium spicy flavor. Place the bagged roast with the marinade in the roasting pan in a 500-degree oven. Reduce the oven temperature to 350 degrees when the marinade begins to boil. Bake for about 3 hours or until the roast is tender. Cut away the oven-cooking bag and discard. Place the roast on a platter; cover loosely with foil. Pour the marinade into a blender container and process until smooth. Serve the hot marinade with the roast. May thicken the marinade to serve as gravy by pouring into a saucepan and adding a small amount of cornstarch dissolved in a small amount of cold water. Cook until thickened, stirring constantly.
Yield: 12 servings.

Paula Johnson, Laureate Alpha Beta
Sandy, Oregon

---

*Jennifer Anderson, Upsilon Gamma, West Salem, Ohio, prepares **Simple Beef Stroganoff** by combining 1 pound stew beef cut into 1-inch cubes with 1 chopped medium onion, 2 cups sliced mushrooms and one 15-ounce can of beef broth in a slow cooker. Cook on Low for 6 to 8 hours. Add 8 ounces of chive and onion cream cheese 10 to 15 minutes before the end of the cooking time. Serve over noodles.*

ROAST BEEF WITH YORKSHIRE PUDDING

1 (4-pound) standing rib roast or boneless roast
3/4 cup dry red wine
1 cup thawed cranberry juice cocktail concentrate
1 cup beef stock
1/4 cup soy sauce
4 large garlic cloves, minced
No-Fail Yorkshire Pudding

Place the roast in a large glass dish. Combine the next 5 ingredients in a bowl and mix well. Pour the wine mixture over the roast and marinate, covered, in the refrigerator for 12 to 24 hours. Roast in a 325-degree oven to desired doneness (to 160 degrees on a meat thermometer for medium). Serve with No-Fail Yorkshire Pudding. Yield: 6 servings.

NO-FAIL YORKSHIRE PUDDING

2 large eggs
1/3 cup milk
Pinch of salt
1 cup minus 2 tablespoons flour

Combine the eggs, milk, salt, flour and 2/3 cup water in a bowl and whisk until smooth. Butter muffin cups and heat in a 450-degree oven just until the butter starts smoking. Fill muffin cups 2/3 full with the flour mixture. Bake at 450 degrees for 15 minutes. Reduce oven temperature to 400 degrees and bake for 10 minutes longer.

Delma J. Waller, Laureate Delta Lambda
Waterloo, Ontario, Canada

BAKED CUBE STEAKS

8 cube steaks
1 small onion, minced
1/4 cup chopped green bell pepper
1/2 teaspoon celery salt
1/2 teaspoon chili powder
1/2 cup grated Parmesan cheese
1 tablespoon parsley flakes
1 (8-ounce) can mushroom pieces, drained
1 (8-ounce) can tomato sauce
Salt and pepper to taste

Brown the steaks on both sides in a skillet over medium heat. Arrange 4 of the steaks in an 8×8-inch baking dish. Combine the onion, bell pepper, celery salt, chili powder, Parmesan cheese and parsley flakes in a bowl and mix well. Layer half the onion mixture and half the mushroom pieces over the cube steaks in the baking dish. Layer the remaining cube steaks, onion mixture and mushroom pieces over the mushroom layer. Drizzle the tomato sauce over the top. Bake, uncovered, at 350 degrees for 45 minutes. Yield: 8 servings.

Kathy Drake, Nu Chi
Bolivar, Missouri

ROUND STEAK ROULADE

1 (2- to 3-pound) boneless round steak
1/2 cup bread crumbs
1/2 teaspoon salt
1/4 teaspoon pepper
1/2 cup chopped onion
4 uncooked bacon slices, or 1/2 pound bulk pork sausage, cooked and crumbled
1 (10-ounce) can cream of mushroom soup
1 soup can red wine

Pound the steak as thin as possible on a flat surface. Layer the bread crumbs over the steak and sprinkle with salt and pepper. Layer the onion and bacon over the top. Roll as for a jelly roll and secure with wooden picks. Coat the roulade in flour and brown in a large greased skillet. Remove to a roasting pan that can be covered. Pour a mixture of the soup, wine and 1/2 soup can of water over the roulade. Bake, covered, at 300 degrees for 2 hours or slightly less, basting occasionally. At serving time, remove to a serving platter and garnish with parsley and spiced crabapples. The roulade may be carved at the table and served by the host. Serve with the self-made gravy. Yield: 6 to 8 servings.

Agnes C. Scannell, Upsilon Master
Dubuque, Iowa

BEEF BURGUNDY

1 (2-pound) round steak, cut into 1/2-inch cubes
4 tablespoons butter
1 envelope onion soup mix
1 (10-ounce) can cream of mushroom soup
1 cup red wine, or 1/2 cup brandy
6 cups cooked rice

Sauté the round steak in the butter in a skillet over medium heat until browned. Combine the steak, onion soup mix, cream of mushroom soup, wine and 1 1/4 cups water in a 3-quart casserole. Bake, covered, at 350 degrees for 2 to 2 1/2 hours or until done to taste. Serve over rice. Yield: 6 servings.

Evelyn Wright, Preceptor Alpha
Peoria, Illinois

---

*Pam Thomas, Alpha Omicron Master, Canon City, Colorado, makes **Mock Steak** by combining 3 pounds ground beef, 1 cup evaporated milk and 1 cup cracker crumbs. Press the meat mixture over the bottom of a jelly roll pan and refrigerate, covered, for 8 to 10 hours. Cut into 10 to 12 pieces. Flour the pieces and brown in hot oil. Transfer the "steaks" to a baking pan. Pour a mixture of 1 can cream of celery soup, 1 can cream of onion soup and 1 cup water over the "steaks." Bake at 275 degrees for 2 hours.*

FRENCH OVEN STEW

2 to 3 pounds beef stew meat
5 or 6 each carrots, celery ribs and potatoes, peeled, cut into chunks
2 cups tomato juice
1/3 cup tapioca
1 tablespoon sugar
1 envelope onion soup mix
Salt and pepper to taste

Combine the stew meat, carrots, celery and potatoes in a roasting pan. Pour a mixture of the tomato juice, tapioca and sugar over the meat mixture. If you use more tomato juice, be sure to use more tapioca. Sprinkle with onion soup mix and season with salt and pepper. Bake, tightly covered, at 300 degrees for 3 hours. Yield: 6 servings.

Kathy Radford, Xi Gamma Alpha
Waterford, Michigan

SLOW-COOKER BEEF STEW

6 slices bacon
3 pounds beef, cut into 1 1/2-inch cubes
3 carrots, peeled and sliced
1 onion, sliced
1 1/2 teaspoons salt
1/8 teaspoon pepper
3 tablespoons flour
1 (10-ounce) can beef broth
1 tablespoon ketchup
2 garlic cloves, minced
1 teaspoon thyme
1 bay leaf
8 ounces small white onions, peeled
8 ounces mushrooms, sliced
2 tablespoons butter
1/2 cup red wine

Crisp-cook the bacon in a large skillet. Remove the bacon to paper towels. Brown the beef in the bacon drippings in the skillet over medium heat. Remove the beef to a slow cooker. Brown the carrots and sliced onion in the skillet. Season with salt and pepper and stir in the flour. Stir in the beef broth. Add the broth mixture to the beef. Stir in the bacon, ketchup, garlic, thyme, bay leaf and onions. Cook on Low for 8 to 10 hours. Sauté the mushrooms in the butter. Stir in the mushrooms and wine for the last hour of cooking. Yield: 6 to 8 servings.

Elaine M. Wilson, Laureate Beta
Warwick, Rhode Island

Ann Latoski, Xi Delta, Portage La Prairie, Manitoba, Canada, prepares ***Quick and Easy Mexican Chili*** *by sautéing 1 pound ground beef with 1 cup chopped green bell pepper and 1/2 cup chopped onion; drain. Add one 16-ounce can stewed tomatoes, one 12-ounce can whole kernel corn, one 10-ounce can mushrooms, 1 chopped garlic clove, 4 teaspoons pepper, 2 teaspoons chili powder and salt to taste. Simmer for 15 minutes.*

CHUCKWAGON STEW

1 1/4 pounds beef, cut into 1-inch cubes
1 tablespoon flour
1 1/2 teaspoons paprika
1/2 teaspoon chili powder
1 onion, chopped
1 or 2 garlic cloves, minced
1 (15-ounce) can diced tomatoes
1 1/2 tablespoons chili powder
1 1/2 tablespoons cinnamon
1 1/2 teaspoons ground cloves
1 cup chopped potatoes
1 cup chopped carrots

Coat the beef cubes with a mixture of the flour, paprika and the 1/2 teaspoon chili powder. Brown in hot oil in a heavy 4-quart kettle. Add the onion and garlic; sauté over medium-low heat for 5 to 10 minutes or until tender. Add the undrained tomatoes, the 1 1/2 tablespoons chili powder, cinnamon and cloves. Simmer, covered, for 2 hours. Add the potatoes and carrots. Simmer, covered, for 45 minutes longer or until vegetables are tender. Yield: 3 or 4 servings.

Lois Coleman, Eta Xi
Bend, Oregon

FIVE-HOUR OVEN STEW

3 pounds lean beef, cut into cubes
3 cups carrot chunks
2 cups sliced celery
1 small onion, thinly sliced
4 potatoes, peeled and cubed
1 tablespoon sugar
3 tablespoon quick-cooking tapioca
Salt and pepper to taste
1 (10-ounce) can beef broth
1 (10-ounce) can golden mushroom soup

Layer the beef, carrots, celery, onion and potatoes in a heavy 5-quart baking pan. Sprinkle with the sugar, tapioca, salt and pepper. Spoon a mixture of the beef broth and soup over the top. Bake, covered with a tight-fitting lid, at 275 degrees for 5 hours; do not remove the lid during that time. Serve with coleslaw and corn bread. Yield: 10 servings.

Lucille Finn, Iota Master
Salem, Oregon

Wanda Gish, Laureate Alpha Rho, Marshall, Michigan, makes ***Cabbage Casserole*** *by browning 1 1/2 pounds ground beef with 1 chopped large onion. Layer 1/2 chopped medium head of cabbage, the ground beef mixture, 3/4 to 1 cup cooked rice, 1/2 cup spaghetti sauce, 1/2 chopped medium head of cabbage, 1 can tomato soup and 1/2 cup spaghetti sauce in a slow cooker. Cook on Low for 6 to 8 hours or on High for 3 to 4 hours.*

BARBECUED BEEF WITH CORNED BEEF

1½ pounds ground beef
2 medium onions, chopped
⅓ cup brown sugar
1 cup ketchup
2 tablespoons Worcestershire sauce
1 (15-ounce) can corned beef

Brown the ground beef with the onions in a skillet, stirring until crumbly; drain. Stir in the brown sugar, ketchup, 1 cup water, Worcestershire sauce and corned beef. Simmer, covered, for at least 1 hour. Yield: 8 to 10 servings.

Shirley M. Lacey, Alpha Iota Master
Springfield, Illinois

ALL-AMERICAN CHEESY MACARONI

1½ pounds ground beef
2 medium onions, chopped
1 medium green bell pepper, diced
1 (6-ounce) can tomato paste
2 (8-ounce) cans tomato sauce
1½ tablespoons salt
¾ teaspoon oregano
¼ teaspoon crushed red pepper
2 cups uncooked elbow macaroni
1 cup creamed cottage cheese
4 ounces Cheddar cheese, shredded (1 cup)

Brown the ground beef in a saucepan, stirring until crumbly; drain. Add the onions and bell pepper; cook for 1 minute longer. Stir in the tomato paste, 1 can tomato sauce, 1½ teaspoons of the salt, oregano and red pepper. Cook, covered, over low heat for 45 minutes. Bring 3 quarts of water to a boil in a large kettle. Add the remaining salt and macaroni and cook until tender; drain. Spread half the macaroni in a 2½-quart casserole. Layer half the beef mixture, cottage cheese and ¼ cup of the cheese over the macaroni. Layer the remaining macaroni, the remaining beef mixture, the remaining can of tomato sauce and the remaining ¾ cup cheese over the cheese layer. Bake, uncovered, at 375 degrees for 15 minutes. Cover loosely with foil and bake for 15 minutes longer. Yield: 8 servings.

Tami Conner, Xi Nu Theta
Carbondale, Illinois

Shirley Howie, Alpha Beta Chi, Okeechobee, Florida, makes ***Spanish Rice*** *by browning 1 pound of ground beef. Add 1 chopped medium onion, ½ chopped bell pepper, 1 cup converted rice, salt and pepper to taste; sauté. Add one 15-ounce can diced tomatoes, ½ teaspoon garlic salt, 1 tablespoon Worcestershire sauce and 2 teaspoons chili powder. Simmer, covered, for 30 minutes, stirring occasionally.*

BURRITO ROLL-UP

For a low-fat dish, use low-fat cheese and low-fat turkey chili with beans.

1½ to 2 pounds ground beef
1 to 2 envelopes taco seasoning mix
2 (15-ounce) cans chili with beans
8 ounces Mexican-style cheese, shredded (2 cups)
10 large flour tortillas

Brown the ground beef in a skillet, stirring until crumbly; drain. Prepare the ground beef with the taco seasoning mix using the directions on the package. Stir in 1 can of the chili with beans. Grease the bottom and sides of a 9×13-inch baking dish. Spoon a moderate amount of the ground beef mixture into the center of each tortilla and sprinkle with a spoonful of cheese. Fold the ends of each tortilla toward the center, roll up to enclose the filling. Place the burritos seam side down in the prepared baking dish. Layer the remaining can of chili with beans and the remaining cheese over the top. Bake, uncovered, at 350 degrees for 20 to 30 minutes or until bubbly. Serve with your choice of black olives, diced tomatoes, shredded lettuce, salsa or picante sauce, sour cream and jalapeño pepper slices. Yield: 10 servings.

Patti Bonta, Preceptor Delta
Crestview, Florida

CHILES RELLENOS BAKE

1 pound ground beef
½ cup chopped onion
½ teaspoon salt
½ teaspoon pepper
2 (7-ounce) cans whole green chiles, drained
6 ounces Mexican-style cheese, shredded (1½ cups)
4 eggs
¼ cup flour
1½ cups milk

Brown the ground beef with the onion, salt and pepper in a skillet, stirring until crumbly; drain. Split the chiles lengthwise. Line a 7×11-inch baking dish with half the green chiles. Add layers of the ground beef, cheese and the remaining green chiles. Beat the eggs in a medium bowl. Add the flour and whisk until smooth. Whisk in the milk gradually. Pour the egg mixture evenly over the chiles. Bake, uncovered, at 350 degrees for 40 to 45 minutes or until puffy and lightly browned. Serve with a green salad and French bread. Yield: 8 servings.

Helen N. Woods, Alpha Master
Riverside, California

BAKED BEEF CHOP SUEY

1 pound ground beef
2 small onions, chopped
1 green bell pepper, chopped
2 cups chopped celery
1 (10-ounce) can cream of mushroom soup
1 (10-ounce) can cream of chicken soup
1/2 cup uncooked quick-cooking rice
4 tablespoons soy sauce
Pinch of salt
1 (10-ounce) can bean sprouts
1 (5-ounce) can chow mein noodles

Brown the ground beef in a skillet, stirring until crumbly; drain. Remove from heat. Add the onions, bell pepper, celery, soups, rice, soy sauce, 1 1/2 cups water, salt and bean sprouts; mix well. Spoon into a 9×13-inch baking dish; cover tightly with foil. Bake at 350 degrees for 1 1/2 hours. Remove the foil, stir and sprinkle the chow mein noodles over the top. Bake, uncovered, for 30 to 40 minutes longer or until bubbly and beginning to brown. Yield: 12 servings.

Irene Greer, Laureate Delta Phi
St. Augustine, Florida

BEEF AND PORK ENCHILADAS

Substitute Monterey Jack cheese for part of the Cheddar if you like.

Pancakes
1 to 2 pounds ground beef
1 pound bulk pork sausage
1 cup chopped onion
1/2 cup chopped green bell pepper
2 garlic cloves, minced
1 tablespoon chili powder
1 teaspoon salt
1 (10-ounce) package frozen chopped spinach, cooked and drained
1 (29-ounce) jar meatless spaghetti sauce
1 (8-ounce) can tomato sauce
2 teaspoons chili powder
Pancakes for Enchiladas
8 ounces Cheddar cheese, shredded (2 cups)

Prepare the Pancakes. Brown the ground beef and sausage in a skillet, stirring until crumbly; drain all but 1 tablespoon of the drippings. Add the onion, bell pepper, garlic, the 1 tablespoon chili powder and salt; simmer for 10 minutes. Stir in the spinach and set aside. Combine the spaghetti sauce, tomato sauce, 1 cup water and the 2 teaspoons chili powder in a bowl and mix well. Spoon a scant 1/4 cup of the ground beef mixture down the center of each Pancake. Fold the sides about an inch over the filling. Roll up and place seam side down in two 9×13-inch baking dishes. Pour the tomato mixture evenly over the top. Top with cheese. Bake, uncovered, at 350 degrees for 30 minutes.

PANCAKES FOR ENCHILADAS

6 eggs, well beaten
3 cups milk
2 cups flour
1/8 teaspoon salt

Combine the eggs and milk in a large bowl and mix well. Add the flour and salt; beat until smooth. Ladle 1/4 cup batter into a hot greased 6- to 8-inch skillet, tilting the skillet so the batter covers the bottom. Turn the pancakes when the surface looks dry. Stack the pancakes while you prepare the remaining pancakes. Yield: about 30.

Shari Richmond, Nu Master
Walla Walla, Washington

SLOW-COOKER ENCHILADAS

1 pound ground beef or ground chicken
1 medium onion, chopped
3 garlic cloves, chopped
2 (10-ounce) cans creamed soup, any style
1 (7-ounce) can green chile salsa
1 cup sour cream
12 flour tortillas
8 ounces Cheddar cheese, shredded (2 cups)

Brown the ground beef with the onion and garlic in a skillet, stirring until crumbly; drain. Season to taste. Stir in the soup, salsa and sour cream; remove from heat. Spray nonstick cooking spray on all inside surfaces of the slow cooker. Alternate layers of the tortillas, beef mixture and cheese in the prepared slow cooker until all ingredients are used, ending with cheese. Cook on Low for 4 to 5 hours. Sprinkle with additional cheese and cook on Low for 15 to 20 minutes longer. Yield: 12 servings.

Cherie Seidel, Xi Theta Nu
Shawnee, Kansas

MEXICAN CORN BREAD CASSEROLE

1 pound ground beef
1 (8-ounce) package corn bread mix
3 eggs
1 cup mild picante sauce
1/3 cup vegetable oil
1 (8-ounce) can cream-style corn
1 small onion, chopped
2 or 3 jalapeño peppers, diced
1/2 cup diced green bell pepper
4 ounces Cheddar cheese, shredded (1 cup)

Brown the ground beef in a skillet, stirring until crumbly; drain well. Combine all the ingredients in a large bowl and mix well. Spoon into a greased 9×13-inch baking dish. Bake, uncovered, at 350 degrees for 50 to 55 minutes or until bubbly and browned.
Yield: 4 to 6 servings.

Ann Spence, Theta Chi
Steinhatchee, Florida

MEXICAN LASAGNA

1 pound lean ground beef
1 (16-ounce) can refried beans
1 small onion, finely chopped
2 teaspoons oregano
1 teaspoon cumin
3/4 teaspoon garlic powder
12 uncooked lasagna noodles
2 1/2 cups picante sauce or salsa
2 cups sour cream
3/4 cup finely chopped green onions
1 (2-ounce) can sliced black olives, drained
4 ounces Monterey Jack cheese, shredded (1 cup)

Combine the first 6 ingredients in a large bowl; mix well. Line a greased 9×13-inch baking dish with 4 uncooked lasagna noodles. Layer half the beef mixture, 4 uncooked lasagna noodles and the remaining beef mixture over the noodles. Top with the remaining 4 uncooked lasagna noodles. Pour a mixture of the picante sauce and 2 1/2 cups water evenly over the top. Bake, tightly covered with aluminum foil, at 350 degrees for 1 1/2 hours. Remove from the oven; remove the foil. Combine the sour cream, green onions and olives in a bowl and mix well. Spread the sour cream mixture over the cooked lasagna; top with cheese. Bake, uncovered, for about 5 minutes or until cheese melts. Let stand for 10 minutes before serving. Cut into squares. Yield: 12 servings.

Mary Helen Goldberg, Preceptor Lambda Mu
Plattsburg, Missouri

MEXICAN MANICOTTI

1 pound ground beef
1 (16-ounce) can refried beans
2 1/2 teaspoons chili powder
1 1/2 teaspoons oregano
16 ounces manicotti shells, cooked al dente
1 (16-ounce) jar picante sauce
2 cups sour cream
1 cup shredded cheese of choice
1/4 cup sliced green onions
1/4 cup sliced green olives

Mix the first 4 ingredients in a bowl. Spoon the ground beef mixture into the manicotti shells. Arrange the stuffed shells in a greased 9×13-inch baking dish. Pour a mixture of the picante sauce and 2 1/2 cups water evenly over the stuffed shells. Chill, covered, for 8 to 10 hours. Bake, covered, at 350 degrees for 1 hour. Spoon the sour cream over the top. Sprinkle with cheese, green onions and olives. Bake, uncovered, for 5 to 10 minutes longer or until cheese is melted. Yield: 8 servings.

June Shelton, Laureate Beta Beta
Colorado Springs, Colorado

HUNGARIAN MEATBALLS

1 pound ground beef
8 potatoes, peeled and shredded
1 teaspoon salt
1 teaspoon pepper
1 (12-ounce) package Cream of Wheat
2 large eggs
Dash of garlic powder, or more to taste

Combine the uncooked ground beef with the potatoes, salt and pepper in a bowl; mix well. Mix in the dry Cream of Wheat. Mix in the eggs and garlic powder. Shape into 3/4-inch balls. Drop the meatballs into a large amount of boiling water and cook for about 45 minutes. Serve with dumplings and gravy.
Yield: 6 servings.

Linda Yaun, Xi Beta Delta
DeFuniak Springs, Florida

TRADITIONAL MEAT LOAF

2 pounds ground round
2 eggs
1 1/2 cups seasoned bread crumbs
1 teaspoon MSG
1 envelope onion soup mix
3/4 cup ketchup

Combine the ground round, eggs, bread crumbs, MSG, 1/2 cup warm water, soup mix and ketchup in a large bowl. Mix very well with the hands. Shape into loaves and place in two 9-inch loaf pans that have been sprayed with nonstick cooking spray. Spread a mixture of 1 scant cup ketchup and 2 tablespoons Worcestershire sauce over the top. Bake, uncovered, at 350 degrees for 50 to 60 minutes or until cooked through. Yield: 6 to 8 servings.

Anne Ledbetter, Iota Chi
St. Charles, Missouri

SAVORY MEAT LOAF

1 pound ground beef
1 egg
1 large onion, chopped
Salt and pepper to taste
1 garlic clove, minced
3/4 cup ketchup
3 slices bread, toasted
3 tablespoons brown sugar
1/4 teaspoon nutmeg
1/2 teaspoon prepared mustard
1 (10-ounce) can vegetable beef soup

Combine the ground beef, egg, onion, salt, pepper, garlic and 1/2 cup of the ketchup in a large bowl and mix well. Pour a little milk over the toasted bread to soften; cut into cubes. Combine the toast cubes, brown sugar, the remaining 1/4 cup ketchup, nutmeg, mustard and soup in a small bowl and mix well. Shape the beef mixture into a loaf and place in a deep baking pan. Poke holes all over the top of the loaf with the end of a wooden spoon. Pour the ketchup mixture over the loaf, allowing it to fill the holes.

Bake, uncovered, at 425 degrees for 1 hour, draining the drippings from the pan after 45 minutes of baking. Let stand at room temperature for 10 minutes. Yield: 4 to 6 servings.

Linda Hinzie
Marion, Iowa

SAUCY MEAT LOAF

1 1/2 pounds ground beef
1 cup bread crumbs or cracker crumbs
1 egg
3/4 cup ketchup
1/2 cup milk
1 large onion, chopped
4 tablespoons apple cider vinegar
4 tablespoons brown sugar
2 tablespoons Worcestershire sauce
1 small onion, finely chopped
Salt and pepper to taste

Combine the ground beef, bread crumbs, egg, 1/4 cup of the ketchup, milk and the large onion in a large bowl and mix well. Shape into a loaf and place in a loaf pan. Combine the vinegar, brown sugar, Worcestershire sauce, the remaining 1/2 cup ketchup, the small onion, salt and pepper in a saucepan over medium-high heat. Bring to a boil. Pour the hot ketchup sauce over the meat loaf. Bake, uncovered, at 350 degrees for 1 hour or until cooked through. Yield: 6 to 8 servings.

Linda Kay Nobles, Xi Alpha Sigma
Pascagoula, Mississippi

BACON BEEF ROLL

2 eggs
1/4 cup ketchup
2 tablespoons Worcestershire sauce
4 ounces Cheddar cheese, shredded (1 cup)
1/4 cup minced onion
2 tablespoons grated Parmesan cheese
1 teaspoon salt
1/4 teaspoon pepper
2 pounds ground beef
12 slices bacon

Combine the eggs, ketchup, Worcestershire sauce, Cheddar cheese, onion, Parmesan cheese, salt and pepper in a large bowl; mix well. Mix in the ground beef. Roll into two 6-inch rolls. Place 6 bacon slices side by side on a large sheet of waxed paper. Place 1 beef roll across the ends of the bacon and roll so that bacon wraps around beef roll; secure with wooden picks. Repeat with the remaining beef roll and bacon slices. Place the wrapped beef rolls in an ungreased 9×13-inch baking dish. Bake at 375 degrees for 45 to 50 minutes to 160 degrees on a meat thermometer or until meat is no longer pink. Discard the wooden picks. Yield: 8 servings.

Cheryl Sheat, Xi Zeta Rho
Lamar, Missouri

SPICY MEAT LOAF

1 3/4 cups ketchup
2 pounds ground beef
2 eggs
1/2 envelope onion soup mix
1/4 cup chopped green bell pepper
1/4 cup sour cream
1/2 teaspoon garlic salt
1 teaspoon salt
2 teaspoons Worcestershire sauce
1 (4-ounce) can chopped green chiles, drained
1 cup herb-seasoned stuffing mix
1 cup packed brown sugar
3 tablespoons Dijon mustard

Combine 1/4 cup of the ketchup and the next 10 ingredients in a large bowl and mix well. Bake at 350 degrees for 1 hour. Spread a mixture of the remaining 1 1/2 cups ketchup, brown sugar and Dijon mustard over the top and bake for 15 minutes longer. Yield: 8 to 10 servings.

Elaine Salazar, Chi Omicron
Aurora, Illinois

LITTLE CHEDDAR MEAT LOAVES

1 1/2 pounds ground beef
3/4 cup rolled oats
1 teaspoon salt
1/2 cup shredded Cheddar cheese
1/4 cup chopped onion
1 egg
3/4 cup milk
1 tablespoon brown sugar
1 tablespoon prepared mustard
1/3 cup ketchup

Combine the first 7 ingredients in a large bowl and mix well. Shape into 6 small loaves and place in a shallow baking pan. Spread a mixture of the brown sugar, mustard and ketchup over the loaves. Bake at 350 degrees for 35 minutes or until cooked through. Yield: 6 to 12 servings.

Karla Grant, Preceptor Alpha Upsilon
Hayden, Idaho

ITALIAN MEAT LOAF

2 pounds ground beef
1/4 cup chopped onion
2 teaspoons salt
1/4 teaspoon pepper
1/2 cup bread crumbs
2 eggs
1 garlic clove, minced
1/4 cup Parmesan cheese
1 (8-ounce) can tomato sauce

Mix the ground beef, onion, salt, pepper, bread crumbs, eggs, garlic and Parmesan cheese in a large bowl. Shape into a loaf and place in a greased baking pan. Spread tomato sauce over the top. Pour 1/4 cup water around the loaf in the pan. Bake, uncovered, at 350 degrees for 1 hour, basting the loaf with the pan liquid at 15-minute intervals. Yield: 8 to 10 servings.

Lois Buford, Lambda Upsilon
Athens, Texas

SAUCY STUFFED PEPPERS

3/4 pound ground beef
1 teaspoon salt
1 teaspoon garlic salt
1 medium onion, chopped
1 cup cooked rice
1 (6-ounce) can tomato paste
3 large green bell peppers
1 (6-ounce) can tomato juice

Brown the ground beef with the salt, garlic salt and onion in a skillet, stirring until crumbly; drain. Stir in the rice, tomato paste and 1/3 cup water; simmer for 10 minutes. Cut the bell peppers in half lengthwise and clean out the seeds. Boil in salted water for 5 minutes or until tender-crisp. Fill the bell pepper halves with the beef mixture and arrange in a foil-lined shallow 9×11-inch baking dish. Drizzle the tomato juice over the peppers. Bake at 300 degrees for 45 minutes. Yield: 6 servings.

Pat Gottschalk, Xi Alpha Omega
Paducah, Kentucky

MEXICAN STUFFED PEPPERS

4 medium green bell peppers
1 (15-ounce) can stewed tomatoes, drained, cut up
1/2 cup Grape-Nuts cereal
1/2 pound ground beef
1 small garlic clove, crushed
1 tablespoon chili powder
1 teaspoon salt
1/2 cup shredded Cheddar cheese

Remove stems and seeds from the bell peppers. Place the bell peppers in a saucepan; add enough cold water to cover. Bring to a boil; boil for 5 minutes. Drain and set aside. Combine 1/2 cup of the tomatoes with the cereal. Brown the ground beef with the garlic in a skillet, stirring until crumbly; drain. Stir in the chili powder, salt and cereal mixture. Arrange the bell pepper halves in a shallow baking pan and fill with the ground beef mixture. Top with the remaining tomatoes and sprinkle with cheese. Bake at 375 degrees for 25 minutes. Yield: 4 servings.

Sheila Merrill, Preceptor Epsilon Beta
Princeton, Missouri

Ava Kiefer, Preceptor Delta Delta, Fort Wayne, Indiana, make ***One-Pan Casserole*** *by crumbling 1 pound ground beef in a 2-quart baking dish and sprinkling with salt and pepper to taste. Layer with 2 thinly sliced onions and 3 thinly sliced potatoes. Spoon 1 can pork and beans over the prepared layers. Spread 1 can tomato soup over the top. Bake, uncovered, at 275 degrees for 70 minues.*

SHEPHERD'S PIE

1 1/2 cups instant mashed potatoes
1 pound ground beef
1/2 teaspoon salt
1/4 teaspoon pepper
1 (12-ounce) jar beef gravy
1 (10-ounce) package frozen mixed vegetables, thawed
3/4 cup grated Parmesan cheese

Prepare 4 servings of mashed potatoes using the package directions, using 1 2/3 cups milk, 2 tablespoons butter and 1/2 teaspoon salt. Brown the ground beef in a broilerproof skillet over medium-high heat, stirring until crumbly; drain. Sprinkle with salt and pepper. Stir in the gravy and mixed vegetables. Cook over medium-low heat for 5 minutes or until hot. Spoon the prepared mashed potatoes around the edge of the skillet, leaving a 3-inch circle in the center. Sprinkle the cheese evenly over the potatoes. Broil 4 to 5 inches from the heat source for 3 minutes or until beef mixture is bubbly and cheese is golden brown. Yield: 4 servings.

Margaret Lawrence, Laureate Phi
Montgomery, New York

BEEF AND CHEESE CRESCENT PIE

4 ounces Cheddar cheese, shredded (1 cup)
4 ounces Monterey Jack cheese, shredded (1 cup)
1 (8-count) can crescent rolls
1 egg, slightly beaten
1 1/4 pounds ground beef
1/2 cup chopped onion
1/2 cup chopped green bell pepper
1 (8-ounce) can tomato sauce with mushrooms
1 (8-ounce) can green beans, drained
Salt and pepper to taste
1/4 teaspoon garlic salt

Combine the Cheddar cheese and Monterey Jack cheese in a bowl and mix well. Unroll the dough. Fit the dough into a 9- to 10-inch pie plate, pressing perforations to seal and trimming to fit. Brush a mixture of the egg and 1/2 cup of the cheese mixture over the dough. Brown the ground beef in a skillet, stirring until crumbly; drain. Stir in the onion, bell pepper, tomato sauce, green beans, salt, pepper and garlic salt; simmer for 10 minutes. Fill the dough shell with the beef mixture. Sprinkle the remaining cheese mixture evenly over the top. Bake at 350 degrees for 30 to 35 minutes or until golden and bubbly. Serve with salsa. Yield: 6 to 8 servings.

Linda Durland, Preceptor Gamma Iota
Elk City, Oklahoma

UPSIDE-DOWN CRESCENT PIZZA

1 pound ground beef
1 tablespoon dried minced onion
1 (26-ounce) jar pasta sauce
Salt and pepper to taste
Pizza toppings such as pepperoni slices
8 ounces mozzarella cheese, shredded (2 cups)
1 (8-count) can crescent rolls
2 tablespoons (about) butter or margarine, melted
Parmesan cheese to taste

Brown the ground beef in a skillet, stirring until crumbly; drain. Stir in the onion, pasta sauce, salt and pepper. Spoon the beef mixture into a 9×13-inch baking dish. Top with pepperoni slices or other pizza toppings. Sprinkle the mozzarella cheese over the top. Unroll the dough and layer over the top. Brush with butter and sprinkle with grated Parmesan cheese. Bake at 350 degrees for 20 to 25 minutes or until golden. Yield: about 8 servings.

Mary Shoup, Laureate Gamma Omega
Casstown, Ohio

STUFFED PASTA SHELLS

1 pound ground beef
1 (26-ounce) jar pasta sauce
1 cup cottage cheese
1/2 cup grated Parmesan cheese
1 cup shredded mozzarella cheese
1 egg
3 tablespoons parsley flakes
1/2 teaspoon pepper
16 ounces jumbo shell pasta, cooked and drained
Italian seasonings to taste

Brown the ground beef in a skillet, stirring until crumbly; drain. Combine the beef and pasta sauce in a bowl and mix well. Combine the next 6 ingredients in a bowl and mix well. Fill the pasta shells with the cottage cheese mixture. Line a 9×13-inch baking dish with the shells. Pour the beef mixture evenly over the shells. Sprinkle with Italian seasonings. Bake, uncovered, at 400 degrees for 25 minutes or until bubbly. Yield: 8 to 10 servings.

Carolyn Cole, Beta Omicron
Fletcher, North Carolina

Mary Beth Mitchell, Xi Beta Xi, Paris, Missouri, makes ***Texas Spaghetti*** *by browning 1 pound ground beef with 1 chopped medium onion; drain. Stir in 1 can spaghetti sauce, one 7-ounce can sliced mushrooms, 1 pound cubed longhorn cheese and 12 ounces drained cooked spaghetti. Spoon the mixture into a 9×13-inch pan and bake at 350 degrees until cheese melts and turns brown.*

BAKED SPAGHETTI

1 cup chopped onion
1 cup chopped green bell pepper
1 tablespoon butter
1 (28-ounce) can diced tomatoes
1 (4-ounce) can mushroom stems and pieces, drained
1 (2-ounce) can sliced black olives, drained
2 teaspoons oregano
1 pound ground beef, browned and drained
16 ounces angel hair pasta, cooked and drained
16 ounces Cheddar cheese
1 (10-ounce) can cream of mushroom soup
Parmesan cheese to taste

Sauté the onion and bell pepper in butter in a large skillet over medium-low heat for 5 to 8 minutes or until tender. Stir in the undrained tomatoes, mushrooms, olives and oregano. Stir in the ground beef. Simmer, uncovered, for 10 minutes. Spread half the pasta in a greased 9×13-inch baking dish. Layer half the tomato mixture and half the Cheddar cheese over the pasta. Repeat the layers. Combine the soup and 1/4 cup water in a bowl and mix well. Pour the soup mixture evenly over the last cheese layer. Sprinkle with Parmesan cheese. Bake, uncovered, at 350 degrees for about 45 minutes or until heated through. Yield: 9 to 12 servings.

Jane Thiel, Preceptor Zeta
Nampa, Idaho

ONE-SKILLET SPAGHETTI

1 pound ground beef
1 cup chopped onion
3/4 cup chopped green bell pepper
1 (28-ounce) can tomatoes, cut up
1 (4-ounce) can mushroom stems and pieces, drained
2 teaspoons salt
1 teaspoon sugar
1 teaspoon chili powder
1/4 teaspoon garlic powder
1/4 teaspoon cayenne pepper (optional)
7 ounces thin spaghetti, broken
4 ounces Cheddar cheese, shredded (1 cup)

Brown the ground beef with the onion and bell pepper in a skillet, stirring until crumbly; drain. Stir in the undrained tomatoes, 1/2 cup water, mushrooms, salt, sugar, chili powder, garlic powder, cayenne pepper and spaghetti. Simmer, covered, for 30 minutes or until spaghetti is tender, stirring frequently and adding small amounts of water if necessary. Sprinkle with cheese. Heat, covered, until cheese is melted. Yield: 6 to 8 servings.

Lavada Harrison, Laureate Delta Sigma
Poplar Bluff, Missouri

HAMBURGER STROGANOFF

1 pound ground beef
1 small onion, chopped
2 tablespoons margarine
2 tablespoons flour
1 teaspoon salt
1 teaspoon garlic salt
Dash of pepper
1 (8-ounce) can chopped mushrooms, drained
1 (10-ounce) can creamy chicken mushroom soup
1 cup sour cream

Brown the ground beef with the onion in a large skillet or Dutch oven, stirring until crumbly; drain. Stir in the flour, salt, garlic salt, pepper and mushrooms and cook for 5 minutes, stirring constantly. Stir in the soup; simmer, uncovered, for about 10 minutes, stirring occasionally. Stir in the sour cream just before serving; cook until heated through. Serve over rice or noodles. Yield: 4 to 6 servings.

Sarah Byerly, Lambda Master
Salisbury, North Carolina

CHILI TAMALE BAKE

2 (15-ounce) cans beef tamales
1 cup finely chopped onion
2 (15-ounce) cans corn, drained
1 cup shredded Cheddar cheese
2 (15-ounce) cans mild chili with beans

Remove the tamales from the cans. Unwrap the tamales and discard the paper. Cut each tamale in half. Place half the tamales in a single layer in a 9×11-inch baking pan. Layer the onion, corn, cheese and chili 1/2 at a time over the tamales. Repeat the layers. Bake, uncovered, at 350 degrees for 30 minutes or until hot and bubbly. Yield: about 6 servings.

Joyce G. Dorius, Eta Master
Salt Lake City, Utah

TAMALE BAKE

1/2 pound bulk pork sausage
1 cup chopped onion
1 pound ground beef
3 teaspoons salt
4 teaspoons chili powder
2 envelopes spaghetti sauce mix
1 (30-ounce) can diced tomatoes, drained
1 (16-ounce) can whole kernel corn, drained
1 cup pitted black olives
3/4 cup yellow cornmeal
4 ounces Cheddar cheese, shredded (1 cup)

Brown the sausage in a large skillet, stirring until crumbly; drain. Add the onion, ground beef, 2 teaspoons of the salt, chili powder and spaghetti sauce mix; mix well. Cook over medium-low heat for about 10 minutes or until ground beef is cooked through, stirring frequently. Add the tomatoes and corn; simmer for 20 minutes, stirring occasionally. Pour into a 10×15-inch baking dish. Press the olives into the sausage mixture with a wooden spoon. Place 2 cups water in a saucepan and bring to a boil. Combine the cornmeal, the remaining 1 teaspoon salt and 1 cup cold water in a bowl and mix until smooth. Add the cornmeal mixture gradually to the boiling water, stirring constantly. Cook over low heat until thickened, stirring frequently. Spread the cornmeal mush over the beef mixture. Sprinkle with cheese. Bake at 350 degrees for 45 minutes or until golden brown.
Yield: 10 to 12 servings.

Marge Liggett, Xi Alpha Theta
Bartlesville, Oklahoma

BEEF TAMALE PIE

1 1/2 pounds ground beef
1/4 cup vegetable oil
1 cup finely chopped onion
1 garlic clove, minced
1/2 cup chopped green bell pepper
2 1/2 cups chopped tomatoes
2 cups drained canned whole kernel corn
2 teaspoons salt
1/4 teaspoon black pepper
1 1/2 tablespoons chili powder
1 (6-ounce) can sliced black olives, drained, juice reserved
1 cup cornmeal
1 1/2 cups milk
2 tablespoons butter
4 ounces sharp Cheddar cheese, shredded (1 cup)
2 eggs, slightly beaten

Brown the ground beef in the vegetable oil in a skillet, stirring until crumbly; drain. Stir in the onion, garlic and bell pepper. Cook over medium-low heat for 5 minutes or until vegetables are tender but not browned. Stir in the tomatoes, corn, 1 teaspoon of the salt, black pepper and chili powder. Simmer for 5 minutes, stirring occasionally. Pour the reserved olive juice into a measuring cup and add enough water to make 1 cup. Combine the olive juice mixture and 1/2 cup of the cornmeal in a bowl and whisk to blend. Add the cornmeal mixture gradually to the beef mixture; stir well. Cook, covered, over low heat for 10 minutes. Stir in the olives. Spoon the beef mixture into an 8×11-inch baking dish. Combine the milk, the remaining 1 teaspoon salt and butter in a saucepan over medium-low heat; cook until heated through. Add the remaining 1/2 cup cornmeal gradually and cook until thickened, stirring constantly. Remove from heat. Stir in the cheese and eggs. Spread over the beef mixture. Bake at 375 degrees for 20 minutes or until golden brown. Yield: 8 to 10 servings.

Norma M. Ellis, Gamma Omicron Master
Yreka, California

CHILI TAMALE PIE

2 pounds ground beef
3 (15-ounce) cans beef tamales
1 (15-ounce) can beanless chili with sauce
1 (15-ounce) can chili with beans
2 cups shredded Mexican-style or nacho cheese

Brown the ground beef in a skillet, stirring until crumbly; drain. Spread the ground beef in a greased 9×13-inch baking pan. Unwrap the beef tamales and arrange over the ground beef layer. Layer the beanless chili, chili with beans and cheese over the tamales. Bake, uncovered, at 350 degrees for 25 to 30 minutes or until hot and cheese is melted.
Yield: 6 servings.

Freda F. Pirtle, Laureate Beta Gamma
West Frankfort, Illinois

STOVETOP TAMALE PIE

1 pound lean ground beef or turkey
1 (8-ounce) can tomato sauce
1 (16-ounce) can kidney beans or black beans
1 envelope taco seasoning mix
1 (8-ounce) package corn muffin mix
1 cup shredded Cheddar cheese
1/4 cup sliced green onions

Brown the ground beef in a skillet, stirring until crumbly; drain. Stir in the tomato sauce, undrained kidney beans, 1/2 cup water and taco seasoning mix. Bring to a boil. Reduce heat and simmer, covered, for 5 minutes. Prepare the corn muffin batter using the package directions. Drop small spoonfuls of the batter over the ground beef mixture in the skillet. Cook, covered, over medium-low heat for 15 to 17 minutes or until corn bread tests done. Top with cheese and green onions. Cook, covered, over low heat until cheese is melted. Yield: 4 to 6 servings.

Kathryn Hill, Xi Mu Pi
Edwardsville, Illinois

SWEET-AND-SOUR BEEF

1 each medium green and red bell pepper
1 medium onion
1 pound ground beef
1 cup chopped celery
1/3 cup brown sugar
2 tablespoons cornstarch
3 tablespoons soy sauce
1/4 cup red wine vinegar
1 (20-ounce) can pineapple chunks, drained, juice reserved

Cut the green and red bell peppers and onion into bite-size pieces. Brown the ground beef in a large skillet, stirring until crumbly; drain. Stir in the bell peppers, onion and celery. Move the ground beef mixture to one side of the skillet. Combine the brown sugar, cornstarch, soy sauce, vinegar and reserved pineapple juice in a small bowl and whisk to blend. Pour the vinegar mixture into the empty side of the skillet and cook over low heat until thickened, stirring constantly. Stir the ground beef mixture and vinegar mixture together. Stir in the pineapple. Serve with rice. Yield: 4 servings.

Kimberlee Reynolds, Xi Beta
Regina, Saskatchewan, Canada

BAKED ZITI

1 pound lean ground beef
1 onion, chopped
2 (26-ounce) jars spaghetti sauce
16 ounces ziti, cooked and drained
6 ounces provolone cheese, sliced
1 1/2 cups sour cream
6 ounces mozzarella cheese, shredded (1 1/2 cups)
2 tablespoons grated Parmesan cheese

Brown the ground beef with the onion in a large skillet over medium heat, stirring until crumbly; drain. Stir in the spaghetti sauce. Simmer, covered, for 15 minutes. Layer half the ziti, provolone cheese, sour cream, half the ground beef mixture, the remaining ziti, mozzarella cheese and the remaining ground beef mixture in a greased 9×13-inch baking dish. Sprinkle Parmesan cheese over the top. Bake, uncovered, at 350 degrees for 30 minutes or until cheeses are melted. Yield: 8 servings.

Gina Alvarez, Beta Nu
Gardner, Kansas

SIRLOIN BEEF PATTIES WITH SWEET-AND-SOUR ONIONS

1 pound lean ground beef
1/4 teaspoon garlic powder
1/4 teaspoon pepper
1/4 teaspoon seasoned salt
2 1/2 cups sliced onions
2 1/2 cups sliced mushrooms
2 tablespoons sugar
2 tablespoons balsamic vinegar
4 slices Swiss cheese

Mix the first 4 ingredients in a bowl. Shape into 4 patties. Brown in a large skillet over medium-low heat, cooking for 5 minutes on each side or until done to taste. Remove the patties to individual plates. Combine the onions, mushrooms, sugar and vinegar in the skillet and cook for 5 to 8 minutes or until tender-crisp, stirring frequently. Top each patty with a slice of cheese. Spoon 1/4 of the hot mushroom mixture over each patty and serve. Yield: 4 servings.

Shelly Allison, Nu Kappa
Guthrie, Oklahoma

SPICY ORIENTAL BURGERS

2 tablespoons butter
1 pound ground beef
1/4 cup chopped onion
1 tablespoon prepared mustard
2 tablespoons tomato paste
2 tablespoons soy sauce
1 1/2 teaspoons garlic powder
1/4 teaspoon pepper
1 1/2 teaspoons horseradish
1 (10-ounce) can bean sprouts, rinsed and drained
1/2 cup sour cream
8 hamburger buns, toasted and buttered

Melt the butter in a large skillet over medium heat. Brown the ground beef with the onion in the butter, stirring until crumbly; drain. Stir in the mustard, tomato paste, soy sauce, garlic powder, pepper, horseradish and bean sprouts. Simmer, covered, for 10 minutes, stirring occasionally. Remove from heat. Stir in the sour cream and spoon over the hamburger buns. Yield: 8 servings.

Martha Crumpacker, Alpha Kappa
Ozark, Arkansas

SOUPER BURGERS

1 pound ground beef
3 tablespoons flour
1/8 teaspoon Worcestershire sauce
1 (10-ounce) can French onion soup
6 hamburger buns
Hamburger-sliced dill pickle chips to taste

Brown the ground beef in a preheated skillet, stirring until crumbly; drain. Stir in the flour. Add the Worcestershire sauce and soup; stir well. Bring to a boil, stirring constantly. Reduce heat and simmer, covered, for 20 minutes. Spoon the ground beef mixture over the bottom halves of the hamburger buns. Layer dill pickle chips over the ground beef mixture and cover with bun tops. Yield: 6 servings.

Muriel M. Hollenbeck, Preceptor Gamma Lambda
Sedalia, Colorado

SLOPPY JOES

1 pound ground beef
1/4 cup chopped onion
1 (6-ounce) can tomato paste
1/2 cup ketchup
1 teaspoon Worcestershire sauce
1/2 teaspoon chili powder
1 tablespoon prepared mustard
2 tablespoons sugar
3 tablespoons ketchup
3 tablespoons white vinegar

Brown the ground beef with the onion in a skillet, stirring until crumbly; drain. Stir in the tomato paste and the 1/2 cup ketchup. Simmer, covered, for 15 to 20 minutes. Stir a mixture of the Worcestershire sauce, chili powder, mustard, sugar, the 3 tablespoons ketchup and vinegar into the ground beef mixture. Cook until heated through. Serve over warm buns. Top with cheese slices and green relish if desired. Yield: 6 to 8 servings.

Billie J. Trahin, Preceptor Xi
Baxter Springs, Kansas

SLOW-COOKER JOES

2 1/2 pounds ground beef
1 small green bell pepper, finely chopped
1 large onion, finely chopped
3 tablespoons sugar
2 tablespoons white vinegar
1 tablespoon mustard
1 (32-ounce) bottle ketchup

Brown the ground beef with the bell pepper and onion in a large skillet, stirring until crumbly; drain. Place in a slow cooker. Add the sugar, vinegar and mustard. Stir in the ketchup. Cook on Medium for 8 to 10 hours. Serve over hamburger buns.
Yield: 10 servings.

Doris Whiston, Xi Master
South Bend, Indiana

PASTIES

A pasty is a pie, usually a meat pie.

1 pound ground beef
1 large potato, peeled and cubed
1 medium onion, diced
1 small rutabaga, cubed
1 tablespoon margarine or butter
Salt and pepper to taste
1 (2-crust) pie pastry

Brown the ground beef lightly in a skillet, stirring until crumbly; drain. Remove ground beef from skillet and set aside. Combine the potato, onion, rutabaga, margarine, salt and pepper in the skillet over medium heat and cook until vegetables are tender, stirring frequently; do not overcook. Combine the ground beef and potato mixture in a large bowl and mix well. Fit 1 of the pie pastries into a pie plate. Spoon half the ground beef mixture into the pastry. Bring the pastry to the center around the ground beef mixture to enclose, sealing the edges to make a small football shape. Repeat with the remaining ground beef mixture and pastry. Bake at 400 degrees for about 30 minutes or until crust is brown.
Yield: 2 servings.

Frances Patterson, Laureate Zeta
Lafayette, Indiana

BIEROX

Bierox is a hearty German dish—pastry stuffed with meat and cabbage.

5 pounds ground beef
2 or 3 large onions, chopped
1 large head green cabbage
1 small head green cabbage
1 quart beer
5 (16-ounce) packages hot roll mix

Brown the ground beef with the onions in a skillet, stirring until crumbly; drain. Place the ground beef mixture in a very large kettle. Shred the cabbage, more coarsely than for coleslaw. Add the cabbage and beer to the ground beef and bring to a simmer over medium heat. Simmer, uncovered, until liquid is nearly gone. Prepare the hot rolls dough using the package directions; let rise. Punch down the dough and roll into small 1/4-inch-thick rectangles. Place 1/4 cup ground beef mixture in the center of each rectangle; fold dough edges to enclose the filling and pinch to seal. Arrange on a nonstick baking sheet. Bake at 350 degrees for 15 to 20 minutes or until golden brown. Yield: 6 dozen (or more).

Lana L. Lukes, Xi Beta Epsilon
Woodward, Oklahoma

ANYTIME SPAGHETTI SAUCE

3 pounds ground beef
1 pound sweet Italian sausage links, casings removed
1 large onion, chopped
1 (29-ounce) can tomato sauce
1 (15-ounce) can tomato sauce
1 (12-ounce) can tomato paste
3 ribs celery, cut into bite-size pieces
1 (8-ounce) jar sliced mushrooms, drained
1 (15-ounce) can stewed tomatoes
1/4 cup brown sugar
1/4 cup butter
2 tablespoons Italian seasoning
1 tablespoon garlic powder
1 tablespoon Worcestershire sauce
1 teaspoon white vinegar

Brown the ground beef and sausage with the onion in a skillet, stirring until ground beef is crumbly; drain. Stir in the tomato sauce, tomato paste, one 12-ounce can of water, celery, mushrooms, undrained stewed tomatoes, brown sugar, butter, Italian seasoning, garlic powder, Worcestershire sauce and vinegar. Simmer, covered, for 3 hours. Serve with good bread and cheese or over pasta. Yield: 8 servings.

Janet Schilf, Laureate Delta
Lincoln, Nebraska

SPICY VENISON BLACK BEAN CHILI

2 pounds ground venison
1 small garlic clove, minced
1 large white onion, chopped
2 (10-ounce) cans tomatoes with green chiles
1 teaspoon chili powder
1/2 teaspoon cumin
1/2 teaspoon paprika
1/4 teaspoon hot red pepper flakes
1/2 teaspoon salt
1/2 teaspoon black pepper
1 (15-ounce) can black beans, drained
1/2 cup sour cream

Brown the ground venison in a skillet over medium heat, stirring until crumbly; drain. Add the garlic and onion and cook until fragrant. Stir in the tomatoes with green chiles, chili powder, cumin, paprika, red pepper flakes, salt and pepper. Simmer, covered, for 30 minutes to 3 hours, the longer the better. Stir in the black beans 5 minutes before serving. Garnish each serving with 1 to 2 tablespoons sour cream and a dash of paprika. 4 to 6 servings.

Melissa Quevillon, Nu Kappa
Guthrie, Oklahoma

VENISON WITH PEAS AND NOODLES

1 pound venison, cut into small pieces
1/2 cup (about) flour
1 onion, chopped
2 tablespoons (about) butter
Onion powder to taste
Garlic powder to taste
Pepper to taste
2 teaspoons minced fresh garlic
1 (10-ounce) can mushroom soup
3/4 soup can of milk
1/2 to 3/4 cup frozen peas, rinsed
1/2 cup sour cream
8 to 10 ounces noodles, cooked al dente, drained

Coat the venison with flour and brown with the onion in the butter in a large skillet, scraping the skillet frequently. Sprinkle with onion powder, garlic powder and pepper. Stir in the fresh garlic and cook for 1 minute longer. Combine the soup and milk in a bowl; whisk to blend. Add the soup mixture to the venison mixture and cook over medium heat until reduced to desired thickness, scraping frequently. Stir in the peas and sour cream. Cook until heated through. Serve over noodles, or stir the noodles into the venison mixture for a one-dish meal.
Yield: 4 servings.

Rita Minard, Xi Epsilon
Nampa, Idaho

VENISON CHILI

Use 1 1/3 (46-ounce) cans of tomato juice to make 60 ounces.

2 pounds ground venison
1 medium-large onion, chopped
2 to 3 tablespoons olive oil
2 (8-ounce) cans tomato sauce
4 (16-ounce) cans kidney beans, partially drained
4 cups chopped tomatoes
1/3 cup sugar
6 teaspoons chili powder
1 teaspoon cumin
2 tablespoons Worcestershire sauce
2 teaspoons salt
60 ounces tomato juice

Brown the venison with the onion in 1 tablespoon of the olive oil in a skillet, stirring until crumbly. Combine the tomato sauce, kidney beans, tomatoes, sugar, chili powder, cumin, Worcestershire sauce, salt and tomato juice in a 12-quart kettle. Stir in the remaining 2 tablespoons olive oil and bring to a boil. Reduce heat and simmer, covered, over low heat for 3 hours, stirring occasionally. Serve with Parmesan cheese and crackers. Yield: 12 servings.

Martha A. Newman, Xi Kappa
Kettering, Ohio

SAVORY VENISON BURRITOS

2 to 3 pounds deer or beef roast
1 large yellow onion, chopped
1 green bell pepper, chopped
2 garlic cloves, minced
1 (7-ounce) can chopped green chiles, drained
1 (8-ounce) can mild salsa
1 (15-ounce) can diced tomatoes, drained
1 (3-ounce) tablet Mexican chocolate
Pinch of cumin
Pinch of chile pepper
Salt and black pepper to taste

Brown the deer in a skillet; do not drain. Add the onion, bell pepper, garlic, green chiles, salsa, tomatoes and Mexican chocolate. Stir in the cumin, chile pepper, salt and black pepper. Cook over low heat, covered, for 1 hour or longer; the longer the cooking time, the tenderer the meat. Serve in warmed tortillas. Yield: 10 servings.

Pam Smith, Xi Chi
Fallon, Nevada

✣ CHEESY GRILLED PORK LOIN

1 (6-pound) boneless pork loin
1/2 cup Dale's bottled marinade
1/2 teaspoon salt
1/2 teaspoon pepper
1/2 teaspoon garlic powder
4 ounces bleu cheese, crumbled
1/2 pound spicy link sausages, chopped
1 cup mayonnaise
3 tablespoons creamy horseradish
3 tablespoons lime juice

Place the pork loin in a large glass dish. Pour the bottled marinade over the loin. Marinate, covered, in the refrigerator for at least 3 hours. Drain the pork loin, discarding the marinade. Make parallel cuts along the length of the loin about 1 inch from each edge and to a depth of about 2/3 of the loin's thickness. Rub the salt, pepper and garlic powder well into the loin. Press the bleu cheese and sausages into the pockets in the meat. Tie the loin together at each end with cooking string. Grill over low to medium coals for 2 1/2 hours. Serve with a sauce made of a mixture of the mayonnaise, horseradish and lime juice.
Yield: 15 to 20 servings.

Jessie Neighbors, Xi Beta Chi
Alexander City, Alabama

ROAST PORK LOIN STUFFED WITH DRIED APRICOTS AND SHALLOTS

4 tablespoons canola oil
1 pound dried apricots, cut into 1/4-inch pieces
2 tablespoons chopped shallots
4 green onions, cut into 1/4-inch slices
1/3 cup raisins
1 tablespoon chopped fresh sage leaves
1/2 cup brandy
2 cups orange juice
1 1/2 cups coarse dry bread crumbs or herb-seasoned stuffing mix
2 large eggs, lightly beaten
1 (4- to 5-pound) boneless pork loin

Heat 2 tablespoons of the canola oil in a skillet over medium-high heat. Stir in the apricots, shallots, green onions, raisins and sage. Sauté for 2 minutes or until sage is fragrant. Stir in the brandy; simmer for 1 minute. Stir in 1 cup of the orange juice and bring to a boil. Reduce heat; cook over medium heat until liquid is reduced by 1/3. Remove from heat and stir in the bread crumbs. Let stand until cool. Stir in the eggs. Cut the pork loin in half lengthwise, leaving one side attached. Fold open and cut out a trough about 1 inch deep and 2 inches wide in the center of each half. Fill the troughs with bread crumb mixture. Fold the two halves together and tie with string. Season with salt and pepper to taste. Heat the remaining 2 tablespoons canola oil in a large ovenproof skillet or roasting pan over high heat. Add the pork loin and brown on all sides. Pour in the remaining 1 cup orange juice. Roast at 400 degrees for 10 minutes. Reduce oven temperature to 350 degrees and roast for 1½ hours, basting every 20 to 25 minutes. Remove from the oven and let stand for 10 to 15 minutes. Cut into 1-inch slices. Serve with the pan juices; add water to the pan juices if desired. Yield: 10 servings.

Joyce Schmidt, Preceptor Beta Sigma
Winterville, North Carolina

HONEY-ROASTED PORK LOIN

¼ cup honey
2 tablespoons Dijon mustard
2 tablespoons peppercorns, crushed
½ teaspoon thyme
½ teaspoon salt
1 (2- to 3-pound) boneless pork loin

Combine the honey, Dijon mustard, peppercorns, thyme and salt in a bowl and mix well. Place the pork loin in a lightly greased roasting pan and brush with half the honey mixture. Roast at 325 degrees for 1 hour. Brush the remaining honey mixture over the loin and roast for 30 minutes longer or to 160 degrees on a meat thermometer. Serve with homemade stuffing or noodles. Yield: 6 to 8 servings.

Violet Soper, Alpha Upsilon Master
Selinsgrove, Pennsylvania

SPICY PORK LOIN ROAST

2 teaspoons garlic powder
2 teaspoons salt
2 teaspoons black pepper
1½ teaspoons dry mustard
1½ teaspoons onion powder
1½ teaspoons paprika
1 teaspoon rubbed sage
½ teaspoon cayenne pepper
1 (3- to 3½-pound) boneless pork loin roast

Rub a mixture of the garlic powder, salt, black pepper, dry mustard, onion powder, paprika, sage and cayenne pepper over the entire roast. Refrigerate, covered, for 8 to 10 hours. Place on a greased rack in a roasting pan. Roast at 350 degrees for 2½ to 2¾ hours or to 160 to 170 degrees on a meat thermometer. Let stand for 10 minutes before serving. Yield: 8 to 10 servings.

Shirley Petersen, Laureate Kappa
Beatrice, Nebraska

✣ STUFFED HOLIDAY ROLL

1 boneless turkey breast
1 boneless pork loin
1 (6-ounce) package herb-seasoned stuffing mix
2 ribs celery, chopped
1 teaspoon sage
½ pound fully cooked bulk pork sausage
Salt and pepper to taste
4 green onions, chopped
½ teaspoon baking powder
1 egg
½ cup dried cranberries
½ cup chopped walnuts
2 cups chicken broth

Tenderize the turkey breast and pork loin and sprinkle each with salt, pepper and sage. Place the turkey on top of the pork and set aside. Combine the dry stuffing mix, celery, the 1 teaspoon sage, sausage, salt, pepper, green onions, baking powder, egg, dried cranberries, walnuts and chicken broth in a bowl and mix well. Spread over the turkey. Roll lengthwise and tie with twine to make a roll. Roast at 350 degrees for about 1½ to 2 hours or until meat is cooked through. Let stand at room temperature for about 15 minutes. Remove the twine and slice the meat. Yield: variable.

Dorothy Steger, Xi Sigma Omicron
San Antonio, Texas

SWEET-AND-SOUR PORK ROAST

½ cup packed brown sugar
⅓ cup teriyaki sauce
⅓ cup red wine
¼ teaspoon ground cloves
½ cup chili sauce
⅛ teaspoon garlic powder
1 (2- to 3-pound) lean pork roast

Combine the first 6 ingredients in a large resealable plastic bag. Place the pork roast in the bag and seal. Marinate in the refrigerator for 8 to 24 hours, turning often. Drain, reserving the marinade. Pour the reserved marinade into a saucepan and bring to a boil; boil for 1 minute. Preheat the grill to high heat; reduce to medium heat. Roast the pork over indirect heat to 160 degrees on a meat thermometer, about 1 to 1½ hours, basting occasionally with the marinade. Yield: variable.

Kris Weishaupt, Omicron
Fruitvale, British Columbia, Canada

---

*Betty A. Kozley, Laureate Delta Nu, Yorba Linda, California, prepares **Arabian Pork Chops** by placing 4 pork chops in a baking dish. Layer 1 sliced onion and 4 tablespoons uncooked rice over the chops. Pour a mixture of one 10-ounce can tomato soup and one 15-ounce can stewed tomatoes over the top. Bake, uncovered, at 350 degrees for 1½ hours.*

KAHLUA PORK

2 (6-pound) pork butts
1/2 cup liquid smoke
3 to 4 tablespoons salt

Make incisions in the meat and rub with liquid smoke and salt. Wrap the pork butts individually in double layers of foil, making sure wrapping is airtight. Bake fat side up on a baking sheet at 400 degrees for 4 1/2 to 5 hours. Unwrap the meat, reserving the juices. Discard the bone and excess fat. Shred the meat into bite-size pieces. Serve hot with the juices. Yield: 20 servings.

Julie Ann Simonik, Eta Omicron
Kingman, Arizona

MEXICAN SHREDDED PORK

1 (2 1/2- to 3-pound) pork loin
2 cups dry pinto beans
4 (4-ounce) cans chopped green chiles, drained
1 (10-ounce) can tomatoes with green chiles
1 medium onion, chopped
Salt and pepper to taste
Minced garlic to taste
Cumin to taste
2 beef bouillon cubes

Combine the pork loin, beans, green chiles, tomatoes with green chiles, onion, salt, pepper, garlic, cumin and bouillon cubes in a slow cooker. Add enough water to cover. Cook on High for 7 to 8 hours or until beans are tender and meat can be shredded. Shred the meat and return it to the slow cooker; mix well. Serve over rice or corn chips. Yield: 7 to 8 servings.

Sarah J. Estes, Zeta Eta
Roosevelt, Arizona

GRILLED PINA COLADA PORK

1 (20-ounce) can sliced pineapple in juice
1 (12-ounce) can piña colada mix
Juice and grated zest of 1 lime
1/2 red bell pepper, chopped
2 tablespoons dark rum
1 tablespoon chopped fresh gingerroot
1 tablespoon chopped fresh garlic
1/2 teaspoon salt
1 (2-pound) boneless pork roast
1 teaspoon cornstarch

Drain the juice from the pineapple into a large resealable bag and set the pineapple aside. Add the piña colada mix, lime juice and zest, bell pepper, rum, gingerroot, garlic and salt to the pineapple juice and mix. Add the pork roast to the pineapple juice mixture and seal the plastic bag. Marinate in the refrigerator for 8 to 10 hours. Remove the pork roast, reserving the marinade. Grill the pork over medium indirect heat to 155 degrees on a meat thermometer, about 1 1/2 hours, turning and brushing with marinade several times. Grill the pineapple slices for 5 to 7 minutes on each side or until brown. Let the grilled roast stand for 10 to 15 minutes. Dissolve the cornstarch in 1 tablespoon cold water. Place the remaining marinade in a small saucepan. Bring to a boil. Boil for 2 to 3 minutes, stirring constantly. Stir in the cornstarch mixture and remove from heat. Cool for 2 minutes or until slightly thickened. Slice the pork roast. Place the pork slices and pineapple slices on a serving plate and drizzle with the thickened marinade. Yield: 6 servings.

Jacqueline V. Perry, Xi Delta Nu
Centerville, Massachusetts

GREEK PORK PITAS WITH TZAZIKI

Instead of stir-frying, you may cook the pork on heavy-duty foil on a grill.

1 pound boneless pork tenderloins
4 tablespoons olive oil
4 tablespoons lemon juice
1 tablespoon prepared mustard
2 garlic cloves, minced
1 teaspoon oregano
1/2 teaspoon dill weed
6 pita bread loaves
Tzaziki

Cut the pork into 1/8- to 1/4-inch-thick strips and place in a glass dish. Pour a mixture of the olive oil, lemon juice, mustard, minced garlic and oregano over the pork. Marinate in the refrigerator, covered, for 1 to 8 hours. Drain the pork. Stir-fry the pork in a nonstick skillet or wok for 2 to 3 minutes or until cooked through. Cut the pita loaves in half and open to form pockets. Fill the pockets with the pork. Serve with lettuce, tomato and Tzaziki. Yield: 6 servings.

TZAZIKI

1 cup plain yogurt
1 cup chopped peeled cucumber
1 garlic clove, minced
1/2 teaspoon dill weed

Combine the yogurt, cucumber, garlic and dill weed in a small bowl and mix well. Chill, covered, until ready to serve.

Molly Quillin, Pi Xi
Vacaville, California

PECAN-CRUSTED PORK TENDERLOIN PINWHEELS

These delectable pinwheels may be prepared and frozen for later use.

1 (1-pound) pork tenderloin
6 thin slices bacon
Carolina Mustard Sauce
1 cup chopped pecans

Cut the pork into 1/4-inch-thick slices the size of the bacon slices. Piggyback a pork slice with a bacon slice; roll into a pinwheel and secure with a wooden pick. Repeat with the remaining pork and bacon slices. Cut each pinwheel in half to make 12 pinwheels. Coat each pinwheel with Carolina Mustard Sauce and pecans. Preheat an uncovered grill to 375 to 400 degrees. Grill the pinwheels on a rack for 6 to 8 minutes on each side or until pork is cooked through. Yield: 6 servings.

CAROLINA MUSTARD SAUCE

3/4 cup prepared mustard
1/2 cup honey
1/4 cup apple cider vinegar
2 tablespoons ketchup
1 tablespoon brown sugar
2 teaspoons Worcestershire sauce
1 teaspoon hot red pepper sauce
1 teaspoon salt
1/2 teaspoon pepper

Combine the mustard, honey, vinegar, ketchup, brown sugar, Worcestershire sauce, hot pepper sauce, salt and pepper in a bowl and mix well.

Judene Juch, Preceptor Xi Theta
Houston, Texas

PORK TENDERLOIN WELLINGTON

Serve with garlic mashed potatoes, sugar snap peas, and candied parsnips for a delightfully elegant meal.

2 tablespoons olive oil
2 slices prosciutto, chopped
3 leeks, white part only, chopped
1 tablespoon Dijon mustard
1/4 cup heavy cream
1/2 teaspoon thyme
1/2 (13-ounce) package frozen puff pastry, thawed
1 egg, beaten
1 (12-ounce) pork tenderloin
Salt and pepper to taste
Port Orange Sauce

Heat the olive oil in a skillet over medium heat. Sauté the prosciutto and leeks in the hot oil for 3 minutes or until leeks are tender. Stir in the Dijon mustard, cream and thyme; bring to a boil. Boil until mixture thickens, about 1 minute. Roll half the puff pastry into a 10×12-inch rectangle. Spread the leek mixture to within 1 inch of the edge of the pastry. Brush the exposed pastry border with beaten egg. Place the pork over the upper third of the pastry; season with salt and pepper. Roll the pastry to enclose the pork. Trim the excess pastry and place the roll seam side down on a nonstick baking sheet. Brush with beaten egg. Bake at 425 degrees for 20 to 25 minutes or until golden. Serve with Port Orange Sauce. Yield: 4 servings.

PORT ORANGE SAUCE

1/2 cup port
1/2 cup orange juice
1 cup chicken stock
1 tablespoon soy sauce
1/4 cup heavy cream

Combine the port, orange juice and stock in a skillet and bring to a boil. Cook over high heat until liquid is reduced to 1 cup. Stir in the soy sauce and cream. Return to a boil and cook over high heat until slightly thickened.

Donna Luus, Alpha Iota Master
Sault Ste. Marie, Ontario, Canada

CHEESY VEGETABLE-STUFFED PORK CHOPS

6 (1 1/4- to 1 1/2-inch-thick) pork rib chops
2 tablespoons margarine or butter
1/2 cup chopped celery
1/2 cup chopped onion
1/2 cup chopped carrot
1/2 cup chopped green bell pepper
4 ounces shredded sharp Cheddar cheese, shredded (1 cup)
1 1/2 teaspoons chopped fresh thyme, or 1/2 teaspoon dried
1/4 teaspoon salt
1/8 teaspoon pepper
2 tablespoons vegetable oil
1/2 teaspoon salt
1/4 teaspoon pepper

Make a pocket in each pork chop by cutting into the meat toward the bone. Melt the margarine in a 12-inch skillet over medium heat. Cook the celery, onion, carrot and bell pepper in the margarine for about 5 minutes or until tender, stirring occasionally. Remove from heat. Stir the cheese, thyme, the 1/4 teaspoon salt and the 1/8 teaspoon pepper into the celery mixture. Fill the pork pockets with celery mixture. Heat the vegetable oil in the skillet over medium heat. Cook the stuffed pork in the oil for about 5 minutes or until light brown, turning once. Sprinkle with the 1/2 teaspoon salt and the 1/4 teaspoon pepper. Place in an ungreased 9×13-inch baking dish. Bake, tightly covered, at 350 degrees for 30 minutes. Bake, uncovered, for 30 minutes longer or until pork is browned and cooked through. Yield: 6 servings.

Geraldine M. Fridmann, Preceptor Alpha Xi
Townbank, New Jersey

CURRIED PORK CHOPS WITH APRICOTS

6 pork loin chops, bones removed
Salt and pepper to taste
1 teaspoon curry powder
1/2 teaspoon dry mustard
1 (10-ounce) can cream of mushroom soup
1/2 cup milk
1 (16-ounce) can whole apricots, drained

Flatten the pork slightly. Brown both sides in a small amount of margarine in a skillet over medium-high heat. Season with salt and pepper. Remove the pork to a 9×13-inch baking dish. Add the curry powder, dry mustard, soup and milk to the drippings in the skillet. Heat, stirring until smooth. Pour the curry mixture over the pork. Bake at 350 degrees for 45 minutes. Garnish with heated apricots.
Yield: 6 servings.

Susan Bremner, Lambda Lambda
Waterford, Michigan

✣ PUERTO RICAN POT ROAST

4 ounces salt pork, rinsed and dried
1 (4-pound) boneless chuck roast
1/2 cup pimento-stuffed olives
2 large green bell peppers, chopped
1 large onion, chopped
1 (4-ounce) can mushrooms, drained
1 (10-ounce) can tomato soup
Pepper and garlic powder to taste

Cut the salt pork into pencil-thick strips 1 to 2 inches long. Sauté in a skillet briefly to render some of the fat; remove the pork from the skillet with a slotted spoon. Poke holes in the roast with a pointed knife. Insert salt pork strips and olives in the holes. Place the roast in a medium roasting pan. Sauté the bell peppers, onion and mushrooms in the salt pork drippings over medium heat for about 5 minutes. Stir in the soup and 1/2 cup water. Season with pepper and garlic powder. Pour the soup mixture over the roast. Roast, uncovered, at 325 degrees for about 5 hours. Yield: 6 to 8 servings.

Lois M. McAleer, Laureate Beta
Sacramento, California

PLANTATION PORK CHOPS

6 (1/2-inch-thick) pork chops
3/4 teaspoon poultry seasoning
Salt and pepper to taste
1 medium green bell pepper, chopped
3 cups boiling chicken broth
1 medium onion, chopped
1 1/2 cups uncooked rice
1 cup uncooked green peas
1 tablespoon Worcestershire sauce

Heat a large skillet and grease the entire inside with fat trimmed from the pork chops. Season the pork with poultry seasoning, salt and pepper and brown both sides in the skillet over medium heat. Remove the pork from the skillet. Combine the bell pepper, chicken broth, onion and rice in the skillet and sauté briefly. Stir in the peas and Worcestershire sauce. Remove the onion mixture to a 9×13-inch baking dish; arrange the pork over the top. Bake, covered, at 350 degrees for 30 to 45 minutes or until pork and rice are cooked through and liquid is absorbed. Fluff the rice and serve. Yield: 6 servings.

Barb Stott, Iota Omicron
Windsor, Colorado

PORK CHOPS WITH BALSAMIC VINEGAR

2 (1/2-inch-thick) boneless center pork loin chops
1 1/2 teaspoons lemon pepper
1 teaspoon olive oil
2 tablespoons chicken broth
3 tablespoons balsamic vinegar
2 teaspoons butter

Pat the pork chops dry and coat with lemon pepper. Heat the olive oil in a heavy skillet over medium-high heat. Brown the chops in the oil for 8 minutes on the first side and 7 minutes on the other side. Remove chops from the skillet and keep warm. Add the chicken broth and vinegar to the drippings in the skillet and cook for 1 to 2 minutes or until syrupy, stirring constantly. Add the butter and stir to blend. Spoon the balsamic sauce over the pork chops. Serve with a salad and a vegetable. Yield: 2 servings.

Sharon Wiggins, Preceptor Alpha Omicron
Deer Park, Texas

PORK CHOP CREOLE

1 large green bell pepper
6 (1-inch-thick) pork tenderloins
Self-rising flour to coat tenderloins
Salt and pepper to taste
1 to 2 tablespoons olive oil
3 cups cooked quick-cooking rice
2 (16-ounce) cans diced tomatoes
1 medium yellow onion, chopped

Cut 6 thin rings crosswise from the center of the bell pepper; dice the remaining bell pepper. Coat the pork in a mixture of the flour, salt and pepper. Heat the olive oil in a large skillet. Brown the pork on both sides in the hot olive oil. Place a bell pepper ring over each tenderloin. Place a scoop of rice in the center of each ring. Pour the undrained tomatoes around the tenderloins and over the edges of the tenderloins; do not pour over the rice. Sprinkle the onion and diced bell pepper over the tomatoes. Simmer, covered, over low heat for about 45 minutes to 1 hour or until cooked through. Serve with fruit salad and yeast rolls. Yield: 6 servings.

Joyce E. Dover, Preceptor Alpha Kappa
Asheville, North Carolina

ALMOND PINEAPPLE SPARERIBS

2 pounds country-style spareribs
1/2 cup flour
2 teaspoons salt
1/2 cup vegetable oil
1 (30-ounce) can sliced pineapple, drained, juice reserved
1 tablespoon white vinegar
2 tablespoons brown sugar
1 small onion
1 green bell pepper
2 tablespoons flour
2 teaspoons soy sauce
2 teaspoons ketchup
1/2 cup chopped toasted almonds

Cut the spareribs into serving pieces. Coat with 1/2 cup flour and sprinkle with salt. Brown in hot oil; drain. Combine the pineapple juice, vinegar, brown sugar and 2 tablespoons water in a bowl and mix until smooth. Pour evenly over the spareribs in the skillet. Cut each pineapple slice into 8 pieces. Quarter the onion. Cut the bell pepper into 1-inch-square pieces. Add the pineapple, onion, bell pepper and 1/2 cup water to the spareribs and simmer, covered, for 20 minutes. Make a smooth paste of the 2 tablespoons flour, soy sauce and ketchup. Remove the spareribs from the skillet to a serving plate. Stir the flour mixture into the skillet juices and cook until slightly thickened, stirring constantly. Drizzle the ketchup mixture over the spareribs. Sprinkle with toasted almonds and serve. Yield: 6 servings.

Ida M. Glass, Preceptor Xi Tau
Magalia, California

BAKED BABY BACK RIBS

1/2 onion, finely chopped
1/4 cup finely chopped green bell pepper
2 (8-ounce) cans tomato sauce
1 tablespoon Worcestershire sauce
1/3 cup apple cider vinegar or wine vinegar
1 (20-ounce) can pineapple tidbits in syrup
1/4 cup packed brown sugar
1/2 teaspoon dry mustard
3 pounds baby back ribs
Salt and pepper to taste

Combine the onion, bell pepper, tomato sauce, Worcestershire sauce, vinegar, undrained pineapple, brown sugar and dry mustard in a small bowl and mix well; let stand until ready to use. Make a cut about halfway through the strips of baby back ribs after every third rib. Sprinkle with salt and pepper and place in a shallow roasting pan. Bake at 350 degrees for 1 1/4 hours. Drain off all excess fat. Pour the pineapple mixture evenly over the ribs. Bake for 45 to 50 minutes longer, basting frequently to coat the ribs with the sauce. Yield: 4 servings.

Gretchen Trepto, Xi Mu Nu
Dunnellon, Florida

BARBECUED RIBS

1/2 cup chopped onion
3 tablespoons white vinegar
3 tablespoons brown sugar
3 tablespoons Worcestershire sauce
1 cup ketchup
1 tablespoon mustard
2 pounds pork ribs

Sauté the onion in butter in a large skillet over medium-low heat for 5 minutes or until golden. Stir in the vinegar, brown sugar, Worcestershire sauce, ketchup, mustard and 1/2 cup water; bring to a boil. Boil gently for 10 to 15 minutes. Place the ribs in a large saucepan or kettle. Add enough water to cover and bring to a boil. Boil for 10 to 15 minutes to render fat from meat; drain. Place the ribs in a slow cooker. Pour the ketchup mixture over the ribs. Cook on Low for about 8 hours. Yield: 4 to 6 servings.

Kara L. Ruffcorn, Epsilon Gamma
Canton, Missouri

CHINESE SPARERIBS

3 pounds country-style spareribs
4 whole cloves
1 onion, whole
4 peppercorns
2 teaspoons salt
1/2 cup molasses
1/2 cup chili sauce
1/4 cup prepared mustard
2 tablespoons soy sauce
1/2 cup chopped onion
1/4 teaspoon pepper
1/2 teaspoon salt

Combine the spareribs, cloves, whole onion, peppercorns and the 2 teaspoons salt in a kettle. Add enough water to cover and bring to a boil. Boil gently for 45 minutes or until spareribs are tender; drain. Discard the seasonings. Place the ribs in a baking dish. Combine the molasses, chili sauce, mustard, soy sauce, the 1/2 cup chopped onion, pepper and the 1/2 teaspoon salt in a small bowl and mix well. Pour the molasses mixture evenly over the ribs. Bake, uncovered, at 325 degrees for 25 minutes. Serve over rice. Yield: 6 to 8 servings.

Karen Casson, Xi Beta Delta
Encampment, Wyoming

MACARONI AND CHEESE

Use several smaller baking dishes if desired.

1 small onion, minced
1 tablespoon vegetable oil
1 (28-ounce) can diced tomatoes, drained
2 (6-ounce) cans tomato paste
1 teaspoon basil
1/2 teaspoon sugar
1/2 teaspoon oregano
8 ounces elbow macaroni, cooked and drained
1 cup cottage cheese
8 ounces Velveeta cheese, cubed
2 cups (or less) chopped cooked ham

About 50 minutes before serving time, sauté the onion in hot oil in a large kettle over medium heat for about 5 minutes. Stir in the tomatoes, tomato paste, basil, sugar and oregano. Simmer, covered, over low heat for 20 minutes, stirring occasionally. Combine the macaroni, cottage cheese, Velveeta cheese and ham in a bowl and mix well. Stir the tomato mixture into the macaroni mixture. Spoon into a buttered 2 1/2-quart baking dish. Bake, covered, at 350 degrees for 30 minutes. Yield: 8 to 10 servings.

Agnes Jackson, Alpha Xi Master
Delta, British Columbia, Canada

JAMBALAYA

A can of shrimp may be substituted for the chicken if desired. Add the shrimp about 10 minutes before the end of cooking time.

1 cup chopped onion
1 cup chopped green bell pepper
1 garlic clove, minced
2 tablespoons vegetable oil
1/4 teaspoon thyme
2 teaspoons salt
2 teaspoons Worcestershire sauce
1 1/2 cups uncooked rice
2 cups chopped cooked chicken
1/2 pound fully cooked ham, chopped

Sauté the onion, bell pepper and garlic in vegetable oil in a 10-inch skillet over medium-low heat for about 5 minutes. Add the thyme, salt, Worcestershire sauce and 3 cups water and simmer for about 10 minutes, stirring occasionally. Mix in the rice, chicken and ham. Simmer, tightly covered, for about 25 minutes. Remove cover. Fluff the rice and cook for 5 minutes longer. Yield: 6 servings.

Joyce Fred, Alpha Iota Master
Springfield, Illinois

HOPPING JOHN

2 (16-ounce) packages frozen black-eyed peas, thawed
1 large onion, chopped
1 hambone
1 (16-ounce) can diced tomatoes
2 cups chopped cooked ham
1 cup uncooked quick-cooking rice
Salt and pepper to taste

Combine the black-eyed peas, onion, hambone and undrained tomatoes in a large kettle. Add enough water to cover. Simmer, covered, for 30 minutes. Stir in the ham and rice; simmer, covered, for 15 minutes or until all ingredients are tender. Season with salt and pepper. Yield: 8 to 12 servings.

Pattie Marshall, Xi Delta Xi
Martinsville, Virginia

ITALIAN BEANS WITH SAUSAGE

2 garlic cloves, minced
1 medium onion, chopped
1 rib celery, chopped
1 pound hot Italian sausage, casings removed
3/4 cup beef broth
1/4 cup red wine
2 tablespoons tomato paste
1 (16-ounce) can kidney or Romano beans
1/2 teaspoon basil
Salt and pepper to taste

Sauté the garlic, onion, celery and sausage in hot oil in a kettle for 5 minutes. Stir in the beef broth, wine and tomato paste; cook over medium heat until liquid is reduced by half. Stir in the kidney beans, basil, salt and pepper. Simmer for 10 minutes and serve. Yield: 4 servings.

Marilyn MacArthur, Preceptor Epsilon Gamma
Pickering, Ontario, Canada

Joan Marie Slingsby, Xi Epsilon Eta, Clearwater, British Columbia, Canada, makes ***Sausage Potato Bake*** *by cutting 2 pounds medium or hot Italian sausage, casings removed, into bite-size pieces and browning in a skillet over medium heat. Place sausage in a casserole. Pour a mixture of one 10-ounce can cream of tomato soup and one soup can water over the sausage. Add 2 tablespoons vegetable oil, 1 teaspoon salt, 1/2 teaspoon pepper, 1 teaspoon basil, 3 chopped, peeled medium potatoes, 1 drained 10-ounce can mushroom pieces and stems, 1 chopped large onion, 3 sliced carrots, 1 teaspoon Worcestershire sauce and 1 teaspoon sugar; mix well. Bake, covered, at 350 degrees for 1 1/2 hours or until meat and vegetables are tender; 1 cup frozen peas may be added during the last 20 minutes of baking.*

BROCCOLI SAUSAGE BAKE

1 pound ground Italian sausage
1 onion, chopped
1 (4-ounce) can sliced mushrooms, drained
Salt and pepper to taste
1 (10-ounce) can cream of mushroom soup
2 (10-ounce) packages frozen broccoli, thawed
8 ounces mozzarella cheese, cubed
1/2 teaspoon Tabasco sauce

Brown the ground sausage with the onion in a large skillet, stirring until crumbly; drain. Add the mushrooms, salt and pepper. Stir in the soup, broccoli, cheese and Tabasco sauce. Spoon the sausage mixture into a deep 1 1/2-quart baking dish. Bake, uncovered, at 350 degrees for 30 minutes. Yield: 4 servings.

Norma Albright, Preceptor Phi
Madison, Wisconsin

TWO-SAUCE LASAGNA

1 pound Italian sausage, casings removed
15 ounces ricotta cheese
16 ounces mozzarella cheese, shredded (4 cups)
1/4 cup freshly grated Parmesan cheese
2 eggs
1 (26-ounce) jar tomato basil pasta sauce
12 lasagna noodles
1 (10-ounce) package frozen chopped spinach, thawed, well drained
1 (16-ounce) jar Alfredo pasta sauce

Brown the sausage in a skillet; drain. Combine the ricotta cheese, mozzarella cheese, 2 tablespoons of the Parmesan cheese and eggs in a bowl; mix well. Spread 1 cup of the tomato basil pasta sauce in a 9×13-inch baking dish. Layer 4 noodles, half the cheese mixture, half the spinach, 1 cup tomato basil pasta sauce and half the sausage over the noodles. Repeat the layers. Top with the remaining noodles. Spread Alfredo pasta sauce over the top; sprinkle with Parmesan cheese. Bake, covered, at 350 degrees for 40 minutes. Bake, uncovered, for 15 minutes. Yield: 20 servings.

Linda McConnell, Preceptor Iota Sigma
Carrollton, Texas

---

*Susan Gascoigne, Xi Delta, Portage La Prairie, Manitoba, Canada, makes **Sweet-and-Sour Sausages** by browning 2 pounds pork sausage links and cutting into bite-size pieces. Place in a 1 1/2-quart baking dish. Add 1 drained 14-ounce can sliced peaches, 3/4 cup sugar, 1 teaspoon curry powder, 1 tablespoon onion flakes, 1 cup chili sauce and 1/2 cup ketchup; mix well. Bake, uncovered, at 350 degrees for 30 minutes. Stir. Bake for 15 to 20 minutes longer.*

MUFFALETTA

Muffaletta is a savory sandwich that originated in New Orleans.

1 round loaf Portuguese bread
1/2 cup mixed chopped olives
1 red bell pepper, blackened, peeled, cut into strips
8 ounces feta cheese, crumbled
1 (8-ounce) can artichoke hearts, drained, sliced
1/4 pound hard salami, thickly sliced
1/4 cup olive oil
2 tablespoons balsamic vinegar
2 garlic cloves, minced
Salt and pepper to taste
1 cup chopped fresh herbs (basil, parsley, oregano)

Cut a horizontal 1-inch-thick slice from the top of the bread. Scoop out the center of the loaf to leave a 1-inch-thick shell. Spread the olives in the bread bowl. Layer the bell pepper, feta cheese, artichoke slices and salami slices over the olives. Drizzle a mixture of the olive oil and vinegar over the salami layer. Replace the top bread slice and wrap well in plastic wrap. Place a heavy weight (like a stack of books) over the top and let stand at room temperature for 8 to 10 hours. Place in the refrigerator and chill until serving time. Cut into wedges and serve.
Yield: 6 to 8 servings.

Connie Painter, Preceptor Beta
Owl's Head, Maine

PEPPERONI QUICHE

1 unbaked (9-inch) deep-dish pie shell
6 ounces mozzarella cheese, shredded (1 1/2 cups)
1/2 cup spaghetti sauce
1/3 cup pepperoni slices
1/4 cup chopped onion
1/4 cup chopped green bell pepper
2 eggs
3/4 cup heavy cream
1/4 teaspoon salt
1/4 teaspoon black pepper

Bake the pie shell for 6 to 8 minutes in a preheated 350-degree oven; let stand until cool. Layer 3/4 cup of the cheese, spaghetti sauce, pepperoni, onion, bell pepper and the remaining 3/4 cup cheese in the pie crust. Combine the eggs, cream, salt and pepper in a medium bowl; mix until smooth. Pour the egg mixture evenly over the cheese layer. Place the pie plate on a baking sheet. Bake at 350 degrees for 45 to 50 minutes or until golden brown and a knife inserted in the center comes out clean. Cool for 15 minutes. Yield: 6 to 8 servings.

Jackie Ann Nelson, Xi Theta Chi
Chesapeake, Virginia

BAKED LEMON CHICKEN

1 (3- to 5-pound) roasting chicken
1 small onion
2 lemons
2 tablespoons olive oil
Lemon pepper

Rinse the chicken and pat dry. Discard the giblets. Place the chicken breast side up in a roasting pan. Cut the onion into quarters and slice the lemons. Stuff the chicken cavity with the onion quarters and lemon slices. Rub the skin with olive oil. Sprinkle lemon pepper over the oiled surface. Bake, covered, at 325 degrees for 1 to 2 hours or until cooked through. Let stand for 15 to 30 minutes before carving. Yield: 4 to 6 servings.

Treva M. Scott, Alpha Pi
Neodesha, Kansas

YOUNG HEN WITH PORT

A young hen is often called a pullet. You may use Cornish game hens in this recipe.

1 small pullet per person
Desired amount of green grapes and red grapes
1 bottle port

Cut the pullets in half and arrange in a baking dish. Sprinkle the grapes over the pullets. Add port to a level halfway up the pullets; grapes will float. Bake, uncovered, at 400 degrees for about 1½ hours or until cooked through; do not overbake or the meat will be tough. Serve with new potatoes and a salad. Yield: variable.

Pam McPherson, Xi Alpha Delta
Austin, Texas

LAZY CHICKEN AND VEGETABLES

You can prepare the chicken before you leave for work and let it cook all day while you are at work. It is a complete meal that requires little effort.

1 frozen chicken
8 to 10 potatoes
8 ounces carrots
1 onion, sliced
Salt and pepper to taste
Garlic powder to taste
Lemon pepper to taste
2 (10-ounce) cans cream of chicken or cream of mushroom soup (or both)

Place the frozen chicken in a roasting pan; leave the giblets and papers for extra flavor. Scrub the potatoes and carrots and cut into serving-size pieces; place in the roasting pan. Arrange the onion slices over the frozen chicken. Season with salt, pepper, garlic powder, lemon pepper and other seasonings to taste. Pour the soup over the chicken. Bake, tightly covered, at 300 degrees for 8 to 10 hours.
Yield: 5 or 6 servings.

Trudy Ruch, Xi Eta
Omaha, Nebraska

CRANBERRY CHICKEN

1 (16-ounce) can whole cranberry sauce
1 (8-ounce) bottle Russian salad dressing
1 envelope onion soup mix
1 teaspoon lemon pepper
½ teaspoon salt
½ teaspoon garlic powder
1 (3- to 3½-pound) chicken, cut up, or 4 to 6 chicken breasts
Hot cooked rice
Pinch of rosemary (optional)

Combine the cranberry sauce, salad dressing, dry onion soup mix, lemon pepper, salt and garlic powder in a bowl and mix well. Rinse the chicken and pat dry. Remove and discard the skin. Arrange the chicken pieces in a single layer in a 9×13-inch baking dish. Pour the cranberry sauce mixture evenly over the chicken. Chill, covered, for 3 to 10 hours. Bake, uncovered, at 300 degrees for 1 1/2 hours or until cooked through, stirring the cranberry sauce and spooning over the chicken once or twice. Serve the chicken and cranberry sauce with hot cooked rice; sprinkle with rosemary. Yield: 4 to 6 servings.

Irene G. Berghoff, Pi Master
Bethalto, Illinois

MUSTARD CHICKEN

Mustard Chicken is also very good when grilled.

1 chicken, cut into pieces
1/2 cup (1 stick) margarine, melted
2 to 3 tablespoons prepared mustard
1 teaspoon lemon juice

Butter a cast-iron skillet. Season the chicken with salt and pepper to taste and place in the prepared skillet. Bake, uncovered, at 350 degrees for 1 hour, basting occasionally with a mixture of the margarine, mustard and lemon juice. Yield: 3 to 4 servings.

Norma J. Boyer, Xi Epsilon Nu
Colorado Springs, Colorado

CRISPY FRIED CHICKEN

This chicken may be deep-fried instead of pan-fried if you prefer.

1 1/2 cups flour
1 tablespoon garlic salt
1 1/2 teaspoons pepper
1 1/2 teaspoons paprika
1/4 to 1/2 teaspoon poultry seasoning
2/3 cup flour
1/2 teaspoon salt
1/4 to 1/2 teaspoon pepper
1 egg, beaten
3/4 cup flat beer or water
1 chicken, cut up
Vegetable oil for frying

Combine the 1 1/2 cups flour, garlic salt, the 1 1/2 teaspoons pepper, paprika and poultry seasoning in a large bowl and mix well. Combine the 2/3 cup flour, salt, the 1/4 to 1/2 teaspoon pepper, egg and beer in another large bowl and mix well. Coat the chicken pieces with the seasoned flour. Dip them in the egg mixture, then coat again with seasoned flour. Fry in 1 inch of vegetable oil in a large skillet over medium-high heat for about 20 minutes or until browned and cooked through, turning twice. Yield: variable.

Elizabeth Hiller, Gamma Zeta
McCune, Kansas

SAUERKRAUT AND SAUSAGE CHICKEN

I like to add more caraway seeds, and I add a bit of sugar.

1 medium onion, chopped
1 garlic clove, minced
1 (27-ounce) can sauerkraut, rinsed and drained
1 pound smoked Polish sausage, cut into 1-inch pieces
1 teaspoon caraway seeds
Desired number of red potatoes, quartered
Desired number of chicken pieces
1/2 teaspoon salt
1/4 teaspoon pepper
1/4 to 1/2 teaspoon thyme

Combine the onion, garlic, sauerkraut, sausage and caraway seeds in a 9×13-inch baking dish. Press the potato quarters into the sausage mixture, "burying" the potatoes. Layer the chicken pieces over the top. Sprinkle with salt, pepper and thyme. Bake, uncovered, at 350 degrees for 1 hour or until chicken is tender. Yield: variable.

JoAnn Panuska, Laureate Delta
Williamsburg, Virginia

SESAME ORANGE CHICKEN

1 or 2 chickens, cut up
2 oranges, halved
1 medium onion, chopped
Dash of salt
Dash of pepper
1 tablespoon butter
1/2 cup sesame seeds

Clean the chicken parts and arrange in a 9×11-inch baking dish. Squeeze the juice from 1 orange, about 1/2 cup. Cut the second orange into slices and arrange over the chicken. Sprinkle with chopped onion, salt and pepper. Drizzle the orange juice over the top and dot with butter. Sprinkle evenly with the sesame seeds. Bake, uncovered, at 375 degrees for 1 hour or until browned and well cooked. Yield: 4 to 6 servings.

Leslie Dorius-Jones, Eta Master
Salt Lake City, Utah

Deborah Bottenfield, Alpha Beta Upsilon, Crestview, Florida, prepares **Chicken Can Can** *for a quick dinner by placing a mixture of 1 cup shredded cooked chicken, one 10-ounce can cream of mushroom soup, one 10-ounce can cream of celery soup, 1 soup can of water and 1 soup can of uncooked minute rice in a 9×13-inch baking dish. Bake, covered, at 350 degrees for 30 minutes. Sprinkle with 1 can of French-fried onion rings and bake for 5 minutes longer or until light brown.*

CREAMY CHICKEN WITH WINE

This dish is delicious served with white rice or mashed potatoes. Do not add salt; pepper is fine.

1 (10-ounce) can cream of mushroom soup
1 (10-ounce) can cream of celery soup
1 (10-ounce) can cream of chicken soup
1 (10-ounce) can Cheddar cheese soup
1/2 cup white wine
2 tablespoons finely chopped onion
6 pounds chicken pieces
1/4 cup grated Parmesan cheese
1/4 cup slivered almonds

Combine the soups, wine and onion in a bowl and mix well. Place the chicken pieces in a roasting pan. Pour the soup mixture evenly over the chicken. Bake, covered, at 325 degrees for 2 1/2 hours. Remove from oven. Layer the Parmesan cheese and almonds over the top. Return to oven and bake, uncovered, for 30 minutes. Yield: 8 to 10 servings.

Esther Colton, Preceptor Epsilon Delta
Garden Grove, California

COQ AU VIN

3 tablespoons butter
1/4 pound bacon, cut up
3/4 cup chopped onion
1 carrot, sliced
3 shallots, minced
1 garlic clove, peeled
Chicken pieces (breasts and thighs are good in this dish)
2 tablespoons minced parsley
2 tablespoons flour
1 teaspoon chervil or marjoram
1 bay leaf
1/2 teaspoon thyme
1 teaspoon salt
1/2 teaspoon pepper
1 1/2 cups dry wine or sherry
8 ounces mushrooms, sliced

Melt the butter in a large kettle over medium heat. Add the bacon, onion, carrot, shallots and garlic and brown in the butter; remove from kettle and set aside. Brown the chicken pieces in the butter; remove and set aside. Stir in the parsley, flour, chervil, bay leaf, thyme, salt, pepper and wine. Return the vegetables and chicken to the kettle. Simmer, covered, for 1 hour, stirring in the mushrooms for the last 5 minutes of cooking time. Yield: 6 to 8 servings.

Elizabeth Gourlay, Laureate Delta Epsilon
Toronto, Ontario, Canada

Janet Molen, Xi Theta Xi, Brandon, Florida, makes ***Cranberry Chicken*** *by dividing 8 to 10 chicken breasts between two 9×11-inch baking dishes. Pour a mixture of 2 cans of whole cranberries, 8 ounces Russian salad dressing and 1 package onion soup mix over the chicken. Bake at 350 degrees for 1 hour.*

BAKED CHICKEN WITH RANCH DRESSING AND CHEDDAR

1 1/2 cups original ranch salad dressing mix
2 tablespoons flour
4 skinless boneless chicken breasts
1/2 cup shredded sharp Cheddar cheese
1/2 cup grated Parmesan cheese

Preheat the oven to 375 degrees. Combine the dry salad dressing mix and flour in a bowl and mix well. Rinse the chicken and pat dry. Coat each chicken breast with the salad dressing mixture and arrange on a nonstick baking sheet. Sprinkle with a mixture of the Cheddar cheese and Parmesan cheese. Bake at 375 degrees for 25 minutes. Yield: 4 servings.

Lynette Bortis, Preceptor Beta Mu
Indianapolis, Indiana

LOW-CARB OVEN-BAKED CHICKEN

1/4 cup margarine, melted
1 egg
1/4 cup skim milk
6 skinless chicken breasts
1/2 (5-ounce) package pork rinds, crushed
Seasonings to taste

Brush the margarine over the bottom of a 9×13-inch baking dish. Beat the egg well with a wire whisk and whisk in the milk. Dip the chicken in the egg mixture and arrange in the prepared baking dish. Sprinkle the pork rinds over the chicken and season with your favorite seasonings. Bake, uncovered, at 350 degrees for 1 hour or until golden brown. Yield: 4 servings.

Barbara Mullen, Tau Omicron
Forsyth, Missouri

YOGURT PARMESAN BAKED CHICKEN

6 skinless boneless chicken breasts
1 cup plain low-fat yogurt
2 tablespoons lemon juice
1 garlic clove, minced
1 teaspoon celery salt
1/4 teaspoon pepper
1 teaspoon salt
3/4 cup dry bread crumbs
1/4 cup grated Parmesan cheese
1/4 cup butter, melted

Rinse the chicken and pat dry. Combine the next six ingredients in a glass dish and mix well. Add the chicken. Marinate, covered, in the refrigerator for 8 to 10 hours. Combine the bread crumbs and Parmesan cheese in a dish. Remove the chicken from the yogurt mixture and roll in the bread crumb mixture to coat. Arrange on a 9×13-inch baking dish and drizzle with butter. Bake, uncovered, at 350 degrees for 1 hour. Yield: 6 to 8 servings.

Laura Amundson, Xi Alpha Delta
Verona, Wisconsin

SLOW-COOKER CHICKEN

4 to 6 chicken breasts
8 ounces cream cheese
2 (10-ounce) cans cream of mushroom soup
1 envelope Italian salad dressing mix
8 ounces mushrooms, sliced (optional)

Combine the chicken, cream cheese, soup, dry salad dressing mix, mushrooms and 1/2 cup water in a slow cooker. Cook on High for 3 or 4 hours, stirring occasionally. Serve over rice or noodles.
Yield: 6 to 8 servings.

Shirlee Farley, Preceptor Phi
Red Lodge, Montana

CHICKEN FINGERS

2 tablespoons whole-grain mustard
6 tablespoons honey
1/2 cup sesame seeds
1/4 cup grated Parmesan cheese
1 pound chicken breasts, skinned, boned, cut into 2 1/2-inch strips
2 teaspoons olive oil
Red leaf lettuce
Strips of orange zest

Blend the whole-grain mustard and honey in a small bowl; set aside. Combine the sesame seeds and Parmesan cheese in a shallow dish and mix well. Roll the chicken strips in the sesame seed mixture. Heat the olive oil in an ovenproof nonstick heavy-bottomed skillet until just below the smoking point. Add the chicken strips and brown on both sides over medium-high heat; do not scorch. Arrange the chicken strips on a baking sheet. Bake in a preheated 425-degree oven for 8 to 10 minutes or until cooked through. Line individual plates with lettuce leaves and arrange the chicken over the lettuce. Garnish with orange zest and serve with honey-mustard sauce. Yield: 4 servings.

Kathleen Denton, Beta Omicron
Fletcher, North Carolina

Naomi S. Murray, Xi Mu Rho, Springfield, Missouri, makes ***Chicken 'n Dressing Casserole*** *by heating 12 ounces Velveeta cheese, one 10-ounce can cream of mushroom soup and 3/4 cup milk in a saucepan over medium heat until cheese melts. Spoon about 1/4 of the cheese mixture over the bottom of a 9×13-inch baking dish. Layer 3 chopped cooked chicken breasts over the cheese mixture and pour the remaining cheese mixture over the chicken. Prepare one 6-ounce package chicken-flavor stuffing using package directions. Fluff stuffing with a fork and crumble over the cheese mixture. Bake at 350 degrees for 30 minutes.*

COUNTRY CHICKEN KIEV

2 whole chicken breasts, split
2/3 cup butter, melted
1/2 cup bread crumbs
2 tablespoons grated Parmesan cheese
1 teaspoon basil
1 teaspoon oregano
1/2 teaspoon garlic powder
1/4 cup white wine
1/4 cup chopped green onions
1/4 cup chopped fresh parsley

Dip the chicken in the melted butter and coat with a mixture of the bread crumbs, cheese, basil, oregano and garlic powder. Reserve the remaining melted butter. Arrange the chicken breasts bone side down in a 10-inch baking dish. Bake, uncovered, at 375 degrees for 50 to 60 minutes or until the chicken is tender and golden brown. Mix the remaining melted butter with the wine, green onions and parsley. Drizzle the mixture over the chicken breasts and bake for 5 minutes longer. Remove the chicken breasts to a serving platter. Spoon the pan juices over the chicken and serve. Yield: 4 servings.

Barbara Kennedy, Laureate Lambda
Fort Pierce, Florida

✣ CHAMPAGNE CHICKEN

2 tablespoons butter
4 boneless skinless chicken breasts
8 ounces small whole mushrooms
2/3 cup champagne
1/4 teaspoon salt
1/4 teaspoon tarragon
1/8 teaspoon white pepper
1/2 cup half-and-half
2 tablespoons cornstarch

Melt the butter in a 10-inch skillet. Add the chicken and cook over medium-high heat for 5 to 7 minutes or until lightly browned on both sides. Reduce heat and add the mushrooms, champagne, salt, tarragon and white pepper. Cook, covered, over medium heat for about 15 minutes longer. Combine the half-and-half and cornstarch in a small bowl and whisk to blend. Remove the chicken and mushrooms from the skillet to a serving platter and cover to keep warm. Stir the half-and-half mixture into the champagne mixture and cook over medium-low heat until thickened, stirring constantly. Cook for 1 minute longer. Spoon over the chicken and mushrooms. Serve immediately. Yield: 4 servings.

Deborah A. Miller, Preceptor Gamma Lambda
Wichita, Kansas

ITALIAN COUNTRY CHICKEN

Fusilli is a corkscrew-shaped pasta.

4½ tablespoons olive oil
1½ large onions, cut into narrow wedges
3 garlic cloves, minced
1½ pounds skinless boneless chicken breasts, cut into strips
1 (14-ounce) can marinated artichokes
1 (12-ounce) jar roasted red peppers
¾ cup pitted olives
Salt and pepper to taste
16 ounces fusilli, freshly cooked and drained
Slices of Monterey Jack cheese

Heat the olive oil in a large heavy skillet over medium heat. Add the onions and garlic and cook for about 10 minutes or until translucent, stirring occasionally. Add the chicken and cook for 5 minutes or until cooked through, stirring constantly. Add the undrained artichokes, undrained roasted peppers and olives; heat through. Season with salt and pepper. Toss with the pasta and pour into 2 baking dishes, one 9×13, the other 9×9. Cover with slices of cheese. Bake, uncovered, at 375 degrees for 10 minutes or until hot and cheese is melted. Yield: 15 servings.

Ethel Armitage, Alpha Xi Master
Delta, British Columbia, Canada

CRAB-STUFFED CHICKEN

4 boneless skinless chicken breasts
2 tablespoons butter
1 tablespoon finely chopped onion
1 tablespoon finely chopped celery leaves
1 cup fine bread crumbs
½ teaspoon salt
⅛ teaspoon black pepper
½ teaspoon dried leaf savory
1 egg
1 (10-ounce) can cream of mushroom soup
2 teaspoons Worcestershire sauce
1 tablespoon lemon juice
1 teaspoon prepared mustard
1 (5-ounce) can crab meat, drained and flaked
¼ cup finely chopped green bell pepper
½ cup flour
¼ teaspoon onion salt
Dash of black pepper
¼ cup vegetable oil

Pound the chicken to ¼-inch thickness and sprinkle with salt. Heat the butter in a skillet over medium-low heat. Add the onion and celery and sauté for 3 minutes. Add the bread crumbs and sauté for 2 minutes longer. Remove from heat. Stir in the ½ teaspoon salt, the ⅛ teaspoon black pepper and savory. Combine the egg, soup, Worcestershire sauce, lemon juice and mustard in a bowl and mix well. Stir the egg mixture into the bread crumb mixture. Stir in the crab and bell pepper. Spread ¼ cup of the crab mixture over each chicken breast; roll up and secure with a small skewer. Coat with a mixture of the flour, onion salt and the dash of black pepper. Pan-fry in vegetable oil for about 15 minutes or until browned, stirring and turning occasionally. Yield: 6 servings.

Beth Johnston, Preceptor Beta Iota
Quesnel, British Columbia, Canada

CHICKEN CACCIATORE

6 boneless skinless chicken breast halves
2 tablespoons olive oil
3 cups small fresh mushrooms
2 medium red or green bell peppers
1 large onion, thinly sliced, separated into rings
2 garlic cloves, minced
¼ teaspoon crushed red pepper
½ cup white wine
1 (28-ounce) can whole tomatoes, cut up
2 tablespoons tomato paste
2 tablespoons lemon juice
2 teaspoons basil
1 teaspoon sugar
1 teaspoon thyme
½ teaspoon salt
¼ teaspoon black pepper

Brown the chicken on all sides in hot oil in a heavy ovenproof skillet or Dutch oven. Remove the chicken and set aside. Add the mushrooms, bell peppers, onion and garlic to the skillet drippings. Cook over medium-low heat for 5 to 10 minutes or until vegetables are tender, stirring frequently. Stir in the crushed red pepper and wine. Bring to a boil. Reduce heat and simmer, uncovered, until almost all liquid has evaporated. Stir in the undrained tomatoes, tomato paste, lemon juice, basil, sugar, thyme, salt and pepper. Return the chicken to the skillet. Bake, uncovered, at 350 degrees for 10 to 15 minutes or until chicken is tender. Serve over pasta.
Yield: 4 to 6 servings.

Joan Robbins, Laureate Beta
East Greenwich, Rhode Island

CHICKEN AND DUMPLINGS

½ chicken, cut up
3 large potatoes, peeled, cut into chunks
2 carrots, cut into chunks
2 ribs celery, cut into chunks
1 medium onion, chopped
Salt and pepper to taste
Chicken bouillon granules to taste
2 cups flour
1 tablespoon baking powder
1 teaspoon salt
¼ cup shortening
1 cup milk

Place the chicken in a kettle. Add enough water to cover and bring to a boil. Reduce heat and simmer for about 30 minutes or until chicken is tender. Drain, reserving the broth. Combine the chicken broth, potatoes, carrots, celery and onion in a kettle and cook until vegetables are tender. Shred the chicken meat and add to the vegetable mixture. Add salt, pepper and bouillon. Combine the flour, baking powder and salt in a bowl. Cut in the shortening until crumbly. Stir in the milk. Drop spoonfuls of the dough into the simmering chicken mixture. Cook, uncovered, for 10 minutes; cover and cook for 10 minutes longer. Yield: 4 to 6 servings.

Charlene Elkin, Xi Delta Lambda
Four Seasons, Missouri

SLOW-COOKER CHICKEN AND DUMPLINGS

6 to 8 frozen boneless skinless chicken breasts
Garlic powder and seasoned salt to taste
1 (10-ounce) can chicken with mushroom soup
1 (10-ounce) can French onion soup
1 (15-ounce) can chicken broth
2 cups baking mix
3/4 cup milk

Sprinkle the chicken with garlic powder and seasoned salt. Place in a slow cooker. Add a mixture of the chicken soup, French onion soup and chicken broth. Cook on Low for 6 to 8 hours. Remove the chicken breasts. Pour the liquid into a large kettle and bring to a boil. Combine the baking mix and milk in a bowl and mix well. Drop the dough by spoonfuls into the boiling liquid. Reduce heat and simmer gently, uncovered, over low heat for 10 minutes. Cover and simmer for 10 minutes longer. Place a chicken breast and 2 dumplings on each plate. Cover with gravy and serve. Yield: 6 to 8 servings.

Kathleen McNiel, Preceptor Epsilon Delta
Garden Grove, California

GRILLED CHICKEN WITH PEACH SAUCE

You may substitute 1/2 cup crushed pineapple for the chopped peach, and strawberry or banana gelatin for the peach gelatin.

1 cup sugar
2 tablespoons cornstarch
2 tablespoons dry peach gelatin mix
1 medium peach, peeled, finely chopped
4 boneless skinless chicken breasts

Combine the sugar, cornstarch and 1 cup water in a saucepan over medium heat; stir until smooth. Bring to a boil; boil for 2 minutes, stirring constantly. Remove from heat. Stir in the dry gelatin and chopped peach; mix well. Remove 1 cup of the peach mixture to a small bowl and set aside. Grill the chicken, uncovered, over medium coals for 3 to 6 minutes on each side, basting with the peach mixture. Grill for 6 to 8 minutes longer or until juices run clear, turning and basting frequently. Serve with the 1 cup reserved peach mixture. Yield: 4 servings.

Joyce Bladorn, Gamma Psi Master
Chico, California

GARLIC AND HERB-SEASONED CHICKEN

3 cups herb-seasoned stuffing mix
1/2 to 3/4 cup grated Parmesan cheese
1 1/2 garlic cloves, minced, or 1 teaspoon garlic salt
3/4 cup slivered almonds
3 teaspoons salt
1/4 teaspoon pepper
1 cup (2 sticks) butter, melted
6 boneless skinless chicken breasts

Combine the stuffing mix, cheese, garlic, almonds, salt and pepper in a bowl and mix well. Add 2/3 of the melted butter and stir. Dip the chicken in the remaining melted butter and coat with the stuffing mixture. Arrange in a buttered 9×13-inch baking dish. Sprinkle with the remaining stuffing mixture and dot with butter. Bake, uncovered, at 350 degrees for about 35 minutes or until chicken is cooked through. Yield: 3 to 6 servings.

Jan Prickel, Theta Nu
Batesville, Indiana

LEMON CHICKEN

4 eggs
1/2 cup grated Parmesan cheese
Chopped fresh parsley to taste
Salt and pepper to taste
6 boneless skinless chicken breasts
Flour to coat the chicken
6 lemon slices
1/4 cup melted butter
Juice of 2 lemons
Sherry to taste

Combine the eggs, cheese, parsley, salt and pepper in a bowl and mix until smooth. Pound the chicken breasts into 1/4-inch thickness. Coat each piece with flour and dip into the egg mixture. Brown quickly in hot oil in a skillet; egg mixture will expand around the edges as for an omelet. Arrange the chicken in a 9×13-inch baking dish. Place a lemon slice over each piece of chicken. Drizzle a mixture of the melted butter and lemon juice over the chicken. Bake, uncovered, at 350 degrees for 45 minutes or until browned and tender. Pour sherry over the chicken just before serving. Yield: 6 servings.

Paula Byrne, Preceptor Gamma Theta
Centennial, Colorado

SPANISH CHICKEN

Use boneless chicken thighs if you prefer dark meat.

2½ pounds boneless skinless chicken breasts
4 garlic cloves, minced
¼ cup oregano
Salt and pepper to taste
½ cup vegetable oil
1 cup pitted dried prunes
½ cup capers, with juice
½ cup pitted Spanish olives
1 bay leaf
1 cup packed brown sugar
1 cup white wine
¼ cup chopped Italian parsley

Place the chicken in a 9×13-inch baking dish. Combine the garlic, oregano, salt, pepper, vegetable oil, prunes, capers, olives, bay leaf, brown sugar, wine and parsley in a bowl and mix well. Pour the marinade evenly over the chicken. Marinate, covered, in the refrigerator for about 12 hours. Bake, uncovered, for 1 hour or less or until tender; do not overcook or white meat may dry.
Yield: 6 to 8 servings.

Margaret H. Keegin, Alpha Zeta Master
Holland, Michigan

CRISPY ONION CHICKEN

½ cup (1 stick) butter or margarine, melted
1 tablespoon Worcestershire sauce
1 teaspoon dry mustard
½ teaspoon garlic salt
¼ teaspoon pepper
4 boneless skinless chicken breasts
1 (6-ounce) can Cheddar or original French-fried onions, crushed

Combine the butter, Worcestershire sauce, dry mustard, garlic salt and pepper in a shallow dish. Dip the chicken pieces in the butter mixture; coat with the crushed French-fried onions. Place in a 9×9-inch baking pan. Top with the remaining onions; drizzle with any remaining butter mixture. Bake, uncovered, at 350 degrees for 30 to 35 minutes or until chicken juices run clear. Yield: 4 servings.

Maureen Hampson, Laureate Beta Theta
Aurora, Colorado

PARMESAN CHICKEN

2 cups crushed butter crackers
½ teaspoon garlic powder
⅓ cup grated Parmesan cheese
2 tablespoons chopped parsley
¼ cup melted butter
6 boneless skinless chicken breasts
2 cups plain yogurt
1 (10-ounce) can cream of chicken soup
1 tablespoon lemon juice

Combine the cracker crumbs, garlic powder, cheese, parsley and butter in a bowl and mix well. Dip the chicken in 1 cup of the yogurt and coat with the cracker mixture. Arrange on a baking sheet. Bake at 350 degrees for 50 minutes. Serve with a warmed mixture of the soup, the remaining 1 cup yogurt and lemon juice. Yield: 6 servings.

Cindy Kruckenberg, Xi Theta Zeta
Gilbert, Iowa

CHICKEN WITH WINE AND CAPERS

4 boneless skinless chicken breasts
1 cup flour
½ teaspoon pepper
2 teaspoons paprika
2 tablespoons extra-virgin olive oil
1 cup low-sodium chicken broth
1 cup dry white wine
2 tablespoons capers
2 teaspoons flour
4 lemon slices

Pound the chicken into ¼-inch thickness. Combine the 1 cup flour, pepper and paprika in a shallow bowl. Coat the chicken in the flour mixture. Heat the olive oil in a large skillet over medium-high heat. Sauté the chicken 3 minutes on each side or until lightly browned. Remove the chicken from the skillet and set aside. Combine the chicken broth, wine and capers in the skillet, scraping to free any hardened drippings. Combine the 2 teaspoons flour and ⅔ cup water in a bowl and whisk until smooth. Add the flour mixture to the broth mixture. Bring to a boil, whisking frequently; cook for 3 to 5 minutes until slightly thickened. Reduce heat to medium low. Add the chicken breasts and place a lemon slice over each one. Cook for 3 to 5 minutes until heated through. Spoon the sauce over the chicken and serve.
Yield: 4 servings.

Mary Louise Hudgins, Xi Epsilon Lambda
Conyers, Georgia

CHICKEN PAPRIKA

2 pounds boneless skinless chicken breasts
4 tablespoons flour
2 teaspoons salt
6 teaspoons paprika
4 tablespoons vegetable oil
2 tablespoons butter or margarine
1 large onion, finely chopped
2 large garlic cloves, minced
2 teaspoons chopped parsley
2 cups chicken broth
1 (6-ounce) can tomato paste

Cut the chicken into bite-size pieces. Coat with a mixture of the flour, salt and 2 teaspoons of the paprika. Sauté in hot vegetable oil in a skillet over medium-low heat for 5 minutes or until golden. Remove the chicken to a serving plate. Add the butter to the skillet drippings. Sauté the onion and garlic over low heat until soft and golden. Add the parsley, remaining paprika, chicken broth and tomato paste and stir briefly. Return the chicken to the skillet. Simmer, covered, for about 15 minutes or until chicken is tender. Yield: 8 servings.

Kathleen Funk, Xi Alpha Psi
Sunbury, Pennsylvania

HOME-STYLE SICILIAN CHICKEN

4 boneless skinless chicken breasts
1/4 cup prepared pesto
2 tablespoons capers
1/4 cup sliced black olives
1/2 cup sliced roasted red peppers
1/2 cup sliced onion
1/2 cup coarsely chopped mushrooms
1 tablespoon balsamic vinegar
1 (15-ounce) can crushed tomatoes
1 teaspoon sugar
1/4 cup red cooking wine
4 slices low-fat mozzarella cheese
2 tablespoons sliced fresh basil

Spray a large nonstick skillet with nonstick cooking spray. Place the skillet over medium-high heat. Spread both sides of each chicken breast with pesto and place the chicken in the skillet. Cook for 3 to 4 minutes on each side or until chicken is tender and golden brown. Remove the chicken from the skillet. Sauté the capers, olives, roasted peppers, onion, mushrooms and vinegar in the skillet over medium heat for 2 minutes. Remove half the vegetable mixture and set aside. Add the undrained tomatoes, sugar and wine to the vegetable mixture in the skillet and stir to combine. Return the chicken to the skillet; cook until hot. Place a slice of cheese over each chicken breast. Cook over low heat, covered, until cheese is melted. Spoon vegetable mixture over the chicken. Garnish with basil. Yield: 4 servings.

Mary Helen Buttman, Xi Alpha Theta
Bartlesville, Oklahoma

Diane Lockwood, Alpha Pi Master, Decatur, Illinois, makes ***Chicken Casserole*** *by placing 6 to 8 chopped cooked chicken breasts in a buttered 7×11-inch baking dish and topping with 1 drained can of sliced water chestnuts. Pour a mixture of 2 cans cream of mushroom soup and 8 ounces sour cream over the prepared layers. Sprinkle a mixture of 1 1/2 crushed sleeves of butter crackers and 2 teaspooons poppy seeds over the soup mixture. Pour 1/2 cup melted margarine over the top. Bake at 350 degrees for 30 to 45 minutes or until bubbly.*

BLACK WALNUT CHICKEN

The recipe can be easily doubled or tripled and adapted to wok cooking. Several of my friends meet annually for a "Wok and Roll" party, and this is always my offering.

1 pound boneless skinless chicken breasts
3 tablespoons soy sauce
1 egg white
2 teaspoons sherry
1/4 teaspoon pepper
1/4 teaspoon onion powder
1 tablespoon cornstarch
1/2 cup black walnuts, finely chopped
5 tablespoons vegetable oil

Cut the chicken into 4 pieces. Pound into 1/2-inch-thick fillets and place in a shallow glass dish. Combine the soy sauce, egg white, sherry, pepper, onion powder and cornstarch in a bowl and mix until smooth. Pour the soy sauce mixture over the chicken and let stand for at least 30 minutes, stirring occasionally. Drain the chicken and coat lightly with the walnuts. Heat the vegetable oil in a skillet over medium heat and fry the coated chicken until tender and golden brown, turning at least once. Yield: 4 servings.

Linda Clemons, Theta Psi
Cookeville, Tennessee

CHICKEN WITH SWEET AND HOT PAPRIKA

1/4 cup vegetable oil
3 medium onions, peeled and chopped
3 garlic cloves, peeled and crushed
2 teaspoons sweet Hungarian paprika
1/2 teaspoon hot Hungarian paprika
3 tomatoes, chopped
2 green bell peppers, cored and chopped
2 teaspoons salt
2 to 3 1/2 pounds boneless skinless chicken thighs
1/2 cup sour cream
2 tablespoons milk

Heat the vegetable oil in a large skillet over medium heat. Add the onions and sauté for 5 minutes or until tender. Reduce heat to medium-low. Stir in the garlic, sweet paprika, hot paprika, tomatoes, bell peppers, salt and 1 cup water. Add the chicken and simmer, covered, for 45 minutes, turning chicken once about halfway through the cooking time. Remove the chicken from the skillet and set aside. Pour the paprika mixture into a blender container; add the sour cream and milk and process until smooth. Remove any skin from the chicken. Return the chicken and sour cream mixture to the skillet and heat through. Serve with pasta, dumplings or fried potatoes. Yield: 4 to 6 servings.

Erika Schultz, Iota Rho
Huntersville, North Carolina

ORANGE CHICKEN

2 dozen skinless chicken thighs
1 cup flour
4 teaspoons paprika
4 teaspoons salt
1/2 teaspoon pepper
3/4 cup butter
3 cups orange juice
4 teaspoons grated orange zest
2 cups orange marmalade
3/4 cup cornstarch
1 cup slivered almonds

Coat the chicken well with a mixture of the flour, paprika, salt and pepper. Melt the butter in a large skillet over medium-low heat. Brown the chicken well in the melted butter. Combine the orange juice, orange zest and marmalade in a small saucepan over medium heat; heat until marmalade is melted, stirring until mixture is uniform. Dissolve the cornstarch in 2 cups cold water and add to the orange juice mixture. Heat until thickened, stirring constantly. Arrange the chicken in 1 or 2 large shallow baking dishes. Cover with orange sauce and sprinkle with almonds. Bake, uncovered, at 325 degrees for 50 minutes or until cooked through. Yield: 12 to 24 servings.

Joy Western, Alpha Psi Master
Port Dover, Ontario, Canada

CREAMY CURRIED CHICKEN

6 to 8 skinless chicken thighs
1/2 cup flour
1 1/2 tablespoons Jamaican yellow curry powder
3 teaspoons seasoning mix
1 to 2 tablespoons vegetable oil
1 medium onion, thinly sliced
1 1/2 tablespoons minced peeled gingerroot
1 to 2 (15-ounce) cans chicken broth
1 whole habanero chile pepper
1/2 (14-ounce) can coconut milk

Rinse the chicken and pat dry. Coat the chicken with a mixture of the flour, curry powder and a seasoning mix made of salt, black pepper, cayenne pepper and garlic powder. Heat a heavy skillet over medium heat and add enough oil to thinly coat the bottom of the skillet. Brown the chicken in the hot oil, stirring in the onion and ginger after a few minutes of cooking. Add enough chicken broth to cover. Pierce the habanero pepper with a knife or fork; stir into the chicken mixture. Bring to a simmer. Simmer for 30 to 40 minutes or until broth has thickened and chicken is tender. Stir in the coconut milk after 30 minutes of simmering. Remove and discard the habanero pepper. Serve over white rice accompanied by mango chutney. Yield: 4 to 8 servings.

Patty Rohleder, Xi Iota
Houston, Texas

TROPICAL CHICKEN STACKS

2 whole chickens, cooked, broth reserved
1 (10-ounce) can cream of chicken soup
1 (10-ounce) can cream of mushroom soup
2 cups uncooked rice, cooked
2 1/2 cups Chinese noodles
1 bunch green onions, chopped
2 cups sliced celery
6 tomatoes, chopped
16 ounces medium Cheddar cheese, shredded (4 cups)
2 (14-ounce) cans crushed pineapple, drained
1 1/2 cups shredded coconut, toasted
2 cups chopped pecans or walnuts

Bone the chicken and chop into bite-size pieces. Combine some of the reserved chicken broth, the soups and your choice of spices in a bowl and mix well. Stir a small amount of the soup mixture into the chicken to moisten. Serve the chicken hot. Instruct guests to stack the ingredients on plates in this order: rice, chicken, noodles, soup mixture, green onions, celery, tomatoes, cheese, pineapple, coconut and pecans. Yield: 10 servings.

Kathleen Lewis, Xi Omicron Rho
Willits, California

CHICKEN AND SAUSAGE IN RICE

2 tablespoons olive oil
1 pound boneless skinless chicken thighs
1 large onion, chopped
1 green bell pepper, chopped
2 garlic cloves, minced
1/2 pound kielbasa, cut into 1/4-inch slices
1 cup uncooked rice
1 (15-ounce) can fat-free chicken broth
2 tablespoons chopped fresh parsley

Heat the olive oil in a large ovenproof skillet over medium-high heat. Brown the chicken on both sides in the hot oil. Remove the chicken from the skillet and set aside. Place the onion, bell pepper and garlic in the skillet and cook for 5 minutes or until beginning to soften, stirring constantly. Stir in the kielbasa and cook for 4 to 5 minutes or until browned, stirring frequently. Stir in the rice and chicken broth. Return the chicken to the skillet. Bake, covered, at 350 degrees for 40 minutes or until rice is tender and chicken is no longer pink. Sprinkle with parsley and serve. Yield: 6 servings.

Bonnie Shepherd, Xi Beta Epsilon
Woodward, Oklahoma

GREEK CINNAMON CHICKEN

1 tablespoon olive oil
2 onions, chopped
4 garlic cloves, minced
6 (4-ounce) boneless skinless chicken thighs
1 (15-ounce) can diced tomatoes
1/4 cup dry white wine
2 bay leaves
1 cinnamon stick
1/2 teaspoon ground cinnamon
1/2 teaspoon coarsely ground pepper
1/4 teaspoon salt
6 cups hot cooked couscous

Heat the olive oil in a large skillet over medium heat. Sauté the onions and garlic in the hot oil for about 5 minutes or until tender. Add the chicken, undrained tomatoes, wine, bay leaves, cinnamon stick, ground cinnamon, pepper and salt; bring to a boil. Reduce heat and simmer, covered, for about 30 minutes or until chicken is cooked through. Remove and discard the bay leaves and cinnamon stick. Serve over couscous. Yield: 2 to 4 servings.

Eileen Rosenthal, Laureate Alpha
Albuquerque, New Mexico

CHICKEN ASPARAGUS CASSEROLE

6 boneless skinless chicken breasts
2 ribs celery, cut up
Pinch of salt
3 (11-ounce) cans asparagus, drained
2 (2-ounce) jars chopped pimentos
3/4 cup slivered almonds
3 (10-ounce) cans cream of mushroom soup
2 (3-ounce) cans French-fried onions

Simmer the chicken with the celery in salted water for 15 minutes or until tender. Remove the chicken and celery to a cutting board; cut the chicken into bite-size pieces. Layer the chicken, celery, asparagus, pimentos, almonds and soup in a casserole. Bake, covered, at 350 degrees for 30 minutes. For the last 5 minutes of baking time, uncover and top with French-fried onions. Yield: 6 to 8 servings.

Janice Tso, Preceptor Eta Phi
Melbourne, Florida

CHEESY CHICKEN BAKE

3 tablespoons butter
1/2 cup chopped onion
1/2 cup chopped green bell pepper
1 (10-ounce) can cream of chicken soup
1 (8-ounce) can sliced mushrooms, drained
1 (2-ounce) jar chopped pimentos, drained
1/2 teaspoon basil
8 ounces noodles, cooked and drained
3 cups chopped cooked chicken
2 cups ricotta cheese
8 ounces Cheddar cheese, shredded (2 cups)
1/4 cup buttered bread crumbs

Melt the butter in a skillet over medium-low heat. Sauté the onion and bell pepper in the butter for 5 minutes or until tender. Remove from heat. Stir in the soup, mushrooms, pimentos and basil; set aside. Combine the noodles, chicken, ricotta cheese and Cheddar cheese in a large bowl; add the mushroom mixture and mix well. Remove to a greased 9×13-inch baking dish. Bake, uncovered, at 350 degrees for 40 to 45 minutes or until bubbly. Sprinkle with bread crumbs and bake for 15 minutes longer.
Yield: 12 to 15 servings.

Sandra E. Moody, Preceptor Delta Psi
Trinity, Florida

CHICKEN DIVAN

2 whole boneless skinless chicken breasts, cooked
1 (6-ounce) package wild rice mix
4 cups chopped cooked broccoli
1 (10-ounce) can cream of broccoli soup
3 tablespoons lemon juice
8 ounces Cheddar cheese, shredded (2 cups)
2 cups buttered bread crumbs

Cut the chicken into 1-inch cubes. Cook the rice using the package directions. Layer the rice, broccoli and chicken in a 9×13-inch baking dish. Mix the soup, lemon juice and cheese in a bowl. Layer the soup mixture over the chicken layer. Sprinkle with bread crumbs. Bake, uncovered, at 350 degrees for 30 minutes or until hot and bubbly. Yield: 4 servings.

Kirsten Merle, Chi
Edmonton, Alberta, Canada

NEVER-FAIL CHICKEN DIVAN

1 (10-ounce) package frozen broccoli, cooked
8 chicken breasts, cooked
1 (10-ounce) can low-fat cream of chicken soup
1 to 2 teaspoons lemon juice
1 cup fat-free mayonnaise or mayonnaise-type salad dressing
1 cup shredded fat-free Cheddar cheese
1 cup bread crumbs

Layer the broccoli in a greased 7×11-inch or 9×13-inch baking dish. Arrange the chicken over the broccoli. Mix the soup, lemon juice and mayonnaise in a bowl. Pour the soup mixture over the chicken. Sprinkle with cheese and bread crumbs. Bake, uncovered, at 350 degrees for 30 minutes or until browned and bubbly. Yield: 8 servings.

Anastasia Hober, Eta Theta
Eastpointe, Michigan

CHICKEN AND TORTILLA DUMPLINGS

8 chicken breasts
2 (15-ounce) cans chicken broth
2 (10-ounce) cans cream of chicken soup
8 ounces cream cheese, softened
1/2 cup (1 stick) butter, softened
12 (6-inch) flour tortillas, cut into 1/2-inch-wide strips

Season the chicken with salt and pepper and place in a slow cooker with the chicken broth. Cook on High for 1 hour or on Low for 6 to 8 hours. Remove the chicken and cut into bite-size pieces. Add the soup, cream cheese and butter to the broth in the slow cooker and stir until smooth. Add the chicken. Stir in the tortilla strips and cook on High for 30 minutes or until tortilla dumplings are tender. Serve in bowls or cups. Yield: 12 servings.

Linda Sobley, Laureate Gamma
Columbus, Mississippi

CREAMY CHICKEN ENCHILADAS

4 boneless skinless chicken breasts, cooked
1/2 cup chopped onion
1/2 cup chopped green bell pepper
1/2 cup chopped red bell pepper
1/2 cup chicken broth
2 cups green enchilada sauce
1 (4-ounce) can chopped green chiles
1 1/2 teaspoons chili powder
1 teaspoon black pepper
2 garlic cloves, minced
3 teaspoons cumin
1/2 cup chopped fresh cilantro
8 ounces low-fat cream cheese
12 flour tortillas
10 ounces shredded Mexican cheese blend (2 1/2 cups)

Shred the chicken meat with a fork. Combine the onion, bell peppers, chicken broth, 1/3 cup of the enchilada sauce and green chiles in a large skillet over medium heat; sauté for 5 minutes. Add the chili powder, black pepper, garlic, cumin, cilantro, cream cheese and chicken; mix well. Simmer until heated through. Place 1/3 cup filling in the center of each tortilla and fold the sides to overlap at the center. Arrange rolled tortillas seam side down in a 9×13-inch baking dish that has been sprayed with nonstick cooking spray. Pour the remaining enchilada sauce evenly over the top and sprinkle with Mexican cheese. Bake, uncovered, at 350 degrees for 20 to 30 minutes or until golden and bubbly. Yield: 6 servings.

Jackie Wiggins, Zeta Iota
Fort Collins, Colorado

GREEN CHILE CHICKEN ENCHILADAS

2 to 3 cups chopped cooked chicken breasts
16 ounces mild Cheddar cheese, shredded (4 cups)
1 (4-ounce) can sliced black olives, drained
1 (4-ounce) can chopped green chiles, drained
1 (28-ounce) can green chile enchilada sauce
1 (10-ounce) can cream of mushroom soup
10 medium flour tortillas

Combine the chicken, cheese, olives and green chiles in a large bowl and mix well. Combine the enchilada sauce and soup in a medium bowl and mix well. Spread a thin layer of the soup mixture in a 9×13-inch baking dish. Place 1/3 cup chicken mixture in the center of each tortilla and fold the sides to overlap at the center. Arrange rolled tortillas seam side down over the soup layer. Pour the remaining soup mixture evenly over and around the tortillas until all are covered. Cover with microwave-safe plastic wrap. Microwave on High for 10 to 15 minutes or until hot and bubbly. Sprinkle shredded cheese over the top after cooking if desired. Yield: 5 to 10 servings.

Leslie Peacock, Xi Upsilon Rho
Oxnard, California

CHEESY CHICKEN TORTILLAS

3 to 4 boneless skinless chicken breasts, cooked
1 small onion, chopped
3 ounces jalapeño peppers, chopped
1 tablespoon butter
12 ounces cream cheese, softened
10 taco-size tortillas
16 ounces Monterey Jack cheese
2 cups heavy cream

Cut the chicken into bite-size pieces. Sauté the onion and jalapeño peppers in butter in a skillet over medium-low heat for 5 to 10 minutes or until tender. Add the cream cheese and chicken and heat until cream cheese is melted, stirring frequently. Place 2 tablespoons chicken mixture in the center of each tortilla and fold the sides to overlap at the center. Arrange seam side down in a 9×13-inch baking dish. Sprinkle the Monterey Jack cheese evenly over the top and drizzle with heavy cream. Bake, uncovered, at 350 degrees for 20 to 25 minutes or until hot and bubbly. Yield: 8 to 10 servings.

Angela Wood, Alpha Epsilon Pi
Williamsville, Missouri

CHICKEN ENCHILADAS

2 cups chopped cooked chicken
1 cup chopped green bell pepper
8 ounces cream cheese, softened
1 (8-ounce) jar salsa
8 (6-inch) flour tortillas
12 ounces Velveeta cheese
1/4 cup milk

Combine the chicken, bell pepper, cream cheese and 1/2 cup of the salsa in a saucepan over low heat. Cook until cream cheese is melted, stirring frequently. Place 1/3 cup chicken mixture in the center of each tortilla and fold the sides to overlap at the center. Arrange seam side down in a greased 9×12-inch baking dish. Combine the Velveeta cheese and milk in a saucepan over low heat. Cook until melted and warmed, stirring frequently. Pour the Velveeta mixture evenly over the tortillas. Cover tightly with foil and bake at 350 degrees for 20 minutes. Pour the remaining salsa over the tortillas and serve.
Yield: 8 servings.

Laura Mikiska, Theta
Vincennes, Indiana

CHICKEN CHILI LASAGNA

6 to 8 ounces cream cheese, softened
1 medium onion, chopped
8 green onions, chopped
8 ounces shredded Mexican cheese blend (2 cups)
2 garlic cloves, minced
3/4 teaspoon cumin
1/2 teaspoon minced parsley
3 cups cubed cooked chicken
1/4 cup butter or margarine
1/4 cup flour
11/2 cups chicken broth
4 ounces Monterey Jack cheese, shredded (1 cup)
1 cup sour cream
1 (4-ounce) can chopped green chiles, drained
1/8 teaspoon thyme
1/8 teaspoon salt
1/8 teaspoon pepper
12 (6-inch) flour tortillas, halved

Combine the cream cheese, onion, green onions, Mexican cheese, garlic, 1/4 teaspoon of the cumin and parsley in a large bowl and mix well. Stir in the chicken and set aside. Melt the butter in a saucepan over medium-low heat. Add the flour, whisking until smooth. Whisk in the chicken broth gradually; bring to a boil. Cook for 2 minutes or until thickened, stirring constantly. Remove from heat. Stir in the Monterey Jack cheese, sour cream, green chiles, thyme, salt, pepper and the remaining 1/2 teaspoon cumin. Spread 1/2 cup of the cheese mixture in a greased 9×13-inch baking dish. Layer 6 tortilla halves, a third of the chicken mixture and a fourth of the cheese mixture over the first layer. Repeat the tortilla, chicken and cheese mixture layers twice. Top with the remaining tortillas and cheese mixture. Sprinkle with additional Mexican cheese. Bake, covered, at 350 degrees for 30 minutes. Bake, uncovered, for 10 minutes longer or until heated through. Let stand for 5 minutes before cutting. Yield: 12 servings.

Clara Riggenbach, Rho Eta
Wooster, Ohio

MEDITERRANEAN CHICKEN WITH FETA CHEESE AND TOMATOES

10 ounces grape tomatoes, quartered
12 kalamata olives, chopped
1/4 cup snipped fresh parsley
1/4 cup capers, rinsed and drained
2 tablespoons red wine vinegar
2 teaspoons olive oil
11/2 teaspoons crumbled dried basil
1 pound boneless skinless chicken pieces
1 (15-ounce) can fat-free chicken broth
1 cup uncooked orzo
2 ounces feta cheese with sun-dried tomatoes and basil, crumbled

Place the tomatoes, olives, parsley, capers, vinegar, olive oil and 1 teaspoon of the basil in a large bowl; toss to combine. Spray a large nonstick skillet with nonstick cooking spray and place over medium-high heat. Cook the chicken smooth side down in the skillet for 20 minutes. Remove the chicken to a platter. Add the chicken broth and orzo to the chicken drippings in the skillet. Bring to a boil, scraping the browned bits in the skillet. Arrange the chicken pieces browned side up over the orzo and sprinkle with the remaining 1/2 teaspoon basil. Simmer, covered, for 12 minutes. Spoon the cooked orzo onto individual plates and top with chicken, tomato mixture and feta cheese. Yield: 4 servings.

Mary Ellen Cramer, Laureate Zeta Lambda
Stroudsburg, Pennsylvania

Shelley Dexter, Gamma Beta, Vernal, Utah, prepares **Chicken Pasta Casserole** *by cooking two 12-ounce bags of medium shell pasta, draining well, and then combining with two 10-ounce cans cream of chicken soup, one undrained 12-ounce can of chicken, 1 small can chopped green chiles and 2 tablespoons butter in a large saucepan. Stir in about 1 cup shredded Monterey Jack cheese until melted. Spoon pasta mixture into a 9×11-inch baking dish and sprinkle with about 1 cup additional shredded Jack cheese. Bake at 400 degrees for 15 to 20 minutes or until heated through and cheese has melted.*

MEXICAN CHICKEN

1 (13-ounce) package nacho cheese Doritos
Chicken broth
4 or 5 boneless skinless chicken breasts, cooked
2 teaspoons chopped onion
1/2 cup chopped green bell pepper
10 ounces Cheddar cheese, shredded (2 1/2 cups)
1 tablespoon each chili powder and garlic powder
3 (10-ounce) cans chicken mushroom soup
1 (10-ounce) can tomatoes with green chiles

Dip the Doritos in chicken broth to soften; spread in a greased 9×13-inch baking dish. Cut the chicken into bite-size pieces and layer over the Doritos. Layer the onion, bell pepper and 2 cups of the Cheddar cheese over the chicken layer. Sprinkle with chili powder and garlic powder. Pour the undiluted soup evenly over the top. Pour the undrained tomatoes with green chiles evenly over the soup layer. Sprinkle with the remaining 1/2 cup shredded Cheddar cheese. Bake, uncovered, at 350 degrees for 45 minutes or until browned and bubbly. Run a spatula around the edges before serving to release some of the liquid. Yield: 6 servings.

Faye Evans, Delta Master
Hendersonville, Tennessee

MONTEREY JACK CHICKEN

1/2 cup cottage cheese
3 ounces cream cheese, softened
1/2 cup sour cream
1 (10-ounce) can cream of chicken soup
1 teaspoon salt
1/8 teaspoon garlic powder
1 (4-ounce) can chopped green chiles, drained
3 cups chopped cooked chicken
3 cups cooked rice
1 cup shredded Monterey Jack cheese
2 tomatoes, chopped
3/4 cup corn chips, crumbled

Combine the cottage cheese, cream cheese and sour cream in a medium bowl and mix well. Combine the soup, salt, garlic powder, green chiles, chicken, rice, cheese and tomatoes in a large bowl and mix well. Stir the cottage cheese mixture into the chicken mixture. Spoon into a greased 9×13-inch baking dish. Sprinkle with corn chips. Bake, uncovered, at 350 degrees for 30 minutes or until browned and bubbly. Yield: 6 to 8 servings.

Marjorie Raiche, Preceptor Iota
Eugene, Oregon

MOROCCAN CHICKEN

3 pounds boneless skinless chicken breasts
1 cup chopped onion
1 cup chopped green bell pepper
1 cup chopped celery
2 garlic cloves, minced
1 (16-ounce) can diced tomatoes
1 teaspoon salt
2 teaspoons chili powder
1/2 teaspoon allspice
1/4 teaspoon cayenne pepper
2 tablespoons chopped parsley
1 teaspoon thyme
2 tablespoons brown sugar
3 tablespoons apple cider vinegar
2 teaspoons curry powder
1 cup dry red wine
1 cup currants
1 cup pine nuts

Cut the chicken into bite-size pieces and coat with a mixture of flour, salt and pepper. Brown in hot olive oil in a large skillet over medium heat. Remove the chicken from the skillet. Place the onion, bell pepper, celery and garlic in the skillet and brown lightly. Add the undrained tomatoes and the next 10 ingredients and bring to a simmer. Simmer, uncovered, for 30 minutes or until thickened. Stir in the currants, pine nuts and chicken. Spoon into a 9×13-inch baking dish. Bake, covered, at 350 degrees for 45 minutes. Serve with couscous, rice or pilaf. Yield: 12 servings.

Beverly Scott, Alpha Phi Master
Elma, Washington

CHICKEN AND HASH BROWN BAKE

1 (32-ounce) package frozen hash brown potatoes, thawed
1 teaspoon salt
1/4 teaspoon pepper
4 cups diced cooked chicken
1 (4-ounce) can sliced mushrooms, drained
1 cup sour cream
2 cups chicken broth
1 (10-ounce) can cream of chicken soup
2 teaspoons chicken bouillon granules
1 tablespoon chopped onion
1 garlic clove, minced
Paprika to taste
1/4 cup sliced almonds

Spread the hash brown potatoes in a 9×13-inch baking dish. Sprinkle with salt and pepper. Layer the chicken and mushrooms over the potatoes. Combine the sour cream, chicken broth, soup, bouillon, onion and garlic in a bowl and mix well. Pour the sour cream mixture evenly over the chicken and mushrooms. Sprinkle with paprika and almonds. Bake, uncovered, at 350 degrees for 50 to 60 minutes or until light brown and bubbly. Yield: 8 to 10 servings.

Anita Prescott, Preceptor Beta Tau
Dallas, Texas

OVERNIGHT CHICKEN BAKE

8 slices day-old white bread, crusts trimmed and reserved
4 cups chopped cooked chicken
1 (4-ounce) jar sliced mushrooms, drained
1 (8-ounce) can sliced water chestnuts, drained
4 eggs
2 cups milk
1/2 cup real mayonnaise
1/2 teaspoon salt
6 ounces (6 to 8 slices) American cheese
1 (10-ounce) can cream of celery soup
1 (10-ounce) can cream of mushroom soup
1 (2-ounce) jar chopped pimentos, drained
2 tablespoons butter or margarine, melted

Arrange the bread slices in a greased 9×13-inch baking dish. Layer the chicken, mushrooms and water chestnuts over the bread. Beat the eggs in a medium bowl. Blend in the milk, mayonnaise and salt. Pour the egg mixture evenly over the water chestnut layer. Arrange the American cheese over the top. Combine the cream of celery soup, cream of mushroom soup and pimentos in a bowl and mix well. Pour the soup mixture evenly over the American cheese layer. Chill, covered, for 8 to 10 hours. Crumble the trimmed bread crusts and toss with the melted butter. Sprinkle over the soup layer. Bake, uncovered, at 350 degrees for 1 1/4 hours or until set. Let stand for 10 minutes before serving. Yield: 8 to 10 servings.

Mary M. Fronczak, Alpha Omega Master
Oviedo, Florida

CHICKEN-STUFFED PASTA

2 (6-ounce) packages cornbread stove-top stuffing mix
2 boneless skinless chicken breasts, cooked, finely chopped
1 cup light mayonnaise
16 ounces jumbo shell pasta, cooked and drained
2 (10-ounce) cans low-fat cream of chicken soup
1/2 cup chicken broth

Prepare the stuffing using the package directions. Combine the stuffing, chicken and mayonnaise in a large bowl and mix well. Fill the pasta shells with the stuffing mixture. Combine the soup and chicken broth in a bowl and mix well. Spread half the soup mixture in a 9×13-inch baking dish. Arrange the stuffed pasta over the soup layer. Pour the remaining soup mixture evenly over the top. Bake, covered, at 350 degrees for 30 to 35 minutes or until hot and bubbly. Yield: 6 to 8 servings.

Loretta F. Hill, Laureate Omicron
Westminster, Maryland

POPPY SEED CHICKEN

4 1/2 dozen butter crackers, crushed
3/4 cup butter, melted
2 (10-ounce) cans cream of chicken soup
2 cups sour cream
2 teaspoons poppy seeds
8 boneless skinless chicken breasts, cooked, chopped

Combine the cracker crumbs and butter in a bowl and mix well. Combine the soup, sour cream and poppy seeds in a bowl and mix well. Layer the chicken, soup mixture and cracker crumbs 1/2 at a time in an 8×12-inch baking dish. Bake, uncovered, at 350 degrees for 40 minutes or until hot and bubbly. Yield: 8 servings.

Amanda Chiappetta, Kappa Tau
Covington, Georgia

SWISS ALMOND CHICKEN PIE

3 cups cubed cooked chicken
1 (10-ounce) can cream of chicken or cream of mushroom soup
1 (4-ounce) can mushroom stems and pieces, drained
1 (8-ounce) can sliced water chestnuts, drained
2/3 cup mayonnaise
1/2 cup chopped celery
1/2 cup chopped onion
1/2 cup sour cream
1 (8-count) can crescent rolls
2/3 cup shredded Swiss cheese
1/2 cup slivered almonds
2 to 4 tablespoons melted butter

Combine the first 8 ingredients in a large saucepan over medium heat. Cook until hot and bubbly, stirring frequently. Pour into an ungreased 8×12-inch baking dish. Unroll the dough. Separate into 2 long rectangles, pressing the perforations to seal. Layer the dough rectangles over the hot chicken mixture. Combine the cheese, almonds and butter in a bowl and mix well. Spread the cheese mixture over the dough. Bake, uncovered, at 375 degrees for 20 to 25 minutes or until golden brown. Yield: 4 to 6 servings.

Kathy McReynolds, Xi Nu
Springfield, Missouri

Marcy Lang, Laureate Beta Eta, Jacksonville, Texas, makes ***Texas Chicken Dressing*** *by preparing an 8-ounce package of corn bread mix, crumbling and combining with 3 chopped cooked chicken breasts, a 10-ounce can cream of mushroom soup, a 10-ounce can cream of chicken soup and a 10-ounce can tomatoes with green chiles. Sauté 1 cup each chopped celery, green bell pepper and onion; add to the chicken mixture. Spoon into a greased 9×13-inch baking dish and bake at 350 degrees for 20 to 25 minutes.*

CHICKEN POT PIE

You may use leftover turkey in place of the chicken.

2 cups diced peeled potatoes
1¾ cups sliced carrots
⅔ cup chopped onion
1 cup (2 sticks) butter or margarine
1 cup flour
1¾ teaspoons salt
1 teaspoon thyme
¾ teaspoon pepper
3 cups chicken broth
1½ cups milk
4 cups chopped cooked chicken
1 cup frozen peas
1 cup frozen corn
2 (2-crust) pie pastries

Combine the potatoes and carrots in a large saucepan. Add enough water to cover and bring to a boil. Reduce heat and simmer, covered, for 8 to 10 minutes. Drain and set aside. Sauté the onion in the butter in a large skillet over medium heat for 5 to 8 minutes or until tender. Add the flour, salt, thyme and pepper; stir to blend. Stir in the chicken broth and milk gradually. Bring to a boil; boil until thickened, stirring constantly (about 2 minutes). Stir in the chicken, peas, corn, potatoes and carrots. Remove from heat. Spoon the chicken mixture into 2 pastry-lined 9-inch pie plates. Top with the remaining pastry, sealing edge and cutting vents. Bake at 425 degrees for 35 to 40 minutes. Reduce oven temperature to 350 degrees and bake for 10 to 15 minutes longer. Yield: 8 to 10 servings.

Patti Akins, Tau Omega
Olmsted Falls, Ohio

CHICKEN ROLLS

6 ounces cream cheese, softened
2 medium green onions, chopped
2 to 3 cups chopped cooked chicken
½ teaspoon pepper
1 (4-ounce) can sliced mushrooms, drained
2 (8-count) cans crescent rolls
¼ cup butter, melted
1 cup dry stove-top stuffing mix, crushed
½ cup finely chopped walnuts or pecans

Combine the cream cheese, green onions, chicken, pepper and mushrooms in a bowl and mix well. Unroll the dough. Separate into triangles; roll to flatten or pull to stretch slightly. Place 2 tablespoons of the chicken mixture over the wide part of each triangle. Roll to enclose the chicken mixture and press the seams to seal. Dip in melted butter and coat with a mixture of the stuffing mix and walnuts. Arrange the rolls in a 9×13-inch baking dish. Bake at 350 degrees for 25 minutes or until golden. Serve with Poulet Sauce. Yield: 16 rolls.

POULET SAUCE

2 tablespoons chopped onion
1 tablespoon butter
1 (10-ounce) can cream of chicken soup
½ cup milk
2 teaspoons lemon juice
2 tablespoons chopped parsley

Sauté the onion in the butter in a skillet for 5 to 8 minutes or until translucent. Add the soup, milk, lemon juice and parsley and cook until heated through, stirring frequently.

Kathryn S. Erickson, Preceptor Alpha Sigma
Russell, Iowa

CHICKEN MUSHROOM ROLL-UPS

2 cups shredded cooked chicken
2 teaspoons lemon pepper
6 ounces cream cheese, softened
2 (4-ounce) cans chopped mushrooms, drained
2 (8-count) cans crescent rolls
2 cups herb-seasoned stuffing mix, crushed
½ cup (1 stick) butter, melted
2 envelopes gravy mix
1 cup sour cream

Combine the chicken, lemon pepper, cream cheese and mushrooms in a bowl and mix well. Unroll the dough. Separate into triangles. Roll to flatten a triangle, stretching the wide end. Place 1 rounded tablespoon of the chicken mixture over the wide end of the triangle. Roll to enclose, pressing seams to seal. Dip the roll in butter and coat with stuffing mix. Repeat with the remaining dough and chicken mixture. Arrange the chicken rolls on an ungreased baking sheet. Bake at 375 degrees for 20 minutes or until golden. Prepare the gravy using the package directions, substituting chicken broth for the water. Stir the sour cream into the thickened gravy. Pour the gravy mixture over the chicken rolls and serve.
Yield: 8 to 10 servings.

Carrie Carr, Alpha Epsilon Iota
Excelsior Springs, Missouri

---

*Emily Inman, Delta Mu Theta, Merced, California, makes **Sweet-and-Sour Chicken** by cutting 1 whole chicken into pieces and arranging the pieces in a single layer in a 9×13-inch baking dish. Spoon a combination of one 10-ounce jar of apricot preserves, one 8-ounce bottle of Catalina salad dressing and 1 envelope onion soup mix over the chicken pieces. Bake at 375 degrees for 1 hour.*

DUCK CASSEROLE

2 medium duck breasts
3 ribs celery
1 onion, halved
1½ teaspoons salt
¼ teaspoon pepper
1 (6-ounce) package long grain and wild rice mix
½ cup margarine
½ cup chopped onion
¼ cup flour
1 (4-ounce) can sliced mushrooms, drained, liquid reserved
1½ cups half-and-half
1 tablespoon chopped parsley
¼ cup slivered almonds

Combine the duck, celery, halved onion, salt and pepper in a saucepan. Add enough water to cover. Simmer, covered, for 1 hour or until tender. Remove the duck to a cutting board, reserving the broth. Cut the cooled duck meat into cubes. Cook the rice using the package directions. Melt the margarine in a skillet; sauté the ½ cup chopped onion in the margarine for 5 to 8 minutes or until translucent. Stir in the flour and add the mushrooms. Add enough duck broth to the mushroom liquid to make 1½ cups; stir the liquid into the onion mixture. Add the duck, rice, half-and-half and parsley to the onion mixture and mix well. Spoon into an ungreased 2-quart casserole. Sprinkle with almonds. Bake, covered, at 350 degrees for 15 to 20 minutes. Uncover and bake for 5 to 10 minutes or until hot and lightly browned. Yield: 6 to 8 servings.

Donna Johnson-Smith, Preceptor Alpha Pi
Little Rock, Arkansas

CRESCENT TURKEY BAKE

3 cups chopped cooked turkey
1 (10-ounce) can cream of chicken soup
½ cup sour cream
⅓ cup mayonnaise
½ cup chopped celery
½ cup chopped onion
1 (8-ounce) can sliced water chestnuts, drained
1 (4-ounce) jar sliced mushrooms, drained
½ teaspoon pepper
1 (8-count) can crescent rolls
3 tablespoons butter, melted
1 (4-ounce) package slivered almonds
3 ounces Swiss cheese, shredded (¾ cup)

Combine the first 9 ingredients in a medium saucepan over medium heat; cook until bubbly, stirring frequently. Spoon into a well-greased 9×13-inch baking dish. Unroll the dough. Separate into triangles and arrange over the turkey mixture. Combine the butter, almonds and cheese in a bowl and mix well. Spread the almond mixture evenly over the dough. Bake at 375 degrees for 20 to 25 minutes or until golden brown. Yield: 6 servings.

Judy Manning, Xi Eta Omicron
Great Bend, Kansas

CRUNCHY TURKEY BAKE

2 large carrots, sliced
¼ cup butter
¼ cup flour
1 (15-ounce) can chicken broth
8 ounces Cheddar cheese, shredded (2 cups)
4 cups chopped cooked turkey or chicken
1 (2-ounce) jar pimentos, drained
1 (8-ounce) package herb-seasoned stuffing

Cook the carrots in a small amount of water in a saucepan over medium heat until not quite tender; drain. Melt the butter in a saucepan over medium heat; whisk in the flour. Add chicken broth gradually and cook until thickened, stirring constantly. Reduce heat; stir in the cheese. Stir in the turkey, carrots and pimentos. Spoon turkey mixture into a 4-quart baking dish. Prepare stuffing using package directions; spread over turkey mixture. Bake, uncovered, at 375 degrees for 30 minutes or until browned and hot. Yield: 6 servings.

Sharron Hambleton, Laureate Iota
Raleigh, North Carolina

TURKEY CROQUETTES

¼ cup shortening
⅓ cup flour
1 teaspoon salt
1 cup milk
2 cups finely chopped cooked turkey
1 tablespoon grated onion
1 tablespoon lemon juice
1 tablespoon chopped parsley
1 egg, beaten
⅓ cup fine bread crumbs
⅓ cup vegetable oil or shortening for frying

Melt shortening in a 10-inch skillet over medium heat. Whisk in the flour and salt. Add the milk gradually. Cook until thickened, stirring constantly. Cook over low heat for 3 minutes. Remove from heat. Stir in the next 4 ingredients. Spread in an 8×8-inch baking pan. Chill, covered, for at least 1 hour. Cut into squares. Dip into beaten egg and coat with bread crumbs. Fry in hot oil in a skillet until brown.
Yield: 6 to 8 servings.

Cherie Bryant, Xi Theta Zeta
Panama City, Florida

Dorothy J. Hall, Alpha Beta Master, Newport News, Virginia, makes ***Crescent Roll Chicken*** *by combining 4 cups chopped cooked chicken, a can of cream of chicken soup, 8 ounces cream cheese, ½ cup softened butter, 1 can drained water chestnuts, ¼ cup milk and 2 tablespoons chopped green onions. Spoon into a 9×13-inch baking dish. Top with a can of crescent roll dough; sprinkle with ¾ cup croutons. Bake at 350 degrees for 50 minutes.*

TURKEY CABBAGE ROLLS

1 head cabbage
1 pound ground turkey
1 egg
6 crackers, crumbled
1 (16-ounce) can Spanish rice
1 onion, chopped
Garlic salt to taste
Salt and pepper to taste
1 (16-ounce) can tomato sauce
1 (16-ounce) can sauerkraut
Ketchup to taste

Place the cabbage with several inches of water in a large Dutch oven or kettle over medium heat. Steam for 10 minutes. Remove the cabbage to a plate and let cool. Combine the ground turkey, egg, cracker crumbs, Spanish rice, onion, garlic salt, salt and pepper in a bowl and mix well. Separate the cabbage leaves carefully 1 at a time. Place a palm-size scoop of turkey mixture in the center of a cabbage leaf and roll up to enclose the filling, tucking in the ends and securing with a wooden pick if necessary. Repeat with the remaining cabbage leaves and turkey mixture. Place the cabbage rolls in the Dutch oven. Pour the tomato sauce and sauerkraut evenly over the cabbage rolls. Bake, covered, at 350 degrees for 1 hour. Yield: 8 to 10 servings.

Debbie Parker, Preceptor Gamma
Columbus, Mississippi

CHAMPAGNE TURKEY FONDUE

2 pounds turkey or veal
1½ bottles champagne or dry white wine
1 tablespoon salt
1 tablespoon sugar
2 teaspoons cinnamon
1 vanilla bean
2 large garlic cloves, minced
10 whole cloves
Pinch of coriander
20 peppercorns

Trim the fat from the turkey and cut the turkey into bite-size cubes. Combine the champagne, salt, sugar, cinnamon, vanilla bean, garlic, cloves, coriander and peppercorns in a glass dish. Add the turkey and mix well. Marinate, covered, in the refrigerator for about 4 hours. Strain the marinade and discard the solids. Pour the marinade into a fondue pot and bring to a boil. Instruct guests to spear a turkey cube with a fondue fork and hold it in the hot marinade until cooked to desired doneness, usually about 3 minutes. Serve with prepared dipping sauces.
Yield: 4 servings.

Sabine Jeannot, Omega
Kirkland, Washington

HOT BROWN

2 tablespoons butter
2 tablespoons flour
½ teaspoon salt
1 cup milk
1 cup shredded sharp Cheddar cheese
4 slices toast, crusts trimmed
4 slices turkey or chicken breast
4 slices tomato, lightly salted
4 slices broiled bacon

Melt the butter in a saucepan over medium heat. Whisk in the flour to make a paste. Stir in the salt, milk and cheese. Cook until thick and creamy, stirring constantly. Keep hot. Cut the toast slices into triangles. Place 4 triangles of toast on each of 4 ovenproof platters. Place turkey slices over the toast. Pour the hot cheese sauce evenly over the turkey. Top with tomato slices. Broil 6 inches from the heat source until tomato is lightly cooked and sauce is bubbly. Garnish with bacon and serve. Yield: 2 to 4 servings.

Eugenia Wallace, Alpha Master
Lexington, Kentucky

MARINATED TURKEY BREAST

Grated zest of 1 lemon
1 cup olive oil
½ cup lemon juice
3 tablespoons crushed dried oregano
3 garlic cloves, crushed
¾ cup dry white wine or chicken broth
1 (5- to 7-pound) turkey breast

Combine the lemon zest, olive oil, lemon juice, oregano, garlic and wine in a large glass ovenproof dish and whisk well. Place the turkey in the dish. Marinate, covered, in the refrigerator for 4 to 10 hours, turning often. Drain the chicken, reserving the marinade. Bake the turkey at 325 degrees to 180 degrees on a meat thermometer, basting with the marinade every 15 minutes. Let stand for at least 10 minutes before slicing. Yield: 6 to 8 servings.

Jean Delzell, Xi Epsilon Omega
Rohnert Park, California

EASY TURKEY POT PIE

1 (10-ounce) can cream of chicken soup
1 (10-ounce) package frozen mixed vegetables, thawed
1 cup cubed cooked turkey or chicken
½ cup milk
1 egg
1 cup baking mix

Combine the soup, vegetables and turkey in a bowl and mix well. Spoon the turkey mixture into a 9-inch pie plate. Pour a mixture of the milk, egg and baking mix evenly over the chicken mixture. Bake at 400 degrees for 30 minutes or until golden brown. Serve with a mixed green salad. Yield: 4 servings.

Carol Sizemore, Preceptor Alpha Upsilon
Northfork, West Virginia

SCALLOPED TURKEY

Turkey breast, baked and skinned
1 1/2 cups cubed Velveeta cheese
1 1/2 cups chopped celery
2 eggs, slightly beaten
4 cups chicken broth
4 cups crushed butter crackers
1/2 cup chopped onion
1 (10-ounce) can cream of mushroom soup
Salt and pepper to taste

Cut the turkey into small bite-size pieces. Combine the Velveeta cheese, celery, eggs, chicken broth, cracker crumbs, onion, soup, salt and pepper in a large bowl. Add to the turkey and mix well. Spoon into a 9×13-inch baking dish that has been sprayed with nonstick cooking spray. Bake, uncovered, at 350 degrees for 1 1/2 hours. Cover any portions that brown too quickly with foil. Yield: 8 servings.

Dixie A. Hatfield, Alpha Delta Master
Arkansas City, Kansas

TURKEY BROCCOLI LASAGNA

1 (10-ounce) can cream of mushroom soup
1 (10-ounce) can cream of chicken soup
1/4 teaspoon garlic salt
1 cup sour cream
1 cup chopped onions
2 to 3 cups chopped cooked turkey or chicken
6 ounces fresh mushrooms, sautéed
9 lasagna noodles, cooked
1 bunch broccoli florets, cooked
2 to 3 cups shredded mixed mozzarella and Cheddar cheeses

Combine the soups, garlic salt, sour cream, onions, turkey and mushrooms in a bowl and mix well. Spread a thin layer of the turkey mixture in a greased 9×13-inch baking dish. Layer 3 lasagna noodles, broccoli florets and 1/3 of the cheese over the turkey mixture. Layer 3 lasagna noodles, half the remaining turkey mixture and half the remaining cheese over the cheese layer. Layer 3 lasagna noodles and the remaining turkey mixture over the cheese. Layer the remaining cheese over the top. Sprinkle with Parmesan cheese if desired. Bake, uncovered, at 350 degrees for 40 to 50 minutes or until hot and bubbly. Let stand for 10 minutes before cutting and serving. Yield: 10 to 12 servings.

Elizabeth A. LeBlanc, Laureate Alpha Rho
Marshall, Michigan

SUMMER TURKEY

1 fresh turkey, or 1 frozen turkey, thawed
1 1/2 cups ketchup
2 teaspoons vinegar
2 tablespoons Worcestershire sauce
2 teaspoons salt
2 teaspoons paprika
1 teaspoon pepper
1 teaspoon chili powder
2 teaspoons sugar or Splenda

Grill the turkey over hot coals or roast in the oven. Cut into pieces to fit on hamburger buns and place in a disposable baking pan. Combine the ketchup, 1/2 cup water, and the remaining ingredients in a bowl and whisk until smooth. Pour the ketchup mixture evenly over the turkey. Bake, uncovered, at 350 degrees for 30 minutes or until very hot. Serve on hamburger buns. Yield: variable.

Connie Novak, Alpha Upsilon Master
Selinsgrove, Pennsylvania

BEST-EVER TURKEY LOAF

1/2 small onion, chopped
2 garlic cloves, minced
1 1/2 to 3 pounds ground turkey
2 eggs
1/4 cup ketchup
1/4 cup Worcestershire sauce
2 slices day-old bread, crumbled
Salt and pepper to taste

Sauté the onion and garlic in hot oil in a small skillet over medium heat for 5 to 8 minutes or until translucent. Mix with the remaining ingredients in a large bowl. Shape into a loaf and place in a shallow baking dish. Spread additional ketchup over the top. Bake, uncovered, for 30 to 40 minutes or until cooked through. Yield: 4 to 6 servings.

Deena Knudsen, Delta Beta Nu
Anaheim Hills, California

POTATO AND TURKEY SAUSAGE BAKE

1 1/2 pounds turkey sausage
3/4 cup chopped onion
1 cup sour cream
8 ounces Cheddar cheese, shredded (2 cups)
1 (10-ounce) can cream of mushroom soup
1 soup can milk
1 (2-pound) package frozen shredded potatoes, thawed

Brown the sausage in a skillet, stirring until crumbly; drain. Spread in a greased 9×13-inch baking dish. Combine the onion, sour cream, cheese, soup and milk in a large bowl; mix well. Layer the potatoes and soup 1/2 at a time over the sausage. Sprinkle with additional cheese if desired. Bake, uncovered, at 350 degrees for 1 hour or until center is hot and bubbly. Yield: 8 to 10 servings.

Kim Motley, Xi Eta Mu
Lansing, Kansas

CEVICHE

1 cucumber
3 tomatoes
2 ribs celery
3 green onions
1 pound cooked peeled shrimp, or 1 (6-ounce) can baby shrimp
1 (6-ounce) can crab meat
1/2 cup clamato juice
1/2 (8-ounce) can spicy vegetable juice cocktail
1 tub fresh salsa (optional)
1 small lime
1/2 teaspoon oregano
Dash of garlic salt
Dash of pepper
1 small avocado, sliced

Cut the cucumber, tomatoes, celery and green onions into very small pieces. Combine the vegetables and the next 5 ingredients in a large bowl; mix well. Squeeze lime juice over the vegetable mixture. Season with oregano, garlic salt and pepper. Chill, covered, for at least 1 hour before serving; 10 hours is better. Stir just before serving. Serve on large tostadas or on small rounded tortilla chips. Serve with avocado. Yield: 8 to 10 servings.

Aileen Bonet, Xi Psi
Douglas, Arizona

FISH FETA STEW

1/2 small onion, chopped
2 tablespoons olive oil
2 garlic cloves, minced
1 (14-ounce) can diced tomatoes
1/2 cup dry white wine
1/2 teaspoon oregano
1/2 teaspoon salt
Bass or other firm white fish, cut into pieces
4 ounces feta cheese, crumbled
2 tablespoons chopped parsley

Sauté the onion in the olive oil in a skillet over medium heat for 3 minutes. Add the garlic and sauté for 1 minute longer. Stir in the undrained tomatoes, wine, oregano and salt. Cook for 10 minutes. Add the fish and cook for 2 or 3 minutes longer. Stir in the cheese and parsley and serve. Yield: 4 servings.

Linda Walker, Xi Rho
North Vancouver, British Columbia, Canada

HADDOCK MILANESE

4 haddock fillets
1 small onion, chopped
2 tablespoons lemon juice
1/3 cup plus 1 tablespoon vegetable oil
Salt and pepper to taste
2 eggs
1 tablespoon milk
Flour to coat
Dry bread crumbs
1/4 cup plus 2 tablespoons butter
1 garlic clove, minced
2 teaspoons chopped parsley

Remove the skin and bones from the fillets. Combine the onion, lemon juice, the 1/3 cup vegetable oil, salt and pepper in a glass dish and mix well. Add the fillets and turn to coat well. Marinate, covered, in the refrigerator for 1 hour, turning the fillets occasionally. Combine the eggs and milk in a shallow bowl and whisk to blend. Drain the fillets and coat lightly with flour. Dip in the egg mixture. Coat with bread crumbs, pressing the bread crumbs firmly. Heat the 1/4 cup butter and the 1 tablespoon vegetable oil in a skillet over medium heat. Add the fillets and cook until golden brown, about 3 minutes on each side. Melt the 2 tablespoons butter in a small skillet over medium heat. Brown the garlic in the butter. Stir in the parsley. Drizzle the garlic mixture over the fillets and serve. Yield: 4 servings.

Judith Wade, Preceptor Xi
West Lafayette, Indiana

HALIBUT BAKE

1 pound halibut
Salt to taste
1 cup mayonnaise
1/2 cup sour cream
1/4 cup minced onion
1 1/2 cups cornflake crumbs
Paprika (optional)

Cut the halibut into 3/8-inch-thick slices; drain on a paper towel. Salt lightly. Combine the mayonnaise, sour cream and onion in a bowl and mix well. Spread a thin layer of the mayonnaise mixture in a baking dish. Arrange a single layer of halibut slices over the mayonnaise mixture. Pour the remaining mayonnaise mixture evenly over the halibut. Sprinkle with cornflake crumbs and paprika. Bake, uncovered, at 450 degrees for about 15 minutes or until bubbly around the edges and center of fish is tender and cooked through; do not overcook. Yield: 4 servings

Doreen McDonald, Xi Alpha Epsilon
Courtenay, British Columbia, Canada

SALMON WITH SPINACH STUFFING

This healthful dish looks so pretty when you slice it to serve: white, red, and green.

1 (10-ounce) jar roasted red peppers
4 pounds salmon fillets
6 ounces fresh spinach
1/4 cup bread crumbs
1/3 cup Dijon mustard
1/3 cup whole grain mustard

Open the roasted red peppers and press flat. Slice the salmon fillets lengthwise 3/4 of the way through. Gently open the salmon. Layer the spinach and roasted red pepper inside the fillets; sprinkle evenly with bread crumbs. Close the fillets. Arrange the fillets on a baking sheet. Spread a mixture of the Dijon mustard and whole grain mustard evenly over the fillets. Bake at 325 degrees for 20 to 24 minutes or until fish flakes easily with a fork. Arrange on a serving plate. Yield: 8 servings.

Marcia Esposito, Xi Alpha Chi
Davie, Florida

BASIL-STUFFED SALMON

1 whole salmon, head and tail removed, boned and butterflied
Dijon mustard to taste
1 red onion, sliced
2 large tomatoes, sliced
Fresh basil to taste, chopped large
Vodka to taste

Open the salmon and remove any large bones that may have been missed. Spread Dijon mustard over both inside halves. Layer the onion rings, sliced tomatoes and basil over one half and drizzle with vodka. Fold over the other half. Wrap heavy-duty foil around the salmon and tighten ends to seal. Place on a baking sheet. Bake at 350 degrees for 1 to 1 1/2 hours or until done to taste. Slice and serve. Yield: 6 to 8 servings.

Helen Durant, Xi Alpha Alpha
Reno, Nevada

SALMON WITH DILL MUSTARD SAUCE

2 tablespoons each fresh lemon juice and fresh lime juice
4 (4-ounce) salmon fillets
1/4 cup fat-free mayonnaise
1 tablespoon Dijon mustard
1 tablespoon chopped fresh dill weed
Dill weed sprigs (optional)

Combine the lemon juice and lime juice in a glass dish. Rinse the salmon and pat dry. Place the salmon in the juices and marinate for 10 minutes, turning once. Combine the mayonnaise, Dijon mustard and the 1 tablespoon chopped dill weed in a small bowl. Drain the salmon and pat dry. Broil the salmon 4 inches from the heat source, 3 to 4 minutes on each side or until it flakes easily in the center. Pour some of the mayonnaise mixture over the salmon and serve the remaining mixture in small dipping cups. Garnish with dill sprigs and serve. Yield: 4 servings.

Sharon Wiggins, Preceptor Alpha Omicron
Deer Park, Texas

FILLET OF SALMON EN PAPILLOTE

1 (18-ounce) salmon fillet, skinned and boned
Butter or oil
Salt and pepper to taste
2 tablespoons olive oil
1/4 green bell pepper, sliced
1/4 onion, sliced
1/2 tomato, chopped
1 teaspoon herbes de Provence
1/4 cup dry white wine
1/4 cup heavy cream or fat-free half-and-half

Rub the salmon fillet with butter. Sprinkle with salt and pepper. Heat the olive oil in a saucepan over medium-low heat. Add the bell pepper, onion, tomato and herbes de Provence and cook until tender, stirring frequently. Deglaze the saucepan with wine. Add the cream and cook over medium-high heat until reduced by 1/3. Place the salmon on a large piece of heavy-duty foil. Drizzle the cream mixture over the salmon. Fold up the sides of the foil to make seams. Fold ends tightly to seal. Bake in a preheated 425-degree oven for 8 minutes per 1-inch thickness. Cut the end of the pouch and slide the contents onto a bed of steamed rice; or serve with baked potatoes. Yield: 4 servings

Waltraud Anguiano, Laureate Epsilon Pi
Fort Walton Beach, Florida

BAKED SALMON WITH FISH MOUSSE

1/2 pound sole or ling cod fillets
1 egg
1/2 cup heavy cream
4 (1-inch-thick) salmon steaks
1 cup (about) dry white wine
1/2 teaspoon thyme leaves
1 tablespoon minced green onions or shallot
1/4 cup butter, cut into 2 pieces
Salt and pepper to taste

Cut the sole fillets into chunks. Place in a food processor container and process until smooth or put through a food mill fitted with a fine blade. Add the egg and 1/4 cup of the cream and mix well. Arrange the salmon steaks side by side in a shallow 9×13-inch baking dish. Spoon the sole mixture evenly over the salmon. At this point it may be refrigerated, covered, for up to 6 hours. Pour wine around the fish to a depth of 3/8 inch. Bake, uncovered, at 450 degrees for 15 to 20 minutes or until the mousse topping is lightly browned and salmon flakes easily when prodded in the thickest portion with a fork. Remove the salmon to a serving platter carefully and keep warm. Pour the cooking liquid through a wire strainer into a wide skillet. Add the remaining 1/4 cup cream, thyme and green onions. Boil rapidly until reduced to 1/2 cup. Remove from heat. Add the butter 1 piece at a time with a wire whisk or wooden spoon, stirring constantly to incorporate the butter as it melts; the sauce is thickened by the butter. Season with salt and pepper. Spoon the cream sauce over or around the salmon. Yield: 4 servings.

Mary Bacchetti, Laureate Alpha Delta
Santa Clara, California

PINK SALMON PATTIES

1/2 cup mayonnaise
1 (6-ounce) can pink salmon, skin and bones removed
2 teaspoons lime or lemon juice
3 scallions, minced
1 medium egg
1/3 cup Italian bread crumbs
1 teaspoon Italian seasoning
2 teaspoons parsley flakes
3 tablespoons extra-virgin olive oil

Combine the mayonnaise, salmon, lime juice, scallions, egg, bread crumbs, Italian seasoning and parsley flakes in a large bowl; mix well. Shape into 6 patties. Heat the olive oil in a medium saucepan over medium heat. Brown the salmon patties in the oil on both sides. Drain on paper towels. Serve with a mixed green salad. Yield: 6 medium patties.

Dorothy L. Robinson, Alpha Nu Master
Jacksonville, Florida

BROCCOLI SALMON BAKE

Substitute two 10-ounce cans of white chicken for the salmon if you like.

1 (16-ounce) package saffron yellow rice
3 tablespoons margarine
2 (10-ounce) cans cream of mushroom soup
1 cup mayonnaise
2 eggs, well beaten
1 medium onion, chopped
4 ounces Cheddar cheese, shredded (1 cup)
2 (7-ounce) cans pink salmon
1 (6-ounce) can cheddar French-fried onions
12 ounces broccoli florets, cooked

Prepare the rice using the package directions, using the 3 tablespoons margarine. Combine the soup, mayonnaise, eggs, onion, cheese, salmon and half the French-fried onions in a large bowl and mix well. Stir in the rice and broccoli. Spread the salmon mixture evenly in a 9×13-inch baking dish. Bake, uncovered, at 350 degrees for 20 minutes. Sprinkle the remaining French-fried onions over the top. Bake for 10 minutes longer. Let stand for 10 minutes before serving. Yield: 8 to 10 servings.

Eileen A. Ford, Xi Xi Gamma
Ocoee, Florida

SALMON PUFF

1 cup bread crumbs
1 teaspoon salt
1 teaspoon prepared mustard
2 cups milk (2%)
4 eggs, separated
1 1/2 cups flaked canned salmon
Dill Sauce

Combine the bread crumbs, salt, mustard, milk and egg yolks in a saucepan over low heat; cook until thickened, stirring constantly. Remove from heat. Stir in the salmon. Beat the egg whites in a large mixing bowl until stiff peaks form. Fold in the salmon mixture. Spoon into a buttered baking dish or individual dishes. Place the baking dish in a larger baking pan. Add water to the larger pan to a depth of 1 inch. Bake at 425 degrees for 30 minutes, pouring Dill Sauce evenly over the puff for the last 10 minutes of baking. Yield: 6 to 8 servings.

DILL SAUCE

6 tablespoons lemon juice
3 tablespoons olive oil
3 tablespoons dill weed
Salt and pepper to taste

Combine the lemon juice, olive oil, dill weed, salt and pepper in a bowl and mix well.

Yvonne Brewer, Alpha Rho Master
Brooksville, Florida

TILAPIA PARMESAN SAUTE

1/4 cup grated Parmesan cheese
2 tablespoons parsley flakes
1 teaspoon garlic powder
1 tablespoon olive oil
2 tablespoons butter
1 tablespoon lemon juice
4 to 6 tilapia fillets

Combine the Parmesan cheese, parsley flakes and garlic powder in a small bowl; mix well and set aside. Heat the olive oil, butter and lemon juice in a large skillet over medium heat. Sauté the tilapia fillets in the olive oil mixture for 2 to 3 minutes per side or until white and flaky. Sprinkle the cheese mixture over the fillets and sauté for 1 minute longer on each side. Yield: 4 servings.

Marjorie L. Myers, Kappa Master
Knoxville, Iowa

LATTICE-TOPPED TUNA BAKE

2 (6-ounce) cans tuna or chicken, drained
1 (10-ounce) package frozen peas, thawed and drained
4 ounces sharp Cheddar cheese, shredded (1 cup)
1/4 cup chopped onion
1/2 cup bread crumbs
1 cup sliced celery
1/4 teaspoon salt
1/8 teaspoon pepper
1 cup mayonnaise-type salad dressing
1 (8-count) package crescent rolls
Sesame seeds (optional)
Cucumber Sauce

Combine the tuna, peas, cheese, onion, bread crumbs, celery, salt and pepper in a large bowl. Add the mayonnaise-type salad dressing and mix well. Spoon into a 6×10-inch baking dish. Unroll the dough. Separate into 2 rectangles, pressing the perforations to seal. Cut the dough into 8 long and 4 short strips; place over the tuna mixture in a lattice design. Brush lightly with additional mayonnaise-type salad dressing and sprinkle with sesame seeds. Bake at 350 degrees for 35 to 40 minutes or until golden brown. Serve with Cucumber Sauce. Yield: 6 to 8 servings.

CUCUMBER SAUCE

1/2 cup mayonnaise-type salad dressing
1/2 cup sour cream
1/2 cup chopped cucumber
1 tablespoon chopped chives
1 teaspoon chopped parsley or dill weed
1/4 teaspoon salt

Combine the ingredients in a small bowl and whisk until smooth.

Jean Engel, Laureate Gamma Omicron
Freeport, Illinois

SPICY TUNA BAKE

1 large onion, chopped
3 ribs celery, minced
1 teaspoon olive oil
1 pound fresh mushrooms, coarsely chopped
3/4 cup red bell pepper, chopped, or chopped pimentos
1 (4-ounce) can chopped green chiles, drained
6 ounces cream cheese, softened
1/2 cup (or more) mayonnaise
2 (10-ounce) cans cream of mushroom soup
1 (7-ounce) pouch albacore (tuna)
1 (10-ounce) package frozen green peas
Pepper to taste
12 ounces spaghetti, cooked and drained
1/2 cup panko (Japanese bread crumbs)

Sauté the onion and celery in the olive oil in a large skillet over medium heat for 5 to 8 minutes or until translucent. Add the mushrooms, bell pepper, green chiles, cream cheese, mayonnaise, soup, albacore, frozen green peas and pepper and cook until thickened and creamy. Remove from heat and stir in the spaghetti. Spread the tuna mixture in a 9×13-inch baking dish that has been sprayed with nonstick cooking spray. Sprinkle with panko and bake at 350 degrees for 30 minutes. Yield: 8 to 10 servings.

Nancy E. Clapp, Preceptor Xi Sigma
Houston, Texas

CRAB CAKES

3 (6-ounce) cans crab meat, drained and flaked, or 2 cups cooked flaked crab meat
2 to 2 1/2 cups soft bread crumbs
1 egg, beaten
3/4 cup mayonnaise
1/3 cup chopped celery
1/3 cup chopped green bell pepper
1/3 cup chopped onion
1 tablespoon seafood seasoning
1 tablespoon minced fresh parsley
2 teaspoons lemon juice
1 teaspoon Worcestershire sauce
1 teaspoon prepared mustard
1/4 teaspoon black pepper
1/8 teaspoon hot red pepper sauce

Combine the crab meat, bread crumbs, egg, mayonnaise, celery, bell pepper, onion, seafood seasoning, parsley, lemon juice, Worcestershire sauce, mustard, black pepper and hot red pepper sauce in a large bowl and mix well. Shape into 8 patties. Broil 6 inches from the heat source, or pan-fry in 2 to 4 tablespoons vegetable oil for 4 minutes on each side or until golden brown. Serve with lemon slices if desired. Yield: 8 servings.

Norma Rowland, Xi Chi Chi
Hemet, California

SWISS CRAB BAKE

1/4 cup plus 1 tablespoon butter
1/2 cup chopped celery
1/4 cup chopped onion
1/4 cup flour
1 teaspoon salt
1/4 teaspoon pepper
2 cups milk
2 cups cooked rice
2 cups shredded Swiss cheese
1 (4-ounce) can sliced mushrooms, drained
1 (4-ounce) can sliced olives, drained
2 (6-ounce) cans crab meat, drained and flaked, or 2 cups cooked flaked crab meat
1/4 cup slivered almonds
1/2 cup dry bread crumbs

Melt the 1/4 cup butter in a skillet over medium-low heat. Sauté the celery and onion in the butter for 5 to 8 minutes or until translucent. Stir in the flour, salt and pepper. Stir in the milk and cook until thickened, stirring constantly. Combine the rice, cheese, mushrooms, olives, crab meat and almonds in a bowl and mix well. Add the flour mixture and toss to combine. Spoon into a 2-quart baking dish. Melt the 1 tablespoon butter and mix with the bread crumbs; sprinkle over the crab mixture. Bake, uncovered, at 350 degrees for 30 minutes. Serve with a salad. Yield: 6 to 8 servings.

Elizabeth Flatt, Alpha Master
Kelso, Washington

CRAB MEAT AND SPINACH ENCHILADAS

1 (10-ounce) can cream of chicken soup
1/2 cup chopped onion
3 to 5 dashes hot red pepper sauce
Dash of nutmeg
Dash of black pepper
1 (10-ounce) package frozen chopped spinach, thawed and drained
1 (8-ounce) package frozen imitation crab meat, thawed and chopped
1 3/4 cups shredded Monterey Jack cheese
8 (5- to 6-inch) corn tortillas
1 cup milk

Mix the first 5 ingredients in a bowl. Combine half the soup mixture, spinach, crab meat and 1 cup of the cheese in a bowl and mix well. Wrap the tortillas in paper towels. Microwave on High for 30 to 60 seconds. Place 1/3 cup crab mixture in the center of each tortilla; roll up and place seam side down in a greased 9×13-inch baking dish. Pour a mixture of the remaining soup mixture and milk over the enchiladas. Bake, covered, at 350 degrees for 12 to 14 minutes. Sprinkle with the remaining cheese. Let stand at room temperature for 10 minutes. Yield: 4 servings.

Edith Oates, Zeta Alpha
Sheridan, Arkansas

MIXED VEGETABLE AND CRAB FETTUCCINI

1 cup (2 sticks) butter or margarine
8 to 12 ounces fettuccini, cooked and drained
1/2 medium green bell pepper, sliced
1/2 medium red bell pepper, sliced
1/2 cup chopped green onions
1 cup broccoli florets
1 cup sliced fresh mushrooms
1 small zucchini, sliced
2 cups flaked crab meat
1 (10-ounce) can cream of mushroom soup
6 to 8 ounces cream cheese, softened
1 cup milk
Black pepper to taste

Add 1/2 cup of the butter to the hot fettuccini in a bowl and toss. Sauté the bell peppers, green onions, broccoli, mushrooms and zucchini in the remaining 1/2 cup butter in a skillet over medium heat for 5 to 10 minutes or until tender. Add the crab meat to the vegetable mixture and sauté until warm. Combine the soup, cream cheese, milk and black pepper in a bowl and mix well. Stir the soup mixture into the vegetable mixture and cook until hot. Serve over the buttered fettuccini. Yield: 4 to 6 servings.

Colette Theel, Xi Zeta
Rapid City, South Dakota

POOR MAN'S RICH CRAB DINNER

This recipe will make a quiet dinner for two seem special because it tastes rich and it will seem that you fussed in the kitchen all day.

3/4 cup uncooked rice
1-inch strip lemon zest
3 tablespoons unsalted butter
8 ounces imitation crab meat
1 tablespoon flour
1 cup heavy cream
1/2 teaspoon dry mustard
1 tablespoon cognac
3 teaspoons Worcestershire sauce
Salt and pepper to taste

Cook the rice with the lemon zest and 1 tablespoon of the butter in 1 1/2 cups water in a tightly covered saucepan for 20 minutes or until tender. Cut the crab meat into 1- to 2-inch pieces. Melt 2 tablespoons of the butter in a large skillet over medium heat. Sauté the crab meat in the butter for about 5 minutes or until warmed; remove the crab meat and set aside. Add the flour to the skillet drippings and stir until blended. Stir in the cream, dry mustard, cognac and 2 teaspoons of the Worcestershire sauce. Simmer until thickened, stirring constantly. Stir in the crab. Add salt, pepper and the remaining Worcestershire sauce if necessary. Serve over rice. Yield: 2 servings.

Carmella Markett, Laureate Gamma Lambda
Downers Grove, Illinois

CRAB SOUFFLE

8 slices bread
2 cups flaked crab meat
1/2 cup mayonnaise
1 medium onion, chopped
1 green bell pepper, chopped
1 cup chopped celery
3 cups milk
4 eggs
1 (10-ounce) can mushroom soup
1 cup shredded Cheddar cheese

Cut half the bread slices into 1/2-inch cubes and layer in an 8×12-inch baking dish. Combine the crab meat, mayonnaise, onion, bell pepper and celery in a bowl and mix well. Spread the crab mixture over the bread layer. Trim the crusts from the remaining 4 slices bread. Layer the trimmed bread slices over the crab mixture. Pour a mixture of the milk and eggs evenly over the bread layer. Chill, covered, for 8 to 10 hours. Bake at 325 degrees for 15 minutes. Remove from the oven and spoon the soup over the top. Sprinkle with cheese and paprika. Return to the oven and bake for 1 hour. Yield: 8 servings.

Betty Gustafson, Laureate Zeta
Nome, Alaska

WILD MUSHROOM AND SCALLOP POT PIE

2 sheets frozen puff pastry, thawed
6 tablespoons butter
1/2 cup sliced shallots
3 garlic cloves, minced
20 ounces assorted fresh mushrooms, chopped
1 ounce dried morels (mushrooms)
2 cups white wine
1 3/4 cups beef broth or stock
2 1/2 cups heavy cream
3 cups packed spinach leaves, chopped
2 tablespoons sliced fresh basil
1 tablespoon fresh lemon juice
1 teaspoon white truffle oil (optional)
Salt and pepper to taste
24 large sea scallops

Cut each pastry sheet into four 4-inch rounds. Chill, covered, until ready to use. Melt 5 tablespoons of the butter in a large heavy kettle over medium heat. Add the shallots, garlic and mushrooms and sauté for 10 minutes. Add the dried morels and wine and cook over high heat for about 10 minutes or until reduced by 1/2. Add 1 1/4 cups of the beef broth and the cream. Boil for about 15 minutes or until thick enough to coat a spoon. Stir in the spinach, basil, lemon juice and truffle oil. Season with salt and pepper. Remove from heat. Arrange 8 custard cups on a baking sheet. Melt the remaining 1 tablespoon butter in a large heavy skillet over high heat. Add the scallops and sauté about 1 minute per side or until golden. Remove the scallops from the skillet and cool. Add the remaining 1/2 cup beef broth to the skillet and bring to a boil. Stir the beef broth mixture into the mushroom mixture. Place equal portions of the mushroom mixture and 3 scallops in each custard cup. Top each with a pastry round, pressing the edge to seal. Bake at 425 degrees for 15 to 20 minutes or until hot and golden. Yield: 8 servings.

Nancy DeMond, Preceptor Mu
Brookings, Oregon

SCALLOPS WITH SAGE AND CORN

1 pound fresh scallops
1 tablespoon lemon juice
Salt to taste
1/4 teaspoon black pepper
2 tablespoons olive oil
1/4 cup chopped fresh sage
1 garlic clove, minced
2 cups fresh or frozen corn kernels
1 large green bell pepper, chopped

Rinse the scallops and pat dry; sprinkle with lemon juice. Season with salt and pepper. Combine the olive oil, sage and garlic in a skillet over medium heat; sauté for 1 minute. Add the scallops and cook for 2 minutes or until scallops turn opaque. Remove the scallops from the skillet and set aside. Add the corn and bell pepper to the skillet drippings and cook for 3 minutes or until tender, stirring frequently. Stir in the scallops and serve immediately. Yield: 4 servings.

Ruth Weiss, Alpha Epsilon Master
Prescott, Arizona

SPICY SHRIMP PASTA

2 tablespoons olive oil
1 teaspoon crushed red pepper
2 garlic cloves, minced
1/2 teaspoon salt
1/4 teaspoon black pepper
12 ounces fresh shrimp, peeled and deveined, or frozen shrimp, thawed
2 cups chopped tomatoes
8 ounces linguini, cooked and drained
Finely shredded Parmesan cheese to taste

Heat the olive oil in a large skillet over medium heat. Add the crushed red pepper, garlic, salt and pepper and sauté for 1 minute. Add the shrimp and sauté for 3 minutes or until opaque. Stir in the tomatoes and heat through. Toss the shrimp mixture with the linguini. Sprinkle with cheese and serve.
Yield: 4 servings.

Connie Leetsch, Gamma Zeta Master
Abilene, Texas

SHRIMP AND RICE BAKE

1 (6-ounce) package long grain wild rice mix
1 cup sliced green onions
1 cup chopped celery
1 cup chopped green bell pepper
1/2 cup (1 stick) butter, melted
10 ounces Mexican Velveeta cheese, melted
1 (10-ounce) can cream of mushroom soup
1 cup milk
2 to 3 cups shrimp, peeled and deveined

Prepare the rice using the package directions. Sauté the green onions, celery and bell pepper in the butter in a skillet over medium-low heat for a few minutes. Combine the rice, onion mixture and cheese in a bowl and mix well. Stir in the soup, milk and shrimp. Spoon into a 9×13-inch baking dish. Bake, uncovered, at 350 degrees for 30 minutes or until hot and bubbly. Yield: 8 to 10 servings.

Sandy Joynor, Xi Delta Tau
Jonesboro, Louisiana

YELLOW SQUASH AND SHRIMP BAKE

6 yellow squash, sliced
1/2 cup (1 stick) butter
1 cup chopped onion
1 cup chopped celery
1/2 cup chopped green bell pepper
1/4 cup chopped garlic
1 1/2 to 2 cups shrimp, peeled and deveined
Salt and pepper to taste
1/4 cup chopped parsley
1 cup Italian bread crumbs

Place the squash in a saucepan with enough lightly salted water to cover and bring to a boil. Cook until tender; drain. Melt the butter in a large skillet over medium heat. Add the onion, celery, bell pepper, garlic and shrimp. Sauté for about 5 minutes or until vegetables are tender and shrimp are pink. Stir in the squash and mix well. Season to taste. Stir in the parsley and bread crumbs. Spoon the squash mixture into a buttered 9×13-inch baking dish. Sprinkle with additional bread crumbs. Bake at 375 degrees for 25 minutes or until golden brown. Yield: 6 to 8 servings.

Sharmaine LaCarbo Eastin, Kappu Chi
Ville Platte, Louisiana

Janice DiBeneditto, Theta Master, Waterbury, Connecticut, makes ***Crab-Shrimp Bake*** *by combining a drained 7-ounce can of crab meat with 1 cup cooked deveined shelled shrimp, 1 cup chopped celery, 3/4 cup mayonnaise, 1/4 cup chopped green bell pepper, 2 tablespoons finely chopped onion, 1 teaspoon Worcestershire sauce, 1/2 teaspoon salt and pepper to taste in a 1-quart casserole. Top with a mixture of 1 cup soft bread crumbs and 1 tablespoon melted butter. Bake at 350 degrees for 30 to 35 minutes.*

SHRIMP WITH THAI LIME BUTTER

16 to 20 large shrimp in the shell
Salt and pepper to taste
1/2 recipe Thai Lime Butter, at room temperature

Split each shrimp lengthwise down the middle of the back but do not cut all the way through. Butterfly the shrimp and season lightly with salt and pepper. Smear the inside of each shrimp with about 2 teaspoons Thai Lime Butter. Place the shrimp 1 inch apart on a rimmed baking sheet. Roast in a preheated 475-degree oven for 6 minutes or just until barely done; shrimp will continue to cook slightly when removed from the oven. Serve immediately. Yield: 4 servings.

THAI LIME BUTTER

1 cup (2 sticks) butter, softened
2 teaspoons minced lime zest
1/4 cup fresh lime juice
1 tablespoon minced lemongrass
2 tablespoons chopped fresh mint
2 tablespoons chopped fresh cilantro
1/4 teaspoon hot red pepper flakes
2 tablespoons minced gingerroot
1/4 teaspoon curry powder
2 teaspoons minced garlic
1 tablespoon Thai fish sauce

Combine the butter, lime zest and juice, lemongrass, mint, cilantro, red pepper flakes, gingerroot, curry powder, garlic and fish sauce in a food processor container and process until smooth. Chill, tightly covered, for up to 1 week. Leftover Thai Lime Butter may be rolled into a log, wrapped tightly in plastic wrap and frozen for up to 3 months.

Sheri Grove, Beta Psi
Phoenix, Arizona

TEQUILA LIME SHRIMP WITH BLACK BEAN SALSA

1/2 cup tequila
1/2 cup triple sec
Juice of 4 limes
Juice of 2 lemons
2 teaspoons minced garlic
Pinch of salt
1 small bunch cilantro, chopped
1 1/2 pounds (21- to 25-count) peeled fresh shrimp with tails, deveined
Black Bean Salsa

Combine the tequila, triple sec, lime juice, lemon juice, garlic, salt and cilantro in a large glass dish; mix well. Toss in the shrimp. Marinate, covered, in the refrigerator for 30 minutes to 1 hour. Drain the shrimp. Grill over very hot coals for 2 to 3 minutes or just until cooked through, turning frequently. Shrimp may be cooked in a hot skillet for 2 to 3 minutes or until browned and opaque, turning frequently if preferred. Chill the shrimp, covered, until serving time. Arrange the shimp on a serving platter and serve with Black Bean Salsa. Yield: 10 servings.

BLACK BEAN SALSA

For an occasional change, omit the picante sauce to make pico de gallo and serve with tortilla chips.

2 (15-ounce) cans black beans
2 small tomatoes, chopped
1 small red onion, diced
3 serrano peppers, seeded and chopped
1/2 bunch cilantro, chopped
Juice of 2 lemons
2 teaspoons chopped garlic
1 (16-ounce) jar picante sauce

Drain the beans, rinse under running water and drain well. Combine the beans, tomatoes, onion, serrano peppers, cilantro, lemon juice, garlic and picante sauce in a bowl and mix well. Chill, covered, until serving time.

Brenda Petru, Xi Lambda Zeta
Gonzales, Texas

✣ TOMATO SHRIMP WITH FETTUCCINE

8 ounces fettuccini
4 garlic cloves, minced
1/4 cup olive oil
2 cups chopped plum tomatoes
1/2 cup white cooking wine
1/4 cup lemon juice
1/2 teaspoon sugar
4 scallions, chopped
1 pound shrimp, peeled and deveined
1/8 teaspoon hot red pepper flakes
4 tablespoons basil
4 tablespoons grated Parmesan cheese

Cook the fettuccine using the package directions for 8 minutes or until tender but still firm. Drain well and keep warm. Sauté the garlic in the olive oil in a large skillet over medium heat for 2 minutes. Add the tomatoes and sauté for 5 minutes. Stir in the wine, lemon juice and sugar. Simmer for 6 minutes. Stir in the scallions, shrimp and red pepper flakes. Cook until shrimp is pink and cooked through, about 3 minutes, stirring constantly. Stir in the basil and Parmesan cheese. Toss with the fettuccine.
Yield: 4 servings.

Mary Ann Valley, Preceptor Gamma Lambda
Goodrich, Michigan

COLD SHRIMP LINGUINI

16 ounces linguini
1 1/2 pounds cooked peeled shrimp
1 (6-ounce) package frozen snow peas, thawed and drained
6 green onions, chopped
4 medium tomatoes, peeled, chopped, drained
3/4 cup olive oil
1/4 cup chopped fresh parsley
1/3 cup wine vinegar
1 teaspoon oregano
1 1/2 teaspoons basil
1/2 teaspoon garlic salt
1/2 teaspoon pepper

Cook the linguini al dente according to the package directions but omitting the salt. Drain and rinse under cold running water. Drain well. Combine the linguini, shrimp, snow peas, green onions and tomatoes in a large bowl. Combine the olive oil, parsley, vinegar, oregano, basil, garlic salt and pepper in a small bowl or jar and mix vigorously. Add to the shrimp mixture and toss gently. Chill, covered, for 2 hours or longer. Toss before serving.
Yield: 8 to 10 servings.

Thelma Kenney, Preceptor Gamma Kappa
Virginia Beach, Virginia

SAVORY SHRIMP BAKE

4 slices bread
1 1/2 cups chopped onions
1 green bell pepper, chopped
2 ribs celery, chopped
2 garlic cloves, crushed
1/2 cup margarine
1 (10-ounce) can tomatoes with green chiles
2 pounds shrimp, peeled and deveined
1 (10-ounce) can cream of mushroom soup
2 cups cooked rice
1/2 cup water
1/4 cup chopped parsley
Salt and pepper to taste
2 tablespoons dry bread crumbs
1 tablespoon (about) margarine

Soak the bread briefly in water; drain and squeeze dry. Set aside. Sauté the onions, bell pepper, celery and garlic in the margarine in a large kettle over medium heat for 5 to 8 minutes or until tender. Add the tomatoes with green chiles and shrimp and cook for 10 minutes, stirring frequently. Add the soup and 1/2 cup water and cook for 5 minutes longer, stirring frequently. Add the soaked bread, rice and parsley to the shrimp mixture and mix well. Season to taste. Spoon into a greased 10×13-inch baking dish. Sprinkle with the dry bread crumbs and dot with margarine. Bake at 350 degrees for 20 minutes or until browned. Yield: 8 to 10 servings.

Cindy Theriot, Xi Delta Pi
Breaux Bridge, Louisiana

SAUCY ROSEMARY SHRIMP

1/2 cup (1 stick) butter
1/2 cup olive oil
1/4 cup crushed rosemary
2 tablespoons oregano leaves
8 large garlic cloves, minced
3 or 4 bay leaves, crushed
2 tablespoons Worcestershire sauce
5 pounds unpeeled shrimp
1/2 cup dry white or red wine
Salt and coarsely ground pepper to taste

Heat the butter and olive oil in a heavy kettle or large deep skillet over medium heat. Add the rosemary, oregano, garlic, bay leaves and Worcestershire sauce; stir and heat. Add the shrimp. Reduce heat, cover and simmer until shrimp turns pink and just begins to pull away from the shell, stirring occasionally. Add the wine quickly. Simmer, covered, for about 5 minutes; the entire cooking time should be 15 to 20 minutes. Season with salt and pepper. Place in a large bowl in the center of the table. Serve with hot crisp bread like sourdough French bread that can be used to sop the pan juices directly from the serving bowl. Yield: 4 or 5 servings.

Maggie Hall, Laureate Delta
Juneau, Alaska

SHRIMP SCAMPI

1/4 cup chopped onion
3 tablespoons chopped garlic
3/4 (11/2 sticks) cup butter
3 pounds jumbo shrimp, peeled and deveined
1 teaspoon salt
1/8 teaspoon pepper
2 tablespoons lemon juice
1/4 cup chopped parsley

Sauté the onion and garlic in the butter in a 12-inch skillet over medium heat for 5 minutes. Add the shrimp and cook for 5 minutes, turning once. Remove shrimp to a serving dish and set aside. Add the salt, pepper and lemon juice to the skillet drippings and cook until heated through, stirring constantly. Drizzle the juices over the shrimp. Sprinkle with parsley and serve. Yield: 4 servings.

Belinda Holland, Xi Zeta Lambda
Ft. Stockton, Texas

***Baked Scallops in the Shell** is an easy specialty from Ruth Blundon, Xi Nu, Deer Lake, Newfoundland, Canada. Divide a pound of scallops among 4 greased scallop shells, top each with 1 tablespoon whipping cream, salt and freshly ground pepper and 1 teaspoon buttered bread crumbs. Bake at 450 degrees for 15 minutes.*

SHRIMP BURGERS

2 pounds shrimp, peeled, deveined, chopped
1/2 cup finely chopped onion
1/4 cup finely chopped green bell pepper
1/2 cup finely chopped celery
1 egg, beaten
1 teaspoon salt
1/4 teaspoon cayenne pepper
1 teaspoon baking powder
3 tablespoons finely chopped green onions
3 tablespoons finely chopped parsley
4 slices stale bread, cut into small cubes
Flour for coating
3 to 6 tablespoons vegetable oil
6 hamburger buns, toasted

Chop the shrimp medium finely. Combine the shrimp, onion, bell pepper, celery and egg in a large bowl. Add the salt, cayenne pepper, baking powder, green onions, parsley and bread; mix well. Chill, covered, for at least 2 hours. Shape the shrimp mixture into 6 patties. Coat the patties lightly with flour. Heat 1 to 2 tablespoons of the vegetable oil in a skillet over medium heat. Fry 2 or 3 patties at a time in the hot oil for 3 to 4 minutes or until brown on both sides. Repeat with the remaining oil and patties. Serve on toasted buns with tartar sauce. Yield: 6 patties.

Hazel Saucier, Beta Master
Westwego, Louisiana

SEAFOOD RICE BAKE

Use more shrimp and this dish is even better.

2 (4-ounce) cans shrimp, drained
1 (6-ounce) can crab meat, drained
1 cup salad dressing of choice
1 (10-ounce) can cream of mushroom soup
1 cup sliced mushrooms
1 green bell pepper, chopped
1 cup diced celery
3 cups cooked rice
1 cup milk
1 teaspoon lemon juice
1/2 cup chopped onion
11/2 teaspoons black pepper
1 cup crushed potato chips

Combine the shrimp, crab meat, salad dressing, cream of mushroom soup, mushrooms, bell pepper, celery, rice, milk, lemon juice, onion and black pepper in a large bowl and mix well. Spoon into a 10×13-inch baking dish. Cover with crushed potato chips. Bake at 350 degrees for 45 minutes to 1 hour or until browned and bubbly. Yield: 10 to 12 servings.

Evelyn Finnegan, Gamma Master
Aiken, South Carolina

CHILLED FRUIT CUPS

1 (12-ounce) can frozen pineapple juice concentrate, thawed
1 (6-ounce) can frozen orange juice concentrate, thawed
1 cup sugar
2 tablespoons lemon juice
3 medium bananas, sliced
1 (16-ounce) package frozen unsweetened strawberries, thawed and drained
1 (15-ounce) can mandarin oranges, drained
1 (8-ounce) can crushed pineapple, drained

Prepare the pineapple juice in a large bowl using the package directions. Stir in the undiluted orange juice concentrate, 1 cup water, sugar, lemon juice, bananas, strawberries, mandarin oranges and crushed pineapple. Spoon 3/4 cup of the fruit mixture into each of eighteen 9-ounce clear plastic cups. Arrange the cups in a baking pan. Cover and freeze. Remove from the freezer 40 to 50 minutes before serving.
Yield: 18 servings.

Pauline Huneycutt, Preceptor Delta Theta
Neodesha, Kansas

FRIED APPLES

1/4 cup butter
6 apples, peeled and sliced
Cinnamon to taste
2 to 4 tablespoons brown sugar
2 to 4 tablespoons granulated sugar
Raisins to taste
Hickory nuts to taste
Marshmallows to taste

Melt the butter in a skillet over medium-low heat. Add the apples and cook, covered, until undersides of apples are brown. Turn and brown the other sides. Stir in the cinnamon, sugars, raisins, hickory nuts and 1/4 cup water. Simmer, covered, for 10 minutes or until apples are tender. Top with marshmallows and sprinkle with cinnamon. Remove from heat when marshmallows are melted and serve immediately.
Yield: 6 to 8 servings.

Lois E. Hinton, Preceptor Zeta Sigma
Chillicothe, Ohio

BAKED APRICOTS

3 (15-ounce) cans apricot halves, drained
1 cup packed light brown sugar
1 roll butter crackers, crushed
1/2 cup unsalted butter, melted

Layer the apricots, brown sugar and butter crackers 1/2 at a time in a buttered 9×13-inch baking dish. Drizzle with melted butter. Bake at 350 degrees for 45 minutes or until browned and bubbly.
Yield: 6 servings.

Lydia Ajhar, Preceptor Alpha Gamma
Cumming, Georgia

---

*Fern W. Hunter, Laureate Beta Omicron, N. Fort Myers, Florida, makes **Cinnamon Apples** by thinly slicing 2 small apples and placing them in a 4×8-inch microwave-safe dish. Sprinkle the apples with 1/4 cup red hot cinnamon candies. Add 2 tablespoons water. Cover with waxed paper and microwave on High for 1 minute. Stir and microwave for 1 minute longer. Let stand for 1 minute to set. Serve immediately.*

CRANBERRY BAKE

2 cups cranberries
3 cups sliced peeled apples
2 tablespoons flour
3/4 cup granulated sugar
1/2 cup margarine, melted
1/3 cup rolled oats
1 teaspoon cinnamon
1 cup chopped walnuts or pecans
1/2 cup packed brown sugar

Combine the cranberries and apples in a large bowl. Sprinkle with flour and toss; add the granulated sugar and toss. Spoon into a 2-quart baking dish. Combine the margarine, rolled oats, cinnamon, walnuts and brown sugar in a small bowl and mix well. Spoon the cinnamon mixture over the apple mixture. Bake at 350 degrees for 45 minutes or until browned and bubbly. Yield: 8 to 10 servings.

Dena M. Hammye, Preceptor Gamma Delta
Lakeland, Florida

BRANDIED PEACHES

2 (15-ounce) cans peach halves, drained, 2 tablespoons syrup reserved
1/4 cup butter, softened
Pinch of cinnamon
1/2 cup packed light brown sugar
3 tablespoons brandy
1/2 to 1 cup sour cream
Nutmeg to taste

Pat the peach halves dry with a paper towel. Combine the butter, cinnamon, brown sugar, brandy and the reserved 2 tablespoons peach syrup. Arrange the peach halves cut side up in a shallow 9×9-inch baking dish. Fill each peach half with a spoonful of the butter mixture. Bake at 350 degrees for 30 minutes or until hot and bubbly. Heat a little additional brandy and drizzle over the peaches before serving. Place a dollop of sour cream in the center of each. Sprinkle with nutmeg and serve.
Yield: 4 to 5 servings.

Joan Pacholko, Xi Kappa
Calgary, Alberta, Canada

PEACHY JARLSBERG LIGHT CHEESE STRATA

4 slices whole grain bread, cut into 1/4-inch cubes
8 dried peaches, coarsely chopped
6 ounces reduced-fat Jarlsberg cheese, cut into 1/4-inch cubes
1 (12-ounce) can evaporated skim milk
1 cup fat-free liquid egg substitute
1 cup fat-free peach yogurt
2 tablespoons sugar
2 teaspoons cinnamon
2 teaspoons vanilla extract

Layer the bread, dried peaches and cheese 1/2 at a time in a buttered 7×11-inch baking dish. Combine the evaporated milk, egg substitute, yogurt, sugar, cinnamon and vanilla in a bowl and mix well. Pour the egg mixture evenly over the cheese layer. Chill, covered, for 8 to 10 hours. Let stand at room temperature for 1 hour before baking. Place in the center of a cold oven. Turn the oven temperature to 300 degrees. Bake, uncovered, for 1 hour or until lightly browned and liquid is absorbed. Yield: 6 servings.

Janet Thompson, Laureate Beta Delta
Roanoke, Virginia

SWEET PINEAPPLE PECAN CRUNCH

To make a dessert, serve warm with ice cream.

1 (18-ounce) package yellow cake mix
1 cup rolled oats
1/2 cup packed brown sugar
1 (20-ounce) can crushed pineapple
1 (20-ounce) can pineapple tidbits
3/4 cup chopped pecans
3/4 (1 1/2 sticks) cup butter or margarine, melted

Combine the dry cake mix, rolled oats and brown sugar in a bowl and mix well. Butter the bottom and sides of a 9×13-inch baking dish. Layer the undrained crushed pineapple, undrained pineapple tidbits and cake mix mixture in the prepared baking dish. Press down with a large wooden spoon and sprinkle with pecans. Drizzle the melted butter evenly over the top. Bake at 350 degrees for 40 to 45 minutes or until lightly browned. Yield: 12 to 18 servings.

Edna Irene Piper, Alpha Beta
Bedford, Indiana

SCALLOPED PINEAPPLE

1/2 cup margarine, softened
2 cups sugar
3 eggs, beaten
1 cup milk
4 cups cubed bread
2 (8-ounce) cans pineapple tidbits, drained well

Combine the margarine and sugar in a mixing bowl and beat until smooth. Beat in the eggs 1 at a time. Beat in the milk. Stir in the bread. Stir in the pineapple. Spoon into a buttered 8×10-inch baking dish. Bake at 350 degrees for 35 to 40 minutes or until lightly browned. Yield: 6 to 8 servings.

Billie J. Hufton, Eta Mu
Virginia Beach, Virginia

FRUIT SALSA WITH CINNAMON CRISPS

1 tablespoon sugar
2 teaspoons cinnamon
6 (8- or 10-inch) flour tortillas
3 tablespoons butter or margarine, melted
1 cup finely chopped pineapple
1 cup finely chopped papaya
1 cup finely chopped mango
1/4 cup chopped cilantro
1 tablespoon finely chopped crystallized ginger
1 tablespoon lemon juice
1/8 teaspoon salt

Mix the sugar and cinnamon together in a small bowl. Brush both sides of the tortillas with melted butter and sprinkle with the cinnamon mixture. Cut each tortilla into 12 wedges. Place the wedges in a single layer on 2 ungreased baking sheets. Broil 6 inches from the heat source for 2 to 4 minutes or until crispy and golden brown, turning once. Cool completely. Combine the pineapple, papaya, mango, cilantro, crystallized ginger, lemon juice and salt in a pretty bowl and mix gently. Serve with the cinnamon crisps. Yield: 24 to 30 servings.

Rhonda Povlot, Kappa Pi
Alpharetta, Georgia

BRANDIED JAM

1 (10-ounce) package frozen unsweetened strawberries
2 cups fresh or frozen cranberries
1 tablespoon grated orange zest
1 1/2 cups sugar
1 envelope no-cook fruit pectin
1/4 cup brandy

Combine the strawberries, cranberries, orange zest, sugar, pectin and brandy in a microwave-safe 2-quart bowl. Microwave on High for 7 minutes, stirring after 3 1/2 minutes. Stir well. Microwave on Medium for 7 minutes, watching carefully to make sure it doesn't boil over. Skim if needed. Pour into sterilized jars and chill. Yield: 3 cups.

Mary Elizabeth Reinhart, Gamma Master
Milwaukee, Wisconsin

*Lisa A. Kartawich, Xi Theta Chi, Robinson, Illinois, prepares **Escalloped Pineapple** by tearing 8 slices of bread into small pieces and combining with a 20-ounce can of crushed pineapple, 1 scant cup packed brown sugar and 1/2 cup melted butter or margarine. Spoon the pineapple mixture into an 8×8-inch baking dish. Bake at 400 degrees for 15 minutes or until lightly browned.*

APRICOT MUSTARD-GLAZED SAUSAGE LINKS

The mustard glaze may be prepared up to the addition of the rosemary, then refrigerated for a day before resuming preparation of sausages.

1/2 cup apricot preserves
1/4 cup sweet hot mustard
Salt and pepper to taste
2 teaspoons chopped fresh rosemary
2 tablespoons vegetable oil
1 (18-ounce) package breakfast sausage links

Heat the preserves in a saucepan over medium heat for about 1 minute or until melted and smooth, whisking constantly. Add the mustard and bring to a simmer, whisking constantly. Remove from heat. Season with salt and pepper and stir in the rosemary. Heat the vegetable oil in a skillet over medium heat; add the sausage links and sauté until brown and heated through. Add the sausages to the mustard glaze and cook over medium heat for about 1 minute or until sausages are glazed, stirring constantly. Remove to a platter and serve. Yield: 6 servings.

Cynthia Albert, Beta Phi
Wilber, Nebraska

SAUSAGE AND CHEESE BALLS

For a firmer texture, add an extra 3 cups baking mix and an extra 2 cups shredded cheese.

16 ounces Cheddar cheese, shredded (4 cups)
1 1/2 cups baking mix
1/2 cup finely chopped celery
1/2 cup finely chopped onion
1/2 teaspoon garlic powder (optional)
2 pounds bulk pork sausage

Combine the cheese, baking mix, celery, onion, garlic powder and sausage in a large bowl and mix well. Shape into 1-inch balls and arrange on an ungreased baking sheet. Bake in a preheated 375-degree oven for 15 minutes or until golden brown. Yield: 6 dozen.

Hazel Irene Ivey, Beta Epsilon Omicron
Brackettville, Texas

*Pauline Dennis, Alpha Alpha Master, Dallas, Texas, makes **Sausage on English Muffins** by browning 2 pounds bulk pork sausage in a skillet until crumbly; drain. Add 16 ounces Velveeta cheese and 3/4 cup margarine to the sausage and stir until melted. Let cool slightly. Spoon sausage mixture onto English muffin halves.*

COUNTRY GRITS AND SAUSAGE BAKE

2 pounds mild bulk pork sausage
1/2 cup uncooked quick-cooking grits
16 ounces sharp Cheddar cheese, shredded (4 cups)
4 eggs, beaten
1 cup milk
1 small green bell pepper, chopped (optional)

Brown the sausage in a skillet, stirring until crumbly; drain. Bring 2 cups salted water to a boil in a saucepan over medium-high heat. Stir in the grits. Reduce heat and simmer, covered, for 4 minutes, stirring occasionally. Combine the hot grits and cheese in a large bowl; stir until cheese is melted. Combine the eggs, milk and a small amount of the grits mixture in another bowl and stir well. Stir the remaining egg mixture into the grits mixture. Stir in the sausage and bell pepper. Spoon into a greased 6×10×2-inch baking dish. Chill, covered, for 8 to 10 hours. Let stand at room temperature for 15 minutes. Bake at 350 degrees for 50 to 55 minutes or until hot and lightly browned. Yield: 6 to 8 servings.

Sarah V. Gilchrist, Preceptor Epsilon Alpha
Lakeridge, Virginia

ORANGE COCONUT BREAKFAST BARS

4 cups quick-cooking oats
1 cup packed brown sugar
1 teaspoon salt
1 1/2 cups chopped pecans
1 cup shredded coconut
3/4 (1 1/2 sticks) cup butter or margarine, softened
1 cup orange marmalade

Combine the oats, brown sugar and salt in a large bowl. Stir in the pecans, coconut, butter and orange marmalade; mix well. Press into a greased 10×15-inch cake pan. Bake at 425 degrees for 15 to 17 minutes or until golden brown. Cool and cut into 24 bars.
Yield: 2 dozen.

Nina Rohlfs, Preceptor Tau
Unadilla, Nebraska

✣ CRUNCHY GRANOLA

4 cups rolled oats
1 cup All-Bran
1/4 cup sesame seeds
1 cup shredded unsweetened coconut
1/2 cup sliced almonds (optional)
1/4 cup cracked flax seed (optional)
1/2 cup sunflower seeds (optional)
1/4 cup honey
2 tablespoons brown sugar
1/2 cup vegetable oil
1 cup dried fruit (such as cranberries, apples, apricots)

Combine the oats, All-Bran, sesame seeds, coconut, almonds, flax seed and sunflower seeds in a large bowl. Combine the honey, brown sugar and vegetable oil in a small bowl and mix well. Drizzle the honey mixture over the oats mixture and mix well. Spread in a shallow pan. Bake at 300 degrees for 30 minutes, stirring every 10 minutes. Let stand until cool, stirring several times. Stir in the dried fruit. Store in an airtight container. Yield: 7 cups.

Eileen Cockburn, Laureate Beta Pi
Keene, Ontario, Canada

SUMMER OATMEAL BREAKFAST TREAT

For a fancy treat, layer in parfait dishes with fresh strawberries and garnish with additional almonds.

1 cup quick-cooking oats or old-fashioned rolled oats
2 (8-ounce) cartons nonfat or low-fat yogurt, any flavor
1 (8-ounce) can crushed pineapple
2 tablespoons sliced almonds (optional)

Combine the oats, yogurt, undrained pineapple and almonds in a medium bowl; mix well. Chill, covered, for 8 to 10 hours. Eat from a bowl for breakfast or a midday snack. Yield: 4 servings.

Thomasine Morris, Preceptor Lambda Theta
Miami, Florida

FAUX EGGS BENEDICT

The poached eggs should be cooked to the point where whites are solid. The recipe may be doubled or tripled.

1 (10-ounce) can cream of mushroom soup
1 cup shredded Cheddar cheese
4 to 5 tablespoons fresh lemon juice
1 teaspoon grated lemon zest (optional)
4 slices Canadian bacon or bacon
2 English muffins, toasted and buttered
4 eggs, poached, whites solid

Combine the soup and 3/4 cup of the cheese in a saucepan over medium-high heat; bring to a simmer. Stir in 3 to 4 tablespoons of the lemon juice and lemon zest. Place 1 slice Canadian bacon or 1 slice bacon, halved, over each English muffin half. Place a poached egg over the bacon. Pour 1/4 cup cheese sauce over each egg and top with 1 tablespoon shredded cheese. Drizzle 1 teaspoon lemon juice over each and garnish with parsley. Yield: 2 servings.

Dottie Bastyr, Alpha Rho Master
Weeki Wachee, Florida

POTATO SAUSAGE BAKE

1/2 (20-ounce) package frozen hash brown potatoes, thawed
12 ounces Cheddar cheese, shredded (3 cups)
2 pounds bulk pork sausage, browned and crumbled
8 ounces mushrooms, sliced
5 eggs
2 cups milk
3/4 teaspoon dry mustard
Pepper to taste
1 (10-ounce) can cream of mushroom soup
1/2 soup can milk

Layer the potatoes, cheese, sausage and mushrooms in a 9×13-inch baking dish that has been sprayed with nonstick cooking spray. Combine the eggs and the 2 cups milk in a bowl and beat well; beat in the dry mustard and pepper. Pour the egg mixture evenly over the mushroom layer. Let stand, covered, in the refrigerator for 5 to 10 hours. Combine the soup and the 1/2 soup can of milk in a bowl and mix well. Pour the soup mixture evenly over the egg layer. Sprinkle with paprika. Bake at 350 degrees for 1 to 1 1/2 hours or until set. Remove from the oven and let stand for 5 to 10 minutes. Yield: 10 to 12 servings.

Loretta McClintock, Xi Beta Gamma
Green River, Wyoming

COUNTRY SAUSAGE BREAKFAST

12 to 16 ounces bulk pork sausage
6 eggs, lightly beaten
1/2 cup milk
1 envelope sausage country gravy mix
8 ounces Cheddar cheese, shredded (2 cups)
6 slices bread, cut into 1-inch cubes
2 tablespoons melted butter (optional)

Brown the sausage in a skillet, stirring until crumbly. Remove the sausage from the skillet and drain on a paper towel. Spread the sausage in a lightly greased 8×11-inch baking dish. Combine the eggs, 1 cup water, milk and dry gravy mix in a bowl and whisk to blend. Sprinkle the cheese over the sausage layer. Pour the egg mixture evenly over the cheese. Layer the bread cubes over the egg mixture and drizzle with butter. Sprinkle with paprika if desired. Bake, uncovered, at 325 degrees for 40 minutes or until a knife inserted in the center comes out clean. Let stand at room temperature for 10 minutes before serving.
Yield: 8 servings.

Claudia M. Long, Kappa Kappa
Meriden, Kansas

EGG PIE WITH FLUFFY MAPLE SAUCE

1/2 pound bacon, diced
9 eggs, beaten
1 cup flour
1/4 teaspoon salt
1 cup milk
Fluffy Maple Sauce

Crisp-cook the bacon in an ovenproof skillet; do not drain. Combine the eggs, flour, salt and milk in a large mixing bowl and beat until smooth. Pour the egg mixture evenly over the cooked bacon in the skillet. Bake at 450 degrees for 30 to 40 minutes or until set and browned. Serve with Fluffy Maple Sauce.
Yield: 4 to 6 servings.

FLUFFY MAPLE SAUCE

1 1/2 cups sifted confectioners' sugar
1/2 cup maple syrup
1/2 cup (1 stick) butter, softened

Combine the confectioners' sugar, maple syrup and butter in a bowl and blend. Chill, covered, until serving time.

Jeanne Dalzell, Xi Gamma
Anchorage, Alaska

CHEESE AND EGGS OLE

1 dozen eggs, beaten
1/2 cup flour
1 teaspoon baking powder
16 ounces Monterey Jack cheese, shredded (4 cups)
2 cups cottage cheese
1/2 cup (1 stick) butter, melted
2 (4-ounce) cans chopped green chiles, drained

Combine all the ingredients in a large bowl and mix well. Pour into a buttered 9×13-inch baking dish. Bake at 350 degrees for 35 minutes or until set and lightly browned. Serve immediately.
Yield: 8 to 10 servings.

Janet Brees, Preceptor Pi
Columbia, Missouri

CHEESY BREAKFAST BAKE

2 or 3 shakes of Mrs. Dash seasoning
10 to 12 eggs, beaten until frothy
1/4 cup dried minced onion
2 tablespoons chopped parsley
3 cups creamed cottage cheese
8 ounces bulk pork sausage
4 ounces Cheddar cheese, shredded (1 cup)
1/2 cup crushed tortilla chips

Sprinkle the Mrs. Dash seasoning over the eggs. Stir in the onion and parsley. Stir in the cottage cheese, sausage, Cheddar cheese and tortilla chips 1 at a time. Pour into a buttered 9×13-inch baking dish. Bake at 350 degrees for 45 to 50 minutes or until set and browned. Yield: 6 to 8 servings.

Ruth Brink, Epsilon Master
Richardson, Texas

EGG AND MUSHROOM BAKE

1 dozen eggs
1 (10-ounce) can cream of mushroom soup
1/2 cup heavy cream or evaporated milk
1 (4-ounce) can mushroom stems and pieces, drained
1 medium onion, diced
1 green bell pepper, chopped (optional)
Salt and pepper to taste
8 ounces Velveeta cheese, diced

Break the eggs into a large bowl and beat well. Blend in the soup and cream; mixture will be slightly lumpy. Sauté the mushrooms, onion and bell pepper in a small amount of butter in a skillet over medium heat for 5 to 8 minutes or until tender. Let the sautéed vegetables stand for several minutes to cool slightly. Stir the mushroom mixture into the egg mixture. Season with salt and pepper. Pour into a buttered 9×13-inch baking dish. Layer the cheese over the top. Bake at 300 degrees for 30 to 35 minutes Check the egg mixture after 15 to 20 minutes. If edges have set but center has not, stir the edges gently to the center. Bake to the desired firmness of scrambled eggs. Yield: 12 servings.

Debbie Jones, Xi Beta Xi
Paris, Missouri

EGGS FLORENTINE

Serve with fresh fruit and coffee cake or pastries for an Easter brunch.

2 (10-ounce) packages frozen chopped spinach, thawed
9 eggs, beaten
2 cups small curd cottage cheese
8 ounces Swiss cheese, shredded (2 cups)
8 ounces feta cheese, crumbled
1/4 cup melted butter
1/2 cup chopped red bell pepper
1/2 cup chopped onion
1 teaspoon nutmeg

Drain the spinach and squeeze between paper towels to remove excess moisture. Combine the eggs, cottage cheese, Swiss cheese, feta cheese, butter, spinach, bell pepper, onion and nutmeg in a large bowl and mix well. Spoon into a greased 9×13-inch baking dish. Bake, uncovered, at 350 degrees for 1 hour or until set. Cover with foil if eggs brown too quickly. Yield: 8 servings.

Linda Leake, Preceptor Alpha Sigma
Beaverton, Oregon

HAM AND EGG BAKE

1 (20-ounce) package frozen hash brown potatoes, thawed
1 medium onion, diced
1/2 green bell pepper, diced
1 cup diced fully cooked ham
1 cup diced fully cooked sausage
4 ounces Mexican-style or Cheddar cheese, shredded (1 cup)
1 cup sliced mushrooms
1 dozen eggs, beaten
1 cup heavy cream
1 teaspoon salt
1 teaspoon black pepper
1 teaspoon dry mustard
1/4 teaspoon Tabasco sauce
2 cups sour cream
1 (8-ounce) jar salsa

Layer the potatoes, onion, bell pepper, ham, sausage, cheese and mushrooms in a greased 9×13-inch baking dish. Combine the eggs, cream, salt, black pepper, mustard and Tabasco sauce in a large bowl and whisk until smooth. Pour evenly over the cheese layer. Bake, uncovered, at 350 degrees for 45 to 50 minutes or until a knife inserted in the center comes out clean. Let stand for 5 minutes before serving. Serve with sour cream and salsa. Yield: 12 servings.

Lois Franz, Preceptor Epsilon
Hayden, Idaho

OVEN OMELET

1/2 cup (1 stick) butter
1 1/2 dozen eggs
1 cup sour cream
1 cup milk
2 teaspoons (or less) salt
1/4 cup chopped green onion

Melt the butter in a 9×13-inch baking dish in a 325-degree oven, tilting the dish to coat the bottom with butter. Combine the eggs, sour cream, milk and salt in a large mixing bowl and beat until blended. Stir in the green onion. Pour into the prepared baking dish. Bake at 325 degrees for 35 minutes or until eggs are set but still moist. Yield: 12 servings.

Mary Ellen Kincaid, Preceptor Tau
Alexandria, Virginia

SAUSAGE AND EGG BREAKFAST BAKE

2 pounds sausage, bacon or ham
4 eggs, beaten
3/4 teaspoon dry mustard
2 cups milk
2 1/2 cups herbed cheese croutons
8 ounces Cheddar cheese, shredded (2 cups)
1 (10-ounce) can cream of mushroom soup
1/2 cup milk

Brown the sausage in a skillet, stirring until crumbly; drain on paper towels. Combine the eggs, dry mustard and milk in a mixing bowl and beat until smooth. Layer the croutons, sausage, cheese and egg mixture in a greased 9×13-inch baking dish. Chill, covered, for 8 to 10 hours. Before baking, pour a mixture of the soup and milk evenly over the top. Bake at 300 degrees for 1 hour and 30 minutes or until browned. Yield: 15 servings.

Jean McGuire, Laureate Tau
Worthing, South Dakota

EGG AND BACON BAKE

6 eggs, slightly beaten
16 ounces sharp Cheddar cheese, shredded (4 cups)
2 1/4 cups milk
2 tablespoons prepared mustard
2 tablespoons minced green onions
1/2 teaspoon Worcestershire sauce
1/2 teaspoon salt
1/2 pound bacon, crisp-cooked, crumbled
1/2 cup sliced mushrooms
1/2 cup diced green bell pepper
Dash of cayenne pepper
10 to 15 slices firm day-old bread, crusts trimmed, cubed

Combine the eggs, cheese, milk, mustard, green onions, Worcestershire sauce, salt, bacon, mushrooms, bell pepper and cayenne pepper in a large bowl and mix well. Layer the bread and the egg mixture 1/2 at a time in a greased 9×13-inch baking dish. Bake at 325 degrees for 50 to 55 minutes or until browned and bubbly; if browning and bubbling begins too soon, cover with a tent of foil while baking. Yield: 8 servings.

Monica Samson, Chi Omicron
Naperville, Illinois

EGG AND CHEDDAR BAKE

3/4 (1 1/2 sticks) cup butter
8 slices bread, crusts trimmed, cubed
5 eggs
2 cups milk
Pepper to taste
8 ounces Cheddar cheese, shredded (2 cups)
1 (10-ounce) can cream of mushroom soup

Melt the butter in a glass 9×13-inch baking dish; tilt to coat the bottom of the dish. Spread the bread cubes over the butter. Combine the eggs, milk and pepper in a large bowl and beat until smooth. Pour the egg mixture evenly over the bread layer. Sprinkle evenly with cheese. Chill, covered, for 8 to 10 hours. Spread a mixture of the soup and 1/2 soup can of water over the top. Bake, uncovered, at 350 degrees for at least 1 hour or until browned. Yield: 8 servings.

Allison Angel, Sigma Epsilon
Cassville, Missouri

GREEN CHILE BREAKFAST BAKE

1/2 pound bulk pork sausage
6 slices white bread, crusts trimmed
1 (4-ounce) can chopped green chiles, drained
16 ounces Monterey Jack cheese, shredded (4 cups)
6 eggs, beaten
2 cups heavy cream

Brown the sausage in a skillet, stirring until crumbly; drain. Butter one side of each bread slice. Place the bread buttered side up in a 9×13-inch baking dish. Layer the sausage, green chiles and cheese over the bread. Combine the eggs and cream in a bowl and beat until smooth. Pour the egg mixture evenly over the cheese layer. Bake at 350 degrees for 45 minutes or until browned. Yield: 8 servings.

Frances Sullivan, Xi Rho Theta
Ennis, Texas

CHEESY SOURDOUGH EGG BAKE

8 slices sourdough bread, crusts trimmed
1/2 cup (1 stick) butter
2 cups sliced mushrooms
1 cup minced onion
2 cups diced cooked ham
8 ounces Cheddar cheese, shredded (2 cups)
8 ounces Monterey Jack cheese, shredded (2 cups)
2 tablespoons flour
2 cups half-and-half
2 tablespoons prepared mustard
1 tablespoon garlic salt
8 eggs

Arrange the bread slices in a buttered 9×13-inch baking dish. Heat the butter in a skillet over medium heat. Sauté the mushrooms and onion in the butter for about 5 minutes. Spoon the mushroom mixture over the bread. Layer the ham over the mushroom mixture. Place the Cheddar cheese, Monterey Jack cheese and flour in a bowl and toss to combine. Sprinkle the cheese mixture over the ham. Combine the remaining ingredients in a bowl and mix until smooth. Pour the egg mixture over the cheese. Chill, covered, for 4 to 10 hours. Bake, uncovered, at 325 degrees for 1 hour. Yield: about 10 servings.

Maxine Harris, Laureate Beta Iota
Merced, California

Norma Jean Jones, Epsilon Master, Broken Arrow, Oklahoma, makes ***Gingered Tea*** *for herself or enough for a crowd. To make 2 servings: Bring 1 cup water to a boil. Add 2 teaspoons honey and 3/4 teaspoon ground ginger. Simmer, covered, for 10 minutes; remove from heat. Add 3 tea bags and steep, covered, for 5 to 7 minutes. Discard tea bags, add milk and heat to serving temperature, but do not boil.*

✤ CHEESY SPINACH BREAKFAST BAKE

1 pound bulk pork sausage
2½ cups herb-seasoned croutons
8 eggs, beaten
2¼ cups milk
1 (10-ounce) can cream of mushroom soup
1 (10-ounce) package frozen chopped spinach, thawed and drained
1 (4-ounce) can sliced mushrooms, drained
4 ounces sharp Cheddar cheese, shredded (1 cup)
4 ounces Monterey Jack cheese, shredded (1 cup)
¼ teaspoon dry mustard

Brown the sausage in a skillet, stirring until crumbly; drain. Spread the croutons in a greased 9×13-inch baking dish. Layer the sausage over the croutons. Place the eggs and milk in a large bowl and whisk to blend. Stir in the soup, spinach, mushrooms, Cheddar cheese, Monterey Jack cheese and dry mustard. Pour the egg mixture evenly over the sausage layer. Chill, covered, for 8 to 10 hours. Bake, uncovered, at 350 degrees for 50 to 55 minutes or until browned and set. Serve with picante sauce if desired. Yield: 10 to 12 servings.

Misty Wells, Omicron Mu
Fort Stockton, Texas

SHREDDED POTATO AND HAM PIE

4 eggs, slightly beaten
1 (15-ounce) can Veg-All, well drained
1 cup chopped cooked ham
Dash of garlic powder (optional)
½ cup milk
¼ teaspoon dried minced onion
1½ cups shredded Cheddar cheese
2 cups thawed frozen hash brown potatoes

Combine the eggs, Veg-All, ham, garlic powder, milk, dried onion and 1 cup of the cheese in a bowl; mix well and set aside. Combine the uncooked hash brown potatoes and ½ cup of the cheese in a bowl and mix well. Press the potato mixture over the bottom and up the side of a 9-inch pie plate. Pour the ham mixture into the potato-lined pie plate. Bake at 350 degrees for 45 to 50 minutes or until center is set. Let stand for 10 minutes before serving.
Yield: 6 servings.

Juanita Prior, Laureate Alpha Gamma
Bella Vista, Arkansas

HAM AND VEGETABLE QUICHE

1½ cups cubed cooked ham
6 ounces Swiss cheese, shredded (1½ cups)
1 cup frozen chopped broccoli or cauliflower, thawed and drained
1 baked (9-inch) pie shell
4 eggs
1 cup milk
½ teaspoon salt
½ teaspoon prepared mustard
½ teaspoon pepper

Layer the ham, cheese and broccoli in the pie shell. Combine the eggs, milk, salt, mustard and pepper in a mixing bowl and beat until smooth. Pour the egg mixture evenly over the vegetable layer. Bake at 375 degrees for 35 to 45 minutes or until a knife inserted in the center comes out clean. Let stand for 10 minutes before serving. Yield: 6 servings.

Mary Brooks, Preceptor Mu Alpha
Escondido, California

CRESCENT CHILI QUICHE

¾ cup shredded Monterey Jack cheese
¾ cup shredded Colby cheese
1 (8-count) can crescent rolls
½ cup diced green chiles
½ cup chopped onion
4 eggs
1 cup milk
⅓ cup Dijon mustard
1 tablespoon chopped cilantro or parsley
1 teaspoon chili powder
¼ cup chopped tomato
¼ cup chopped green bell pepper

Combine the Monterey Jack cheese and Colby cheese in a bowl and mix. Unroll the dough. Shape into 1 large rectangle, pressing the perforations to seal. Press over the bottom and 1 inch up the sides of a greased 9×13-inch baking dish. Bake at 375 degrees for 8 minutes. Remove from oven. Sprinkle with half the cheese mixture. Sprinkle with the green chiles and onion. Combine the eggs, milk, Dijon mustard, cilantro and chili powder in a bowl and mix well. Pour the egg mixture evenly over the cheese layer. Sprinkle the remaining cheese mixture evenly over the top. Bake at 375 degrees for 30 minutes or until set. Let cool for 5 minutes. Garnish with tomato and bell pepper. Cut into 2-inch squares and serve.
Yield: 12 servings.

Margie Roselle, Xi Gamma
Miles City, Montana

Joan Mize, Xi, Brandon, Mississippi, makes ***Mock Champagne Punch*** *by mixing a 2-liter bottle of chilled gingerale with 64 ounces white grape juice and garnishing with fresh mint and strawberries.*

SPINACH AND BACON QUICHE

This breakfast quiche also makes a nice Sunday supper when served with cantaloupe slices, strawberries, and grapes, and sherbet and cookies for dessert.

1 unbaked (10-inch) pie shell
3 eggs, beaten
1 1/2 cups milk
1 (10-ounce) package frozen spinach, thawed and drained
1 cup diced red bell pepper
1/4 cup sliced green onions
1/4 teaspoon salt
1/8 teaspoon black pepper
Dash of nutmeg
1 cup cubed Canadian bacon
1 cup chopped pecans (optional)
1 1/2 cups shredded cheese of choice
1 tablespoon flour

Line the unpricked pie shell with a double thickness of foil. Bake at 450 degrees for 5 minutes. Remove the foil and bake for 5 to 7 minutes longer. Remove from oven. Reduce oven temperature to 325 degrees. Combine the eggs, milk, spinach, bell pepper, green onions, salt, pepper and nutmeg in a large bowl and mix well. Stir in the Canadian bacon and pecans. Toss the cheese and flour together and stir into the egg mixture. Pour the egg mixture into the hot pie shell. Bake at 325 degrees for 40 to 45 minutes or until a knife inserted in the center comes out clean. Let stand for 10 minutes before cutting. Serve warm.
Yield: 6 servings.

Gloria Behrens, Xi Gamma Rho
Bull Shoals, Arkansas

NO-CRUST QUICHE

4 eggs
1 cup milk
1/4 cup flour
1 cup shredded Cheddar cheese
1 cup shredded Monterey Jack cheese
1 cup shredded Swiss cheese
1 tablespoon melted margarine
2 tablespoons chopped chives
Salt and pepper to taste

Place the eggs in a large mixing bowl and beat until smooth. Beat in the milk. Beat in the flour. Beat in the Cheddar cheese, Monterey Jack cheese and Swiss cheese. Beat in the margarine, chives, salt and pepper. Pour into a buttered 9-inch pie plate. Top with additional shredded cheese. Bake at 425 degrees for 25 minutes or until set and browned.
Yield: 6 to 8 servings.

Cid Knight, Preceptor Zeta
Carthage, Missouri

HAM AND BROCCOLI QUICHE

1 (1-crust) pie pastry
1/2 pound ham, cut up
1/2 (16-ounce) package frozen broccoli, thawed and drained
2 cups shredded Cheddar cheese
2 cups shredded mozzarella cheese
5 eggs
1 cup milk
Salt and pepper to taste

Fit the pastry into a 10-inch pie plate and flute the edge. Bake at 350 degrees for 10 minutes. Layer the ham, broccoli, Cheddar cheese and mozzarella cheese in the crust. Combine the eggs, milk, salt and pepper in a mixing bowl and beat until smooth. Pour the egg mixture evenly over the cheese. Bake at 350 degrees for 40 minutes or until browned.
Yield: 8 servings.

Cathy Close, Xi Gamma Tau
Carbondale, Colorado

HAM BREAKFAST IN ONE DISH

1 1/2 cups shredded Cheddar cheese or Swiss cheese
1 unbaked (9-inch) pie shell
1 1/2 cups diced cooked ham
1/4 cup finely chopped onion
1/3 cup flour
1/2 teaspoon salt
1/4 teaspoon pepper
1/4 teaspoon caraway seeds
1 cup milk
5 eggs

Spread 1/2 cup of the cheese in the pie shell. Layer half the ham and half the onion over the cheese. Combine the flour, salt, pepper and caraway seeds in a mixing bowl. Beat in the milk gradually. Add the eggs 1 at a time, beating well after each addition. Stir in the remaining ham, onion and cheese. Spoon evenly over the onion layer. Bake at 350 degrees for 45 to 50 minutes or until a knife inserted in the center comes out clean. Let stand for 5 to 10 minutes before cutting. Yield: 6 to 8 servings.

Muriel V. Rush, Laureate Alpha Rho
Grove City, Ohio

***Bacon Roll-Ups** are easy to make and delicious. Brenda Marsden, Xi Delta Alpha, Stoney Creek, Ontario, Canada, trims the crusts from white bread slices and rolls the bread flat with a rolling pin. Spread the slices with Cheez Whiz. Roll each up as for a jelly roll. Wrap each with 1/2 bacon slice; secure with a wooden pick. Arrange on rack in a broiler pan and broil (not too close to the heat source) for 15 minutes or until bacon is crisp, turning as necessary.*

QUICHE IN A FLASH

1/2 cup flour
2 teaspoons baking powder
Salt and pepper to taste
1 cup shredded Cheddar or Swiss cheese
1 cup milk
4 eggs
1/2 cup diced onion (optional)
1/2 cup chopped broccoli (optional)
1/4 cup chopped parsley (optional)
1/2 cup creamed corn (optional)
1/2 cup mixed frozen vegetables (optional)
1/2 cup crumbled cooked bacon (optional)
1/2 cup grated carrot (optional)
1/2 cup cubed ham (optional)

Combine the flour, baking powder, salt, pepper, cheese, milk and eggs in a large bowl and mix well. Stir in 2 or 3 of the optional ingredients, or make your own selection from whatever you have on hand. Spoon into a greased 10-inch pie plate. Bake at 350 degrees for 40 minutes or until beginning to brown. Let stand for 5 minutes before serving.
Yield: 8 servings.

Kelly Rogney, Beta Upsilon
Ashland, Oregon

SALMON QUICHE

1 cup croutons
1 (15-ounce) can salmon, drained
1/2 teaspoon chopped parsley
2 tablespoons chopped green bell pepper
3 eggs
Pinch of cayenne pepper
Pinch of nutmeg
Dash of black pepper
1 cup milk
1/4 cup shredded Cheddar or Swiss cheese

Sprinkle the croutons evenly over the bottom of a greased 9- or 10-inch pie plate. Spread the salmon evenly over the croutons. Sprinkle with parsley and bell pepper. Combine the eggs, cayenne pepper, nutmeg, black pepper and milk in a bowl and blend with a fork. Pour evenly over the salmon. Sprinkle with cheese. Bake at 425 degrees for 10 minutes. Reduce oven temperature to 375 degrees and bake for 20 minutes longer or until beginning to brown.
Yield: 6 to 8 servings.

Suzanne Wilson, Alpha Rho
Cambridge, Ontario, Canada

Terri Dill, Preceptor Beta Lambda, Bristow, Oklahoma, serves fresh fruit in season for an appetizer, dessert or other treats. This ***Yummy Fruit Dip*** *makes any fresh fruit special. Cut 8 ounces Velveeta cheese into small pieces and combine with a small carton of whipped topping and a 15-ounce can cream of coconut in a food processor. Process until smooth.*

CREAMY SALMON QUICHE

1 cup flour
1/2 teaspoon salt
6 tablespoons vegetable oil
2/3 cup plus 1/2 cup shredded Cheddar cheese
1/4 teaspoon paprika
1 (15-ounce) can salmon, drained, liquid reserved
1 cup sour cream
1/4 cup mayonnaise
3 eggs
1/4 teaspoon dill weed
1 tablespoon chopped onion
3 drops of Tabasco sauce (optional)

Combine the flour, salt, vegetable oil, the 2/3 cup cheese and paprika in a bowl and mix well. Reserve 1/2 cup of the flour mixture for the topping and press the remaining flour mixture into a 9-inch pie plate. Bake at 400 degrees for 10 minutes. Remove from oven. Reduce oven temperature to 325 degrees. Add enough water to the salmon liquid to make 1/2 cup. Combine the salmon liquid mixture, sour cream, mayonnaise and eggs in a bowl and blend well. Stir in the salmon, the 1/2 cup cheese, dill weed, onion and Tabasco sauce. Pour the salmon mixture into the pie crust. Sprinkle with the reserved flour mixture. Bake at 325 degrees for 45 minutes or until set and beginning to brown. Yield: 6 to 8 servings.

Cheri Hruskocy, Laureate Beta Kappa
Michigan City, Indiana

CRAB QUICHE

1 unbaked (9-inch) pie shell
1 tablespoon flour
1 cup shredded Swiss cheese
1 cup shredded Monterey Jack cheese
1 pound lump crab meat
1 tablespoon dried minced onion
3 eggs, well beaten
1 1/2 cups half-and-half
1/2 cup sour cream
1/2 teaspoon salt
1/2 teaspoon Old Bay seafood seasoning
1/4 teaspoon nutmeg
1/2 cup mayonnaise
1/2 teaspoon lemon juice
1 teaspoon paprika

Warm the pie shell in a 350-degree oven for 1 minute. Prick the shell all over with a fork and bake for 3 minutes longer. Dust the bottom with 1 tablespoon flour. Combine the Swiss cheese and Monterey Jack cheese in a bowl and mix well; reserve 1/2 cup of the cheese mixture for the topping. Add the crab meat and onion to the cheese mixture and mix well. Spoon the crab meat mixture into the pie crust. Combine the eggs, half-and-half, sour cream, salt, seafood seasoning and nutmeg in a bowl and whisk to blend. Pour the egg mixture evenly over the crab mixture. Bake at 350 degrees for 35 minutes. Remove from oven.

Combine the mayonnaise, lemon juice and paprika in a small bowl and whisk to blend. Spread gently over the top of the quiche. Sprinkle with the reserved cheese mixture. Bake for 15 minutes longer. Let stand for 10 minutes before cutting. Yield: 6 to 10 servings.

Virginia H. Jones, Laureate Beta Beta
Newport News, Virginia

TOMATO QUICHE

Substitute canned vegetables for the canned tuna if you prefer.

$\frac{1}{2}$ cup light mayonnaise
$\frac{1}{2}$ cup milk
$\frac{1}{3}$ cup chopped onion
2 tablespoons flour
1 (7-ounce) can tuna or other canned meat, drained
2 eggs
12 ounces Cheddar or Swiss cheese, shredded (3 cups)
1 unbaked (1-crust) pie shell
$\frac{1}{2}$ small Roma tomato, sliced

Combine the mayonnaise, milk, onion, flour, tuna, eggs and 2 cups of the cheese in a large bowl and mix well. Spoon into the pie shell. Bake at 350 degrees for 35 minutes. Remove from oven. Arrange the tomato slices over the top and sprinkle with the remaining 1 cup cheese. Bake for 10 minutes longer. Let cool before cutting. Yield: 8 servings.

Brenda Brotsch, Xi Epsilon
Tukwila, Washington

CRUSTLESS ZUCCHINI QUICHE

1 cup thinly sliced onion
1 garlic clove, minced
3 tablespoons olive oil
2 cups thinly sliced zucchini
$\frac{1}{2}$ cup cubed mozzarella cheese
1 teaspoon salt
4 eggs
$\frac{1}{2}$ cup milk
1 cup heavy cream
$\frac{1}{2}$ cup baking mix

Sauté the onion and garlic in the olive oil in a skillet over medium heat for 5 to 8 minutes or until tender. Stir in the zucchini. Remove from heat. Place the cheese in a food processor container and pulse until shredded. Add the salt, eggs, milk, cream and baking mix and process until well mixed. Mix in the zucchini mixture. Pour into a nonstick 8×8-inch baking dish or 10-inch pie plate. Bake at 375 degrees for 30 minutes or until set. Cut into squares and serve warm. Yield: 6 to 10 servings.

Wendelyn Stamer, Xi Beta Rho
Sparta, New Jersey

FIESTA BRUNCH EGGS

$\frac{1}{2}$ cup (1 stick) butter, softened
8 slices day-old bread
8 ounces shredded ham
8 ounces sharp Cheddar cheese, shredded (2 cups)
1 (4-ounce) can chopped green chiles, drained
6 eggs
2 cups half-and-half
1 cup milk
Cayenne pepper to taste
Dry mustard to taste
Onion powder to taste
$\frac{1}{2}$ teaspoon salt

Butter both sides of bread slices and cut into cubes. Layer bread cubes, ham, cheese and green chiles in a buttered 9×13-inch baking dish. Combine the eggs, half-and-half, milk, cayenne pepper, dry mustard, onion powder and salt in a mixing bowl and beat until smooth. Pour the egg mixture over the contents of the baking dish. Chill, covered, for 8 to 10 hours. Bake, uncovered, at 325 degrees for 45 minutes or until lightly browned. Yield: 8 to 10 servings.

Coriece Estes, Zeta Kappa
Roosevelt, Arizona

EGG POTATO BAKE

10 to 12 eggs, beaten
2 cups cottage cheese
8 ounces Cheddar cheese, shredded (2 cups)
1 (20-ounce) package frozen hash brown potatoes, thawed
8 to 10 dashes of Tabasco sauce
Salt and pepper to taste
Garlic salt to taste
1 pound bacon, cooked, not crisp

Combine the eggs, cottage cheese, Cheddar cheese, potatoes, Tabasco sauce, salt, pepper and garlic salt in a large bowl and mix well. Spoon into a buttered 9×13-inch baking dish. Chop the bacon and sprinkle over the top. Bake at 325 degrees in the prepared baking dish for $1\frac{1}{2}$ hours (bake at 350 degrees if the baking pan is metal). Yield: 10 to 12 servings.

Shauna Spees, Beta Upsilon
Medford, Oregon

Joan Skipper, Laureate Lambda, West Vancouver, British Columbia, Canada, makes **Scotch Eggs** *by peeling 12 hard-cooked eggs and rolling in flour to coat. She covers each egg with sausage to enclose completely. Dip each in an egg wash of 1 egg beaten with 1 tablesoon water and roll in fine bread crumbs to coat. Arrange in a shallow baking pan and bake at 350 degrees for 30 minutes or until sausage is cooked through. Drain on paper towels. Cut each egg lengthwise into quarters and arrange on a serving plate with honey mustard for dipping.*

SAVORY SPINACH MONTEREY BAKE

6 large eggs
2 cups low-fat milk
1/4 teaspoon each thyme, salt and pepper
Pinch of nutmeg
1 cup shredded Monterey Jack cheese
1 (10-ounce) package frozen spinach, thawed, squeezed dry
8 slices firm white bread, cut into 1-inch pieces

Combine the eggs, milk, thyme, salt, pepper and nutmeg in a large bowl and whisk until smooth. Stir in the cheese, spinach and bread pieces. Spoon the mixture into a buttered 9×13-inch baking dish. Bake at 375 degrees for 25 to 30 minutes or until browned and puffed and a knife inserted in the center comes out clean. Yield: 10 to 12 servings.

Dottie Hay, Iota Iota
Blairsville, Georgia

SPINACH QUICHE

1 dozen eggs, beaten
8 ounces Monterey Jack cheese, shredded (2 cups)
8 ounces Cheddar cheese, shredded (2 cups)
1 cup cottage cheese
1 teaspoon salt
1 teaspoon baking powder
1/4 cup flour
6 tablespoons butter
1 (10-ounce) package frozen spinach, thawed and drained
1 (4-ounce) can chopped green chiles, drained

Combine the first 7 ingredients in a large bowl and mix well. Melt 4 tablespoons of the butter and stir it into the egg mixture. Stir in the spinach and green chiles. Melt the remaining butter in a 9×13-inch baking dish, tilting to coat the bottom. Spoon the egg mixture into the dish. Bake at 450 degrees for 15 minutes. Reduce oven temperature to 350 degrees and bake for 20 to 30 minutes longer or until top is light brown and sides are bubbly. Let stand for 10 minutes before serving. Yield: 10 to 12 servings.

Mary Ann Fossen, Xi Delta
Ponca City, Oklahoma

Elizabeth Daley, Xi Delta Phi, Independence, Missouri, shares her grandmother's ***German Rice Pudding.*** *Cook 1/2 cup rice in 2 cups water until water is absorbed, stirring occasionally. Add 3 cups milk and simmer for 20 minutes, stirring occasionally. Stir in 1/4 cup sugar and 1/2 teaspoon salt. Cook for 20 minutes or until creamy. Add 1 teaspoon vanilla; pour into a baking dish. Sprinkle with 1/4 cup sugar and cinnamon to taste. Dot with butter and broil until butter melts.*

SPINACH CAKES

Use mushrooms and cauliflower in place of the spinach if you prefer.

1 (10-ounce) package frozen spinach
4 eggs, beaten
2 tablespoons Italian-style shredded cheese
1/2 teaspoon parsley flakes
1/8 teaspoon salt
Dash of pepper
1 tablespoon bread crumbs
Vegetable oil for frying

Cook the spinach using the package directions; drain very well. Combine the eggs, cheese, parsley, salt, pepper and bread crumbs in a large bowl and mix well. Stir in the spinach. Heat 1/4 inch vegetable oil in a skillet over medium heat. Pour the spinach mixture 1/4 cup at a time onto the skillet. Cook until brown on both sides, turning once. Serve hot. Yield: 3 servings.

Dorothy P. Wegmann, Preceptor Theta Xi
Wichita Falls, Texas

SWISS SPINACH QUICHE

1 (10-ounce) package frozen chopped spinach
6 large eggs, beaten
1 (5-ounce) can evaporated milk
1/3 cup shredded Parmesan cheese
1 cup shredded Swiss cheese
1 (4-ounce) can sliced mushrooms, drained (optional)
1 baked (9- or 10-inch) pie shell

Thaw the spinach and press to dry. Combine the eggs and evaporated milk in a large bowl and blend well. Stir in the spinach, Parmesan cheese, Swiss cheese and mushrooms. Pour the mixture into the pie shell. Cover the edge with foil to prevent burning and bake at 350 degrees for 45 to 50 minutes or until a knife inserted in the center comes out clean. Let stand for 5 minutes before serving. Yield: 6 to 8 servings.

Deb Patton, Xi Eta Sigma
Gowrie, Iowa

PIMENTO CHEESE SPREAD

Do not use preshredded cheese for this spread.

1 (10-ounce) can original tomatoes with green chiles, drained
1 cup mayonnaise
1 teaspoon Worcestershire sauce
1/2 teaspoon salt
1 (4-ounce) jar chopped pimentos, drained
16 ounces sharp Cheddar cheese, shredded (4 cups)

Combine the tomatoes with green chiles, mayonnaise, Worcestershire sauce and salt in a large bowl and mix well. Stir in the pimentos and cheese. Spread on seven-grain bread and serve. Yield: 2½ cups.

Edna Earle Raper, Xi Alpha Zeta
Wilson, North Carolina

✣ PECAN SANDWICH MIX

1 cup pecans
1 large onion
1 large green bell pepper
8 hard-cooked eggs
Salt and pepper to taste
Mayonnaise
2 large loaves sliced white bread, crusts trimmed

Put the pecans, onion, bell pepper and hard-cooked eggs through a food mill and place in a large bowl; mix well. Season with salt and pepper. Mix in enough mayonnaise to moisten. Chill, covered, until serving time. Make into sandwiches. Cut in thirds or halves. Yield: 3 to 4 cups.

Bonnie Pearson, Xi Delta Psi
Franklin, Tennessee

GRILLED MUSHROOM SANDWICHES

1 tablespoon butter or margarine
1 small onion, finely chopped
1 small garlic clove, minced
16 ounces fresh mushrooms, finely chopped
6 ounces cream cheese, softened
½ teaspoon salt
½ teaspoon Worcestershire sauce
Dash of pepper
12 slices bread

Melt the butter in a medium skillet over medium heat. Sauté the onion and garlic in the butter for 5 to 8 minutes or until onion is tender. Add the mushrooms and cook for 3 minutes or until tender. Remove from heat. Add the cream cheese, salt, Worcestershire sauce and pepper and mix until smooth. You may chill, covered, until serving time, but bring to room temperature before using. Spread ¼ cup mushroom mixture over 1 slice of bread and top with second slice. Butter the sandwich and grill until bread is golden. Yield: 6 servings.

Barbara Leber, Xi Epsilon Iota
Kirkwood, Missouri

APPLE ENCHILADAS

Great for a breakfast buffet.

1 (21-ounce) can apple pie filling
6 (8-inch) flour tortillas
1 teaspoon cinnamon
⅓ cup butter
½ cup sugar
½ cup firmly packed brown sugar

Spoon the filling evenly down the center of each tortilla. Sprinkle with cinnamon. Roll up and place seam side down in a lightly greased 2-quart baking dish. Combine the butter, sugar, brown sugar and ½ cup water in a saucepan over medium-high heat; bring to a boil. Reduce heat and simmer for 3 minutes, stirring constantly. Pour the sugar mixture evenly over the enchiladas. Let stand for 3 minutes and serve. Yield: 6 servings.

Jean C. Hove, Laureate Gamma Iota
Tallahassee, Florida

BRUNCH ENCHILADAS

2 (4-ounce) cans chopped green chiles, drained
4 cups shredded American cheese
3 cups (24 ounces) cottage cheese
1 garlic clove, minced
½ teaspoon salt
½ teaspoon pepper
12 corn tortillas
1 cup sour cream
1 (15-ounce) can enchilada sauce

Combine the green chiles, half the American cheese, cottage cheese, garlic, salt and pepper in a large bowl; mix well. Spoon 1 generous tablespoon of the cheese mixture in the center of each tortilla. Roll up and place seam side down in a 9×13-inch baking dish. Spoon the remaining cheese mixture over the center of each enchilada. Combine the sour cream and enchilada sauce in a bowl and mix well. Pour the sour cream mixture evenly over the enchiladas. Sprinkle with the remaining American cheese. Bake at 350 degrees for 25 to 30 minutes or until lightly browned and bubbly. Yield: 6 servings.

Carolyn J. Pock, Alpha Psi Master
Pensacola, Florida

BACON TOMATO PIE

3 medium tomatoes, cut into ¼-inch slices
1 baked (9-inch) deep-dish pie shell
10 slices bacon, crisp-cooked, crumbled
4 ounces Cheddar or Swiss cheese, shredded (1 cup)
1 cup real mayonnaise

Layer the tomato slices in the pie shell and sprinkle with bacon. Combine the cheese and mayonnaise in a bowl and mix well. Spoon the cheese mixture evenly over the bacon to within 1 inch of the pie's edge. Bake at 350 degrees for 30 to 40 minutes or until golden brown; cover edge with foil if necessary to prevent overbrowning. Yield: 6 servings.

Jean Kraft, Alpha Eta Master
New Albany, Indiana

BLENDER POTATO PANCAKES

2 eggs
1 small onion, quartered, or 1 tablespoon minced dried onion
1 teaspoon salt
3 tablespoons flour
1/4 cup milk
3 cups chopped peeled potatoes

Combine the eggs, onion, salt, flour and milk in a blender container and process until smooth. Add the potatoes and process briefly; do not overblend. Pour 1/2 cup at a time onto a hot, lightly greased griddle. Cook until brown on both sides, turning once. Drain on paper towels. Yield: 11 or 12 pancakes.

Bette Bartels, Laureate Beta Delta
Sierra Vista, Arizona

BREAKFAST PIZZA

1 pound bulk pork sausage
1 green bell pepper, chopped
1 small onion, chopped
1 (8-count) can crescent rolls
1 cup thawed frozen hash brown potatoes
5 eggs, beaten
1/4 cup milk
Salt and pepper to taste
1 cup shredded Cheddar cheese

Brown the sausage with the bell pepper and onion in a skillet, stirring until crumbly; drain. Unroll the dough and use to line a 12-inch pizza pan, pressing to fit and pushing up the side of the pan. Layer the sausage mixture and potatoes in the prepared pan. Combine the next 4 ingredients in a mixing bowl and blend well. Pour the egg mixture over the potato layer. Sprinkle with cheese. Bake at 350 degrees for 20 to 25 minutes or until browned. Yield: 6 servings.

LaVonna Phy, Theta Psi
Cookeville, Tennessee

HOMINY BAKE

1/2 cup chopped onion
1/2 cup chopped celery
2 teaspoons butter
2 (20-ounce) cans yellow hominy, drained
1/4 cup milk
1 (10-ounce) can cream of mushroom soup
1/2 cup shredded Cheddar cheese
1 1/2 cups bread crumbs

Sauté the onion and celery in the butter in a skillet over medium heat for 5 to 8 minutes or until tender. Combine the onion mixture, hominy, milk, soup and cheese in a large bowl and mix well. Spoon into a buttered 9×13-inch baking dish. Spread bread crumbs over the top. Bake at 350 degrees for 40 minutes or until hot and bubbly. Yield: 9 to 12 servings.

Barbara M. Stanphill, Alpha Kappa
Hope, Arkansas

CHEESE GRITS PUFF

For a fluffy soufflé, separate the eggs and beat the egg whites until stiff peaks form. Add the beaten egg yolks to the hot grits mixture and fold in the stiffly beaten egg whites.

2 teaspoons salt
2 cups uncooked grits
1 (6-ounce) roll nippy (sharp) cheese
1 (6-ounce) roll garlic cheese
1 cup melted butter
4 eggs, beaten
1/2 cup milk
Salt and pepper to taste

Place 7 cups water and the 2 teaspoons salt in a saucepan and bring to a boil. Add the grits. Reduce heat to low and simmer, covered, for 25 minutes or until thickened, stirring frequently. Cut the nippy cheese and garlic cheese into small cubes. Stir the cheese, butter, eggs, milk, salt and pepper into the hot grits. Pour into a 3-quart baking dish. Bake at 350 degrees for 1 hour or until puffed and brown.
Yield: 12 servings.

Jacquie Patterson, Preceptor Epsilon Omega
Joplin, Missouri

CHOCOLATE GRAVY

2 cups flour
3 1/2 cups sugar
1/2 cup baking cocoa
1/2 cup (1 stick) butter
2 tablespoons vanilla extract

Combine the flour, sugar and baking cocoa in a bowl and mix well. Bring 6 cups of water to a rapid boil in a saucepan over high heat. Pour the cocoa mixture into the boiling water and whisk well until thickened and smooth. Remove from heat. Add half the butter and the vanilla and stir to blend. Serve over biscuits with the remaining butter. Yield: 8 to 12 servings.

Jennifer Garner, Alpha Kappa
Hot Springs, Arkansas

Syble A. Lamons, Xi Mu, McCalla, Alabama, makes ***Crispy Sausage Grits*** *by browning and draining a pound of mild sausage. She cooks 3/4 cup grits with 2 1/2 cups salted water for 6 minutes and stirs in 6 tablespoons butter and a 4-ounce jar of cheese spread until melted. Beat 3 eggs with 1/2 cup milk; stir a small amount of the hot grits mixture into the eggs and eggs into the hot grits. Mix in the sausage and spoon into a greased casserole. Layer 1/2 cup shredded Cheddar cheese and a mixture of 1 cup crushed cornflakes and 1/2 cup melted butter on top. Bake at 350 degrees for 40 minutes.*

CHEESY GARLIC BISCUITS

2 cups baking mix
2/3 cup milk
1/2 cup shredded Cheddar cheese
1/4 cup butter, melted
1/4 teaspoon garlic powder

Combine the baking mix, milk, cheese, butter and garlic powder in a bowl and stir to make a soft dough. Beat vigorously, 30 strokes with a wooden spoon. Drop the dough by spoonfuls 2 inches apart on a buttered baking sheet. Bake at 450 degrees for 8 to 10 minutes or until golden brown.
Yield: 10 to 12 biscuits.

Louise Snyder, Chi Iota
Troy, Illinois

OVERNIGHT BUNS

Mix the dough at six p.m. Punch the dough down at seven p.m. Shape into balls, arrange on a baking sheet, cover with a tea towel, and let rise overnight. Bake in the morning!

1 tablespoon dry yeast
1 teaspoon sugar
1/2 cup lukewarm water
3 eggs, beaten
3/4 cup sugar
2 cups warm water
1/2 cup vegetable oil
1 teaspoon salt
8 to 9 cups flour

Dissolve the yeast and the 1 teaspoon sugar in 1/2 cup lukewarm water; let stand for about 10 minutes. Combine the eggs, the 3/4 cup sugar, 2 cups warm water, vegetable oil and salt in a large bowl and mix well. Add the yeast mixture and mix gently. Mix in 8 cups of the flour. Add enough of the remaining 1 cup flour to make the dough of the desired consistency. Let rise, covered, for 1 hour. Punch the dough down. Shape into 1 1/2-inch balls and arrange on greased baking sheets. Let rise, covered with a tea towel, in the refrigerator for 8 to 10 hours. Bake at 350 degrees for 15 to 20 minutes or until golden. Yield: 3 dozen.

Glenda Polis, Beta Phi
Westlock, Alberta, Canada

LEMON YOGURT SCONES

They're light and flaky and can be prepared very fast to make for company.

2 cups flour
2 tablespoons sugar
1 tablespoon baking powder
1/2 teaspoon baking soda
1/2 teaspoon salt
1/2 cup cold butter or margarine
1 cup plain yogurt
1 tablespoon grated lemon zest

Preheat the oven to 425 degrees. Sift the flour, sugar, baking powder, baking soda and salt together into a large bowl. Cut in the butter with 2 knives until crumbly. Combine the yogurt and lemon zest in a small bowl and mix well. Add the yogurt mixture to the flour mixture and stir just until moistened. Shape into a ball and place on a lightly floured surface. Flatten to 1-inch thickness. Cut with a floured biscuit cutter or water glass. Arrange on an ungreased baking sheet. Bake at 425 degrees for 12 to 14 minutes or until lightly browned. Yield: 12 servings.

Donna Osborne, Laureate Tau
Edmonton, Alberta, Canada

TEA BISCUITS

2 cups flour
3 teaspoons baking powder
3/4 teaspoon salt
2 teaspoons sugar
1/4 cup butter or margarine
1 cup milk

Combine the flour, baking powder, salt and sugar in a bowl and mix with a fork. Cut in the butter until mixture resembles coarse crumbs. Add the milk, stirring just enough to blend without overmixing. Roll to 1-inch thickness on a floured surface. Cut with a floured biscuit cutter. Arrange on a parchment paper-lined baking sheet; do not prick the dough. Bake at 435 degrees for about 12 minutes or until lightly browned. Yield: 1 dozen.

Dianne S. Hebb, Laureate Lambda
Lower Sackville, Nova Scotia, Canada

EASY CINNAMON ROLLS

2 cups flour
4 teaspoons baking powder
1 tablespoon granulated sugar
1/2 teaspoon salt
1/2 cup shortening
2/3 cup milk
3 tablespoons butter or margarine, softened
2 tablespoons cinnamon
4 tablespoons brown sugar

Combine the flour, baking powder, granulated sugar and salt in a bowl and mix well. Cut in the shortening until mixture resembles coarse crumbs. Add the milk and mix just until moistened. Place on a floured surface and knead 4 or 5 strokes. Pat or roll into a 1/4-inch-thick 8×10-inch rectangle. Spread with the butter and sprinkle with cinnamon and brown sugar. Roll as for a jelly roll. Cut into 1-inch slices and arrange in a 9×13-inch baking dish. Bake at 425 degrees for 12 to 15 minutes or until golden. Serve plain or with favorite frosting.
Yield: 12 or more servings.

Della Mae Warner, Preceptor Delta
Coffeyville, Kansas

DANISH PASTRY

2 cups flour
1 cup (2 sticks) butter
1 teaspoon almond extract
3 eggs
1/2 to 2/3 cup chopped walnuts or pecans

Combine 1 cup of the flour, 1/2 cup of the butter and 2 tablespoons water in a bowl and mix well. Divide the dough into halves. Roll each half into a 2×12-inch strip and place on an unbuttered baking sheet. Combine the remaining 1/2 cup butter and 1 cup water in a saucepan over high heat and bring to a rolling boil. Add the almond extract; remove from heat. Add the remaining 1 cup flour all at once, stirring quickly to prevent lumping. When smooth and thick, add the eggs 1 at a time, beating until smooth after each addition. Spread the egg mixture evenly over the dough strips. Bake at 325 degrees for 1 hour. Frost with a cream cheese frosting. Sprinkle with chopped nuts. Let cool. Slice and serve.
Yield: 20 to 24 pastries.

Phyllis Abbott, Preceptor Xi
Baxter Springs, Kansas

OLD-FASHIONED DOUGHNUTS

1/2 cup milk
1/2 cup granulated sugar
2 teaspoons baking powder
1/4 teaspoon nutmeg
1/2 teaspoon salt
1 tablespoon butter, melted
1 egg, beaten
1 3/4 cups (about) flour
Vegetable oil or shortening for deep-frying
Confectioners' sugar or granulated sugar for dusting

Combine the milk, granulated sugar, baking powder, nutmeg, salt, butter and egg in a large bowl and mix well. Mix in the flour gradually, adding enough to make a dough that is firm enough to handle yet as soft as possible. Chill, covered, for 1 hour. Knead on a lightly floured board for a few minutes. Roll 1/2 inch thick. Cut with a 3-inch doughnut cutter, saving the centers. Place on lightly floured waxed paper to rest for 5 minutes. Heat 4 inches of vegetable oil to 360 degrees in a heavy kettle over medium-high heat. Fry the doughnuts 3 or 4 at a time in the hot oil until brown on both sides, turning once. Fry the doughnut centers if desired. Drain on paper towels and dust with confectioners' sugar. Yield: 2 dozen.

Joycee Davis, Laureate Alpha Epsilon
Lowell, Arkansas

APPLE CAKE

4 apples, cored, peeled, sliced
1/2 teaspoon cinnamon
2 1/2 cups sugar
1 cup (2 sticks) butter, melted
4 eggs
3 cups flour
1 teaspoon baking powder
1/4 teaspoon salt
1/2 cup orange juice

Combine the apples, cinnamon and 1/2 cup of the sugar in a large bowl and toss to coat. Combine the butter and the remaining 2 cups sugar in a separate bowl and mix well. Mix in the eggs. Stir in a mixture of the flour, baking powder and salt. Stir in the egg mixture. Stir in the orange juice. Layer the orange juice mixture and sliced apples alternately in a buttered bundt pan, ending with a layer of apples. Bake

at 350 degrees for 50 minutes to 1 hour or until the cake pulls away from the side of the pan.
Yield: 16 servings.

Bonnie Davis, Nu Epsilon
New Port Richey, Florida

APPLE KUCHEN

1 (2-layer) golden cake mix
1/2 cup (1 stick) butter, softened
1/2 cup shredded coconut
1 (21-ounce) can apple pie filling
1/4 cup sugar
1 teaspoon cinnamon
1 cup sour cream
1 egg

Place the dry cake mix in a large bowl. Cut the butter into the cake mix with a pastry blender. Stir in the coconut. Press into a 9×13-inch baking dish. Bake at 350 degrees for 10 minutes. Remove from oven. Layer the apple pie filling over the cake layer. Sprinkle with a mixture of the sugar and cinnamon. Drizzle with a mixture of the sour cream and egg. Bake for 20 to 25 minutes longer. Serve warm.
Yield: 12 servings.

Donna Vanden Bergh, Alpha Pi Master
Newmarket, Ontario, Canada

RASPBERRY COFFEE CAKE

1 cup flour
1/3 cup granulated sugar
1/2 teaspoon baking powder
1/4 teaspoon baking soda
1/4 teaspoon salt
1 egg, beaten
2 tablespoons margarine, melted
1/2 cup plain yogurt
1 teaspoon vanilla extract
3 tablespoons brown sugar
1 cup unsweetened fresh or frozen raspberries
Sliced almonds

Combine the flour, granulated sugar, baking powder, baking soda and salt in a large bowl and mix well. Combine the egg, margarine, yogurt and vanilla in a small bowl and blend well. Add the egg mixture to the dry ingredients and stir just until moistened. Spoon 2/3 of the batter into a buttered 8-inch cake pan. Layer a mixture of the brown sugar and raspberries over the top. Spoon the remaining batter over the raspberry layer. Sprinkle with almonds. Bake at 350 degrees for 35 to 40 minutes or until the cake tests done. Drizzle with a glaze made of 1/4 cup confectioners' sugar, 1 teaspoon milk and 1/4 teaspoon vanilla. Yield: 8 servings.

Sharon Mashek, Beta Delta
Spillville, Iowa

✣ APRICOT COCONUT COFFEE CAKE

1/2 cup (1 stick) butter, softened
8 ounces cream cheese, softened
1 1/4 cups granulated sugar
2 eggs
1/4 cup milk
1 teaspoon vanilla extract
2 cups flour
1 teaspoon baking powder
1/2 teaspoon baking soda
1/4 teaspoon salt
1 (12-ounce) can apricot pie filling
1/2 cup (1 stick) butter, softened
2/3 cup packed brown sugar
1 teaspoon cinnamon
2 cups flaked coconut

Cream 1/2 cup butter, cream cheese and sugar in a mixing bowl until light and fluffy. Add the eggs 1 at a time, mixing well after each addition. Beat in the milk and vanilla. Mix the flour, baking powder, baking soda and salt together. Add the flour mixture to the cream cheese mixture and beat just until moistened. Spread half the batter in a buttered 9×13-inch baking dish. Spread the pie filling carefully over the batter; spread the remaining batter over the top. Bake at 350 degrees for 35 to 40 minutes or until golden brown. Combine the remaining 1/2 cup butter, brown sugar and cinnamon in a medium bowl and blend well. Stir in the coconut. Spoon the coconut mixture evenly over the cooled cake. Broil 4 inches from the heat source for 1 to 2 minutes or until coconut layer is golden brown. Cool in the pan on a wire rack.
Yield: 12 to 15 servings.

Joyce Boor, Theta Master
Great Bend, Kansas

BLUEBERRY MUFFINS

1 1/2 cups flour
3/4 teaspoon salt
1/2 teaspoon baking soda
1 cup sugar
2 eggs, well beaten
1/2 cup vegetable oil
1/2 teaspoon vanilla extract
1/8 teaspoon almond extract
1 1/4 cups fresh blueberries

Combine the flour, salt, baking soda and sugar in a large bowl and mix well. Make a well in the center of the dry ingredients and add the eggs, vegetable oil and vanilla and almond extracts; stir just until moistened. Stir in the blueberries gently. Fill buttered muffin cups 2/3 full. Bake at 350 degrees for 20 to 25 minutes or until golden brown. Yield: 12 muffins.

Janet Walker, Xi Beta Epsilon
Woodward, Oklahoma

BANANA MUFFINS

1/2 cup (1 stick) butter or shortening
1/2 cup sugar
2 eggs
1 cup mashed ripe banana
1 teaspoon baking soda
1 cup flour
1/2 teaspoon salt
1 cup granola
1/2 cup chocolate chips or walnuts or both

Cream the butter and sugar in a large mixing bowl until light and fluffy. Beat in the eggs. Mix in the banana. Dissolve the baking soda in 3 tablespoons hot water and stir into the banana mixture; mixture will be lumpy. Stir in the flour and salt. Stir in the granola and chocolate chips. Fill muffin cups 2/3 full. Bake at 350 degrees for 20 minutes or until muffins test done. Yield: 12 muffins.

Laurel Pethick, Beta Eta
Meadow Lake, Saskatchewan, Canada

BRAN MUFFINS

1 cup flour
1/4 cup sugar
3 teaspoons baking powder
1 1/4 cups All-Bran
1 cup milk
1/4 cup molasses
3/4 cup raisins, chocolate chips or nuts
1 egg

Combine the flour, sugar and baking powder in a bowl and mix well. Combine the All-Bran, milk, molasses, raisins and egg in a separate bowl and mix well; let stand for 10 minutes. Add the All-Bran mixture to the flour mixture and stir just until moistened. Fill lightly buttered muffin cups 2/3 full. Bake at 350 degrees for 20 minutes or until muffins test done.
Yield: 12 muffins.

Val Spear, Epsilon Sigma
South Mountain, Ontario, Canada

BIG BATCH BRAN MUFFINS

The batter may be kept in the refrigerator for up to 1 month before baking.

1 (17-ounce) can sliced peaches
3 cups sugar
1 cup canola oil
4 large eggs
1 tablespoon plus 2 teaspoons baking soda
1 tablespoon plus 1 teaspoon cinnamon
2 teaspoons salt
5 cups flour
1 quart buttermilk
1 (15-ounce) package Raisin Bran
1 cup chopped pecans

Purée the undrained peaches in a blender. Combine the peach purée, sugar, canola oil, eggs, baking soda, cinnamon, salt, flour, buttermilk and Raisin Bran in a large mixing bowl; beat at medium speed for 2 minutes. Stir in the pecans. Fill lightly buttered or paper-lined muffin cups 2/3 full. Bake at 400 degrees for 16 to 18 minutes or until muffins test done. Remove from muffin cups immediately.
Yield: about 4 1/2 dozen.

Jeanette E. Felger, Iota Master
New Braunfels, Texas

CRANBERRY ORANGE MUFFINS

Blueberries, rhubarb, apples, raspberries, or other fruit may be substituted for the cranberries, and you may use lemon zest instead of orange.

1 3/4 cups flour
2/3 cup packed brown sugar
1 tablespoon baking powder
Grated zest of 1 orange
1 1/2 cups fresh or frozen cranberries
1 cup milk
2 eggs, beaten
3 tablespoons melted butter or vegetable oil
1 teaspoon vanilla extract

Combine the flour, brown sugar, baking powder and orange zest in a large bowl and mix well. Sprinkle the cranberries over the dry ingredients and stir together gently. Combine the milk, eggs, butter and vanilla in a separate bowl and whisk to blend. Pour the egg mixture over the dry ingredients and stir until moistened. Fill muffin cups 2/3 full. Bake at 400 degrees for 20 to 25 minutes or until muffins test done.
Yield: 12 muffins.

June Bean, Beta Master
Courtenay, British Columbia, Canada

GINGER MUFFINS

1/4 cup shortening
1/4 cup sugar
1 egg
1/2 cup molasses
1 1/2 cups sifted flour
3/4 teaspoon baking soda
1/4 teaspoon salt
1/2 teaspoon cinnamon
1/2 teaspoon ginger
1/4 teaspoon ground cloves

Cream the shortening and sugar in a mixing bowl until light and fluffy. Beat in the egg and molasses; mix well. Sift the flour, baking soda, salt, cinnamon, ginger and cloves into a bowl. Stir the flour mixture into the molasses mixture. Add 1/2 cup hot tap water gradually, beating until smooth. Fill buttered muffin cups 2/3 full. Bake at 375 degrees for 20 to 25 minutes or until muffins test done. Serve warm with a pat of butter. Yield: 1 dozen.

Kathi Maxson, Kappa Mu
Westminster, Colorado

SUGARLESS PINEAPPLE MUFFINS

1/2 cup (1 stick) butter, softened
3 eggs
1 cup pineapple juice
1 teaspoon lemon juice
2 1/2 cups flour
1 teaspoon baking soda
2 teaspoons baking powder
1/2 teaspoon salt
1 cup well-drained crushed pineapple
Cream Cheese Pineapple Frosting
1/2 cup ground pecans

Combine the butter and eggs in a mixing bowl and beat until light and smooth. Add the pineapple juice and lemon juice; mix well. Add a mixture of the flour, baking soda, baking powder and salt; beat until smooth. Stir in the pineapple. Fill 14 paper-lined muffin cups 2/3 full. Bake at 350 degrees for 20 minutes or until muffins test done. Let cool. Frost with Cream Cheese Pineapple Frosting and sprinkle with pecans. Yield: 14 muffins.

CREAM CHEESE PINEAPPLE FROSTING

8 ounces cream cheese, softened
2 tablespoons butter, softened
2 tablespoons well-drained crushed pineapple

Combine the cream cheese and butter in a mixing bowl and beat until smooth. Stir in the pineapple.

Patty Dahlman, Preceptor Epsilon
Dalton Gardens, Idaho

SPICED YAM MUFFINS

1/3 cup butter, softened
1 cup sugar
1 cup mashed canned yams
1 egg
1 cup sifted flour
3/4 teaspoon cinnamon
3/4 teaspoon nutmeg
1/4 teaspoon allspice
1/4 teaspoon ground cloves
1/4 teaspoon salt
1/2 teaspoon baking powder
1/2 teaspoon baking soda
1/3 cup buttermilk
1/2 cup raisins
1/2 cup chopped pecans

Cream the butter and sugar in a mixing bowl until light and fluffy. Beat in the yams and egg. Add a mixture of the flour, cinnamon, nutmeg, allspice, cloves, salt, baking powder and baking soda to the yam mixture and beat at medium speed until smooth. Blend in the buttermilk. Stir in the raisins and pecans. Fill muffin cups that have been sprayed with nonstick cooking spray 2/3 full. Bake at 350 degrees for 25 to 30 minutes or until muffins test done. Yield: 18 muffins.

Carole S. Knapp, Preceptor Omega
Beaufort, South Carolina

MINIATURE PECAN PIE MUFFINS

1 cup packed light brown sugar
1/2 cup flour
2 eggs
2/3 cup (1 1/3 sticks) butter, melted
1 cup chopped pecans
2 1/2 to 3 dozen pecan halves

Combine the brown sugar, flour, eggs, butter and pecans in a bowl; mix well with a wooden spoon. Fill buttered miniature muffin cups 2/3 full. Top each muffin with a pecan half. Bake at 350 degrees for 12 to 15 minutes or until golden brown.
Yield: 2 1/2 to 3 dozen.

Joan Herman, Xi Alpha Omega
Gilbertsville, Kentucky

OVERNIGHT APPLE FRENCH TOAST

Texas Toast can be found in the frozen food section of many supermarkets.

1 cup packed brown sugar
1/2 cup margarine
2 tablespoons corn syrup
2 or 3 large apples, peeled and sliced
2 teaspoons cinnamon
3 eggs
1 cup milk
1 teaspoon vanilla extract
7 to 9 slices Texas Toast

Combine the brown sugar, margarine and corn syrup in a small saucepan over medium-low heat. Cook until thickened, about 7 to 10 minutes, stirring constantly. Pour immediately into an unbuttered 9×13-inch baking dish and spread evenly across the bottom of the pan. Layer the apple slices over the top. Sprinkle with cinnamon. Combine the eggs, milk and vanilla in a bowl and blend well. Dip the Texas Toast slices in the egg mixture and place in a single layer over the apples. Chill, covered, for 8 to 10 hours. Remove from the refrigerator 30 minutes before baking. Bake, uncovered, at 350 degrees for 35 to 40 minutes or until a knife inserted in the center comes out clean. Yield: 4 or 5 servings

Tracy Wilson, Xi Beta
Regina, Saskatchewan, Canada

Ruth Edwards, Preceptor Beta Tau, King City, Oregon, makes ***Cottage Cheese Pancakes*** *by combining 1 cup cottage cheese, 4 eggs, 1/4 cup flour and a pinch of salt, if desired, in a blender and pulsing just until mixed. Add a small amount of additional flour if necessary and process to desired consistency. Ladle onto a hot lightly greased skillet or griddle and brown lightly on both sides, turning once.*

FRENCH APPLE PANCAKES

3/4 cup flour
1/2 teaspoon salt
2 tablespoons sugar
1 teaspoon baking powder
2 eggs, beaten
2/3 cup milk
1/2 teaspoon grated lemon zest
3 apples, peeled, very finely chopped

Sift the flour, salt, sugar and baking powder into a bowl. Add the eggs, milk, 1/3 cup water and lemon zest to make a thin batter; beat until smooth. Sauté the apples briefly in butter in a skillet over medium heat. Ladle the pancake batter 1/4 cup at a time into a hot, lightly buttered iron skillet. When the underside is golden brown, spread a layer of apple over the pancake. Turn the pancake and brown on the apple side. Dust with confectioners' sugar. Serve hot.
Yield: 8 to 12 medium pancakes.

Della Garrett
Brandon, Florida

STUFFED FRENCH TOAST

1 loaf fresh French bread
8 ounces cream cheese with pineapple, softened
1/2 cup chopped pecans
4 large eggs, beaten
1 cup heavy cream
1/2 teaspoon vanilla extract
1 teaspoon ginger
1/2 cup orange juice
1 (12-ounce) jar apricot preserves

Cut the bread into 1 1/2-inch-thick slices. Cut a slit in each slice to make a pocket. Combine the cream cheese and pecans in a small bowl and beat well with a wooden spoon. Stuff the pocket of each bread slice with cream cheese mixture. Combine the eggs, cream, vanilla and ginger in a large bowl and whisk until smooth. Dip each stuffed bread slice in the egg mixture and cook on a hot, lightly buttered griddle until golden brown on both sides, turning once. Combine the orange juice and apricot preserves in a small saucepan over low heat. Cook until melted, stirring to blend. Drizzle over the French toast and serve. Yield: 8 to 10 servings.

Nita Ivey, Xi Beta Phi
Birmingham, Alabama

OVERNIGHT STICKY FRENCH TOAST

1 loaf French bread
3 eggs, beaten
1 cup half-and-half
1 teaspoon vanilla extract
2 to 3 tablespoons sugar
1/2 cup melted butter
1/2 cup maple syrup
1/2 cup chopped walnuts or pecans

Cut the bread into 3/4-inch slices. Combine the eggs, half-and-half, vanilla and sugar in a mixing bowl and beat until smooth. Combine the butter, syrup and walnuts in a separate bowl and mix well. Spread the walnut mixture evenly over a baking sheet. Dip the bread slices in the half-and-half mixture and arrange over the coated baking sheet. Let stand, covered, in the refrigerator for 8 to 10 hours. Bake at 350 degrees for 30 minutes or until golden. Yield: variable.

Rose Gundy, Preceptor Rho
Pasco, Washington

CRANBERRY APPLE FRENCH TOAST

1 cup packed brown sugar
1/2 cup (1 stick) butter, melted
3 teaspoons cinnamon
3 tart apples, peeled, thinly sliced
1/2 cup dried cranberries
1 baguette, cut into 1-inch slices
6 large eggs
1 1/3 cups milk
1 tablespoon vanilla extract

Place the brown sugar, butter and 1 teaspoon of the cinnamon in a 9×13-inch baking dish; stir to combine. Add the apples and cranberries and toss to coat. Spread the apple mixture evenly over the bottom of the dish. Place the baguette slices over the apple layer. Combine the eggs, milk, vanilla and the remaining 2 teaspoons cinnamon in a bowl; mix until smooth. Pour the egg mixture evenly over the bread. Chill, covered, for 4 to 24 hours. Bake, covered with foil, at 375 degrees for 40 minutes. Remove the foil and bake for 5 minutes longer or until light brown. Let stand for 5 minutes before serving.
Yield: 8 servings.

Shelly Benzon, Laureate Epsilon Phi
Danville, California

OLD-FASHIONED BUCKWHEAT CAKES

1 envelope dry yeast
2 cups buckwheat flour
1 cup all-purpose flour, sifted
1 teaspoon salt
1 teaspoon baking soda
1 tablespoon molasses or brown sugar
1/4 cup butter, melted

Dissolve the yeast in 1/2 cup warm water in a bowl. Stir in 2 cups cold water. Sift the buckwheat flour and all-purpose flour together into the bowl. Stir in the salt. Beat vigorously until smooth. Chill, covered, for 8 to 10 hours. Dissolve the baking soda in 1/2 cup hot water. Stir the molasses, butter and baking soda mixture into the batter. Let stand at room temperature for 30 minutes. Pour 1/4 cup at a time onto a hot, lightly buttered griddle. Cook until brown on both sides, turning once. Yield: 3 dozen 4-inch pancakes.

Judy Livingston, Xi Epsilon Alpha
Paonia, Colorado

More Breads

BEER CORN BREAD

1 cup yellow cornmeal
1 cup flour
1/2 teaspoon salt
1/2 cup corn kernels (canned and drained or frozen and thawed)
2 tablespoons chopped green onions
1/4 cup sugar
4 teaspoons baking powder
1/2 cup milk
1/2 cup lager beer
1 tablespoon butter
1/2 cup shredded Cheddar cheese
1 egg, beaten with a fork

Combine the cornmeal, flour, salt, corn kernels, green onions, sugar and baking powder in a medium mixing bowl; mix well. Stir in the milk, beer, butter, cheese and egg; mix well. Pour into a greased 8×8-inch baking pan. Bake at 425 degrees for 20 minutes or until golden brown. Yield: 6 to 8 servings.

Verlyne Wilson, Xi Tau Delta
Vacaville, California

LIGHT CORN BREAD

2 cups cornmeal
1/2 cup sugar
1 cup flour
1 1/2 teaspoons salt
1 teaspoon baking soda
2 tablespoons melted shortening
2 cups buttermilk

Combine the cornmeal, sugar, flour, salt and baking soda in a bowl and mix well. Stir the shortening and buttermilk into the dry ingredients. Pour into a loaf pan and bake at 350 degrees for 1 hour.
Yield: about 12 servings.

Doris Rushing, Zeta Alpha
Marion, Kentucky

BUTTERMILK CORN BREAD

1 cup flour
1 cup cornmeal
1/2 cup sugar
4 teaspoons baking powder
1 teaspoon salt
2 eggs
3/4 cup buttermilk
1 (8-ounce) can cream-style corn

Combine the flour, cornmeal, sugar, baking powder and salt in a bowl and mix well. Add the eggs, buttermilk and corn and mix well. Pour into a buttered square or round 9-inch baking pan. Bake at 425 degrees for 25 minutes or until a wooden pick inserted in the center comes out clean.
Yield: 8 servings.

Tricia Evans, Laureate Alpha
Lebanon, Oregon

DELICIOUS APPLE CINNAMON BREAD

3 eggs
2 cups sugar
1 cup vegetable oil
1 tablespoon vanilla extract
2 cups flour
1 teaspoon baking soda
1 teaspoon cinnamon
4 cups chopped peeled apples
1 cup chopped pecans or walnuts (optional)

Combine the eggs, sugar, vegetable oil and vanilla in a large mixing bowl and mix well. Sift the flour, baking soda and cinnamon into the bowl; beat until smooth. Stir in the apples and pecans. Pour into a 5×9-inch loaf pan. Bake at 350 degrees for 70 minutes. Cool in the pan. Remove from the pan when cooled completely. Yield: 1 loaf.

Becky Jones, Laureate Epsilon Gamma
Queen City, Missouri

TANGY APRICOT BREAD

8 ounces dried apricots
1/2 cup chopped pecans
2 cups flour
1 cup sugar
2 tablespoons butter or margarine, softened
1 egg, beaten
2 teaspoons baking powder
1/4 teaspoon baking soda
1/4 teaspoon salt
1/2 cup orange juice

Soak the apricots in warm water for 30 minutes; drain well and cut into 1/4-inch pieces. Coat a mixture of the apricots and pecans with 1/4 cup of the flour; set aside. Combine the sugar and butter in a bowl and mix well. Beat in the egg. Place the remaining 1 3/4 cups flour, baking powder, baking soda and salt in a bowl and stir to combine. Add to the creamed mixture alternately with a mixture of the orange juice and 1/4 cup water, beginning and ending with flour mixture and mixing lightly after each addition. Stir in the apricot mixture. Spoon into a waxed paper-lined and greased 5×9-inch loaf pan. Let stand at room temperature for 20 minutes. Bake at 350 degrees for 1 hour or until a wooden pick inserted in the center comes out clean. Remove to a wire rack to cool. Yield: 1 loaf.

Frances Parks, Alpha Sigma Master
Saint Charles, Missouri

BANANA NUT BREAD

3/4 cup (1 1/2 sticks) butter, softened
1 1/2 cups sugar
3 soft bananas
1 teaspoon vanilla extract
2 eggs, well beaten
1 teaspoon baking soda
3/4 teaspoon salt
2 cups flour
1/2 cup buttermilk
3/4 cup chopped pecans

Cream the butter and sugar in a mixing bowl until light and fluffy. Beat in the bananas. Beat in the next 4 ingredients. Add the flour and buttermilk; stir until well mixed. Stir in the pecans. Spoon into a 5×9-inch loaf pan. Bake at 325 degrees for 1 hour and 15 minutes or until the bread tests done. Yield: 12 to 16 slices.

Verian Duggin, Laureate Alpha Iota
Bel Aire, Kansas

BANANA BREAD

5 tablespoons butter
1/2 cup granulated sugar
1/2 cup packed brown sugar
2 eggs
1 teaspoon vanilla extract
1 1/2 cups mashed bananas
1 3/4 cups flour
1 teaspoon baking soda
1/2 teaspoon salt
1/4 teaspoon baking powder
1/2 cup heavy cream or milk
1/3 cup chopped walnuts (optional)

Cream the butter and sugars in a medium mixing bowl until light and fluffy. Beat in the eggs and vanilla. Add the bananas and beat at high speed for 30 seconds. Place the flour, baking soda, salt and baking powder in a small bowl and stir to combine. Add to the creamed mixture alternately with the cream, ending with flour mixture and mixing lightly after each addition. Add the walnuts and mix well. Spoon into a 5×9-inch loaf pan that has been sprayed with nonstick cooking spray. Bake at 350 degrees for 1 hour and 15 minutes or until a wooden pick inserted in the center comes out clean. Cool in the pan for 10 minutes. Remove to a wire rack to cool completely. Yield: 1 loaf.

Maurene Humphrey, Xi Beta Pi
Post Falls, Idaho

BOSTON BROWN BREAD

1 1/2 cups raisins
2 rounded teaspoons baking soda
1/4 cup margarine, softened
2 cups sugar
2 eggs, well beaten
4 cups flour
1 teaspoon vanilla extract
1/2 cup chopped walnuts or pecans (optional)

Place the raisins in a large bowl and toss with the baking soda. Pour 2 cups boiling water over the raisin mixture. Let stand until cooled completely. Combine the margarine, sugar and eggs in a bowl and mix well. Stir the egg mixture into the raisin mixture. Stir in the flour, vanilla and walnuts. Fill three greased 1-pound coffee cans 1/2 full. Bake at 350 degrees for 1 hour. Cool in the coffee cans. Serve with butter or cream cheese. Yield: 3 loaves.

Erma Braswell, Laureate Alpha Eta
Sikeston, Missouri

BUTTER PECAN NUT BREAD

Make two at a time—this delicious bread freezes well.

1 (2-layer) package butter pecan cake mix
1 (4-ounce) package coconut instant pudding mix
1 cup vegetable oil
4 eggs, beaten
1 cup chopped pecans

Combine the dry cake mix, dry pudding mix, vegetable oil, eggs and 1 cup hot water in a large bowl and mix well. Stir in the pecans. Pour into two 5×9-inch loaf pans. Bake at 325 degrees for 45 minutes or until the bread tests done. Yield: 2 loaves.

Louise U. Redding, Laureate Sigma
Asheboro, North Carolina

SAVORY CHEESE BREAD

2 cups flour
4 teaspoons baking powder
1 tablespoon sugar
1/2 teaspoon onion salt
1/2 teaspoon crushed oregano
1/4 teaspoon dry mustard
1/4 cup shredded Cheddar cheese
1 egg, well beaten
1 cup milk
1 tablespoon melted butter

Combine the flour, baking powder, sugar, onion salt, oregano, dry mustard and cheese in a large bowl and mix well. Combine the egg, milk and butter in a separate bowl and beat until smooth. Add the egg mixture all at once to the dry ingredients; stir just until moistened. Spread the batter in a buttered loaf pan. Bake at 350 degrees for 45 minutes or until the bread tests done. Yield: 1 loaf.

Jacquie Forbes, Xi Delta
Portage La Prairie, Manitoba, Canada

COTTAGE CHEESE LOAF

6 eggs, beaten
1 cup chopped onion
1 cup margarine, softened
4 cups cottage cheese
1 envelope onion soup mix
6 cups Special-K
1/2 cup chopped walnuts or pecans

Combine the eggs, onion, margarine, cottage cheese, dry soup mix, Special-K and walnuts in a large bowl and mix well. Pour into a buttered loaf pan. Bake at 350 degrees for 1 hour. Yield: 20 to 24 servings.

Mickey Thaxton, Preceptor Gamma Phi
Anna, Texas

CRANBERRY PUMPKIN BREAD

1 cup canned or cooked pumpkin
1 cup sugar
1/2 cup milk
2 eggs
1/4 cup margarine, melted
2 teaspoons baking powder
2 cups flour
1 teaspoon cinnamon
1/2 teaspoon baking soda
1/2 teaspoon nutmeg
1/2 teaspoon ginger
1 cup chopped walnuts
1 cup fresh or frozen cranberries

Combine the pumpkin, sugar, milk, eggs and margarine in a large mixing bowl; beat until smooth. Combine the baking powder, flour, cinnamon, baking soda, nutmeg and ginger in a separate bowl and mix well. Stir the dry ingredients into the pumpkin mixture. Fold in the walnuts and cranberries. Pour into 2 buttered loaf pans. Bake at 350 degrees for 70 minutes or until a wooden pick inserted in the center comes out clean. Cool in the pan for 10 minutes. Remove to a wire rack to cool completely before placing in plastic bags. Yield: 1 loaf.

Julia Gatsos, Laureate Beta Omicron
New Albany, Indiana

IRISH SODA BREAD

3 1/2 cups flour
2/3 cup sugar
1 teaspoon salt
1 tablespoon baking powder
1 teaspoon baking soda
1 1/2 cups seedless raisins
2 tablespoons caraway seeds
2 eggs, lightly beaten
1 1/2 cups buttermilk
2 tablespoons melted butter

Sift the flour, sugar, salt, baking powder and baking soda into a bowl. Add the raisins and caraway seeds and mix well. Combine the eggs, buttermilk and butter in a separate bowl and mix until smooth. Add the egg mixture to the flour mixture and mix lightly to moisten. Pour into a buttered loaf pan. Bake at 375 degrees for 50 minutes or until the bread tests done. Yield: 1 loaf.

Kay Howkins, Preceptor Theta Zeta
Cocoa Beach, Florida

NUTTY SEED BREAD

This delectable wholesome bread freezes well. It's great to take along as a pick-me-up on hiking trips.

1 egg
1 cup buttermilk
1/3 cup canola oil
1 cup all-purpose flour
1 cup whole wheat flour
1 cup packed brown sugar
1/3 cup finely chopped walnuts or pecans
2 tablespoons wheat germ
2 tablespoons flax seeds
2 tablespoons sesame seeds
2 tablespoons sunflower seeds
2 tablespoons poppy seeds

Combine the egg, buttermilk and canola oil in a large mixing bowl and mix well. Combine the all-purpose flour, whole wheat flour, brown sugar, walnuts, wheat germ, flax seeds, sesame seeds, sunflower seeds and poppy seeds in a separate bowl and mix well. Add the dry ingredients to the buttermilk mixture and stir just until moistened. Spread in a buttered 5x9-inch loaf pan. Bake at 350 degrees for 50 to 60 minutes or until the bread tests done. Cool in the pan for 10 minutes. Remove to a wire rack to cool completely. Yield: 1 loaf.

Ellen Ouellette, Xi Alpha Epsilon
Courtenay, British Columbia, Canada

✣ JALAPENO PULL-APART BREAD

2 (4-ounce) cans chopped jalapeño peppers
2 bunches green onions, chopped
1 cup shredded Cheddar cheese
1 cup shredded Swiss cheese
2 (10-count) cans biscuits
1/2 cup (1 stick) butter or margarine, melted
1 cup shredded Monterey Jack cheese

Sauté the jalapeños and green onions in hot oil in a skillet over medium heat for 5 minutes or until tender. Mix the Cheddar cheese and Swiss cheese together in a bowl. Separate the biscuits and cut into quarters. Spray a bundt pan with nonstick cooking spray. Dip the biscuit quarters in melted butter and layer alternately with the jalapeño mixture and cheese mixture, beginning and ending with a layer of biscuits. There should be 3 layers of biscuits and 2 layers of mixed cheese. Bake at 350 degrees for 30 to 35 minutes or until golden brown.
Yield: 12 servings.

Karen Stowers, Xi Alpha Sigma
Amarillo, Texas

LEMON YOGURT BREAD

3 eggs
1 cup vegetable oil
2 1/4 cups sugar
3 cups (24 ounces) lemon yogurt
1 tablespoon lemon extract
3 cups flour
1/2 teaspoon baking powder
1 teaspoon baking soda
1/4 cup lemon juice
Orange Butter

Combine the eggs, vegetable oil, 1 3/4 cups of the sugar, yogurt and lemon extract in a large bowl and mix well. Stir in a mixture of the flour, baking powder and baking soda; beat until smooth. Spray three 5×9-inch loaf pans or 1 bundt pan with nonstick cooking spray and sprinkle with sugar. Pour the batter into the prepared pans. Bake at 350 degrees for 45 to 60 minutes or until a wooden pick inserted in the center comes out clean. Drizzle a mixture of the lemon juice and the remaining 1/2 cup sugar over the warm bread. Serve with Orange Butter.
Yield: 3 loaves.

ORANGE BUTTER

1/2 cup (1 stick) butter, softened
3 ounces cream cheese, softened
2 tablespoons grated orange zest
1 tablespoon frozen orange juice concentrate

Combine the butter, cream cheese, orange zest and orange juice concentrate in a small mixing bowl and beat until smooth. Chill, covered, until ready to use.

Marna Frick, Xi Chi
Watford City, North Dakota

POPPY SEED BREAD

2 1/4 cups sugar
1 cup plus 2 tablespoons vegetable oil
3 eggs
3 cups flour
1 1/2 teaspoons salt
1 1/2 teaspoons baking powder
1 1/2 cups milk
1 1/2 teaspoons vanilla extract
1 1/2 teaspoons butter flavoring
1 1/2 teaspoons almond extract
3 tablespoons poppy seeds
Almond Orange Glaze

Combine the sugar, vegetable oil and eggs in a mixing bowl and beat until smooth. Sift the flour, salt and baking powder into the sugar mixture and mix well. Combine the milk, vanilla, butter flavoring and almond extract in a separate bowl and mix well. Add the milk mixture to the flour mixture gradually. Stir in the poppy seeds. Pour into 2 buttered loaf pans. Bake at 350 degrees for 55 to 60 minutes or until a wooden pick inserted in the center comes out clean. Cool in the pan for 5 minutes. Drizzle Almond Orange Glaze over the bread and cool in the pan for 5 minutes longer. Remove to a wire rack to cool completely. This bread freezes well. Yield: 2 loaves.

ALMOND ORANGE GLAZE

1/4 cup orange juice
1/2 teaspoon vanilla extract
1/2 teaspoon butter flavoring
1/2 teaspoon almond extract
3/4 cup sugar

Combine all the ingredients in a bowl and mix until smooth.

Brenda Staggenborg, Preceptor Zeta
Marysville, Kansas

PISTACHIO CHRISTMAS NUT BREAD

1 (2-layer) package yellow cake mix (without pudding)
1 (4-ounce) package pistachio instant pudding mix
4 eggs
1/4 cup vegetable oil
1 cup sour cream
3/4 cup maraschino cherries, minced
1/2 cup chopped walnuts
2 to 4 drops of green food coloring
1/4 cup sugar
1 tablespoon cinnamon

Combine the dry cake mix, dry pudding mix, eggs, vegetable oil, 1/2 cup water, sour cream, cherries, walnuts and food coloring in a large bowl; mix well with a wooden spoon. Butter 2 loaf pans. Dust the bottoms of the pans with a mixture of the sugar and cinnamon, reserving the remaining mixture for the tops of the loaves. Pour the batter into the prepared pans and sprinkle with cinnamon mixture. Bake at 350 degrees for 45 minutes or until the bread tests done. Let cool. Chill, wrapped in foil, until serving time. This bread freezes well. Yield: 20 slices.

LouAnn Rochford, Xi Alpha Sigma
North Platte, Nebraska

PEANUT BUTTER BREAD

2 cups flour, sifted
4 teaspoons baking powder
1 teaspoon salt
2/3 cup peanut butter
1/2 cup sugar
1 cup milk

Measure the flour and sift with the baking powder and salt into a large bowl. Add the peanut butter and sugar, working the peanut butter into the dry ingredients with the fingertips. Add the milk; mix lightly but completely. Oil a small loaf pan generously or spray heavily with nonstick cooking spray. Pour the batter into the prepared pan. Bake at 420 degrees for 30 to 35 minutes or until a wooden pick inserted in the center comes out clean. Cool in the pan for 10 minutes. Remove to a wire rack to cool completely. Yield: 6 to 8 servings.

Nancy Brake, Alpha Kappa
Hot Springs, Arkansas

PUMPKIN BREAD

3 cups flour, sifted
2 cups sugar
1 teaspoon baking soda
1 teaspoon salt
1 tablespoon cinnamon
1/2 teaspoon nutmeg
1/2 teaspoon ginger
1/2 teaspoon allspice
4 eggs, beaten
1 1/4 cups vegetable oil
1 (15-ounce) can pumpkin (2 cups)
1 cup chopped pecans

Combine the flour, sugar, baking soda, salt, cinnamon, nutmeg, ginger and allspice in a large bowl and mix well. Make a deep well in the dry ingredients and fill with a mixture of the eggs, vegetable oil and pumpkin; stir lightly just until moistened. Stir in the pecans. Spoon into 3 buttered small coffee cans or 2 buttered 9-inch loaf pans. Bake at 350 degrees for 1 hour and 15 to 20 minutes or until a wooden pick inserted in the center comes out clean. Cool in the pan for 10 minutes. Remove to a wire rack to cool completely. Yield: 2 or 3 loaves.

Sue Powell, Laureate Pi
Carrollton, Texas

PORK AND BEAN BREAD

1 cup raisins
1 (15-ounce) can pork and beans
2 cups sugar
3 eggs, beaten
1 cup vegetable oil
1 teaspoon vanilla extract
3 cups flour
1 teaspoon cinnamon
1/2 teaspoon baking powder
1 teaspoon baking soda
1 cup chopped walnuts or pecans

Place the raisins in a small bowl. Add 1 cup of boiling water and set aside. Place the pork and beans in a large bowl and mash with a fork until smooth. Add the sugar, eggs, vegetable oil and vanilla and mix well. Sift the flour, cinnamon, baking powder and baking soda into the bowl and fold into the egg mixture. Drain the raisins. Fold the raisins and walnuts into the batter. Spoon the batter into 2 or 3 greased and floured medium loaf pans. Bake at 325 degrees for 1 hour and 15 minutes or until a knife inserted in the center comes out clean. Yield: 3 loaves.

Betty West, Laureate Omicron
Pahrump, Nevada

ZUCCHINI PINEAPPLE BREAD

3 eggs
2 cups sugar
1 cup vegetable oil
1 teaspoon vanilla extract
3 cups flour
2 teaspoons baking soda
1 1/2 teaspoons baking powder
1 teaspoon salt
1 1/2 teaspoons cinnamon
1 teaspoon nutmeg
2 cups shredded peeled zucchini
1 (8-ounce) can crushed pineapple, drained
1/2 cup golden raisins
1 cup chopped pecans or walnuts
1 (4-ounce) package vanilla instant pudding mix

Combine the eggs, sugar, vegetable oil and vanilla in a large mixing bowl and beat until foamy and uniformly mixed. Sift the flour, baking soda, baking powder, salt, cinnamon and nutmeg into the bowl; stir to combine. Stir in the zucchini, pineapple, raisins, pecans and dry pudding mix. Pour into 2 greased and floured 5x9-inch loaf pans. Bake at 350 degrees for 1 hour or until a wooden pick inserted in the center comes out clean. Cool in the pan for 5 to 10 minutes. Remove to a wire rack to cool completely. Chill, wrapped in plastic wrap, for 8 to 10 hours. Yield: 2 loaves.

Margaret Budney, Preceptor Eta Phi
Indian Harbour, Florida

SWISS BRAID

1 envelope dry yeast
1 1/4 cups milk
4 tablespoons butter
1/2 cup sugar
1 1/2 teaspoons salt
4 1/2 cups flour, sifted
1 egg yolk

Dissolve the yeast in 1/4 cup warm water. Heat the milk in a saucepan over medium-low heat until a film wrinkles on the surface. Remove from heat and stir in the butter, sugar and salt. Cool to lukewarm. Mix in the yeast mixture and as much flour as possible. Place the remaining flour on a flat surface. Knead the dough, incorporating all the flour in the dough. Remove to a buttered bread board and brush with additional soft butter. Let rise, covered, in a warm place until doubled in bulk. Punch the dough down. Divide in half. Divide each half into 3 portions. Roll each portion with the palm of the hand into a rope about 12 inches long with one end thicker than the other. Braid 3 ropes of dough together and place on a large baking sheet. Braid the remaining ropes of dough and place over the first braid. Thick ends should all be at the same end. Brush the surface of the loaf with a mixture of the egg yolk and a little water. Let rise, covered, in a warm place until doubled in bulk. Bake at 350 degrees for 30 to 40 minutes or until the bread tests done. Yield: 20 to 25 servings.

Ruth Rightmer, Laureate Beta Omicron
Mayer, Arizona

CASSEROLE HERB BREAD

1 envelope dry yeast
1 3/4 cups flour
2 tablespoons sugar
2 tablespoons shortening
1 teaspoon salt
1 teaspoon parsley flakes
1/2 teaspoon marjoram
1/2 teaspoon oregano
1/4 teaspoon garlic powder
2 eggs
3/4 cup hot milk

Combine the yeast, flour, sugar, shortening, salt, parsley flakes, marjoram, oregano, garlic powder, eggs and milk in a large mixing bowl and beat at medium speed for 3 minutes, scraping down the batter with a rubber spatula if it climbs the beaters. Spoon into a well-buttered 2-quart baking dish or bundt pan. Let rise, covered, in a warm place for 30 minutes or until light. Bake at 350 degrees for 25 to 30 minutes or until golden brown. Remove from the pan to a wire rack immediately. Yield: 6 servings.

Phyllis Hawk
Pueblo, Colorado

TRADITIONAL CZECH BRAIDS

Use a whole box of raisins if you love raisins the way my family does!

2 cakes yeast
1/2 cup sugar
1/2 cup (1 stick) butter or margarine
4 teaspoons salt
2 cups milk, scalded
9 cups flour
2 eggs
1/4 teaspoon mace
1 cup raisins
1 cup blanched almonds

Dissolve the yeast in 1/2 cup lukewarm water. Stir the sugar, butter and salt into the scalded milk and cool to lukewarm. Add 1 cup of the flour and beat until smooth. Add the yeast mixture, eggs, mace and raisins; mix well. Add enough flour to make a soft dough. Knead until smooth and elastic. Let rise, covered, in a warm place until doubled in bulk. Punch the dough down. Divide into 4 large portions and 5 small ones. Shape each portion into a log. Shape the four large logs into a loose braid and place on a greased baking stone. Press the almonds into the braid. Braid 3 of the small logs and place over the larger braid. Twist the remaining 2 small logs together and place over the smaller braid. Let rise, covered, until doubled in bulk. Brush with beaten egg white. Bake at 350 degrees for 1 hour and 10 minutes or until browned. Decorate cooled bread with icing if desired. Yield: 12 servings.

Marlene Mallon, Mu Theta
Salina, Kansas

POPPY SEED CRESCENTS

5 3/4 to 6 3/4 cups unsifted flour
1/2 cup sugar
1 1/2 teaspoons salt
2 envelopes dry yeast
1 cup milk
1/4 cup margarine
2 eggs, at room temperature
Poppy Seed Filling

Combine 1 3/4 cups of the flour, sugar, salt and yeast in a large mixing bowl; stir to blend. Combine the milk, 2/3 cup water and margarine in a saucepan over low heat; cook to 120 to 130 degrees on a candy thermometer, stirring frequently. Add the milk mixture to the dry ingredients gradually, beating at medium speed. Add the eggs and 1/2 cup flour; beat at high speed for 2 minutes. Stir in enough flour to make a stiff dough. Knead on a lightly floured board until smooth and elastic, about 8 to 10 minutes. Cover with plastic wrap and a towel; let stand for 20 minutes. Punch the dough down and divide into 3 equal portions. Roll each portion into a 12-inch circle on a lightly floured surface. Brush with melted margarine. Cut each circle into 12 wedges. Place 2 teaspoons Poppy Seed Filling over the wide end of each wedge.

Roll up tightly from the wide ends and press the points to seal. Arrange point side down on a greased baking sheet, curving to make a crescent shape. Cover loosely with waxed paper brushed with vegetable oil. Let stand in the refrigerator, covered, for 2 to 24 hours. Uncover dough and let stand at room temperature for 10 minutes before baking. Bake at 400 degrees for 12 to 15 minutes or until golden brown. Yield: 3 dozen.

POPPY SEED FILLING

1/4 cup poppy seeds
1 tablespoon margarine
1/2 cup confectioners' sugar
3 tablespoons honey
3/4 cup raisins
1 egg white, stiffly beaten

Crush the poppy seeds in a blender. Melt the margarine in a small skillet over medium-low heat. Add the poppy seeds and cook for about 4 minutes, stirring constantly. Stir in the confectioners' sugar, honey and raisins. Fold in the egg white.

Elaine Willey, Laureate Beta
Milford, Delaware

COOL-RISE DINNER ROLLS

2 envelopes dry yeast
1/2 cup sugar
1 cup warm milk
2 eggs
1/4 cup margarine or shortening, softened
5 to 6 cups flour
1 1/2 teaspoons salt

Dissolve the yeast in 2/3 cup warm water in a medium bowl. Stir in the sugar. Stir in the milk, eggs and margarine. Add 3 cups of the flour and the salt. Mix until smooth with a wooden spoon. Add the remaining flour gradually to make a soft dough, mixing with a wooden spoon. Knead on a floured surface until smooth and elastic. Cover with plastic wrap and place a kitchen towel over the wrap. Let stand for 15 minutes. Roll to desired thickness and cut into rolls. Arrange in an oiled 9×13-inch baking dish and brush with melted margarine. Let the rolls stand, covered, in the refrigerator until ready for use; or let rise, covered, in a warm place for 1 1/2 to 2 hours or until doubled in bulk. Bake at 375 degrees for 20 to 25 minutes or until golden brown. Yield: 20 to 24 rolls.

Linda Whisenhunt, Preceptor Alpha Beta
Mena, Arkansas

Patricia Loebig, Alpha Eta Master, New Albany, Indiana, makes ***Mayonnaise Biscuits*** *by combining 1 cup self-rising flour, 1 cup milk and 1 tablespoon mayonnaise. Spoon the dough into 6 greased muffin cups. Bake at 425 degrees for 10 to 15 minutes.*

REFRIGERATOR BUTTERHORNS

1 envelope dry yeast
1 tablespoon plus 1/2 cup sugar
5 cups flour
3 eggs
1/2 cup melted butter
1 teaspoon salt

Mix the yeast, the 1 tablespoon sugar and 1/2 cup warm water together in a bowl; let stand for about 5 minutes. Add the flour, eggs, butter and salt and mix well. Let stand, covered, in the refrigerator for 8 to 10 hours. Divide the dough into halves. Roll each half into a circle and brush with additional melted butter. Cut each circle into 16 wedges; roll up from the wide ends. Shape into crescents on a baking sheet that has been sprayed with nonstick cooking spray. Bake at 375 to 400 degrees for 10 minutes. Brush tops with additional melted butter. Yield: 32 rolls.

Kim Thompson, Xi Omega
Washington, Indiana

BUTTERY BUTTERHORNS

1 envelope dry yeast
2 cups warm milk
1/2 cup sugar
1 egg, beaten
1 teaspoon salt
6 cups flour
3/4 (1 1/2 sticks) cup butter, melted

Dissolve the yeast in 2 tablespoons warm water in a large mixing bowl. Add the milk, sugar, egg, salt and 3 cups of the flour; beat at medium speed until smooth. Beat in the butter and the remaining flour. Dough will be slightly sticky; do not knead. Place in a greased bowl, turning to coat the surface. Let rise, covered, in the refrigerator for 8 to 10 hours. Punch the dough down and divide into halves. Roll each half into a 12-inch circle on a lightly floured surface. Cut each circle into 8 wedges; roll up from the wide ends. Shape into crescents. Arrange point side down and 2 inches apart on a buttered baking sheet. Let rise, covered, in a warm place until doubled in bulk, about 1 hour. Bake at 350 degrees for 15 to 20 minutes or until golden brown. Brush tops with additional melted butter. Yield: 16 rolls.

Crystal W. Vincent, Preceptor Alpha Kappa
Twin Falls, Idaho

Tina Reneé Bennett, Delta Sigma, Flowood, Mississippi, makes ***Parmesan Biscuits,*** *a perfect complement to pasta dishes, by splitting 1 can of biscuits into halves horizontally. Dip biscuit halves into 4 tablespoons melted butter and roll in 3/4 cup grated Parmesan cheese. Place the biscuits on a baking sheet coated with nonstick cooking spray. Bake at 350 degrees for 10 minutes.*

POTATO ROLLS

1 cup milk
2 tablespoons sugar
2 teaspoons salt
1/4 cup margarine
1 envelope dry yeast
2 eggs, beaten, at room temperature
1 cup instant mashed potato mix
4 1/2 to 5 1/2 cups flour

Scald the milk in a saucepan over medium heat. Remove from heat and stir in the sugar, salt and margarine. Cool to lukewarm. Measure 1 cup warm water (105 degrees) into a large warm bowl. Sprinkle the yeast over the water to dissolve. Stir in the lukewarm milk mixture, eggs, dry mashed potato mix and 3 cups of the flour; beat until smooth. Add enough flour to make a stiff dough. Knead on a lightly floured surface until smooth and elastic. Place in a greased bowl, turning to coat the surface. Let rise, covered, until doubled in bulk, about 1 hour. Punch the dough down and divide into halves. Divide each half into 12 pieces. Shape into smooth balls and place 12 in each of 2 buttered 9-inch pans. Let rise, covered, in a warm place for 30 minutes. Bake at 400 degrees for 20 minutes or until golden brown. Remove from pan to a wire rack to cool. Yield: 2 dozen.

Estelle D. Seachrist, Preceptor Beta Theta
Webster, Massachusetts

BEER BREADSTICKS

1 envelope yeast
3/4 cup beer, room temperature
3/4 cup vegetable oil
4 1/2 cups flour
Parmesan cheese

Dissolve the yeast in 3/4 cup warm water (100 to 110 degrees) in a large bowl. Stir in the beer and vegetable oil. Stir in the flour; be sure to measure flour precisely. Knead on a lightly floured surface until smooth and elastic. Place in a greased bowl, turning to coat. Let rise in a warm place, covered, until doubled in bulk. Punch the dough down. Grease a baking sheet and sprinkle with salt. Pinch off a bit of the dough and roll into a pencil-size log. Roll in grated cheese to coat. Repeat with remaining dough and arrange on a nonstick baking sheet. Bake at 350 degrees for 30 minutes or until lightly browned. Yield: variable.

JoAnn Omafray, Gamma Zeta
Mobridge, South Dakota

SOFT FLOUR TORTILLAS

1 cup flour
1/2 cup cornmeal
1/4 teaspoon salt
1 egg

Combine the flour, cornmeal, salt, egg and 1 1/2 cups water in a bowl and mix well; batter will be thin. Ladle enough batter into an electric skillet at 350 degrees to make 6-inch circles; cook until light brown on both sides, turning once. Fill with Mexican-style ingredients and serve warm. Yield: 8 servings.

Lois A. Bennett, Laureate Omicron
Helena, Montana

YORKSHIRE PUDDING

12 teaspoons vegetable oil
1 cup flour
1/2 teaspoon salt
1 cup milk
2 eggs

Place 1 teaspoon vegetable oil in each of 12 muffin cups and heat in a 400-degree oven while preparing the batter. Sift the flour and salt together into a bowl. Add the milk. Beat with a wire whisk or hand beater until mixture is the thickness of cream. Beat the eggs in a separate bowl until thick and pale yellow. Add the eggs to the flour mixture and beat hard for 2 to 3 minutes. Pour the batter evenly into the heated muffin cups. Bake at 400 degrees for 15 minutes. Reduce oven temperature to 350 degrees and bake for 10 minutes longer or until browned and puffed very high. Yield: 12 servings.

Margaret Shortreed, Preceptor Beta Beta
Lilburn, Georgia

PIZZA DOUGH

1 envelope dry yeast
2 3/4 cups flour
1/4 cup nonfat dry milk powder
3 tablespoons sugar
1 teaspoon salt
1/4 cup butter or margarine

Dissolve the yeast in 3/4 cup warm water (85 to 105 degrees) and let it stand until it bubbles. Combine the flour, milk powder, sugar and salt in a large bowl. Cut in the butter until mixture resembles heavy cornmeal. Add the yeast mixture all at once, stirring to combine. Do not let rise. Divide the dough into halves, working quickly to spread in lightly greased 14-inch pizza pans; crimp the edges. Add desired toppings. Bake at 425 degrees for 20 minutes or until done to taste. Yield: 6 to 8 servings.

Jan Srejma, Xi Upsilon
Minot, North Dakota

Karen Crook, Preceptor Laureate Alpha Eta, Moses Lake, Washington, prepares ***Beer Bread*** *by combining 3 cups self-rising flour, one 12-ounce can of room-temperature beer and 3 tablespoons sugar. Pour the dough into a greased loaf pan. Bake at 350 degrees for 35 minutes. Butter the top of the loaf and bake for an additional 10 minutes.*

CORN BREAD DRESSING

6 cups corn bread crumbs
2 cups biscuit crumbs
1/2 teaspoon salt
1 teaspoon pepper
1 1/2 tablespoons rubbed sage
2 cups chopped celery
1 1/2 cups finely chopped onion
1/2 cup (1 stick) butter or margarine
2 cups chicken broth
1/2 cup vegetable oil
3 eggs, lightly beaten

Combine the corn bread crumbs, biscuit crumbs, salt, pepper and sage in a large bowl and mix well; set aside. Combine the celery, onion, butter and 1/3 cup water in a saucepan over medium heat. Bring to a boil; remove from heat. Stir the celery mixture into the corn bread mixture. Add the chicken broth, vegetable oil and eggs; mix well. Pour into a greased shallow 2 1/2-quart baking dish. Bake, uncovered, at 375 degrees for 45 minutes or until golden brown. Yield: 12 to 14 servings.

Gloria C. Swager, Xi Zeta Mu
Belle Glade, Florida

SLOW-COOKER DRESSING

12 to 13 cups dry bread crumbs
1 cup margarine
2 cups chopped onion
2 cups chopped celery
1/4 cup chopped parsley
2 (8-ounce) cans sliced mushrooms, drained
2 eggs, well beaten
1 1/2 teaspoons salt
1 teaspoon poultry seasoning
1 1/2 teaspoons sage
1 teaspoon thyme
1/2 teaspoon marjoram
1/2 teaspoon pepper
3 1/2 to 4 1/2 cups chicken or turkey broth

Place the bread crumbs in a very large bowl. Melt the margarine in a skillet over medium-low heat. Sauté the onion, celery, parsley and mushrooms in the margarine for 5 to 8 minutes or until tender. Pour over the bread crumbs and stir in the eggs, salt, poultry seasoning, sage, thyme, marjoram and pepper. Add the broth and mix well. Spray the slow cooker interior with nonstick cooking spray. Spoon the dressing into the slow cooker and cook on High for 45 minutes. Reduce temperature to Low and cook for 4 to 8 hours longer. Yield: 10 servings.

Barbara J. Schmidt, Xi Kappa Tau
Hardin, Missouri

DELUXE MACARONI AND CHEESE

7 ounces elbow macaroni, cooked and drained
2 cups small curd cottage cheese
1 cup sour cream
1 egg, slightly beaten
3/4 teaspoon salt
Dash of pepper
8 ounces Cheddar cheese, shredded (2 cups)
Cornflake crumbs (optional)

Combine the macaroni, cottage cheese, sour cream, egg, salt, pepper and cheese in a large bowl. Spoon into a greased 9×13-inch baking dish. Chill, covered, for 8 to 10 hours to enhance the flavors. Sprinkle with cornflake crumbs. Bake, uncovered, at 350 degrees for 45 minutes or until bubbly and beginning to brown. Yield: 8 servings.

Juanita V. Fox, Xi Theta Chi
Robinson, Illinois

SLOW-COOKER MACARONI 'N CHEESE

1 1/2 cups skim milk
1 (15-ounce) can evaporated skim milk
1 egg
1/4 teaspoon salt
1/8 teaspoon pepper
1 1/2 cups shredded sharp Cheddar cheese
8 ounces uncooked elbow macaroni

Measure the skim milk into a 4-cup or larger glass measuring cup. Add the evaporated milk, egg, salt and pepper and mix well. Pour the milk mixture into a slow cooker that has been sprayed with nonstick cooking spray. Add the cheese and macaroni and stir gently. Cook on Low for 3 1/2 to 4 hours or until set in center and macaroni is tender. Serve at once. Yield: 6 servings.

Theresa Viola, Pi Iota
Prairie Village, Kansas

MUSHROOM NOODLE BAKE

1/4 cup minced onion
3/4 cup chopped parsley
1/2 cup (1 stick) butter
2 cups sliced fresh mushrooms
1/4 cup white wine
Oregano, paprika and pepper
1 (10-ounce) can cream of celery soup
2 (10-ounce) cans cream of chicken soup
2 cups sour cream
18 ounces wide noodles, cooked and drained

Sauté the onion and parsley in the butter in a skillet over medium-low heat for 2 minutes or until tender. Stir in the mushrooms and wine and sprinkle with oregano, paprika and pepper. Combine the soups and sour cream in a saucepan over low heat and stir in the mushroom mixture. Spread a thin layer of the mushroom mixture in an 11×15-inch baking dish. Set aside 1/2 cup of the mushroom mixture. Combine the remaining mushroom mixture and noodles in a large bowl and mix well. Spoon into the prepared baking dish; top with reserved mushroom mixture. Sprinkle with Parmesan cheese. Bake, covered with foil, at 350 degrees for 1 hour. Yield: 8 servings.

Roberta Terrell, Xi Rho Xi
Visalia, California

FRESH TOMATO SPAGHETTI

12 firm medium Roma tomatoes (about 1 3/4 pounds)
6 garlic cloves, minced
1/2 cup chopped parsley
1/2 cup olive oil
2 tablespoons butter or margarine, at room temperature
1/2 cup fresh whole basil, or 2 tablespoons crumbled dried basil
16 ounces spaghetti, cooked and drained
Salt and pepper to taste
Grated Parmesan cheese to taste (optional)

Cut the tomatoes in half lengthwise. Arrange cut sides up in a 9×13-inch baking dish and sprinkle lightly with salt and pepper. Combine the garlic, 1/3 cup of the parsley and 2 tablespoons of the olive oil in a small bowl and mix well; pat the garlic mixture over the cut sides of the tomatoes. Drizzle another 2 tablespoons olive oil over the top. Bake at 425 degrees for about 1 hour or until browned on top; pan juices may become dark. Combine the butter, the remaining parsley, the remaining 1/4 cup olive oil, basil and 4 of the tomato halves in a warm large serving bowl. Remove and discard most of the tomato skins; coarsely mash the tomatoes. Stir in the cooked spaghetti. Add the remaining baked tomatoes and pan juices; mix gently. Add salt, pepper and Parmesan cheese. Yield: 6 to 8 servings.

Angela E. Taylor, Laureate Alpha Xi
Roy, New Mexico

GARDEN SPECIAL PRIMAVERA

2 cups fresh wax or green beans (about 6 ounces)
1/2 cup diagonally sliced carrots
6 ounces asparagus, cut into 2-inch pieces
1 cup broccoli florets
12 ounces fettuccine
1 small red bell pepper, cut into strips
1 small yellow bell pepper, cut into strips
1 small zucchini, sliced
1 small onion, cut into wedges
2 garlic cloves, minced
2 tablespoons butter
3/4 cup chicken broth
3/4 cup heavy cream
2 tablespoons flour
1/2 cup grated Parmesan cheese
2 ounces cooked ham
2 green onions, chopped
2 tablespoons sliced fresh basil

Cook the beans and carrots in a small amount of boiling salted water in a large saucepan over medium heat for 10 minutes. Add the asparagus and broccoli and return to a boil. Cook for 5 minutes longer; drain. Cook the fettuccine in a large kettle using the package directions. Add the bell peppers and zucchini for the last 3 minutes of boiling time; drain. Stir the bean mixture into the fettuccine mixture and keep warm. Sauté the onion and garlic in the butter in a medium saucepan over medium heat for 5 to 8 minutes or until tender. Stir in the chicken broth. Combine the cream and flour in a small bowl and whisk until smooth. Place the cream mixture in a saucepan over medium-low heat and cook until thickened, stirring constantly. Stir in the cheese, ham, green onions and basil. Spoon over the fettuccini mixture and serve. Yield: 8 servings.

Marilyn A. Williams, Preceptor Epsilon Xi
Athens, Ohio

✤ SIX-CHEESE PENNE PASTA

2 cups heavy cream
1 (15-ounce) can crushed tomatoes, drained
1/2 cup freshly grated Romano cheese
1/2 cup freshly shredded fontina cheese
4 ounces fresh mozzarella cheese, thinly sliced
1/4 cup crumbled Gorgonzola cheese
4 tablespoons ricotta cheese
6 fresh basil leaves, chopped
16 ounces penne pasta
1/4 cup unsalted butter
1/2 cup grated Parmesan cheese

Combine the first 8 ingredients in a bowl and mix well. Parboil the penne in 5 quarts of boiling water in a kettle for 4 to 5 minutes; drain well. Stir the penne into the cheese mixture. Divide the penne mixture among 8 baking dishes or pour the entire mixture into a 10×15-inch baking dish. Dot with butter and sprinkle with Parmesan cheese. Bake at 500 degrees for 8 to 10 minutes or until bubbly and brown. Yield: 8 servings.

Patricia Soard, Theta Psi
Cookeville, Tennessee

LAZY PEROGIES

2 cups cottage cheese
1 egg
10 lasagna noodles, cooked and drained
3 cups mashed potatoes
1/2 cup chopped onion
1 1/2 cups shredded Cheddar cheese
1/4 teaspoon salt
1/4 teaspoon pepper
1 cup chopped onion
1 cup (2 sticks) butter

Combine the cottage cheese and egg in a bowl and mix well. Line a 9×13-inch baking dish with 4 lasagna noodles. Spread the cottage cheese mixture over the noodles. Combine the next 5 ingredients in a bowl and mix well. Layer 3 noodles and the potato mixture over the cottage cheese layer. Top with the remaining lasagna noodles. Sauté 1 cup chopped onion in the butter in a skillet over medium-low heat for 5 to 8 minutes. Spread the onion mixture over the lasagna. Bake, covered, at 350 degrees for 30 minutes.
Yield: 6 to 8 servings.

Lois Wark, Laureate Epsilon
Brandon, Manitoba, Canada

---

*Marie Stephenson, Laureate Chi, Chattanooga, Tennessee, makes **Green Chiles and Rice Casserole** by combining 1 can cream of celery soup, 1 1/2 cups instant white rice, 16 ounces sour cream, two 4-ounce cans of green chiles, 1 cup each shredded Cheddar cheese and shredded American white cheese, salt to taste and 2 chopped seeded jalapeños. Spoon the mixture into a lightly buttered 9×13-inch baking dish. Bake at 350 degrees for 50 minutes.*

VEGETABLES WITH KOREAN NOODLES

1 bunch fresh spinach (optional)
1 tablespoon vegetable oil
15 green onions, cut into 1-inch diagonal pieces
1/2 cup white or yellow onion, julienned
1 large carrot, julienned
1 1/4 cups sliced fresh mushrooms
2 teaspoons minced garlic
1 1/2 tablespoons dark soy sauce
3 tablespoons dark brown sugar (optional)
1 tablespoon dark sesame oil
16 ounces rice vermicelli or bean thread vermicelli, cooked and drained
1/2 teaspoon sesame seeds

Tear the spinach into pieces and drop into boiling water; boil for 1 minute. Drain and set aside. Heat the vegetable oil in a large skillet or wok over high heat. Stir-fry the green onions, white onion, carrot, mushrooms and garlic in the hot oil for several minutes. Add a mixture of the soy sauce and brown sugar and heat for 1 or 2 minutes, tossing and stirring to coat the vegetables and dissolve the brown sugar. Toss in the sesame oil. Remove from heat. Spread the vermicelli in a large shallow serving bowl. Spread the spinach over the vermicelli. Spread the vegetable mixture over the spinach. Gently work the vegetables into the vermicelli with a wooden spoon. Sprinkle with sesame seeds and serve. Yield: 12 to 24 servings.

Lori Andriesian, Preceptor Alpha
Warrenton, Oregon

CREAMY RICE AND CHEESE

2 (4-ounce) cans mild green chile peppers
1 cup chopped onion
1/4 cup butter or margarine
4 cups freshly cooked rice
1 cup cream-style cottage cheese
2 cups sour cream
1/2 teaspoon salt
1/8 teaspoon pepper
8 ounces Cheddar cheese, shredded (2 cups)

Drain the chile peppers and cut in half lengthwise; do not remove the seeds (be sure not to use hot chiles). Brown the onion in the butter in a large skillet over medium-high heat. Remove from heat. Stir in the rice, cottage cheese, sour cream, salt and pepper; toss lightly to mix well. Layer the rice mixture, chile peppers and cheese 1/2 at a time in a lightly greased 11×13-inch baking dish. Sprinkle with chopped parsley. Bake at 350 degrees for 25 minutes or until lightly browned and bubbly. Yield: 12 servings.

Mary Edna King, Laureate Epsilon
Ocean Springs, Mississippi

CHEESY BEANS AND RICE

1 cup uncooked rice
1 (15-ounce) can red kidney beans, rinsed and drained
3 tablespoons butter
1 cup chopped onions
1/3 cup chopped celery
1/2 cup chopped green bell pepper
1 (16-ounce) can tomatoes, chopped
1/2 teaspoon chili powder
1/4 teaspoon salt
1 (4-ounce) can chopped green chile peppers, drained
8 ounces sliced Cheddar cheese
1/2 cup shredded Cheddar cheese

Cook the rice using the package directions. Combine the rice and beans in a large bowl and mix well. Melt the butter in a skillet over medium-low heat. Sauté the onions, celery and bell pepper in the butter for about 5 minutes. Stir in the undrained tomatoes. Simmer, uncovered, for 5 minutes. Stir in the chili powder, salt and green chile peppers. Layer 1 cup of the bean mixture, half the cheese slices and 1/3 of the tomato mixture in a 7×11-inch baking dish. Repeat the layers. Layer the remaining rice mixture and the remaining tomato mixture over the top. Bake at 350 degrees for 45 minutes. Remove from the oven and sprinkle with shredded cheese. Return to the oven for about 3 minutes to melt the cheese.
Yield: 4 servings.

Betsy Fisher, Delta Master
Nashville, Tennessee

INDIAN RICE AND VEGETABLES

1 cup uncooked basmati rice
1 medium onion, cut into wedges
2 tablespoons vegetable oil
1 tablespoon cashews (optional)
1 tablespoon raisins (optional)
1 cup green peas or mixed vegetables
1-inch cinnamon stick
4 whole cloves
1 teaspoon cumin
1-inch piece of gingerroot, sliced
Salt and cayenne pepper to taste

Soak the rice in 2 cups of water. Brown the onion in hot vegetable oil in a 3- to 4-quart kettle over medium-high heat. Stir in the cashews and raisins. Remove the onion, cashews and raisins from the kettle when browned. Add the peas, cinnamon stick, cloves, cumin and gingerroot to the oil in the kettle and stir-fry for 3 to 5 minutes. Drain the rice and add to the kettle. Gently stir in 2 cups of water and bring to a boil. Reduce heat to low and cook, covered, for 10 minutes; cooked rice grains should remain separate, whole and firm. Season with salt and cayenne pepper. Stir with a fork. Garnish with the browned onion mixture and serve. Serve with a gravy dish or plain yogurt if desired. Yield: 4 servings.

Usha Puri, Laureate Omicron
St. Cloud, Minnesota

CORN RELISH

1 (32-ounce) can corn
1/2 medium green bell pepper, chopped
2 1/2 tablespoons chopped pimentos
5 ribs celery, finely chopped
1 large onion, minced
2/3 cup vegetable oil
2 1/2 tablespoons wine vinegar
2 1/2 teaspoons salt
1 1/4 teaspoons pepper
1 1/4 teaspoons dry mustard

Drain the corn for several minutes while chopping the vegetables. Combine the corn, bell pepper, pimentos, celery and onion in a large bowl and toss to mix. Pour a mixture of the vegetable oil and vinegar over the vegetables. Season with salt, pepper and dry mustard. Toss lightly to combine. Chill, covered, for 2 or 3 hours to blend the flavors. Yield: 2 quarts.

June Sawyer, Alpha Lambda Master
Northglenn, Colorado

CRANBERRY CHUTNEY

2 (20-ounce) cans pineapple chunks, drained, juice reserved
2 cups sugar
16 ounces fresh cranberries
1 cup golden raisins
1/2 teaspoon ginger
1 teaspoon cinnamon
1/4 teaspoon allspice
1/4 teaspoon salt
1 cup chopped walnuts or pecans

Combine the pineapple juice, sugar, cranberries, raisins, ginger, cinnamon, allspice and salt in a saucepan over medium-high heat; bring to a boil. Reduce heat and simmer, covered, for 25 minutes. Stir in the pineapple and walnuts. Remove from heat. Let stand until cool. Store in airtight containers in the refrigerator. Yield: 12 or more servings.

Grace M. Baylor, Laureate Theta
Waynesboro, Pennsylvania

CRANBERRY CONSERVE

12 ounces fresh cranberries
1 1/2 cups sugar
1 Granny Smith apple, peeled, cored, chopped
Grated zest of 1 orange
Juice of 1 orange
Grated zest of 1 lemon
Juice of 1 lemon
1/2 cup golden raisins
1/4 cup dark raisins
3/4 cup chopped pecans or walnuts

Combine the cranberries, sugar and 1 cup water in a large saucepan over low heat; simmer for about 5 minutes or until cranberry skins pop open. Add the apple, orange zest and juice, and lemon zest and juice and simmer for 15 minutes longer. Remove from heat. Stir in the raisins and pecans. Let cool. Chill, covered, until serving time. This conserve freezes well. Yield: 4 cups.

Pat Flynn, Laureate Iota
Raleigh, North Carolina

CRANBERRY PINEAPPLE RELISH

1 (8-ounce) can pineapple tidbits, drained, juice reserved
12 ounces fresh cranberries, washed, stems removed
2 cups sugar
1 (3-ounce) package cherry gelatin
1 cup pecan halves
1 cup maraschino cherries

Add enough water to the pineapple juice to make $1^1/_2$ cups liquid. Pour into a saucepan over medium heat. Add the cranberries and sugar and bring to a boil. Boil the cranberries until the skins pop open. Remove from heat immediately. Dissolve the dry gelatin mix in the hot liquid. Cool partially. Stir in the pineapple, pecans and cherries. Chill, covered, for at least 1 week before using or freezing. Yield: 6 cups.

Ramona Brunswick, Alpha Lambda Master
Westminster, Colorado

SWEET PEAR RELISH

6 tomatoes, peeled and chopped
6 pears, peeled and chopped
1/2 cup sultana raisins
1/2 cup chopped onion
1 cup sugar
1 teaspoon salt
1/2 teaspoon black pepper
1/2 teaspoon ginger
1/2 teaspoon dry mustard
Pinch of cayenne pepper
1/2 cup finely chopped red or green bell pepper
1/2 cup white vinegar

Combine the tomatoes, pears, raisins, onion, sugar, salt, black pepper, ginger, dry mustard, cayenne pepper, bell pepper and white vinegar in a saucepan over medium heat. Bring to a boil. Boil gently until thickened, stirring with a wooden spoon to prevent sticking. Reduce heat and simmer, covered, for 45 to 50 minutes, stirring occasionally. Pack the relish into hot sterilized jars and seal with paraffin.
Yield: 6 cups.

Ida Jolly, Alpha Beta Master
Courtenay, British Columbia, Canada

RED PEPPER RELISH

Serve a dollop of Red Pepper Relish on a cracker spread with cream cheese.

6 large red bell peppers
1 tablespoon salt
1 1/2 cups sugar
1 cup white vinegar

Dice the red peppers and sprinkle with salt. Let stand at room temperature, covered, for 8 to 10 hours. Rinse with cold water. Place in a saucepan over medium heat with the sugar and vinegar. Simmer until thickened, about 1 hour, stirring occasionally. Store in an airtight container in the refrigerator.
Yield: 6 servings.

Evelyn Smysniuk, Laureate Upsilon
Saskatoon, Saskatchewan, Canada

ZESTY PICKLES

The taste of these pickles is great—it is not too hot, and it has a touch of sweetness.

1 gallon sliced dill pickles
4 to 5 pounds sugar
1 (12-ounce) bottle Tabasco sauce
2 teaspoons minced garlic

Drain the pickles completely, for about 1 hour. Pour the sugar over the pickles in the jar. Add the Tabasco sauce and garlic. Tighten the lid on the jar and lay the jar on its side in the refrigerator. Turn the jar several times a day for about 10 days. Yield: 1 gallon.

Lynda Mears-Richnow, Laureate Iota
Texarkana, Texas

NORWEGIAN CHRISTMAS PUDDING

This rich Norwegian side dish, known as Rommegrot, is a must on our holiday table.

1 cup (2 sticks) butter (no substitute)
3/4 cup flour
Dash of salt
4 cups half-and-half
1/2 cup sugar
1 teaspoon cinnamon

Melt the butter in a large saucepan over low heat. Add the flour and salt and stir to make a paste. Heat the half-and-half in a separate saucepan over medium-low heat; do not boil. Add the half-and-half to the flour paste gradually over low heat until the consistency of pudding, beating constantly with a wire whisk. Whisk in the sugar. Pour into a serving bowl. Sprinkle with cinnamon and a little additional sugar. Keep warm until serving time.
Yield: about 8 servings.

Sharon M. Roher, Preceptor Zeta
Calmar, Iowa

GREEN TOMATO KETCHUP

$1^1/_2$ gallons (24 cups) ground green tomatoes
6 red or green bell peppers, ground
6 onions, ground
3 hot chile peppers, ground
1 medium head cabbage, ground
6 cups sugar
$^1/_2$ cup salt
3 cups white vinegar
1 tablespoon pickling spice

Let the ground tomatoes stand in a colander for 20 minutes to drain. Combine the tomatoes, bell peppers, onions, chile peppers, cabbage, sugar, salt, vinegar and picking spice in a large kettle over medium heat. Bring to a boil. Boil gently for 5 minutes. Pour into hot sterilized jars, leaving $^1/_4$ inch headspace; seal with 2-piece lids. Invert jars of hot ketchup for 5 minutes. Yield: 8 jars (variable).

LaVerna Trimble, Xi Alpha Omega
Paducah, Kentucky

ROASTED ORANGE SAUCE

1 cup coarsely chopped orange, including peel
12 ounces fresh or frozen cranberries
1 cup packed brown sugar
1 teaspoon cinnamon
1 (15-ounce) can chicken broth ($1^3/_4$ cups)

Remove the seeds from the orange. Combine the orange, cranberries, brown sugar and cinnamon in a 15×17-inch roasting pan. Pour the chicken broth over the cranberry mixture. Bake at 450 degrees for 25 minutes or until thickened. Chill, covered, for 8 to 10 hours or until serving time. Yield: $2^1/_2$ cups.

Judy Harned, Xi Delta Xi
Martinsville, Virginia

STRAWBERRY FIG PRESERVES

3 cups firm ripe strawberries
3 cups ripe figs, halved
5 cups sugar
$^1/_3$ cup lemon juice

Wash the strawberries and remove the stems; do not use any strawberries with hollow stems. Combine the strawberries, figs and sugar in a bowl and let stand at room temperature for 3 to 4 hours. Place in a saucepan over medium heat and bring to a boil gradually, stirring occasionally until sugar dissolves. Stir in the lemon juice. Cook over medium heat until thickened, about 15 minutes, stirring frequently. Pour into a shallow baking dish. Let stand, covered, in a cool place for 12 to 24 hours, shaking the dish occasionally to distribute the berries throughout the syrup. Pour into hot sterilized jars, leaving $^1/_4$ inch headspace; seal with 2-piece lids. Process in a boiling water bath for 20 minutes. Yield: 4 cups.

LaDonna Tiller, Alpha Omicron Kappa
Gainesville, Texas

CHEESE ASPARAGUS PIE

1 (8-count) can crescent rolls
1 (16-ounce) can cut asparagus, drained
$^1/_2$ cup mayonnaise
1 cup packed brown sugar shredded Cheddar cheese
1 teaspoon lemon juice

Unroll the dough. Separate into 8 triangles and place in an 8- or 9-inch pie plate. Press the seams to form a single layer covering the bottom and side of the pie plate. Place the asparagus, mayonnaise, cheese and lemon juice in a bowl and toss lightly to combine. Spread in the unbaked pie shell. Bake at 350 degrees for 35 minutes or until golden brown.
Yield: 6 to 8 servings.

Pat Jones, Xi Alpha Delta
Babson Park, Florida

BLUE RIBBON BEANS

While attending a barbecue cook-off with my husband, I entered the bean contest on a whim with the beans I had cooked for our lunch. I won!

1 (1-gallon) can pinto beans, drained
$^1/_2$ cup Worcestershire sauce
3 cups Head Country Barbecue Sauce
1 onion, chopped
$1^1/_2$ cups chopped red, yellow and green bell peppers
$^1/_4$ cup dry barbecue rubbing spices
2 cups chopped barbecue rib meat

Combine the all the ingredients in a large slow cooker. Cook on High for 1 hour. Reduce temperature to Low and heat until serving time.
Yield: 25 servings.

Bonnee Blue Pierson, Xi Gamma Omicron
Pryor, Oklahoma

QUICK BAKED BEANS

5 (15-ounce) cans pork and beans
1 (16-ounce) can cranberry sauce
1 tablespoon prepared mustard
$^1/_2$ cup maple syrup
1 medium onion, minced or chopped
$1^1/_2$ cups cubed cooked ham
1 envelope onion soup mix

Combine the pork and beans, cranberry sauce, mustard, maple syrup, onion, ham and dry onion soup mix in a slow cooker and mix well. Cook, uncovered, on High for 4 to 5 hours, stirring occasionally; cook longer if you prefer drier beans.
Yield: 10 to 12 servings.

Wanda Brown, Xi Epsilon Sigma
Sylmar, California

FOUR-BEAN BAKE

1 pound sliced bacon
4 large Spanish onions, chopped
1 (16-ounce) can kidney beans, drained
1 (15-ounce) can lima beans, drained
1 (15-ounce) can butter beans, drained
2 (15-ounce) cans pork and beans, drained
1 cup packed brown sugar
1 teaspoon dry mustard
1 teaspoon salt
1/2 teaspoon garlic powder
1/2 cup white vinegar

Cut the bacon into 1-inch pieces and brown in a skillet until crisp. Remove the bacon. Sauté the onions in the bacon drippings for 5 to 10 minutes over medium heat. Combine the bacon, onions, kidney beans, lima beans, butter beans, pork and beans, brown sugar, dry mustard, salt, garlic powder and vinegar in a large bowl and mix well. Pour into a greased 9×13-inch baking dish. Bake, covered, at 350 degrees for 30 to 45 minutes or until hot and bubbly.
Yield: 15 servings.

Dorothy Spears, Preceptor Beta Sigma
Niagara Falls, New York

WHITE BEAN PROVENCAL

1 teaspoon toasted garlic-flavored olive oil
2 cups thinly sliced leeks
2 (16-ounce) cans white beans, drained
1 (14-ounce) can Italian tomatoes
2 tablespoons chopped black olives
1 tablespoon rice vinegar
1/4 teaspoon salt
1/4 teaspoon pepper

Grease a skillet or wok with the oil and place over medium-high heat. Sauté the leeks in the oil for 5 minutes. Add the beans and tomatoes; sauté over medium heat for 5 minutes. Stir in the olives, vinegar, salt and pepper and cook until heated through. Serve over rice or spaghetti. Yield: 4 servings.

Rose Denslinger, Preceptor Alpha Nu
The Dalles, Oregon

MOUNTAIN BEAN AND RICE STEW

16 ounces dry pinto beans, cooked until tender
1 cup uncooked rice, cooked until tender
1 (28-ounce) can diced tomatoes
1/2 pound bacon, cut into small strips
1 onion, diced
2 or 3 garlic cloves, sliced
2 teaspoons paprika
Salt and pepper to taste

Combine the pinto beans and rice in a large kettle. Stir in the undrained tomatoes. Brown the bacon in a skillet over medium heat. Add the onion and cook just until tender. Stir in the garlic. Add the bacon mixture to the bean mixture. Season with paprika, salt and pepper. Yield: 8 to 12 servings.

Nancy L. Cummins, Preceptor Delta Theta
Neodesha, Kansas

MUSHROOM GREEN BEAN BAKE

16 ounces fresh mushrooms, sliced
1 large onion, chopped
1/2 cup (1 stick) butter or margarine
1/4 cup flour
1 cup half-and-half
1 (16-ounce) jar process cheese sauce
2 teaspoons soy sauce
1/2 teaspoon black pepper
1/8 teaspoon red hot pepper sauce
1 (8-ounce) can sliced water chestnuts, drained
2 (16-ounce) packages frozen French-style green beans, thawed and drained
1/4 cup slivered almonds

Sauté the mushrooms and onion in the butter in a skillet over medium-low heat for 5 to 10 minutes or until tender. Whisk in the flour. Add the half-and-half, cheese sauce, soy sauce, black pepper and hot red pepper sauce gradually and heat until cheese is melted, stirring constantly. Remove from heat. Stir in the water chestnuts. Spread the green beans in an ungreased 3-quart baking dish. Pour the cheese mixture evenly over the top. Sprinkle with almonds. Bake, uncovered, at 375 degrees for 25 to 30 minutes or until bubbly. Yield: 14 to 16 servings.

Hilda Stankunas Jones, Laureate Omega
Decatur, Illinois

Byron Tindle, Xi Mu, Bessemer, Alabama, makes ***Ballpark Dipping Sauce*** *for chicken fingers, French fries and more by combining 16 ounces of sour cream, one 9-ounce jar of horseradish sauce, 1 jar of chili sauce, 1 cup mayonnaise and cayenne pepper to taste. Store, covered, in the refrigerator.*

BROCCOLI CHEESE CUSTARD

2 (10-ounce) packages frozen chopped broccoli
1/2 cup shredded Swiss cheese
1/2 cup grated Parmesan cheese
1/2 cup sour cream
1/2 teaspoon salt (optional)
1/4 teaspoon pepper
1/4 teaspoon garlic powder
1/4 cup flour
1/4 teaspoon baking powder
3 eggs, well beaten
1 tablespoon butter or margarine

Combine the frozen broccoli and 1/2 cup boiling water in a covered saucepan; bring to a boil. Simmer for 5 minutes or until broccoli is broken up; drain well. Combine the broccoli, Swiss cheese, Parmesan cheese and sour cream in a medium bowl and mix well. Combine the salt, pepper, garlic powder, flour and baking powder in a small bowl and mix well. Add the flour mixture to the broccoli mixture; mix well. Stir in the eggs. Spoon the broccoli mixture into a buttered 1 1/2-quart baking dish. Bake, uncovered, at 350 degrees for 35 to 40 minutes or until set. Serve hot or warm. Yield: 4 to 6 servings.

Griff Jappé, Laureate Delta Xi
Lehigh Acres, Florida

BROCCOLI WITH ORANGE SAUCE

To eliminate broccoli odor when cooking, place a rib of celery in the boiling water.

2 tablespoons butter
1 teaspoon olive oil
1/4 cup chopped green onions
1 garlic clove, minced
1/3 cup fresh orange juice
1/4 cup dry white wine
16 ounces broccoli, cleaned
2 teaspoons grated orange zest

Melt the butter with the olive oil in a small saucepan over low heat. Add the green onions and garlic and cook for 3 to 4 minutes. Add the orange juice and wine. Simmer until syrupy, about 4 to 5 minutes, stirring often. Remove from heat and set aside; keep warm. Boil 2 quarts of salted water in a large kettle. Add the broccoli and simmer for about 7 to 10 minutes or until tender-crisp. Drain well and pat dry. Layer the broccoli in a serving dish. Pour the hot orange juice mixture over the broccoli; toss gently to combine. Sprinkle with orange zest. Serve very hot. Yield: 4 to 6 servings.

Frances Fischer, Laureate Theta
Rock Hill, South Carolina

CHEESY BROCCOLI RANCH BAKE

1 envelope ranch salad dressing mix
8 ounces cream cheese, softened
3/4 cup milk
16 ounces broccoli, parboiled
3/4 cup shredded sharp Cheddar cheese

Combine the dry salad dressing mix, cream cheese and milk in a blender and process until smooth. Pour over the broccoli in a large bowl and stir to combine. Spread in a 9-inch baking dish and sprinkle with cheese. Bake, uncovered, at 350 degrees for 25 minutes or until lightly browned and bubbly.
Yield: 4 servings.

Gina Birkmaier, Beta Nu
Enterprise, Oregon

BROCCOLI MUSHROOM PIE

2 cups milk
3 tablespoons uncooked grits
3 tablespoons butter or margarine
1 teaspoon salt
3 eggs
Black pepper to taste
1 cup broccoli florets, chopped
1 1/2 cups fresh mushrooms, sliced
2 tablespoons chopped pimentos or chopped red bell pepper
1 green onion, finely chopped
1 tablespoon flour
Dash of nutmeg or cayenne pepper
1 (9-inch) pie shell, prebaked for 3 to 4 minutes

Combine the milk, grits, 1 tablespoon of the butter and salt in a medium saucepan over medium-low heat; bring to a simmer. Cook until thickened and grits are tender, stirring frequently. Set aside. Combine the eggs and black pepper in a small mixing bowl and beat until frothy. Stir the egg mixture into the grits mixture. Sauté the broccoli, mushrooms, pimentos and green onion in the remaining 2 tablespoons butter in a small skillet over medium-low heat for about 5 minutes. Sprinkle with the flour and nutmeg and stir well. Add the broccoli mixture to the grits mixture; stir well. Pour into the pie shell. Bake for 40 to 45 minutes or until top is slightly browned. Yield: 6 to 8 servings.

Fay J. Wiley, Beta Master
Pascagoula, Mississippi

BRUSSELS SPROUTS WITH BACON

1 1/2 pounds brussels sprouts
3 slices bacon
1 tablespoon extra-virgin olive oil
1 shallot, chopped
Salt and pepper to taste
1 cup chicken broth

Trim the brussels sprouts; leave the small ones whole and halve the larger ones. Cut the bacon into 1-inch (or smaller) squares. Crisp-cook the bacon in a skillet over medium-high heat; remove to a paper towel to drain. Add the olive oil to the bacon drippings in the skillet and sauté the shallot for 1 to 2 minutes. Add the brussels sprouts and stir to coat well in the oil. Season with salt and pepper. Cook for 2 to 3 minutes or until brussels sprouts begin to soften. Add the chicken broth and bring to a simmer. Reduce heat to medium-low and cook, covered, for 10 minutes or until brussels sprouts are tender. Remove to a serving dish with a slotted spoon. Top with the bacon bits and serve. Yield: 4 servings.

Dora M. Terry-Miley, Xi Theta Chi
Hutsonville, Illinois

HUNGARIAN CABBAGE AND NOODLES

5 slices bacon, crisp-cooked
1 tablespoon sugar
1 1/2 teaspoons salt
6 cups thin wedges of cabbage
4 ounces medium egg noodles, cooked and drained
1/2 cup sour cream

Remove the bacon from the skillet and crumble. Add the sugar, salt and cabbage to the bacon drippings in the skillet and stir to coat. Cook over medium-low heat for 10 minutes. Add the noodles and bacon and mix well. Pour into a buttered 1 1/2-quart casserole. Bake, covered, at 325 degrees for 45 minutes. Spoon the sour cream over the top and sprinkle with paprika. Return to the oven to bake, uncovered, for 5 minutes longer. Yield: 4 servings.

Susan C. Miller, Preceptor Gamma Eta
Melbourne, Florida

SWEET-AND-SOUR CABBAGE

1/2 head red cabbage
1/2 head green cabbage
1 or 2 tart apples, chopped
1 cup sugar
1 cup white vinegar
1/2 teaspoon salt
1/2 cup (1 stick) margarine
1 teaspoon cinnamon
1/2 teaspoon ground cloves

Cut the red and green cabbage into large pieces. Combine the cabbage, apples, sugar, vinegar, salt, margarine, cinnamon, cloves and 1 cup water in a large skillet over low heat. Cook, covered, for 1 hour. Yield: 8 to 10 servings.

Diana A. Burge, Preceptor Beta Chi
Niles, Michigan

TOMATO CABBAGE

Allspice is the dried berry of the allspice tree, a tropical evergreen plant that can grow to the height of a three-story building.

1 medium onion, chopped
1 teaspoon vegetable oil
1 garlic clove, chopped
1 beef bouillon cube
2 cups vegetable juice cocktail
1 1/2 teaspoons paprika
8 berries whole allspice
1 small head green cabbage, chopped
Salt and pepper to taste
1/2 cup sour cream

Sauté the onion in oil in a large skillet over medium-low heat for 5 to 10 minutes or until translucent, stirring in the garlic during the last few minutes. Dissolve the bouillon cube in 1 cup of boiling water and stir into the onion mixture. Add the vegetable juice cocktail, paprika, allspice berries and cabbage; bring to a boil. Reduce heat and simmer, covered, for 45 to 50 minutes. Season with salt and pepper. Remove the whole allspice. Pour into a 5-quart slow cooker or warming dish. Stir in the sour cream just before serving. Yield: 8 to 10 servings.

Evelyn Brandby, Xi Delta Sigma
Old Hickory, Tennessee

CANDIED CARROTS

5 medium carrots, peeled, cut into 1/2-inch diagonal slices
1/4 cup butter
1/4 cup canned cranberry sauce
2 tablespoons light brown sugar
1/2 teaspoon salt

Cook the carrots, covered, in a saucepan in a small amount of boiling water just until tender, about 6 to 10 minutes; drain. Combine the butter, cranberry sauce, brown sugar and salt in a skillet over medium-low heat. Heat slowly until cranberry sauce is melted, stirring frequently. Stir in the carrots. Heat for about 5 minutes or until glazed on all sides, stirring occasionally. Yield: 4 servings.

Aileen Irvin Tarver, Theta Master
Raleigh, North Carolina

Judy Fox, Xi Nu Gamma, Fort Pierce, Florida, makes **Cabbage Salsa with Parmesan Cheese** *by cutting 1 head of cabbage into small sections and placing the sections in a slow cooker with 1 cup water. Cook on Low for 8 to 10 hours. Sprinkle with garlic salt and all-purpose seasoning to taste. Drain the cooking liquid. Pour 1 jar of medium salsa over the cabbage and sprinkle with 2 tablespoons Parmesan cheese.*

CINNAMON CARROT BAKE

2 pounds carrots, sliced
1 cup (2 sticks) butter
1/3 cup flour
2 cups sugar
1/4 teaspoon cinnamon
2 teaspoons baking powder
4 eggs

Cook the carrots in a small amount of water in a saucepan over medium heat for 10 minutes or until tender; drain. Combine the hot carrots and butter in a blender and process until smooth. Blend in a mixture of the flour, sugar, cinnamon and baking powder. Add the eggs 1 at a time, blending after each addition. Pour the carrot mixture into a greased 2-quart baking dish. Bake at 350 degrees for 1 hour or until firm. Yield: 8 servings.

Barbara LaChapelle, Xi Epsilon Pi
Fayetteville, Georgia

CARROTS IN ORANGE JUICE

2 pounds carrots, cooked
1/4 cup margarine
2/3 cup sugar
1 (12-ounce) can frozen orange juice, thawed
1 tablespoon cornstarch
Salt to taste

Cut the carrots into bite-size pieces and place in a bowl. Melt the margarine in a saucepan over medium-low heat. Add the sugar, orange juice, cornstarch and salt and cook until thickened, stirring constantly. Pour over the carrots and marinate, covered, in the refrigerator for 8 to 10 hours. Heat in a 325-degree oven or microwave oven and serve.
Yield: 6 to 8 servings.

Sarah Stephens, Tau Master
Austin, Texas

MAPLE CARROTS WITH CHERRIES

A great side dish like this one is hard to find!

1 1/2 pounds carrots, peeled and sliced
1/2 cup chopped tart cherries
3 tablespoons maple syrup
2 tablespoons butter
1/2 teaspoon nutmeg
1/4 teaspoon ginger

Cook the carrots, covered, in a small amount of water in a saucepan over medium heat for 8 to 10 minutes or until tender. Stir in the cherries, maple syrup, butter, nutmeg and ginger. Cook, uncovered, for 3 to 4 minutes or until sauce is bubbly.
Yield: 6 (1/2-cup) servings.

Cynthia Snipes, Xi Eta Theta
Carmel, Indiana

SWEET-AND-SOUR CARROTS

1 or 2 medium red onions, sliced into rings
1 or 2 large green bell peppers, cut into strips
3 or 4 (15-ounce) cans sliced carrots, drained
1 cup sugar
1 (10-ounce) can tomato soup
1/2 cup vegetable oil
3/4 cup white vinegar
1 teaspoon salt
1 teaspoon black pepper

Place the onions, bell peppers and carrots in a large bowl and stir to combine. Combine the sugar, tomato soup, vegetable oil, vinegar, salt and black pepper in a saucepan over medium-high heat. Bring to a boil, stirring until sugar is dissolved. Cook for 1 minute, stirring constantly. Remove from heat and let stand for 2 or 3 minutes. Pour over the vegetable mixture and stir. Chill, covered, for at least 12 hours before serving. Serve cold. This dish can be store in the refrigerator for a long time. Yield: variable.

Jackie Brown, Laureate Mu
Garner, North Carolina

✣ MOCK POTATO BAKE

If you prefer a smoother consistency, purée the cauliflower with the butter in a blender or food processor.

1 (16-ounce) package frozen cauliflower florets
2 tablespoons butter
4 ounces cream cheese, softened
1 pound bacon, chopped, crisp-cooked
8 ounces Cheddar cheese, shredded (2 cups)
2 tablespoons chopped green onions

Place the frozen cauliflower with 2 tablespoons water in a microwave-safe bowl. Microwave on High, covered, for 10 to 15 minutes until very soft; drain. Place in an ovenproof 8×8-inch baking dish with the butter and mash with a potato masher. Stir in the cream cheese. Stir in the bacon, Cheddar cheese and green onions. Bake at 350 degrees for 20 to 25 minutes or until brown and bubbly. Yield: 9 servings.

Sharon Ann Robinson, Zeta Pi
Fort Worth, Texas

CREAMY SLOW-COOKER CORN

1 (16-ounce) package frozen corn
8 ounces cream cheese, softened
1/2 cup (1 stick) butter
3 to 4 tablespoons sugar

Combine the frozen corn, cream cheese, butter, sugar and 3 tablespoons water in a slow cooker. Cook on Low for 8 to 10 hours. Stir. Keep warm on Low until serving time. Yield: 10 servings.

Ethel M. Cantrell, Preceptor Laureate Theta
Boise, Idaho

MEXICAN CORN BAKE

2 (10-ounce) cans Cheddar cheese soup
2 (15-ounce) cans diced tomatoes, drained
2 (15-ounce) cans black beans, drained
16 ounces cream cheese, softened
1 to 2 teaspoons chili powder or cumin
1 (16-ounce) package frozen corn, thawed
2 to 3 tablespoons cornmeal or dry instant mashed potatoes

Combine the soup, tomatoes, beans, cream cheese and chili powder in a large bowl and mix until smooth. Stir in the corn. Stir in the cornmeal. Spoon into a greased 9×13-inch baking dish. Bake at 350 degrees for 25 minutes or until bubbly.
Yield: 8 to 10 servings.

Patricia Cosenza, Preceptor Gamma Chi
Mishawaka, Indiana

SPAGHETTI CORN

1 (15-ounce) can corn, drained
1 (15-ounce) can cream-style corn
1 cup broken uncooked spaghetti
1 cup cubed Velveeta cheese
1/4 cup butter
1 tablespoon dried minced onion
1 (6-ounce) can French-fried onions

Combine the corn, cream-style corn, spaghetti, cheese, butter and dried onion in a large bowl and mix well. Spread in a greased 9×13-inch baking dish. Bake at 350 degrees for 40 minutes. Sprinkle with French-fried onions and bake for 20 minutes longer. Yield: 9 to 12 servings.

Linda R. Brown, Xi Delta Alpha
Hyannis, Nebraska

CORN AND SPAGHETTI BAKE

1 (15-ounce) can corn
1 (15-ounce) can cream-style corn
1 cup broken (1- to 1 1/2-inch pieces) uncooked spaghetti
1/4 cup milk
1 cup shredded Cheddar cheese
1/4 cup margarine
2 to 3 teaspoons chopped onion
Buttered bread crumbs

Combine the undrained corn and the cream-style corn in a large bowl and mix well. Stir in the spaghetti. Add the milk, cheese, margarine and onion; mix well. Spread in a greased 9×13-inch baking dish. Sprinkle with bread crumbs. Bake at 350 degrees for 40 minutes or until browned and bubbly. Yield: 8 servings.

Sara E. Broberg, Laureate Beta Theta
Aurora, Colorado

SCALLOPED MUSHROOMS

1 1/2 pounds fresh medium mushrooms
1/2 green bell pepper, chopped
1/2 medium onion, chopped
1/2 teaspoon crushed red pepper
1/4 cup butter
1/2 cup heavy cream
2 cups shredded Monterey Jack or Colby cheese or a mixture of both

Sauté the mushrooms, bell pepper and onion with the crushed red pepper in the butter in a skillet over medium heat for 5 minutes. Add the cream and cook over medium-low heat for 5 minutes, stirring frequently. Spread in a greased 9×13-inch baking dish. Layer the cheese over the top. Bake at 400 degrees for 20 to 25 minutes or until browned and bubbly.
Yield: 10 to 12 servings.

Nancy Evans, Preceptor Delta Sigma
Columbus, Kansas

ONION PIE

6 medium onions, sliced
1/2 cup (1 stick) butter or margarine, melted
2 eggs, beaten
1/2 cup light cream
2 cups shredded Cheddar cheese
2 rolls butter crackers, crushed
1/2 cup (1 stick) butter or margarine, melted

Sauté the onions in 1/2 cup butter in a skillet over medium-low heat for 5 to 8 minutes or until tender. Let cool. Combine the eggs and cream in a bowl and mix well. Stir in the cheese and cooled onions. Toss the crushed crackers with 1/2 cup melted butter. Pat the cracker mixture over the bottoms and sides of two 9-inch pie plates, making a shell. Pour the egg mixture carefully into the cracker crumb shells. Bake at 350 degrees for 45 minutes or until browned.
Yield: 6 to 12 servings.

Lynn A. Ireland, Delta Nu
Hyannis, Massachusetts

PEAS FOR A PARTY

This dish is so easy to make, and so good . . . you don't need to have a party to serve it!

1/4 cup butter
2 tablespoons sugar
2 teaspoons salt
1/4 teaspoon pepper
2 (10-ounce) packages frozen peas
6 cups shredded lettuce (about 1 head)

Combine 1/2 cup water, butter, sugar, salt and pepper in a medium saucepan over medium-high heat; bring to a boil. Reduce heat. Stir in the peas and simmer for about 5 minutes or until tender-crisp. Remove from heat and stir in the lettuce. Let stand, covered, for 2 minutes to steam; drain. Serve hot.
Yield: 8 to 10 servings.

Joan M. Summers, Laureate Zeta Xi
Austin, Texas

CHEESY CREAMY POTATOES

5 large unpeeled potatoes
1 bunch green onions, chopped
16 ounces Velveeta cheese, shredded
Salt and pepper to taste
2 cups heavy cream

Scrub the potatoes and place in a saucepan. Add enough water to cover and bring to a boil. Reduce heat and simmer, covered, for 30 to 35 minutes or until tender. Let the potatoes stand, covered, in the refrigerator until completely cool. Remove and discard the peels. Shred the potatoes into a greased 9×13-inch baking dish. Stir in the green onions, cheese, salt and pepper. Pour the cream evenly over the top. Bake at 350 degrees for 45 to 50 minutes or until browned and bubbly. Sprinkle with paprika and serve. Yield: 6 servings.

Cynthia Haden, Xi Xi
Lone Tree, Colorado

RANCH POTATO BAKE

8 to 10 medium red potatoes
1 cup sour cream
1 cup ranch salad dressing
2 tablespoons parsley flakes
1 3/4 cups shredded Cheddar cheese
1/4 cup real bacon bits
2 cups slightly crushed cornflakes
1/4 cup butter, melted

Scrub the unpeeled potatoes and place in a saucepan. Add enough water to cover. Boil for 30 to 35 minutes or until tender. Let cool. Combine the sour cream, ranch dressing, parsley flakes, 1 cup of the cheese and bacon in a bowl; mix well. Place the potatoes a few at a time in the ranch dressing mixture and toss gently to coat; arrange the coated potatoes in a greased 9×13-inch baking dish. Sprinkle the remaining 3/4 cup cheese over the top. Sprinkle with a mixture of the cornflakes and melted butter. Bake, covered, at 350 degrees for 25 minutes. Uncover and bake for 15 to 20 minutes longer or until browned.
Yield: 10 to 12 servings.

Betty R. Dannels, Xi Upsilon
Pensacola, Florida

CREAMY MASHED POTATO BAKE

3 cups hot mashed potatoes
1 cup sour cream
1/4 cup milk
1/4 teaspoon garlic powder
1 1/3 cups French-fried onions
1 cup shredded Cheddar cheese

Combine the mashed potatoes, sour cream, milk and garlic powder in a large bowl; mix well. Spoon half the potato mixture into a greased 2-quart baking dish. Sprinkle with 2/3 cup of the French-fried onions and half the cheese. Layer the remaining potato mixture over the top. Bake at 350 degrees for 30 minutes or until piping hot. Sprinkle with the remaining French-fried onions and cheese. Bake for 5 minutes or until onions are golden. Yield: 6 or more servings.

Carolyn Trimpe, Alpha Nu Master
Columbus, Indiana

OVEN GARLIC POTATOES

5 or 6 large unpeeled potatoes
1/2 cup (1 stick) butter, melted
2 tablespoons garlic powder
1 medium onion, sliced into thin rings
Salt and pepper to taste

Scrub the potatoes and cut into 1/4-inch slices. Spread a mixture of the butter and garlic powder in the bottom of a shallow 11×16-inch baking dish. Layer the potatoes and onion rings in the dish. Sprinkle with salt and pepper. Bake at 350 degrees, covered, for 50 to 60 minutes or until potatoes are tender.
Yield: 6 servings.

Deborah Fuller, Alpha Beta
Jacksonville, Florida

Esther Westfall, Laureate Psi, Grand Island, New York, makes ***Special Sweet Potatoes*** *by layering 3 pounds cooked or canned sweet potato pieces and a can of apple pie filling in a baking dish. Top with 1/4 cup butter, 2 tablespoons lemon juice and 2 teaspoons cinnamon. Bake at 350 degrees for 30 minutes.*

SPANISH SQUASH BAKE

2 pounds fresh summer squash, or 3 (10-ounce) packages frozen squash
1/2 teaspoon salt
1 green bell pepper, chopped
1 onion, chopped
1 (4-ounce) can chopped mild green chiles
2 eggs, beaten
1/2 cup mayonnaise
1/2 cup shredded Cheddar cheese
Salt and pepper to taste
Parmesan cheese

Combine the squash, 1/2 teaspoon salt, bell pepper, onion and green chiles in a saucepan. Add a small amount of water and steam over medium heat for 10 minutes or until tender; drain well. Beat the squash mixture with an electric mixer in a large mixing bowl until mixture appears chopped. Add the eggs, mayonnaise, Cheddar cheese and salt and pepper to taste; mix well. Pour into a buttered 8×8-inch baking dish. Sprinkle with Parmesan cheese. Bake at 325 degrees for 45 minutes to 1 hour or until browned and bubbly. Yield: 8 to 10 servings.

Beth Menefee, Xi Beta Alpha
Artesia, New Mexico

COCONUT SWEET POTATO BAKE

3 cups mashed sweet potatoes
6 tablespoons margarine, softened
2 eggs
1 cup granulated sugar
1 cup unsweetened shredded coconut
1 teaspoon vanilla extract
Pinch of salt
1/2 cup flour
1 cup chopped pecans or walnuts
1 cup packed brown sugar

Combine the sweet potatoes, 4 tablespoons of the margarine, eggs, granulated sugar, coconut, vanilla and salt in a bowl and mix well. Spread in a 1 1/2-quart baking dish that has been sprayed with nonstick cooking spray. Sprinkle with a mixture of the flour, pecans, brown sugar and the remaining 2 tablespoons margarine. Bake at 375 degrees for 30 minutes. Yield: 15 to 20 servings.

Edna Faye Williams, Delta Omicron
Kennett, Missouri

Caroline Driessen, Preceptor Omicron Alpha, Dana Point, California, makes a pot luck ***Ranch-Style Corn Casserole*** *by mixing 2 cans cream-style corn with 1/2 cup ranch dip, 1/2 cup French-fried onions, 1/4 cup chopped green bell pepper, 1 teaspoon sugar and 1 tablespoon flour. Pour into a greased casserole and top with corn chips. Bake at 350 degrees for 25 to 30 minutes.*

SAUCY MIXED MUSHROOM AND SWEET POTATO CASSEROLE

1 tablespoon vegetable oil
1 large onion, peeled and chopped
3 cups chopped mixed mushrooms
1 teaspoon thyme
1 cup half-and-half
1/2 teaspoon salt
1/2 teaspoon pepper
3 sweet potatoes, peeled and sliced (about 1 1/2 pounds)
1/2 cup shredded Swiss cheese

Heat the vegetable oil in a skillet over medium heat. Sauté the onion in the hot oil for 5 minutes. Turn heat to medium-high and add the mushrooms. Brown the mushrooms, stirring frequently. Stir in the thyme. Remove from heat and set aside. Combine the half-and-half, salt and pepper in a large measuring cup and mix well. Layer the sweet potatoes and mushroom mixture 1/2 at a time in a buttered 8-cup casserole. Pour the half-and-half mixture evenly over the top. Bake, covered, at 350 degrees for 20 minutes. Sprinkle the cheese evenly over the top. Bake, uncovered, for 40 minutes longer. Yield: 6 servings.

Sue Newton, Preceptor Gamma Epsilon
Kitimat, British Columbia, Canada

GARLIC SWEET POTATOES WITH CARROTS

2 1/2 pounds sweet potatoes, peeled and cubed
2 pounds carrots, peeled and chopped
3/4 cup orange juice
1/4 cup maple syrup
1 teaspoon nutmeg
2 garlic cloves, minced
1 teaspoon salt
2 tablespoons plus 1/3 cup butter, melted
1 1/2 cups fresh bread crumbs
1/2 cup chopped pecans
1 tablespoon chopped fresh parsley

Combine the sweet potatoes and carrots in a saucepan. Add enough salted water to cover and bring to a boil. Reduce heat and simmer, covered, for 20 minutes or until tender; drain. Purée in a blender or food processor. Add the orange juice, maple syrup, nutmeg, garlic, salt and the 2 tablespoons butter; process just until mixed. Spoon into a greased 9×13-inch baking dish. You may chill, covered, for up to 2 days before baking. Sprinkle with a mixture of the bread crumbs, pecans, the 1/3 cup butter and parsley. Bake at 350 degrees for 45 minutes or until browned and bubbly. Yield: 8 to 10 servings.

Linda Bertram, Preceptor Zeta
Minnedosa, Manitoba, Canada

SCALLOPED YAMS WITH PRALINE TOPPING

1/4 cup packed brown sugar
3 tablespoons flour
3 tablespoons butter, at room temperature
1/3 cup finely chopped pecans
6 medium yams (about 3 pounds), peeled, cut into 1/2-inch-thick sticks
1 1/2 cups heavy cream, heated

Combine the brown sugar, flour and butter in a bowl and blend well. Stir in the pecans. Place the yams in a saucepan and add enough salted water to cover. Bring to a oil. Reduce heat and simmer for 5 minutes or until tender-crisp; do not overcook. Rinse in cold water and drain. Arrange the yams in overlapping rows in a lightly buttered 9×13-inch baking dish. Pour the warm cream evenly over the top. Bake at 375 degrees for 20 minutes. Crumble the pecan mixture evenly over the top. Bake for 20 to 30 minutes longer or until yams are tender and topping is browned. Yield: 12 to 15 servings.

Sarah Kapla, Chi Omicron
Romeoville, Illinois

CARAMELIZED SWEET POTATOES

1 (29-ounce) can sweet potatoes, drained
6 marshmallows
1 teaspoon salt
1/2 cup packed brown sugar
1/2 cup granulated sugar
2 tablespoons flour
2 tablespoons butter
1 cup half-and-half
1/2 cup chopped pecans or walnuts

Cut the sweet potatoes into 1 1/2-inch-thick slices. Arrange in a 9×13-inch baking dish. Press in the marshmallows. Sprinkle with a mixture of the salt, brown sugar, granulated sugar and flour. Dot with butter and pour the half-and-half evenly over the top. Bake at 325 degrees for 45 minutes or until thick and creamy. Sprinkle with pecans and serve.
Yield: 6 servings.

Gleora Strauss, Laureate Alpha Lambda
Randolph, Kansas

TOMATO PIE

1 unbaked (9-inch) pie shell
3 large tomatoes, thickly sliced, drained
Salt and pepper to taste
3 green onions, chopped
8 ounces Mexican-blend shredded cheese
1/2 cup mayonnaise

Bake the pie shell at 425 degrees for 5 minutes; let cool. Arrange the tomato slices in the pie shell; season them with salt and pepper and sprinkle with green onions. Spread a mixture of the cheese and mayonnaise over the top. Bake at 400 degrees for 35 minutes. Cool and serve. Yield: 8 servings.

Donna Pool, Preceptor Beta Tau
Mesquite, Texas

TURNIP PUFF

1 medium to large turnip
2 tablespoons butter
2 eggs, beaten
3 tablespoons flour
1 tablespoon brown sugar
1 teaspoon baking powder
3/4 teaspoon salt
1/8 teaspoon pepper
Pinch of nutmeg
1/2 cup fine bread crumbs
2 tablespoons melted butter

Place the turnip on 5 or 6 layers of paper towel in a microwave oven. Microwave on High until tender, about 20 to 30 minutes depending on the size of the turnip; let cool. Peel the turnip and place in a bowl. Mash it and stir in the 2 tablespoons butter and eggs. Combine the flour, brown sugar, baking powder, salt, pepper and nutmeg; stir into the turnip mixture. Spread in a greased medium or large baking dish. Toss the bread crumbs with the 2 tablespoons melted butter and sprinkle over the turnip mixture. Bake at 375 degrees for 20 to 25 minutes or until beginning to brown. Yield: 20 to 25 servings.

Doris H. Cosco, Preceptor Gamma Phi
Sioux Lookout, Ontario, Canada

INDIAN VEGETABLES

Use "California blend" frozen vegetables if you can find them.

1 teaspoon chili powder
1 teaspoon coriander
1 tablespoon cumin seeds
Salt to taste
2 (16-ounce) packages frozen mixed vegetables, thawed
Cilantro leaves to taste

Sauté the chili powder, coriander, cumin seeds and salt in hot oil in a skillet over medium heat for about 2 minutes, stirring constantly. Add the mixed vegetables and mix well. Cook, covered, over low heat for 5 to 10 minutes or until vegetables are tender. Stir in the cilantro. Serve with Indian bread (nan) or pita bread. Yield: 4 to 6 servings.

Joyce Ahmad, Xi Theta Epsilon
Centerville, Ohio

MARVELOUS VEGETABLE MEDLEY

2 tablespoons butter
2 cups frozen cut green beans, thawed
3 carrots, sliced
1 green bell pepper, cut into strips
1 large onion, thinly sliced
2 cups sliced celery
1 1/2 teaspoons salt
1/2 teaspoon white pepper
1 tablespoon sugar
2 tablespoons cornstarch
1 (32-ounce) can whole tomatoes, drained
3 tablespoons butter, softened

Melt the 2 tablespoons butter in a 3-quart casserole or baking dish. Layer the green beans, carrots, bell pepper, onion and celery in the casserole. Combine the salt, white pepper, sugar and cornstarch in a bowl and blend. Sprinkle the cornstarch mixture over the celery layer. Spread the tomatoes over the top; dot with the softened 3 tablespoons butter. Bake, covered, at 350 degrees for 1 hour or until vegetables are tender. Yield: 8 to 10 servings.

Nancy F. Otte, Preceptor Laureate Pi
Freeport, Illinois

OVEN-ROASTED ROOT VEGETABLES

2 cups cubed peeled rutabaga
2 cups cubed peeled parsnips
2 cups cubed peeled butternut squash
2 medium onions, chopped
1 to 2 tablespoons olive oil
1/2 teaspoon salt
1/8 teaspoon pepper
1 tablespoon minced fresh thyme, or 1 teaspoon dried
1 tablespoon minced fresh sage, or 1 teaspoon dried

Combine the rutabaga, parsnips, squash and onions in a large bowl. Add the olive oil, salt and pepper; toss to coat. Arrange in a single layer in a 10×15-inch baking pan that has been sprayed with nonstick cooking spray. Bake, uncovered, at 400 degrees for 40 to 50 minutes, stirring occasionally. Sprinkle with thyme and sage about halfway through baking time. Yield: 6 to 8 servings.

Mary Ellen Grossman, Laureate Beta Nu
Lawrenceburg, Indiana

---

*For a multi-purpose treat, Paige Curtis, Alpha Nu, Westminster, Colorado, prepares **Mango Chutney**. She chops 3 to 4 tablespoons fresh ginger, sautées in olive oil until brown, adds 2 or 3 sliced mangoes, and cooks until soft. Blend in 1/4 cup sherry. Good with chicken or pork or over cream cheese.*

SPICY TEX-MEX VEGETABLE PIZZA

1 (12-inch) pizza crust or Italian bread shell
2 (6-ounce) packages sliced provolone cheese
1 cup bottled roasted red pepper sauce or roasted garlic sauce
2 teaspoons Mexican seasoning or 1 teaspoon chili powder
1 cup frozen whole kernel corn, thawed
1 cup canned black beans, rinsed and drained

Place the pizza crust on a baking sheet. Arrange half the provolone slices over the crust. Spread a mixture of the red pepper sauce and Mexican seasoning over the provolone. Layer the corn and black beans over the top and cover with the remaining provolone. Bake at 450 degrees for about 12 minutes or until cheese is melted and crust is golden brown.
Yield: 6 to 8 servings.

Susan Osburn, Preceptor Delta Gamma
Muskegon, Michigan

VEGETARIAN LASAGNA

1 garlic clove, minced
3 tablespoons parsley flakes
1 tablespoon basil
1/2 tablespoon sugar
1 teaspoon salt (optional)
1 (15-ounce) can diced tomatoes
1 (12-ounce) can tomato paste
1 (14-ounce) can spinach, drained
12 lasagna noodles
3 cups cream-style cottage cheese
2 eggs, beaten
1/2 teaspoon pepper
1/2 cup grated Parmesan cheese
16 ounces Mozzarella cheese, shredded (4 cups)

Combine the garlic, 2 tablespoons of the parsley flakes, basil, sugar, 1/2 teaspoon of the salt, undrained tomatoes, tomato paste and spinach in a saucepan over medium heat and mix well. Simmer, uncovered, for 30 minutes. Cook the lasagna noodles using the package directions. Combine the cottage cheese, eggs, the remaining 1/2 teaspoon salt, pepper, the remaining tablespoon parsley flakes and Parmesan cheese in a bowl and mix well. Layer 6 lasagna noodles in a 9×13-inch baking dish. Layer 1 1/2 cups of the cottage cheese mixture, 2 cups of the mozzarella cheese and 1 1/2 cups tomato mixture over the noodles. Repeat the layers. Bake at 375 degrees for 45 minutes. Let stand for 10 to 15 minutes before cutting. Yield: 9 to 12 servings.

June De Long, Xi Eta Theta
Indianapolis, Indiana

Cakes

APPLE CAKE WITH WARM BUTTER SAUCE

1/2 cup shortening
3 cups sugar
2 eggs
2 cups flour
1/4 teaspoon nutmeg
2 teaspoons baking soda
1/2 teaspoon salt
1 teaspoon cinnamon
1/2 cup chopped English walnuts
4 cups chopped peeled apples
1 cup half-and-half
1/2 cup (1 stick) butter
1 teaspoon vanilla extract

Cream the shortening and 2 cups of the sugar in a mixing bowl until light and fluffy. Beat in the eggs. Sift the flour, nutmeg, baking soda, salt and cinnamon together and mix into the egg mixture. Stir in the walnuts and apples. Pour into a buttered and floured 9×13-inch baking pan. Bake at 350 degrees for 45 to 50 minutes or until the cake tests done. Cool in the pan. Combine the remaining 1 cup sugar, half-and-half, butter and vanilla in a saucepan over medium-low heat. Cook until thick and buttery, stirring constantly. Pour evenly over the cooled cake. Top individual pieces with whipped cream and a maraschino cherry. Yield: 20 servings.

Bonnie J. Hula, Xi Omicron
Clarksville, Arkansas

APPLE CIDER CAKE

1 (2-layer) yellow cake mix
1 (4-ounce) package vanilla instant pudding mix
4 eggs
1 cup apple cider
1/2 cup vegetable oil
3/4 teaspoon cinnamon
1/4 teaspoon ground cloves

Combine the dry cake mix, dry pudding mix, eggs, apple cider, vegetable oil, cinnamon and cloves in a large mixing bowl and beat until smooth. Pour into a bundt pan that has been sprayed with nonstick cooking spray and dusted with flour. Bake at 350 degrees for 42 to 48 minutes or until the cake tests done. Cool in the pan for 20 minutes. Invert onto a serving plate. Drizzle with a mixture of 1 cup confectioners' sugar, 1 tablespoon melted margarine and enough apple cider to make a glaze. Yield: 12 to 16 servings.

Becky Larson, Xi Eta Pi
Mallard, Iowa

APPLE WALNUT SPICE CAKE

3 1/4 cups sifted flour
1 teaspoon baking soda
1 teaspoon baking powder
1/2 teaspoon nutmeg
1/2 teaspoon cinnamon
1/2 teaspoon salt
5 cups chopped peeled Granny Smith apples
2 1/2 cups sugar
1 cup margarine, softened
3 eggs
1 teaspoon vanilla extract
1 1/2 cups walnuts, chopped
Orange Glaze

Sift the flour, baking soda, baking powder, nutmeg, cinnamon and salt into a bowl. Combine the apples and sugar in a large mixing bowl and toss to coat. Add the margarine, eggs and vanilla and beat well at medium speed. Beat in the flour mixture. Add the walnuts and mix well. Spoon into a buttered and floured tube pan. Bake at 350 degrees for 1 hour and 15 minutes or until a wooden pick inserted in the center comes out clean. Invert on a funnel to cool partially. Loosen the warm cake carefully from the side of the pan. Invert onto a plate. Drizzle with Orange

Glaze and sprinkle with confectioners' sugar. Slide onto a doily on a cake plate. Yield: 15 to 20 servings.

ORANGE GLAZE

2 teaspoons grated orange zest
1/2 cup fresh orange juice
1/4 teaspoon sugar

Combine the orange zest and juice, sugar and 1/4 teaspoon water in a small saucepan over medium-high heat and bring to a boil. Boil gently for 10 minutes.

Helen Turner, Preceptor Alpha Tau
Lawton, Oklahoma

FRENCH VANILLA APPLE CAKE

1 (21-ounce) can apple pie filling
1 (2-layer) package yellow cake mix
3 eggs
1/2 cup canola oil
1/2 cup walnut pieces
1/4 teaspoon cinnamon
2 (16-ounce) cans French vanilla frosting
Fresh apple slices
Lemon juice
Walnut halves

Combine 1/4 of the apple pie filling, dry cake mix, eggs and canola oil in a mixing bowl and beat at low speed for 30 seconds. Beat at medium speed for 2 minutes. Pour into 2 buttered and floured 8-inch cake pans. Bake at 350 degrees for 30 minutes or until the cake tests done. Cool in the pan for 15 minutes. Remove to a wire rack to cool. Spread the walnut pieces on a baking sheet and bake at 350 degrees for 6 minutes or until lightly browned; let cool. Stir the cinnamon into the frosting. Place 1 cake layer on a serving plate. Spread 3/4 cup frosting over the top. Layer the remaining apple pie filling over the frosting. Place the second cake layer over the pie filling. Spread frosting over the top and side of the cake. Top with apple slices that have been tossed with lemon juice. Decorate with walnut halves. Yield: 16 servings.

Shirley N. Longobucco, Gamma Master
Torrington, Connecticut

CARAMEL APPLE CUPCAKES

1 (18-ounce) package spice cake or carrot cake mix
2 cups chopped peeled tart apples
20 caramels
3 tablespoons milk
1 cup finely chopped walnuts or pecans

Prepare the cake mix using the package directions; fold in the apples. Fill 12 buttered or paper-lined jumbo muffin cups 3/4 full. Bake at 350 degrees for 20 minutes or until the cake tests done. Cool in the pan for 10 minutes. Remove to a wire rack to cool completely. Combine the caramels and milk in a saucepan over low heat. Cook until caramels are melted and mixture is smooth, stirring frequently. Spread the caramel mixture over the cooled cupcakes. Sprinkle with walnuts. Insert a popsicle stick in the center of each cupcake. Yield: 1 dozen.

Cherie Kenealy, Xi Alpha Alpha
Council Bluffs, Iowa

SUMMER COOLER APRICOT ORANGE CAKE

1 (2-layer) orange cake mix
1/2 cup vegetable oil
1 (3-ounce) package vanilla instant pudding mix
4 eggs
1/4 cup vodka
1/4 cup apricot brandy
3/4 cup apricot nectar
Summer Cooler Glaze

Combine the dry cake mix, vegetable oil, dry pudding mix, eggs, vodka, apricot brandy and apricot nectar in a large mixing bowl and beat at medium speed for 4 minutes. Pour into a buttered and floured tube pan or bundt pan. Bake at 350 degrees for 45 to 50 minutes or until the cake tests done. Invert onto a serving plate to cool. Drizzle warm Summer Cooler Glaze over the cooled cake. Yield: 12 to 20 servings.

SUMMER COOLER GLAZE

1 cup confectioners' sugar
2 tablespoons vodka
2 tablespoons apricot brandy
2 tablespoons apricot nectar

Combine the confectioners' sugar, vodka, apricot brandy and apricot nectar in a saucepan over medium-low heat. Cook until warm and smooth, stirring frequently.

Dyanna L. Lawson, Laureate Eta Iota
Aledo, Texas

Lona M. Fisher, Laureate Beta Theta, Odessa, Missouri, shares her method for making ***Microwave Petits Fours.*** *Cut the lids from 4 clean styrofoam egg cartons; reserve the lids. Spray the cups with nonstick cooking spray. Prepare any flavor cake mix using the package directions. Spoon the batter into the prepared egg cups, filling 3/4 full. Cover with the reserved lids. Microwave 1 carton at a time on High for 2 minutes. Check for doneness: If the tops of the cakes are moist, microwave for 1 minute longer or until cakes are spongy. Invert cakes onto waxed paper to cool. Discard the egg cartons. Frost with your own frosting or use canned frosting microwaved for 1 to 2 seconds. Decorate as desired.*

TANGY GLAZED APRICOT CAKE

1 (2-layer) package lemon cake with pudding in the mix
$1/2$ cup sugar
1 cup apricot nectar
$2/3$ cup vegetable oil
4 eggs
1 cup confectioners' sugar
Grated lemon zest to taste
Juice of 1 lemon

Combine the dry lemon cake mix, sugar, apricot nectar and vegetable oil in a large mixing bowl and mix well. Add the eggs 1 at a time, mixing well after each addition. Pour into a buttered and floured tube pan or bundt pan. Bake at 325 degrees for 1 hour. Combine the confectioners' sugar, lemon zest and lemon juice in a small bowl and mix until smooth. Remove the cake from the oven and let cool in the pan on a wire rack for 5 minutes. Invert the cake onto a serving plate. Drizzle the lemon glaze over the hot cake. Yield: 16 servings.

Lucille Greenfield, Kappa Master
West Richland, Washington

BANANA UPSIDE-DOWN CAKE

3 medium bananas
1 cup sugar
2 tablespoons water
$1/4$ cup ($1/2$ stick) butter
$1\frac{1}{2}$ cups flour
2 teaspoons baking powder
$1/2$ teaspoon salt
$1/2$ cup (1 stick) butter
1 cup sugar
2 eggs
$1/2$ cup buttermilk
1 teaspoon vanilla extract

Quarter the bananas by cutting lengthwise and crosswise. Layer the banana pieces cut side down in a nonstick 8-inch cake pan. Combine 1 cup sugar and 2 tablespoons water in a saucepan over high heat. Cook until sugar is caramelized, stirring constantly. Stir in the $1/4$ cup butter. Drizzle over the bananas. Sift the flour, baking powder and salt into a bowl. Cream the $1/2$ cup butter and 1 cup sugar in a mixing bowl until light and fluffy. Beat in the eggs, buttermilk and vanilla. Beat in the flour mixture gradually. Pour the batter carefully over the bananas. Bake at 325 degrees for 50 minutes or until the cake pulls away from the side of the pan and the top springs back when lightly pressed with a finger. Cool in the pan for 5 minutes. Invert onto a serving plate. Serve warm or at room temperature. Yield: 12 servings.

Marie Smith, Alpha Zeta Master
St. Petersburg, Florida

BLUEBERRY WINE CAKE

1 (2-layer) package white cake mix
1 (3-ounce) package blackberry gelatin
4 eggs
$1/2$ cup vegetable oil
$1\frac{1}{2}$ cups blackberry wine
$1/2$ cup chopped pecans
1 cup confectioners' sugar
$1/2$ cup (1 stick) butter or light margarine

Combine the dry cake mix and dry gelatin mix in a mixing bowl. Add the eggs, vegetable oil and 1 cup of the blackberry wine; beat at low speed until moistened. Beat at medium speed for 2 minutes, scraping the bowl frequently. Sprinkle the pecans in a buttered and floured bundt pan. Pour in the batter. Bake at 325 degrees for 45 to 50 minutes or until the cake tests done. Combine the confectioners' sugar, butter and the remaining $1/2$ cup blackberry wine in a saucepan and bring to a boil. Pour half the glaze over the hot cake in the pan. Let cool in the pan for 30 minutes. Stir additional confectioners' sugar into the remaining glaze to thicken. Invert the cake onto a serving plate and drizzle with the thickened glaze.
Yield: 8 to 10 servings.

Paula Lyens, Laureate Epsilon Theta
Treasure Island, Florida

BLUEBERRY POUND CAKE

You may use fresh blueberries if you prefer.

1 (2-layer) package golden butter recipe cake mix
8 ounces cream cheese, softened
$1/2$ cup vegetable oil
3 eggs
1 (20-ounce) can blueberries, drained

Combine the dry cake mix, cream cheese, vegetable oil and eggs in a large mixing bowl and beat at medium speed for 3 to 4 minutes. Fold in the blueberries. Pour into a buttered bundt pan. Bake at 300 degrees for 1 hour. Cool in the pan for 15 minutes. Invert onto a serving plate. Yield: 16 servings.

Flo Brouillette, Laureate Chi
Natchitoches, Louisiana

CARAMEL PUDDING CAKE

$1/2$ cup (1 stick) butter or margarine, softened
$1/2$ cup granulated sugar
$1\frac{1}{2}$ cups flour
1 teaspoon baking powder
$1/2$ teaspoon salt
$1/2$ cup milk
$1/2$ cup raisins
1 cup packed brown sugar

Cream the butter and granulated sugar in a mixing bowl until light and fluffy. Mix the flour, baking powder and salt together and add to the creamed mixture. Add the milk and stir until smooth. Stir in the raisins. Spread in a buttered 8×8-inch baking pan. Mix the brown sugar and 2 cups cold water together and pour evenly over the batter. Bake at 350 degrees for 40 minutes or until golden brown. Serve warm. Yield: 9 servings.

Myrt Kruse, Preceptor Alpha Phi
Glendale, Arizona

FAKE BOSTON CREAM PIE

We needed a Boston Cream Pie to serve at a dinner play, but we would not be able to keep it refrigerated. I recalled a room-temperature filling from an old recipe. It "saved the play"!

1 (2-layer) package yellow cake mix
1/2 cup (1 stick) plus 3 tablespoons margarine
1/2 cup shortening
1 cup granulated sugar
3/4 cup evaporated milk
1 tablespoon plus 3/4 teaspoon vanilla extract
3 tablespoons baking cocoa
1 cup confectioners' sugar

Prepare and bake the cake in two 9-inch cake pans using the package directions. Cool in the pan for 10 minutes. Remove to a wire rack to cool completely. Cut the cakes in half horizontally, making 4 layers. Cream the 1/2 cup margarine and shortening in a mixing bowl until smooth. Add the sugar to the margarine mixture alternately with the evaporated milk, mixing well after each addition. Add the 1 tablespoon vanilla. Beat at high speed until all sugar is incorporated. Spread half the evaporated milk mixture between 2 cake layers. Repeat with the remaining filling and cake layers. Combine the 3 tablespoons margarine and baking cocoa in a small mixing bowl and mix until smooth. Beat in the confectioners' sugar, the 3/4 teaspoon vanilla and 2 tablespoons hot water. Drizzle the cocoa mixture over the tops of the pies; it should drip down the side. Yield: 16 to 20 servings (2 pies).

Annette Krinhop, Zeta Zeta
Junction City, Kansas

DELUXE CARROT CAKE

1 1/2 cups (3 sticks) butter
2 1/2 cups packed dark brown sugar
5 extra-large eggs
1 tablespoon vanilla extract
4 cups shredded carrots
1 cup chopped almonds or pecans or both
3 cups flour
2 teaspoons baking powder
1 teaspoon baking soda
Cream Cheese Frosting

Cream the butter and brown sugar in a mixing bowl until fluffy. Add the eggs 1 at a time, mixing well after each addition. Beat in the vanilla. Stir in the carrots. Add the almonds and mix well. Add 1 cup of the flour and mix well. Mix in the baking powder and baking soda. Add the remaining 2 cups flour and beat until well mixed. Spoon the batter into three 8-inch cake pans. Bake at 350 degrees for 30 minutes or until the cake tests done. Cool the cake layers in the pans on wire racks for 5 to 10 minutes. Remove from the pans to wire racks to cool completely. Spread Cream Cheese Frosting between the layers and over the top of the cooled cake.
Yield: 12 servings.

CREAM CHEESE FROSTING

1/2 cup (1 stick) butter, softened
8 ounces cream cheese, softened
3 cups (about) confectioners' sugar

Combine the butter and cream cheese in a mixing bowl and blend well. Beat in enough confectioners' sugar to make of spreading consistency.

Anne G. Wilson, Laureate Beta Gamma
Kingman, Arizona

SWEET CHERRY CAKE

3/4 cup milk
1/4 cup maraschino cherry juice
2 1/2 cups sifted cake flour
1 1/2 cups sugar
3 1/2 teaspoons baking powder
1 teaspoon salt
1/2 cup shortening
1 teaspoon vanilla extract
2 teaspoons almond extract
4 egg whites
18 maraschino cherries, well drained, finely chopped
1/2 cup finely chopped walnuts

Combine the milk and cherry juice in a small bowl; whisk to blend. Sift the cake flour, sugar, baking powder and salt into a mixing bowl. Add the shortening, 3/4 of the cherry juice mixture, vanilla and almond extract. Beat at low speed for 2 minutes, scraping the bowl and beaters when necessary. Add the remaining cherry juice mixture and unbeaten egg whites. Beat at low speed for 2 minutes. Stir in the cherries and walnuts. Pour into 2 buttered deep 9-inch cake pans. Bake at 375 degrees for 20 to 25 minutes or until the cake tests done. Frost the cooled cake with a seven-minute icing. Yield: 12 servings.

Pat Ireland, Laureate Beta Lambda
Green Valley, Arizona

CHERRY BUNDT CAKE

1 (5-ounce) can evaporated milk
1 (10-ounce) jar maraschino cherries, drained, stems removed, juice reserved
1 cup (2 sticks) butter or margarine
1/2 cup shortening
3 cups sugar
1 teaspoon vanilla extract
1 teaspoon butternut extract
5 eggs
3 cups flour
1 cup chopped pecans

Pour the evaporated milk into a measuring cup. Add enough of the reserved cherry juice to make 1 cup liquid. Cream the butter and shortening in a bowl with a wooden spoon until light and fluffy. Beat in the sugar 1 cup at a time. Add the vanilla and butternut extracts. Add the eggs 1 at a time, mixing well after each addition. Add 2 1/2 cups of the flour to the egg mixture alternately with the cherry juice mixture, mixing well after each addition. Place the cherries and pecans in a small bowl; toss with the remaining 1/2 cup flour to coat. Stir the cherry mixture into the batter. Spoon into a buttered and floured bundt pan. Bake at 300 degrees for 2 hours. Cool in the pan for 5 minutes. Remove to a wire rack to cool completely. Yield: 20 to 24 servings.

Blanche N. Goldsmith, Eta Master
Las Cruces, New Mexico

AMARETTI TORTE

10 amaretti (cookies)
4 ounces semisweet baking chocolate, coarsely chopped
1 cup unsalted butter, at room temperature
1 cup sugar
5 eggs, separated, at room temperature
1/2 cup flour

Butter the bottom and side of a 9-inch springform pan or cake pan. Line the pan with parchment paper. Butter and flour the paper; shake off excess flour. Break the amaretti into pieces and process in a food processor or blender to make about 1/3 cup fine crumbs. Melt the chocolate with 1 tablespoon water in the top of a double boiler over simmering water, stirring occasionally until smooth. Remove from heat; let cool. Beat the butter in a large mixing bowl until creamy. Beat in the sugar gradually until well blended. Add the egg yolks 1 at a time, mixing well after each addition. Beat at medium speed for about 5 minutes or until batter is light and fluffy. Add the flour to the batter alternately with the amaretti crumbs 1/2 at a time, beating well after each addition. Fold in the chocolate. Beat the egg whites in a medium mixing bowl with clean beaters until stiff peaks form. Fold the egg whites into the batter. Pour the batter into the prepared pan. Bake at 350 degrees for 40 to 45 minutes or until a wooden pick inserted in the center comes out clean. Cool in the pan on a wire rack for about 10 minutes. Invert onto a serving plate. Remove the pan and peel off the parchment paper. Cool completely. Sprinkle with confectioners' sugar just before serving. Garnish with a dollop of sour cream if desired. Yield: 10 to 12 servings.

Gail Shannon, Laureate Epsilon Tau
Houston, Texas

CREAMY CHOCOLATE BUNDT CAKE

Be sure not to omit the pinch of salt called for in each part of the recipe. It is important for the taste.

2 cups semisweet chocolate chips
1 (2-layer) super-moist devil's food cake mix
1 cup sour cream
1 cup packed dark brown sugar
Pinch of salt
1/2 cup vegetable oil
4 extra-large eggs
Chocolate Cream Cheese Frosting

Place the chocolate chips in a large glass measuring cup and add 1/4 cup water. Microwave on High for 1 1/2 minutes; stir until smooth and creamy. Combine the dry cake mix, sour cream, brown sugar, salt, vegetable oil, another 1/4 cup water and eggs in a large mixing bowl. Mix at low speed until moistened. Mix in the chocolate mixture. Pour evenly into a buttered large bundt pan. Tap the pan on the counter 2 or 3 times to release air bubbles. Bake at 350 degrees for 1 hour. Cool in the pan for 30 minutes. Invert onto a cake plate. Cool completely and frost heavily with Chocolate Cream Cheese Frosting.
Yield: 12 to 16 servings.

CHOCOLATE CREAM CHEESE FROSTING

8 ounces cream cheese, at room temperature
1/2 cup (1 stick) butter or margarine, at room temperature
Pinch of salt
2 teaspoons vanilla extract
1/2 cup baking cocoa
Slightly more than 1 pound confectioners' sugar

Combine the cream cheese, butter, salt and vanilla in a mixing bowl and beat until smooth. Add the baking cocoa and confectioners' sugar. Beat until stiff and creamy.

Tammy Easterling, Beta Beta Chi
Cedar Hill, Texas

CHOCOLATE COCONUT CAKE

1 (18-ounce) package golden pound cake mix
4 ounces semisweet baking chocolate, melted and cooled
1/3 cup sour cream
2 eggs
1/3 cup flaked coconut
2 tablespoons honey or light corn syrup

Butter a 12-cup bundt cake pan generously and flour lightly. Combine the dry cake mix, 2/3 cup water, 3 ounces of the chocolate, sour cream and eggs in a medium mixing bowl and beat at low speed for 30 seconds. Beat at medium speed for 3 minutes. Fold in the coconut. Pour into the prepared bundt pan. Bake at 325 degrees for 45 to 50 minutes or until a wooden pick inserted in the center comes out clean. Cool in the pan for 10 minutes. Remove to a wire rack to cool completely. Combine the remaining 1 ounce chocolate and honey in a small bowl and mix well. Drizzle the honey mixture over the cake. Sprinkle with additional flaked coconut. Yield: 12 servings.

Helen Slate, Alpha Omicron
Canon City, Colorado

✣ CHOCOLATE ITALIAN CREAM CAKE

5 eggs, separated
1/2 cup (1 stick) butter
1/2 cup shortening
2 cups sugar
1 teaspoon vanilla extract
2 cups flour
1 teaspoon baking soda
1/4 cup baking cocoa
1 cup buttermilk
1 cup shredded coconut
1 cup chopped pecans
Cocoa Pecan Frosting

Butter and flour three 8-inch cake pans. Beat the egg whites until stiff peaks form. Cream the butter, shortening and sugar in a mixing bowl until light and fluffy. Beat in the egg yolks 1 at a time. Beat in the vanilla. Sift the flour, baking soda and baking cocoa together. Add the dry ingredients to the creamed mixture alternately with the buttermilk, blending well after each addition, beginning and ending with dry ingredients. Stir in the coconut and pecans. Fold in the stiffly beaten egg whites. Pour into the prepared cake pans. Bake at 350 degrees for 25 to 30 minutes or until the cake tests done. Spread Cocoa Pecan Frosting between the layers and over the top and side of the cooled cake. Yield: 10 servings.

COCOA PECAN FROSTING

8 ounces cream cheese, softened
1/2 cup (1 stick) butter, softened
4 cups sifted confectioners' sugar
1/4 cup baking cocoa
1 teaspoon vanilla extract
1 cup chopped pecans
1 cup shredded coconut

Combine the cream cheese and butter in a mixing bowl and beat until smooth and creamy. Sift the confectioners' sugar and baking cocoa into the creamed mixture gradually, beating well after each addition. Beat in the vanilla. Stir in the pecans and coconut.

Tommie May, Laureate Zeta Gamma
Houston, Texas

CHOCOLATE NUT ZUCCHINI CAKE

1/2 cup plus 1 tablespoon baking cocoa
3 cups flour
1 1/2 teaspoons baking powder
1 teaspoon baking soda
1 teaspoon salt
4 eggs
3 cups sugar
1 1/2 cups vegetable oil
3 cups grated zucchini
1 cup chopped pecans

Combine the baking cocoa, flour, baking powder, baking soda and salt in a bowl and mix well. Combine the eggs, sugar and vegetable oil in a mixing bowl and beat well. Mix in the zucchini. Mix in the flour mixture. Stir in the pecans. Spoon into a buttered and floured bundt pan. Bake at 350 degrees for 1 hour and 15 minutes or until a wooden pick inserted in the center comes out clean.
Yield: 16 to 20 servings.

Margaret Head, Preceptor Alpha Tau
Elgin, Texas

CHOCOLATE POTATO CAKE

1 cup shortening
3 cups sugar
6 eggs
3 cups flour
2 tablespoons baking powder
1 teaspoon nutmeg
1/4 teaspoon salt
1 teaspoon ground cloves
3/4 cup baking cocoa
1/2 teaspoon cinnamon
1 1/2 cups mashed potatoes
1 teaspoon vanilla extract
3/4 cup milk or strong coffee
1 1/2 cups chopped walnuts

Combine the shortening, sugar and eggs in a large mixing bowl and beat at high speed until the consistency of thick whipped cream. Sift the flour, baking powder, nutmeg, salt, cloves, baking cocoa and cinnamon into the egg mixture and mix well. Add the mashed potatoes, vanilla and milk; mix well. Stir in the walnuts. Spoon into two buttered 9-inch cake pans. Bake at 350 degrees for 50 to 60 minutes or until the cake tests done. Spread chocolate frosting between the layers and over the top and side of the cooled cake. Yield: 12 servings.

Amelia Pira, Laureate Beta Iota
Merced, California

EGGLESS MILKLESS BUTTERLESS CHOCOLATE CAKE

3 cups flour
2 cups sugar
6 tablespoons baking cocoa
1 teaspoon salt
2 teaspoons baking soda
2 tablespoons vinegar
2 teaspoons vanilla extract
3/4 cup vegetable oil
1 1/3 cups confectioners' sugar
1/4 cup margarine, softened
2 tablespoons milk
1 ounce baking chocolate, melted

Place the flour, sugar, baking cocoa, salt and baking soda in a large mixing bowl and mix with a fork. Combine 2 cups cold water, the vinegar, 1 teaspoon of the vanilla and vegetable oil in a separate bowl and mix well. Add the liquid ingredients to the dry ingredients all at once; beat until well blended. Pour into a generously buttered and floured 9×13-inch baking dish. Bake at 350 degrees for 30 minutes or until the cake tests done. To make the frosting, combine the confectioners' sugar, margarine, milk, chocolate and the remaining 1 teaspoon vanilla in a mixing bowl and beat until smooth. Spread the frosting between the layers and over the top and side of the cooled cake. Yield: 15 servings.

Janet A. Stuemke, Preceptor Beta
Lake Oswego, Oregon

ITALIAN RICOTTA CAKE

1 (2-layer) package fudge marble cake mix
2 pounds ricotta cheese
4 large eggs
1 teaspoon vanilla extract
3/4 cup sugar
1 (4-ounce) package chocolate instant pudding mix
1 cup milk
8 ounces whipped topping

Prepare the cake mix using the package directions. Pour the batter into a buttered and floured 9×13-inch baking dish. Combine the ricotta cheese, eggs, vanilla and sugar in a mixing bowl and beat at medium speed until blended. Spoon the ricotta mixture evenly over the cake batter. Do not mix; the cake will rise above the ricotta mixture. Bake at 350 degrees for 1 hour. Cool in the pan. To make the frosting, combine the dry pudding mix and milk in a mixing bowl and beat at low speed until smooth. Add the whipped topping and beat at low speed until creamy. Spread over the top of the cooled cake. Store the cake in the refrigerator. Yield: 12 servings.

Rose Marie Conroy, Laureate Phi
Montgomery, New York

MAYONNAISE CAKE

2 cups flour
2 cups sugar
2 teaspoons baking soda
6 tablespoons baking cocoa
1 cup mayonnaise
2 eggs
Creamy Chocolate Icing

Combine the flour, sugar, baking soda and baking cocoa in a bowl and mix well. Add 1 cup cold water, the mayonnaise and eggs; mix well. Pour into a buttered and floured 9×13-inch baking pan. Bake at 350 degrees for 45 minutes or until a wooden pick inserted in the center comes out clean. Pour the Creamy Chocolate Icing evenly over the warm cake. Yield: 12 servings.

CREAMY CHOCOLATE ICING

1 2/3 cups sugar
1 1/2 tablespoons baking cocoa
Pinch of salt
7 tablespoons half-and-half
1 teaspoon vanilla extract
1 tablespoon light corn syrup

Combine the sugar, baking cocoa, salt, half-and-half, vanilla and corn syrup in a saucepan over medium-high heat; bring to a boil. Boil for 1 1/2 minutes, stirring constantly. Place the saucepan in a baking pan filled with cold water. Let cool, stirring until the icing coats the spoon without running.

Stephanie Miller, Zeta Lambda
Russell, Iowa

KAHLUA CAKE

1 (2-layer) package yellow cake mix
1 (4-ounce) package chocolate instant pudding mix
4 eggs
1/2 cup vegetable oil
1/3 cup Kahlúa
1/3 cup vodka
Kahlúa Frosting

Combine the dry cake mix, dry pudding mix, eggs, vegetable oil, Kahlúa, vodka and 3/4 cup water in a large mixing bowl and mix until smooth. Pour into an unbuttered bundt pan. Bake at 350 degrees for 50 minutes or until the cake tests done. Cool in the pan. Drizzle Kahlúa Frosting over the cake.
Yield: 16 servings.

KAHLUA FROSTING

1 tablespoon instant coffee granules
1 tablespoon Kahlúa
1 cup sifted confectioners' sugar

Dissolve the coffee granules in 2 tablespoons hot water in a bowl. Stir in the Kahlúa and confectioners' sugar.

Henrietta M. Martz, Preceptor Nu Omega
Sutter Creek, California

COCOA BUTTERMILK CAKE

4 cups sugar
4 cups flour
1 teaspoon salt
1 cup (2 sticks) butter
1 cup vegetable oil
1/2 cup baking cocoa
4 eggs, beaten
2 teaspoons baking soda
1 cup buttermilk
2 teaspoons vanilla extract
Cocoa Icing

Mix the sugar, flour and salt together in a large bowl. Combine the butter, vegetable oil, baking cocoa and 2 cups water in a saucepan over medium-high heat. Bring to a boil and add to the flour mixture; mix well. Combine the eggs, baking soda, buttermilk and vanilla in a bowl and blend well. Add to the flour mixture; mix well. Pour into a buttered and floured 9×13-inch baking dish. Bake at 375 degrees for 45 minutes to 1 hour or until the cake tests done. Frost the warm cake with Cocoa Icing.
Yield: 12 to 16 servings.

COCOA ICING

3/4 cup milk
1 cup margarine
6 tablespoons baking cocoa
2 (1-pound) packages confectioners' sugar
2 cups chopped pecans (optional)

Combine the milk, margarine and baking cocoa in a saucepan over medium-high heat and bring to a boil. Boil gently for 2 to 3 minutes. Remove from heat. Stir in the confectioners' sugar and pecans.

Kathy McConaghy, Chi Omicron
Naperville, Illinois

MOCHA BUTTERMILK CAKE

1 cup (2 sticks) butter, softened
2 1/2 cups sugar
5 eggs, separated
3 cups flour
4 teaspoons baking cocoa
1 teaspoon baking soda
Pinch of salt
1 cup buttermilk
2 teaspoons vanilla extract
5 tablespoons strong coffee
Mocha Icing

Cream the butter and sugar in a mixing bowl until light and fluffy. Add the egg yolks 1 at a time, mixing after each addition. Add a mixture of the flour, baking cocoa, baking soda and salt to the egg mixture alternately with the buttermilk, mixing after each addition. Beat in the vanilla and coffee. Beat the egg whites in a mixing bowl until stiff peaks form. Fold into the batter. Pour into 3 buttered 9-inch cake pans. Bake at 375 degrees for 25 to 30 minutes or until cake tests done. Spread Coffee Icing between the layers and over the top and side of the cooled cake. Yield: 8 large pieces.

COFFEE ICING

1 cup (2 sticks) butter, softened
2 (1-pound) packages confectioners' sugar
2 egg yolks, beaten
4 teaspoons baking cocoa
6 tablespoons strong coffee
2 teaspoons vanilla extract

Cream the butter and confectioners' sugar in a large mixing bowl until light and fluffy. Beat in the egg yolks, baking cocoa, coffee and vanilla. Beat until fluffy.

Sherry Eanes, Xi Alpha Tau
Dandridge, Tennessee

OREO CAKE

24 chocolate sandwich cookies, chopped
1/3 cup semisweet chocolate chips
1/3 cup flour
1/4 cup margarine, softened
1 (2-layer) package butter cake mix with pudding in the mix
1 cup confectioners' sugar
3 tablespoons milk

Combine the chopped cookies, chocolate chips, flour and margarine in a large bowl and mix well. Prepare the cake mix using the package directions. Pour half the cake batter into a 9×13-inch baking dish that has been sprayed with nonstick cooking spray. Sprinkle 2 cups of the cookie mixture evenly over the top. Repeat the layers. Bake at 350 degrees for 45 minutes or until a wooden pick inserted in the center comes out clean. Mix the confectioners' sugar and milk together to make a glaze. Drizzle over the warm cake. Yield: 12 servings.

Kim Rolfes, Xi Eta Sigma
Gowrie, Iowa

Lucylee Lively, Preceptor Iota Sigma, Dallas, Texas, prepares ***Peanut Rolls*** *by mixing a cake mix with 1 1/3 cups water, 2 tablespoons vegetable oil and 3 eggs and baking in an 11×13-inch cake pan at 350 degrees for 32 to 35 minutes. When cool, she cuts into 20 pieces, rolls in a thin glaze of confectioners' sugar and milk and then in ground unsalted peanuts to coat completely.*

WARM SOFT CHOCOLATE CAKE

9 tablespoons unsweetened butter
4 ounces bittersweet chocolate
2 eggs
2 egg yolks
1/4 cup sugar
6 teaspoons flour
1 tablespoon baking cocoa

Butter four 4-ounce individual baking dishes with 1 tablespoon of the butter. Dust with flour, tapping out the excess. Arrange the prepared baking dishes on a baking sheet. Combine the chocolate and the remaining 8 tablespoons butter in the top of a double boiler over simmering water. Heat for about 10 minutes or until almost completely melted. Combine the eggs, egg yolks and sugar in a mixing bowl and beat for 2 to 3 minutes or until thick and pale yellow. Whisk the chocolate mixture until smooth and add to the egg mixture, stirring just until combined. Whisk in the flour. Pour into the prepared ramekins. Bake in a preheated 450-degree oven for 7 minutes; center of cake will be very soft. Invert onto 4 individual dessert plates. Let stand undisturbed for about 10 seconds. Lift up an edge of each to allow the cake to spill out onto the plate. Dust with baking cocoa and serve immediately with a small scoop of vanilla ice cream. Yield: 4 servings.

Janet Semsak, Preceptor Alpha Chi
DuPont, Washington

WHITE CHOCOLATE CAKE

4 ounces white chocolate
1 cup (2 sticks) butter
2 cups sugar
4 eggs, slightly beaten
2 1/2 cups sifted cake flour
1/4 teaspoon baking soda
1 teaspoon baking powder
1 cup buttermilk
1 teaspoon vanilla extract
1 (8-ounce) can shredded coconut
1 cup floured pecans
Creamy Chocolate Frosting

Melt the white chocolate in the top of a double boiler over simmering water. Cream the butter and sugar in a mixing bowl until light and fluffy. Beat in the eggs and melted white chocolate. Sift the flour, baking soda and baking powder together into a bowl. Stir into the egg mixture gradually. Stir in the buttermilk and vanilla. Stir in the coconut and pecans. Pour into two buttered 9-inch cake pans. Bake at 350 degrees for 20 to 25 minutes or until the cake tests done. Frost the cooled cake with Creamy Chocolate Frosting. Yield: 8 servings.

CREAMY CHOCOLATE FROSTING

2 cups sugar
1 cup (2 sticks) butter
1 (5-ounce) can evaporated milk
1 teaspoon vanilla extract
4 ounces baking chocolate

Combine the sugar, butter, evaporated milk, vanilla and chocolate in a saucepan. Cook, uncovered, over medium heat to 234 to 240 degrees on a candy thermometer, soft-ball stage, stirring constantly; beat well until of spreading consistency.

Mae Carmody, Xi Alpha Tau
Morristown, Tennessee

CRANBERRY CAKE WITH BUTTER SAUCE

2 tablespoons melted butter
2 cups flour
1 cup sugar
1 cup milk
2 teaspoons baking soda
1 teaspoon salt
2 cups fresh cranberries
Butter Sauce

Combine the butter, flour, sugar, milk, baking soda and salt in a large mixing bowl and mix well. Fold in the cranberries; mixture will be thick. Spoon into a buttered 9×9-inch cake pan. Bake at 350 degrees for 40 minutes or until a wooden pick inserted in the center comes out clean. Drizzle individual servings of the warm cake with Butter Sauce. Yield: 9 servings.

BUTTER SAUCE

1 cup sugar
1/2 cup butter
1/2 cup heavy cream
1 teaspoon vanilla extract

Combine the sugar, butter, cream and vanilla in a saucepan over medium heat. Bring to a full boil. Boil for 3 minutes. Store leftovers in the refrigerator and reheat.

Sharon J. Simon, Gamma Zeta
Mobridge, South Dakota

ORANGE SLICE CAKE

1 cup margarine
2 cups sugar
4 eggs
1 teaspoon vanilla extract
3 1/2 cups flour
1 teaspoon baking soda
1 teaspoon salt
8 ounces chopped dates
1 pound orange slice candy, finely chopped
1 cup shredded coconut
2 cups chopped pecans
1/2 cup buttermilk
Orange Glaze

Cream the margarine and sugar in a mixing bowl until light and fluffy. Add the eggs 1 at a time, mixing well after each addition. Mix in the vanilla. Sift the flour, baking soda and salt together into a bowl. Sprinkle 1/2 cup of the flour mixture over the dates, candy, coconut and pecans in a bowl; mix to coat well. Add the flour mixture to the creamed mixture alternately with the buttermilk. Fold in the candy mixture. Pour into a buttered 9×13-inch cake pan. Bake at 250 degrees for 3 hours. Drizzle warm cake with Orange Glaze. Yield: 9 to 12 servings.

ORANGE GLAZE

1/2 cup sugar
1/2 cup orange juice

Combine the sugar and orange juice in a saucepan over medium heat and bring to a boil.

Sue Warden, Laureate Alpha Rho
Salem, Virginia

FUZZY NAVEL CAKE

1 (2-layer) package yellow cake mix
1/2 cup vegetable oil
1 (6-ounce) package vanilla instant pudding mix
4 eggs
1 cup peach schnapps
1/2 cup plus 2 tablespoons orange juice
1/2 teaspoon orange extract
1 cup sifted confectioners' sugar

Combine the dry cake mix, vegetable oil, dry pudding mix, eggs, 3/4 cup of the peach schnapps, the 1/2 cup orange juice and orange extract in a mixing bowl; blend well. Pour into a buttered and lightly floured 9 1/2-inch bundt pan. Bake at 350 degrees for 45 to 50 minutes or until the top springs back when lightly pressed. Remove from oven. Combine the remaining 1/4 cup peach schnapps, the 2 tablespoons orange juice and confectioners' sugar in a bowl; stir until smooth. Poke holes in the warm cake and pour the orange juice mixture into the holes. Cool in the pan for at least 2 hours. Remove to a serving plate.
Yield: 16 servings.

Nelda Wheeldon, Xi Eta Xi
Rushville, Indiana

BRAZIL NUT SENSATION

3/4 cup sifted flour
3/4 cup sugar
1/2 teaspoon baking powder
1/2 teaspoon salt
3 cups shelled Brazil nuts (2 pounds unshelled or 1 pound shelled)
2 (1-pound) packages pitted dates
1 cup well-drained maraschino cherries
3 eggs
1 teaspoon vanilla extract

Butter a 5×9-inch loaf pan and line with waxed paper. Place the flour, sugar, baking powder and salt in a flour sifter. Combine the nuts, dates and cherries in a large bowl. Sift the flour mixture over the nut mixture. Stir until well coated. Beat the eggs in a small bowl until foamy; stir in the vanilla. Stir the egg mixture into the nut mixture. Spread evenly in the prepared loaf pan. Bake at 300 degrees for 1 hour and 45 minutes or until the cake tests done. Cool in the pan on a wire rack. Remove to a wire rack to cool completely. Wrap in foil when completely cool. Store in the refrigerator. Yield: 8 to 10 servings.

Rose C. Gaspari, Beta Chi Master
Santa Rosa, California

EGGLESS MILKLESS BUTTERLESS RAISIN CAKE

This is my husband's favorite cake. My mother-in-law acquired the recipe during World War II when so many foods were rationed.

16 ounces raisins
1 3/4 cups sugar
1/2 cup shortening
4 cups flour
1 tablespoon baking soda
1/2 teaspoon salt
1 teaspoon cinnamon
1/2 teaspoon ground cloves
1/2 teaspoon nutmeg

Pour 2 cups boiling water over the raisins in a bowl. Let stand for 15 minutes. Add 1 cup cold water. Stir in the remaining ingredients; mix well. Spoon into a 9×13-inch cake pan that has been sprayed with nonstick cooking spray. Bake at 325 degrees for 45 minutes. Yield: 15 to 18 servings.

Wilma E. Jolly, Nu Master
Arvada, Colorado

FLAN CAKE

1 (2-layer) package devil's food cake mix
5 tablespoons Mexican caramel (cajeta)
1 (12-ounce) can evaporated milk
1 (14-ounce) can sweetened condensed milk
3 eggs
1 teaspoon vanilla extract

Prepare the cake mix using the package directions. Pour the caramel into a bundt pan that has been sprayed with nonstick cooking spray. Combine the remaining ingredients in a blender and process until smooth. Pour the milk mixture over the caramel layer. Pour the cake batter over the milk mixture. Bake at 350 degrees for 45 minutes. Cool in the pan for 15 minutes. Invert onto a serving plate.
Yield: 16 servings.

Diana G. Artalejo, Laureate Gamma Zeta
El Paso, Texas

FIG CAKE

1 cup buttermilk
1 cup light olive oil
3 eggs
1 1/2 cups sifted flour
1 teaspoon baking soda
1 teaspoon salt
1 teaspoon vanilla extract
1 teaspoon cinnamon
1 teaspoon allspice
1 cup chopped pecans
2 cups drained fig preserves
Buttermilk Sauce

Combine the buttermilk, olive oil and eggs in a mixing bowl and mix well. Sift the flour, baking soda, salt, vanilla, cinnamon and allspice over the buttermilk mixture and mix well. Stir in the pecans and fig preserves. Pour into a buttered and floured tube pan. Bake at 300 degrees for 1 hour. Cool in the pan for 10 minutes. Invert onto a serving plate. Spoon Buttermilk Sauce over the cooled cake and serve. Yield: 16 servings.

BUTTERMILK SAUCE

1/2 cup buttermilk
1/2 teaspoon baking soda
1 cup sugar
6 tablespoons butter

Combine the buttermilk, baking soda, sugar and butter in a saucepan. Cook over medium heat to 234 to 240 degrees on a candy thermometer, soft-ball stage. Beat until slightly cooled.

Sandi Dragg, Beta Kappa Sigma
Hilltop Lakes, Texas

LEMON SHEET CAKE

1 (2-layer) package lemon cake mix
4 eggs
1 (16-ounce) can lemon pie filling
3 ounces cream cheese, softened
1/2 cup (1 stick) butter or margarine, softened
2 cups confectioners' sugar
1 1/2 teaspoons vanilla extract

Combine the dry cake mix and eggs in a large mixing bowl and beat until smooth. Fold in the pie filling. Spread in a buttered 10×15-inch cake pan. Bake at 350 degrees for 18 to 20 minutes or until a wooden pick inserted in the center comes out clean. Remove to a wire rack to cool. Combine the cream cheese, butter and confectioners' sugar in a mixing bowl and beat until smooth. Stir in the vanilla. Spread over the top and sides of the cooled cake. Store in the refrigerator. Yield: 35 small pieces or 15 large.

Marjorie Buckner, Beta Kappa Master
Welland, Ontario, Canada

LEMON LOAF CAKE

1 cup (2 sticks) butter or margarine
2 1/2 cups granulated sugar
4 eggs
1/4 cup shredded lemon peel
3/4 cup buttermilk
3/4 cup lemon juice
3 cups flour
1/2 teaspoon baking soda
1 teaspoon salt
1/2 teaspoon baking powder
1 teaspoon vanilla extract
2 cups confectioners' sugar

Butter 2 loaf pans and line the bottom with parchment paper. Cream the butter and 2 cups of the sugar in a large mixing bowl until light and fluffy. Beat in the eggs. Beat in the lemon peel and buttermilk. Beat in 1/4 cup of the lemon juice. Add a mixture of the flour, baking soda, salt and baking powder and beat at medium speed for 2 to 3 minutes. Pour into the prepared loaf pans. Bake at 350 degrees for 45 to 50 minutes or until the cake tests done. Combine the remaining 1/2 cup sugar and the remaining 1/2 cup lemon juice in a saucepan over medium heat and cook until slightly thickened, stirring constantly. Spoon over the warm cake. Let cool. Combine the confectioners' sugar and enough additional lemon juice to make a thin glaze in a bowl; mix well. Drizzle over the cooled cake. Best the next day and several days afterwards. Yield: 10 to 12 servings.

Beverley Neff, Rho Master
South Charleston, West Virginia

LEMON JELLY ROLL

1 cup cake flour
1 teaspoon baking powder
1/4 teaspoon salt
3 large eggs
1 cup sugar
1 teaspoon vanilla extract
1 (8-ounce) package lemon pie filling

Sift the flour, baking powder and salt together into a bowl. Place the eggs in a large mixing bowl and beat at high speed for about 5 minutes or until thick and pale yellow. Beat in the sugar gradually. Beat in the vanilla and 1/3 cup cold water. Add the flour mixture; beat at low speed until smooth. Spread evenly in a buttered 10×15-inch cake pan that has been lined with waxed paper. Bake at 375 degrees for 12 to 15 minutes or until the cake tests done. Dust a clean kitchen towel with confectioners' sugar. Invert the cake onto the towel. Remove the waxed paper and trim the edges. Roll the warm cake in the towel from the short side and place on a wire rack to cool. Prepare the lemon pie filling with 1 egg yolk using the package directions. Unroll the cooled cake carefully and remove the towel. Spread the lemon filling to the edge and reroll. Wrap in plastic wrap. Chill until serving time. Serve with whipped cream if desired. Yield: 8 to 10 servings.

Elizabeth Thomey, Xi Nu
Deer Lake, Newfoundland, Canada

OATMEAL CAKE

1 1/2 cups boiling water
1 cup old-fashioned rolled oats
1 1/2 cups flour
1 teaspoon baking soda
1 teaspoon cinnamon
1 teaspoon nutmeg
1/2 teaspoon salt
1/2 cup (1 stick) butter or margarine
1 cup firmly packed brown sugar
1 cup granulated sugar
2 large eggs
Coconut Topping

Pour the water over the rolled oats in a bowl; mix well. Cool to room temperature. Whisk the flour, baking soda, cinnamon, nutmeg and salt together in a medium bowl. Cream the butter and sugars in a mixing bowl until light and fluffy. Beat in the eggs. Stir in the flour mixture just until moistened. Stir in the cooled oat mixture. Pour into a buttered 9×13-inch baking dish. Bake at 350 degrees for 30 to 35 minutes or until the cake tests done. Remove from the oven and preheat the broiler. Drop small spoonfuls of Coconut Topping over the top of the cake and spread evenly. Broil 6 inches from the heat source for 2 to 5 minutes or until topping is bubbly and lightly browned. Yield: 12 servings.

COCONUT TOPPING

1/4 cup firmly packed brown sugar
1/2 cup granulated sugar
1 cup sweetened flaked coconut
6 tablespoons butter or margarine, melted
1/4 teaspoon vanilla extract
1/4 cup cream or evaporated milk

Combine the sugars, coconut, butter, vanilla and cream in a mixing bowl and beat until well mixed.

Pat Foesch, Laureate Delta
Salem, Oregon

Irene Berghoff, Pi Master, Bethalto, Illinois, makes **Root Beer Cake** *using 1-step angel food cake mix, 1 cup root beer, 1/4 cup water and 1 teaspoon nutmeg. Prepare and bake using the package directions. Glaze with a mixture of 1 cup confectioners' sugar, 2 tablespoons root beer and 1/4 teaspoon nutmeg.*

TROPICAL ITALIAN CREAM CAKE

1/2 cup plus 2 tablespoons margarine
1/2 cup shortening
1 1/4 cups sugar
6 egg yolks
1 teaspoon vanilla extract
1 cup buttermilk
1 teaspoon baking soda
2 1/4 cups sifted flour
1/4 cup drained crushed pineapple
1 cup flaked coconut
1 cup toasted chopped pecans
6 egg whites
Pineapple Glaze
Coconut Frosting

Cream the margarine, shortening and sugar in a mixing bowl until light and fluffy. Add the egg yolks 1 at a time, mixing well after each addition. Beat in the vanilla. Add a mixture of the buttermilk and baking soda to the creamed mixture alternately with the flour, mixing well after each addition. Stir in the pineapple, coconut and pecans. Beat the egg whites in a mixing bowl until stiff peaks form. Fold into the pineapple mixture. Pour into 3 buttered and floured 9-inch cake pans. Bake at 350 degrees for 25 minutes. Pour Pineapple Glaze evenly over the warm cake layers. Let cool. Spread Coconut Frosting between the layers and over the top of the cooled cake.
Yield: 12 to 15 servings.

PINEAPPLE GLAZE

1 cup peach juice
1/4 cup drained crushed pineapple
Juice of 1 lemon
2 cups sugar

Combine the peach juice, pineapple, lemon juice and sugar in a saucepan over medium-high heat. Boil gently for 5 minutes or until a thin syrup is formed, stirring constantly.

COCONUT FROSTING

8 ounces cream cheese, softened
1/2 cup (1 stick) margarine, softened
1 (1-pound) package confectioners' sugar
1 teaspoon vanilla extract
1 cup shredded coconut
1 cup chopped walnuts or pecans

Combine the cream cheese, margarine, confectioners' sugar, vanilla, coconut and walnuts in the order listed in a mixing bowl, mixing at medium speed after each addition.

Patsy Rene Baggett, Laureate Gamma Chi
Gallatin, Texas

COMPANY PLUM CAKE

1/2 cup packed brown sugar
1 teaspoon cinnamon
1/2 cup butter, softened
2 egg yolks, slightly beaten
1 cup granulated sugar
1 1/2 cups flour
1 teaspoon baking powder
1/2 cup plus 1 tablespoon milk
2 egg whites
2 cups halved pitted plums
3/4 cup confectioners' sugar
1/2 teaspoon almond extract

Mix the brown sugar, cinnamon and 1/4 cup of the butter together in a bowl; set aside. Cream the remaining 1/4 cup butter, egg yolks and sugar in a mixing bowl until light and fluffy. Sift the flour and baking powder together into a bowl. Add the flour mixture to the egg yolk mixture alternately with the 1/2 cup milk, mixing well after each addition. Beat the egg whites in a mixing bowl until stiff peaks form. Fold into the batter. Pour the batter into a buttered 9×9-inch baking pan. Arrange the plums neatly over the top. Sprinkle evenly with the brown sugar mixture. Bake at 350 degrees for 45 minutes or until golden brown. Combine the confectioners' sugar, the 1 tablespoon milk and almond extract in a small bowl and blend well. Pour evenly over the top of the warm cake. Yield: 9 to 12 servings.

Sue Flagel, Omicron
Trail, British Columbia, Canada

POPPY SEED ANGEL FOOD CAKE

1 (16-ounce) package angel food cake mix
2 tablespoons poppy seeds
1 1/2 teaspoons almond extract
1 1/2 cups sifted confectioners' sugar
1/4 cup sliced almonds

Prepare the cake mix using the package directions, stirring in the poppy seeds and 1 teaspoon of the almond extract. Pour into an unbuttered 10-inch tube pan. Bake at 350 degrees for 40 to 45 minutes or until top is golden brown. Invert on a funnel to cool completely. Remove the cake to a serving plate; do not invert. Combine the confectioners' sugar, the remaining 1/2 teaspoon almond extract and 2 tablespoons water in a small bowl and whisk to blend; add more water if necessary to make of drizzling consistency. Drizzle over the cake. Sprinkle with almonds.
Yield: 16 servings.

Joy Boudreaux, Preceptor Nu
Frederick, Maryland

PRUNE CAKE

1/2 cup vegetable oil
2 1/2 cups sugar
2 eggs
2 1/2 cups flour
3/4 teaspoon baking powder
1 1/4 teaspoons baking soda
1 teaspoon allspice
1 teaspoon cinnamon
1 1/2 cups buttermilk
1 cup chopped prunes
1/2 cup black walnuts
1/2 cup (1 stick) margarine

Cream the vegetable oil and 1 1/2 cups of the sugar in a mixing bowl until light and smooth. Beat in the eggs, flour, baking powder, 1 teaspoon of the baking soda, allspice, cinnamon and 1 cup of the buttermilk. Stir in the prunes and black walnuts. Spoon into a buttered 9×13-inch baking dish. Bake at 350 degrees for 30 minutes or until top of cake springs back when lightly pressed. Combine the margarine, the remaining 1 cup sugar and the remaining 1/2 cup buttermilk in a saucepan over medium heat. Cook until bubbly, stirring frequently. Remove from heat. Stir in the remaining 1/4 teaspoon baking soda. Spoon the buttermilk mixture over the warm cake as soon as it comes out of the oven. Yield: 12 to 15 servings.

Cynthia Strayer, Preceptor Iota Theta
Titusville, Florida

PUMPKIN BUNDT CAKE

1/4 cup butter or margarine, softened
1 cup granulated sugar
1 cup packed brown sugar
4 eggs
1 (15-ounce) can pumpkin, or 1 3/4 cups cooked pumpkin
3 cups baking mix
1 cup confectioners' sugar
1 tablespoon milk
1/2 teaspoon vanilla extract

Cream the butter, granulated sugar and brown sugar in a mixing bowl until light and fluffy. Add the eggs 1 at a time, mixing well after each addition. Add the pumpkin and mix well. Add the baking mix gradually; mix well. Pour into a buttered 10-inch fluted tube pan. Bake at 350 degrees for 55 to 60 minutes or until a wooden pick inserted near the center comes out clean. Cool in the pan for 10 minutes. Remove to a wire rack to cool completely. Combine the confectioners' sugar, milk and vanilla in a small bowl and whisk to blend. Drizzle over the cooled cake.
Yield: 12 to 16 servings.

Tosha Schroeder, Xi Nu Iota
St. Elmo, Illinois

PUMPKIN PECAN CAKE GLAZED WITH MAPLE BOURBON SYRUP

1 1/2 cups flour
2 teaspoons cinnamon
1 teaspoon baking soda
1 teaspoon baking powder
1/2 teaspoon salt
2 large eggs
1 cup canned pumpkin
1 cup sugar
3/4 cup applesauce
1/2 cup chopped pecans
1/4 cup maple syrup
1/4 cup bourbon

Mix the flour, cinnamon, baking soda, baking powder and salt together in a bowl. Combine the eggs, pumpkin, sugar and applesauce in a separate bowl and mix well. Add the pumpkin mixture to the flour mixture, stirring just until moistened. Stir in the pecans. Spoon into a lightly buttered 9-inch cake pan. Bake at 350 degrees for 40 to 45 minutes or until a wooden pick inserted in the center comes out clean. Remove to a wire rack to cool. Combine the maple syrup and bourbon in a small saucepan and bring to a simmer. Brush over the top of the cake until absorbed completely. Serve with whipped cream or ice cream if desired. Yield: 8 to 10 servings.

Vicky Williams, Xi Alpha Phi
Campbell River, British Columbia, Canada

ITALIAN RASPBERRY TORTE

1 1/4 cups flour
1/2 teaspoon baking soda
1/2 teaspoon baking powder
1/4 teaspoon salt
2/3 cup plus 1/4 cup sugar
3/4 cup sour cream
1/2 cup (1 stick) butter, melted
2 eggs
1/2 teaspoon vanilla extract
1/2 teaspoon almond extract
8 ounces cream cheese, softened
2 cups raspberries
Sprigs of mint

Mix the flour, baking soda, baking powder and salt together in a small bowl. Combine the 2/3 cup sugar, 1/2 cup of the sour cream and the melted butter in a large mixing bowl. Add the eggs, vanilla and 1/4 teaspoon of the almond extract; mix until combined. Stir in the flour mixture. Pour into a buttered 9-inch springform pan. Bake at 350 degrees for 15 minutes. Place the pan on a wire rack. Combine the cream cheese and the 1/4 cup sugar in a mixing bowl and beat until smooth. Beat in the remaining 1/4 cup sour cream and the remaining 1/4 teaspoon almond extract. Spoon over the hot cake carefully to the edge. Return to oven and bake for 20 to 25 minutes longer or until top is set and edge is brown. Cool in the pan on a wire rack. Mound the raspberries over the top. Let stand for 10 minutes. Loosen the cake from the side of the pan. Let stand for 30 minutes longer. Remove from the pan. Chill, covered, until serving time. Garnish with mint sprigs and serve.
Yield: 12 to 16 servings.

Jan Meredith, Laureate Beta Gamma
Fredericksburg, Virginia

RHUBARB CAKE

1/2 cup shortening
2 cups packed brown sugar
1 egg
2 cups flour
1 teaspoon baking soda
1 cup buttermilk
1 teaspoon vanilla extract
2 cups chopped rhubarb
1 cup chopped walnuts or pecans
1 tablespoon butter, softened

Cream the shortening and half the brown sugar in a mixing bowl until fluffy. Beat in the egg. Add a mixture of the flour and baking soda to the egg mixture alternately with the buttermilk. Stir in the vanilla and rhubarb. Pour into a buttered 8×10-inch cake pan. Combine the remaining brown sugar, walnuts and butter in a bowl; mix well. Spread over the batter. Bake at 350 degrees for 45 minutes.
Yield: 16 servings.

Barbara Herbst-Anderson, Zeta Master
Seattle, Washington

GREEN TOMATO CAKE

2/3 cup margarine
1 3/4 cups sugar
2 eggs
1 teaspoon vanilla extract
2 ounces unsweetened chocolate, melted
2 1/2 cups flour
1/2 cup baking cocoa
2 teaspoons baking powder
2 teaspoons baking soda
1/4 teaspoon salt
1 cup green tomato pulp
1 cup beer

Cream the margarine and sugar in a mixing bowl until light and fluffy. Beat in the eggs, vanilla and melted chocolate. Add a mixture of the flour, baking cocoa, baking powder, baking soda and salt alternately with the green tomato pulp and beer, mixing well after each addition. Pour into 3 buttered and floured 9-inch cake pans. Bake at 350 degrees for 30 minutes or until the cake tests done. Cool the layers on wire racks for 5 to 10 minutes and remove from the pans to cool completely. Spread your favorite cream cheese frosting between the layers and over the top and side of the cooled cake.
Yield: 12 servings.

Rosemary Hohman, Xi Epsilon Psi
Brookport, Illinois

TOMATO CAKE

1 1/2 cups raisins
3/4 cup shortening
1 1/4 cups sugar
1 cup tomato juice
3 cups flour
1 teaspoon baking soda
1 tablespoon baking powder
1 1/2 teaspoons cinnamon
1 1/2 teaspoons nutmeg
1 teaspoon ground cloves
3/4 teaspoon salt
1 1/2 cups chopped walnuts or pecans

Soak the raisins in enough water to cover. Cream the shortening and sugar in a mixing bowl until light and fluffy. Beat in the tomato juice and 3/4 cup water. Sift the flour, baking soda, baking powder, cinnamon, nutmeg, cloves and salt over the sugar mixture; stir to combine. Drain the raisins and stir into the batter. Stir in the walnuts. Pour into a cake pan that has been sprayed with nonstick cooking spray; you may use a pan of almost any size, as the cake keeps like a fruitcake. Place in a cold oven. Turn oven temperature to 350 degrees. Bake the cake for 45 minutes or until browned and the center springs back when lightly pressed with a finger. Yield: variable.

Laura Hannan, Xi Eta Theta
Wamego, Kansas

✣ TIRAMISU CAKE

1 (2-layer) package moist white cake mix
2 cups strong coffee, at room temperature
4 egg whites
4 small chocolate-covered toffee candy bars, very finely chopped
Tiramisu Frosting

Combine the dry cake mix, 1 cup of the coffee and egg whites in a large mixing bowl; beat at low speed until moistened. Beat 2 minutes at high speed. Fold in the chopped toffee bars. Divide the batter evenly between 2 buttered and floured 9-inch cake pans. Bake at 350 degrees for 20 to 30 minutes or until a wooden pick inserted in the center comes out clean. Cool in the pan for 10 minutes. Remove to a wire rack to cool completely. Halve each layer horizontally to make 4 thin layers. Drizzle the cut side of each layer with 1/4 cup coffee. Place 1 layer coffee side up on a serving plate; spread 3/4 cup Tiramisu Frosting over the top. Place a second layer coffee side up over the first layer; spread 3/4 cup Tiramisu Frosting over the top. Place a third layer coffee side up over the second layer; spread 3/4 cup Tiramisu Frosting over the top. Top with the fourth layer, coffee side down. Frost the top and side with the remaining Tiramisu Frosting. Garnish with chocolate curls or additional chopped toffee bars. Chill, covered, until serving time. Store in the refrigerator. Yield: 12 servings.

TIRAMISU FROSTING

2/3 cup sugar
1/3 cup chocolate syrup
4 ounces cream cheese, softened
2 cups heavy cream
2 teaspoons vanilla extract

Combine the sugar, chocolate syrup and cream cheese in a medium mixing bowl and beat until smooth. Add the cream and vanilla; beat until light and fluffy. Chill, covered, until ready to use.

Juanita Bean, Theta Master
Sparks, Nevada

TOFFEE TREASURE BUNDT CAKE

1/4 cup plus 1 cup sugar
1 teaspoon cinnamon
2 cups flour
1 1/2 teaspoons baking powder
1 teaspoon baking soda
1/4 teaspoon salt
1 teaspoon vanilla extract
1 cup sour cream
1/2 cup (1 stick) butter or margarine, softened
2 eggs
1/4 cup chopped walnuts or pecans
6 (7-ounce) chocolate candy bars, frozen and crushed
1/4 cup melted butter or margarine

Mix the 1/4 cup sugar and cinnamon together in a small bowl. Combine the flour, the 1 cup sugar, baking powder, baking soda, salt, vanilla, sour cream, the 1/2 cup softened butter and eggs in a large mixing bowl and beat at low speed until moistened. Beat at medium speed for 3 minutes, scraping the bowl occasionally. Pour half the batter into a buttered and floured bundt pan and sprinkle with half the cinnamon mixture. Spoon the remaining batter over the top and sprinkle with the remaining cinnamon mixture. Layer the walnuts and crushed candy over the top. Drizzle with the 1/4 cup melted butter. Bake at 325 degrees for 45 minutes. Cool in the pan for 15 minutes. Invert onto a serving plate. Sprinkle with confectioners' sugar. Yield: 10 to 12 servings.

Romita Carol Cohee, Preceptor Delta Theta
Neodesha, Kansas

Vicki Gauger, Xi Delta Kappa, Abilene, Texas, makes ***Vanilla Wafer Cake*** *by creaming 1 cup butter with 2 cups sugar, then beating in 6 eggs 1 at a time. Stir in 1 teaspoon vanilla, a 12-ounce package of vanilla wafer crumbs, a 7-ounce can of flaked coconut and a cup of chopped pecans. Bake in a 9×13-inch cake pan at 275 degrees for 1 1/4 hours or until the cake pulls away from the sides of the pan.*

Pies

BLACKBERRY APPLE FANTASY PIE

1 cup sugar
4 teaspoons quick-cooking tapioca
1/2 teaspoon cinnamon
2 cups fresh blackberries
2 cups sliced peeled apples
1 (2-crust) pie pastry

Mix the sugar, tapioca and cinnamon in a mixing bowl. Add the blackberries and apples; toss gently to coat. Let stand for 15 minutes. Spoon into a pastry-lined pie plate. Dot with butter. Top with the second pastry; seal edge and cut vents. Brush with milk. Cover the top loosely with foil. Bake at 375 degrees for 25 minutes. Remove the foil and bake for 25 minutes longer. Yield: 8 servings.

MaryAnn Pitts, Preceptor Xi
Riverton, Kansas

CARAMEL APPLE PIE

1 cup firmly packed brown sugar
1/2 cup vanilla ice cream
1/4 cup butter or margarine
6 cups sliced peeled cooking apples
2 tablespoons cornstarch
1 (2-crust) pie pastry

Combine the brown sugar, ice cream and butter in a medium saucepan over medium-high heat. Bring to a boil; boil gently for about 1 minute or until sugar dissolves, stirring constantly. Remove from heat. Combine the apples and cornstarch in a bowl; toss to coat. Spoon into a pastry-lined pie plate. Pour the ice cream mixture over the apples. Top with the second pastry; seal edge and cut vents. Bake at 425 degrees for 30 to 45 minutes or until golden. Yield: 6 to 8 servings.

Marcy M. Evans, Preceptor Beta
Kearney, Nebraska

SOUTHERN AMBROSIA PIE

1/2 cup packed brown sugar
1/2 cup apple juice
2 tablespoons butter or margarine
2 tablespoons cornstarch
1/4 teaspoon salt
4 cups thinly sliced peeled baking apples
2 teaspoons lemon juice
1 baked (9-inch) pie shell
1 egg
2/3 cup evaporated milk
1/2 cup granulated sugar
1/2 cup flaked coconut
2 teaspoons vanilla extract
1 teaspoon cinnamon
Pecan Cream Topping

Combine the brown sugar, apple juice, butter, cornstarch and salt in a large saucepan over medium heat; bring to a boil. Stir in the apples and lemon juice. Simmer for 5 to 8 minutes or until apples are tender-crisp, stirring constantly. Pour into the pie shell. Mix the next 6 ingredients in a bowl. Pour over the apple mixture. Bake at 350 degrees for 40 to 45 minutes or until set. Cool on a wire rack. Spread with Pecan Cream Topping. Chill, covered, for 4 to 6 hours. Yield: 8 servings.

PECAN CREAM TOPPING

8 ounces cream cheese, softened
1/2 cup granulated sugar
3/4 cup chopped pecans, toasted
1 teaspoon vanilla extract
8 ounces whipped topping

Combine the cream cheese and sugar in a mixing bowl and beat until fluffy. Stir in the pecans and vanilla. Fold in the whipped topping.

Veronica "Ronnie" Graves, Theta Master
Rogers, Arkansas

CANTALOUPE PIE

1 ripe cantaloupe
2 cups sugar
1 1/4 cups flour
1 egg
1 cup melted butter or margarine
1 teaspoon vanilla extract
2 (1-crust) pie shells

Scoop the cantaloupe flesh into a blender and purée. Combine the cantaloupe purée, sugar, flour, egg, butter and vanilla in a mixing bowl and beat until well mixed. Pour into the pie shells. Bake at 350 degrees for 30 minutes or until a knife inserted halfway between the outside and center of the custard comes out clean. Cool for 15 to 30 minutes. Chill, covered, until ready to serve. Serve with whipped topping if desired. Yield: 12 servings.

Linda Lance, Kappa Nu
Warner Robins, Georgia

CARAMEL PIE

1 1/2 cups plus 6 teaspoons sugar
2 tablespoons flour
1 cup milk
3 eggs, separated
1/4 cup margarine
1 teaspoon vanilla extract
1 baked (9-inch) pie shell

Cook 1/2 cup of the sugar in a saucepan over low heat until caramel-colored, stirring constantly. Combine 1 cup of the sugar, flour, milk, egg yolks, margarine and vanilla in a bowl and mix well. Mix in the caramelized sugar. Pour into the pie shell. Beat the egg whites in a mixing bowl until foamy. Add the 6 teaspoons sugar gradually, beating until stiff peaks form. Top the pie with the meringue, sealing to the edge. Bake in a 350-degree oven until lightly browned. Cool and serve. Yield: 6 to 8 servings.

Betty Jones, Beta Pi Master
Paris, Texas

FREEZER PECAN PIE

It tastes like an ice cream pie and is great in the summertime.

1/2 cup (1 stick) butter
1 (14-ounce) package shredded coconut
2 cups chopped pecans
8 ounces cream cheese, softened
1 (14-ounce) can sweetened condensed milk
16 ounces whipped topping
3 baked (8-inch) pie shells
1 (20-ounce) squeeze bottle caramel sundae syrup

Melt the butter in a large saucepan over medium-low heat. Stir in the coconut and pecans. Heat until all the butter is absorbed, stirring constantly. Let cool. Combine the cream cheese and condensed milk in a mixing bowl and beat until well blended. Beat in the whipped topping. Spread a 1-inch-thick layer of cream cheese mixture in each pie shell. Drizzle with sundae syrup in a crisscross pattern. Layer 1/6 of the coconut mixture over the top. Repeat the layers until all ingredients are used, ending with coconut mixture. Cover tightly with foil and freeze. Thaw for about 15 minutes before serving.
Yield: 6 to 8 servings per pie.

Pat Howell, Preceptor Delta
Big Spring, Texas

CHOCOLATE LAYER PIE

The chocolate sinks to the bottom, creating a nice treat.

2 ounces unsweetened chocolate
2/3 cup plus 3/4 cup sugar
1/4 cup butter
2 teaspoons vanilla extract
1 cup flour
1/2 teaspoon salt
1 teaspoon baking powder
1/4 cup shortening
1/2 cup milk
1 egg
1 unbaked deep-dish (9-inch) pie shell
1/2 cup chopped walnuts or pecans

Combine the chocolate and 1/2 cup water in a heavy saucepan over medium-low heat; cook until chocolate is melted. Stir in the 2/3 cup sugar. Bring to a boil, stirring constantly. Remove from heat. Stir in the butter and 1 1/2 teaspoons of the vanilla. Mix the flour, the 3/4 cup sugar, salt and baking powder together in a mixing bowl. Add the shortening, milk and the remaining 1/2 teaspoon vanilla; beat at medium speed for 2 minutes. Add the egg and beat for 2 minutes longer. Pour into the pie shell. Stir the chocolate mixture and drizzle carefully over the batter. Sprinkle with walnuts. Bake at 350 degrees for 55 to 65 minutes or until a wooden pick inserted in the center comes out clean. Yield: 6 to 8 servings.

Martha L. Taylor, Laureate Alpha Xi
Roy, New Mexico

Charlotte Ballard, Preceptor Lambda, Plattsburg, Missouri, makes a light ***Sherbet Fluff Pie*** *by beating 8 ounces cream cheese with 7 ounces marshmallow creme, then blending in 1 cup sherbet of any flavor and 2 cups whipped topping. Spread in a crumb crust and freeze until firm.*

RED GRAPEFRUIT PIE

4 ruby red grapefruit, peeled
4 tablespoons cornstarch
3/4 cup sugar
3 tablespoons red hot cinnamon candies
1 baked (9-inch) pie shell
8 ounces whipped topping

Separate the grapefruit sections, collecting the juice in a measuring cup and placing the grapefruit flesh in a bowl. Remove and discard the seeds and membranes. Dissolve the cornstarch in the grapefruit juice and pour into a small saucepan over medium heat. Cook until thickened, stirring constantly. Add the sugar and stir to dissolve. Add the red hot cinnamon candies. Cook until smooth and thick and candies are dissolved. Pour the hot sugar mixture over the grapefruit sections and stir gently. Pour the grapefruit mixture into the pie shell. Let stand until cool. Top with whipped topping and serve. Yield: 6 to 8 servings.

Mildred O'Banion, Preceptor Xi
Baxter Springs, Kansas

NO-BAKE PEANUT BUTTER ICE CREAM PIE

2 envelopes hot cocoa mix (1/3 cup)
1 1/4 cups creamy peanut butter
1 ready-made (9-inch) chocolate or honey graham crumb crust
3 cups vanilla ice cream, softened

Combine the dry cocoa mix and 2 tablespoons hot water in a small bowl and whisk until smooth. Microwave 3/4 cup of the peanut butter in a microwave-safe bowl until melted. Brush the inside of the crumb crust with the melted peanut butter. Freeze for 15 minutes to set. Microwave the remaining 1/2 cup peanut butter until soft but not melted. Fill the pie shell quickly with the softened ice cream. Drizzle the softened peanut butter over the top. Drizzle with the cocoa mixture. Freeze until firm. Keep frozen until ready to use. Yield: 6 to 8 servings.

Shelley Fulton, Nu Beta
Indianapolis, Indiana

LEMON CHIFFON PIE

5 or 6 eggs, separated
Juice and grated zest of 2 lemons
1 cup sugar
1 baked (9-inch) pie shell

Place the egg yolks in a mixing bowl and beat until light. Mix in the lemon juice, lemon zest and sugar. Place in the top of a double boiler and cook over simmering water until thickened and smooth, stirring constantly. Let cool. Beat the egg whites in a mixing bowl until stiff peaks form. Fold 3/4 of the stiffly beaten egg whites into the cooled lemon mixture. Spoon into the pie shell. Add sugar to the remaining stiffly beaten egg whites, about 2 tablespoons for every egg white. Spread over the top of the pie, sealing to the edge. Brown in a 325-degree oven for 8 to 10 minutes. Yield: 6 to 8 servings.

Marion A. Ratliff, Xi Beta Alpha
Artesia, New Mexico

LEMON PIE

4 tablespoons cornstarch
1 cup plus 6 tablespoons sugar
1/4 cup lemon juice
1/4 teaspoon grated lemon zest (optional)
2 egg yolks, slightly beaten
1 tablespoon butter or margarine
1 baked (9-inch) pie shell
2 egg whites
1/4 teaspoon cream of tartar
1/4 teaspoon vanilla extract

Combine the cornstarch and the 1 cup sugar in a saucepan. Pour 1 1/4 cups boiling water over the cornstarch mixture and mix well. Cook over medium heat until thickened, stirring constantly. Remove from heat. Combine the lemon juice, lemon zest and egg yolks in a bowl and whisk to blend. Add a small amount of the hot sugar mixture and whisk to blend. Return the mixture to the saucepan and cook for 2 or 3 minutes longer until thickened, stirring constantly. Remove from heat. Add the butter and stir until melted. Let cool. Pour into the pie shell. Beat the egg whites with the cream of tartar in a mixing bowl until soft peaks form. Beat in the 6 tablespoons sugar 1 tablespoon at a time until stiff peaks form. Beat in the vanilla. Spread over the pie, sealing to the edge. Bake at 350 degrees for 8 to 10 minutes or until lightly browned. Yield: 6 to 8 servings.

Zelma Newman, Master Kappa
Brookfield, Missouri

Carol Zeiss, Delta Tau, St. Peters, Missouri, makes ***Malted Milk Ball Pie*** *for kids of all ages. Crush 7 ounces of malted milk balls. Mix with 1 cup chocolate sandwich cookie crumbs and 3 tablespoons melted butter and press into a pie plate sprayed with nonstick cooking spray to form a crust. Chill for 30 minutes, then fill with scoops of 1/2 gallon tin roof ice cream and store in the freezer. Drizzle with 1/2 cup marshmallow ice cream topping just before serving.*

KEY LIME PIE

5 or 6 eggs, separated
4 tablespoons sugar
1 (14-ounce) can sweetened condensed milk
1/2 cup Key lime juice
1 baked (9-inch) pie shell

Beat the egg whites in a mixing bowl until soft peaks form. Add the sugar gradually, beating until stiff peaks form. Combine the egg yolks and condensed milk in a mixing bowl and mix well. Add the lime juice very slowly, blending well. Pour into the pie shell. Top with the meringue, sealing to the edge. Bake at 300 degrees for 15 minutes or until honey-colored. Chill until serving time.
Yield: 6 to 8 servings.

Patricia Roberson, Alpha Beta Master
Plantation, Florida

NO-BAKE KEY LIME PIE

1 small package sugar-free lime gelatin
12 ounces Key lime light yogurt
8 ounces fat-free whipped topping
1 ready-made reduced-fat graham cracker pie shell

Dissolve the dry gelatin mix in 1/4 cup boiling water in a large heat-resistant bowl. Whisk in the yogurt. Fold in the whipped topping with a wooden spoon. Spread in the pie shell. Chill, covered, for 2 to 10 hours. Garnish as desired and serve. Refrigerate leftovers. Yield: 8 servings.

Patty Brooks, Preceptor Alpha Gamma
Aztec, New Mexico

PEACHES AND CREAM PIE

This pie is always such a big hit that it has almost become famous. People will walk up to me and say, "I heard you have the most delicious pie!"

3/4 cup flour
1/2 teaspoon salt
1 teaspoon baking powder
1 (4-ounce) package vanilla instant pudding mix
1 egg
3 tablespoons melted butter
1/2 cup milk
1 (16-ounce) can sliced peaches, drained, 3 tablespoons syrup reserved
8 ounces cream cheese, softened
1/2 cup plus 1 tablespoon sugar
1/2 teaspoon cinnamon

Combine the flour, salt, baking powder, dry pudding mix, egg, butter and milk in a mixing bowl and beat until smooth. Spread over the bottom and up the side of a buttered 9-inch pie plate to form a shell. Spread the peaches in the shell. Combine the cream cheese, the 1/2 cup sugar and the reserved 3 tablespoons peach syrup in a mixing bowl and beat at medium speed for 2 minutes. Spread evenly over the peaches. Sprinkle with a mixture of the 1 tablespoon sugar and cinnamon. Yield: 8 servings.

Dinah Braune, Xi Lambda Zeta
Gonzales, Texas

PECAN PIE

2 eggs, beaten
1/2 cup sugar
2 rounded tablespoons flour
1 cup light corn syrup
1 tablespoon butter or margarine, melted
1 teaspoon vanilla extract
3/4 cup (or more) pecan halves
1 unbaked (9-inch) pie shell

Combine the eggs, sugar and flour in a mixing bowl and mix well. Add the corn syrup, butter and vanilla and mix well. Stir in the pecans. Pour into the pie shell. Bake at 350 degrees for 10 minutes. Reduce oven temperature to 200 degrees and bake for 40 minutes longer or just until set.
Yield: 6 to 8 servings.

Eloise Brandt, Gamma Chi Master
Coleman, Texas

BOURBON PECAN PIE

Pat-in-Pan Pastry
3 eggs
1 cup packed brown sugar
1/2 cup plus 2 tablespoons corn syrup
1/4 cup bourbon or rye whiskey
2 tablespoons butter, melted
1/2 teaspoon cinnamon
1/4 teaspoon nutmeg
1/4 teaspoon ground cloves
1/4 teaspoon allspice
1 1/2 cups pecan halves
2 tablespoons corn syrup

Prepare the Pat-in-Pan Pastry shell. Combine the eggs, brown sugar, the 1/2 cup corn syrup, bourbon, butter, cinnamon, nutmeg, cloves and allspice in a bowl and whisk to blend. Stir in the pecans. Pour into the Pat-in-Pan Pastry shell. Bake at 375 degrees for 45 minutes or until firm. Remove from oven and brush with the 2 tablespoons corn syrup. Let cool. Serve with whipped cream or ice cream. Yield: 12 servings.

PAT-IN-PAN PIE PASTRY

1 3/4 cups flour
2 tablespoons sugar
1/4 teaspoon salt
1/3 cup cold butter, cut up
1 teaspoon white vinegar

Combine the flour, sugar and salt in a food processor container. Add the butter by pulsing 5 or 6 times until mixture resembles fine crumbs. Add the vinegar and 2 tablespoons water by pulsing 4 or 5 times until blended but still crumbly. Pat evenly and firmly over the bottom and up the side of a 9-inch tart or springform pan.

Barbara Rankin, Laureate Omega
Guelph, Ontario, Canada

CHOCOLATE CHIP PECAN PIE

2 eggs
1 cup sugar
1/2 cup flour
1/2 cup (1 stick) butter, melted
1 cup chopped pecans
1 cup chocolate chips
1 teaspoon bourbon
1 teaspoon vanilla extract
1 unbaked (9-inch) pie shell
Whipped cream

Beat the eggs at high speed in a small mixing bowl until thick and pale yellow. Beat in the sugar gradually. Add the flour and melted butter and beat at low speed until combined. Stir in the pecans, chocolate chips, bourbon and vanilla. Pour into the pie shell. Bake at 350 degrees for about 40 minutes or until golden brown. Serve warm with dollops of whipped cream. Yield: 6 to 8 servings.

Theda Bray, Laureate Gamma Pi
Jay, Florida

HONEY CRUNCH PECAN MACADAMIA PIE

4 eggs, slightly beaten
1 cup light corn syrup
1/4 cup plus 1/3 cup packed brown sugar
1/4 cup granulated sugar
2 tablespoons melted butter
1 tablespoon bourbon
1 teaspoon vanilla extract
1/2 teaspoon salt
1 cup chopped pecans
3/4 cup chopped macadamia nuts
1 unbaked (9- to 10-inch) pie shell
3 tablespoons butter
3 tablespoons honey
1 cup pecan halves

Combine the eggs, corn syrup, the 1/4 cup brown sugar, granulated sugar, the 2 tablespoons melted butter, bourbon, vanilla and salt in a large mixing bowl and mix well. Stir in the chopped pecans and macadamia nuts. Pour into the pie shell. Bake at 350 degrees for 40 to 45 minutes. Prepare the topping during the last 15 minutes of baking time. Combine the 1/3 cup brown sugar, the 3 tablespoons butter and honey in a heavy saucepan over medium heat for about 2 or 3 minutes or until sugar is dissolved, stirring constantly. Add the pecan halves and stir until well coated. Spoon over the top of the pie and bake for 10 minutes longer. Yield: 8 servings.

Evelyn Burke, Alpha Alpha Master
Evans, Colorado

PINEAPPLE COCONUT CHESS PIE

5 eggs, beaten
1/2 cup (1 stick) butter, melted
3 cups sugar
2 1/2 tablespoons flour
1 (20-ounce) can crushed pineapple, drained
1 (7-ounce) package flaked coconut
2 unbaked (10-inch) deep-dish pie shells

Combine the eggs, butter, sugar and flour in a large mixing bowl and beat at medium speed until fluffy. Stir in the pineapple and coconut. Pour into the pie shells. Bake at 325 degrees for about 40 minutes or until set. Yield: 2 pies.

Pamela Kelly, Mu Phi
Frederick, Oklahoma

NO-BAKE PUMPKIN PIE

1 (14-ounce) can sweetened condensed milk
1 egg, slightly beaten
1 teaspoon cinnamon
1/4 teaspoon ginger
1/2 teaspoon nutmeg
1/2 teaspoon salt
1 envelope unflavored gelatin
1 (16-ounce) can pumpkin
1 baked (9-inch) graham cracker pie shell

Combine the condensed milk, egg, cinnamon, ginger, nutmeg and salt in a mixing bowl and blend well. Sprinkle the gelatin over 2 tablespoons water in a medium saucepan; let stand for 1 minute. Cook over low heat for about 2 minutes until gelatin is dissolved, stirring constantly. Stir in the egg mixture. Cook for 5 minutes or until slightly thickened, stirring constantly. Stir in the pumpkin. Pour into the pie shell. Chill until firm. Garnish with whipped cream and serve. Yield: 8 servings.

Martha T. Batson, Laureate Rho
Greenville, South Carolina

Elizabeth Elaine Biles, Laureate Lambda, Broken Arrow, Oklahoma, beats 2 cartons any flavor yogurt with a medium carton of whipped topping, spreads in a graham cracker crust, and chills for 4 hours or longer to make ***Simple and Delicious Yogurt Pie.***

NO-CRUST PUMPKIN PIE

3/4 cup sugar
1/2 cup (1 stick) margarine
1 (12-ounce) can evaporated milk
2 eggs
1 (16-ounce) can pumpkin
2 1/2 teaspoons pumpkin pie spice
2 teaspoons vanilla extract

Combine the sugar, margarine, evaporated milk, eggs, pumpkin, pumpkin pie spice and vanilla in a blender and process until smooth (or beat for 2 minutes in a bowl with a hand mixer). Pour into a buttered 10-inch pie plate. Bake at 350 degrees for 55 to 60 minutes or until a knife inserted in the center comes out clean. Yield: 6 servings.

Frances Gwaltney, Alpha Beta Master
Williamsburg, Virginia

SOUR CREAM RAISIN PIE

3/4 cup sugar
2 tablespoons flour
1/4 teaspoon ground cloves
1/2 teaspoon cinnamon
Dash of nutmeg
2 large eggs, separated
1/3 cup (or more) raisins
1 cup sour cream
1 baked (8-inch) pie shell
1/4 teaspoon cream of tartar

Combine 1/2 cup of the sugar, flour, cloves, cinnamon and nutmeg in a small bowl and mix well. Beat the egg yolks in a large mixing bowl. Add the flour mixture, raisins and sour cream and mix well. Pour into the top of a double boiler and cook over simmering water until thickened, stirring almost constantly. Pour into the pie shell. Beat the egg whites with the cream of tartar in a mixing bowl until soft peaks form. Add the remaining 1/4 cup sugar gradually, beating until stiff peaks form. Top the pie with the meringue, spreading almost to the edge. Bake at 450 minutes just until lightly browned.
Yield: 5 or 6 servings.

Catherine Baker, Laureate Alpha Pi
Sedona, Arizona

✣ CHOCOLATE RASPBERRY PIE

1 unbaked (9-inch) pie shell
3 tablespoons plus 1/3 cup sugar
1 tablespoon cornstarch
2 cups fresh or (thawed) frozen unsweetened raspberries
8 ounces cream cheese, softened
1/2 teaspoon vanilla extract
1/2 cup whipping cream, whipped
2 ounces semisweet chocolate
3 tablespoons butter or margarine

Line the unpricked pie shell with a double thickness of heavy-duty foil. Bake at 450 degrees for 8 minutes. Remove the foil and bake for 5 minutes longer. Cool. Combine the 3 tablespoons sugar and cornstarch in a saucepan. Stir in the raspberries. Bring to a boil. Boil for 2 minutes, stirring constantly. Remove from heat. Cool for 15 minutes. Spread in the pie shell. Chill, covered, while preparing the topping. Combine the cream cheese, the 1/3 cup sugar and vanilla in a mixing bowl and beat until smooth. Fold in the whipped cream. Spread over the raspberry layer. Chill, covered, for at least 1 hour. Melt the chocolate with the butter in the top of a double boiler over simmering water or in the microwave oven. Cool for 4 or 5 minutes. Drizzle over the whipped cream layer. Chill, covered, for at least 2 hours before serving.
Yield: 6 to 8 servings.

Kay Nelson, Laureate Upsilon
Grimes, Iowa

RASPBERRY PIE

2 cups fresh mulberries
2 cups fresh raspberries
2/3 teaspoon quick-cooking tapioca, or 2 tablespoons cornstarch
1 1/2 tablespoons lemon juice
2/3 cup sugar
1 (3-ounce) package raspberry gelatin
1 (3-ounce) package lemon gelatin
1 (2-crust) pie pastry
2 tablespoons butter

Combine the mulberries, raspberries, tapioca, lemon juice, sugar and dry gelatin mixes in a large mixing bowl; beat until smooth. Pour into a pastry-lined 9-inch pie plate. Dot with butter. Brush milk over the edge of the pastry. Top with the second pastry, sealing edge and cutting vents. Sprinkle with a mixture of cinnamon and sugar if desired. Bake at 450 degrees for 10 minutes. Reduce oven temperature to 350 degrees and bake for 40 minutes or until golden.
Yield: 8 servings.

Diana Prochazka, Beta Phi
Wilber, Nebraska

RHUBARB CUSTARD PIE

3 eggs, slightly beaten
3 tablespoons half-and-half or canned milk
2 tablespoons cornstarch
2 cups sugar
Dash of salt
1/4 teaspoon almond extract
4 cups chopped rhubarb
1 unbaked (9-inch) pie shell

Combine the eggs, half-and-half, cornstarch, sugar, salt and almond extract in a mixing bowl and beat until smooth. Stir in the rhubarb. Pour into the pie shell. Top with shapes cut from unused pie pastry if

desired. Bake at 375 degrees for 1 hour to 1 hour and 15 minutes or until slightly browned and the rhubarb is tender. Top with whipped cream.
Yield: 6 to 8 servings.

Sheryl A. Noel, Xi Mu Epsilon
Princeton, Illinois

STRAWBERRY PIE

1 (3-ounce) package strawberry gelatin
1/4 cup sugar
1 (10-ounce) package frozen strawberries
1 cup chopped pecans
3 bananas, sliced
1 baked (9-inch) pie shell

Dissolve the dry gelatin mix and sugar in 1 cup hot water in a large bowl. Stir in the frozen strawberries. Stir in the pecans and bananas. Let stand until it begins to thicken. Pour into the pie shell. Chill, covered, until serving time. Garnish with whipped cream and serve. Yield: 8 servings.

Kay Frances Williams, Laureate Xi
Belle Fourche, South Dakota

SWEET POTATO PIE

1 cup chopped cooked sweet potato
2 cups sugar
2 eggs
1/2 cup (1 stick) butter
2/3 cup evaporated milk
2 tablespoons flour
1 teaspoon vanilla extract
1 teaspoon lemon extract
1 unbaked (9-inch) pie shell

Combine the sweet potato, sugar, eggs, butter, evaporated milk, flour, vanilla and lemon extract in a large mixing bowl and beat until smooth. Pour into the pie shell. Bake at 450 degrees for 10 minutes. Reduce oven temperature to 350 degrees and bake for 1 hour. Yield: 6 to 8 servings.

Teresa Savell, Xi Alpha Sigma
Foley, Alabama

SHERRY WALNUT PIE

3 eggs
1/2 cup (1 stick) butter
2 tablespoons flour
1/2 cup dark corn syrup
1/3 cup sherry
1 cup sugar
1 cup broken walnuts
1 unbaked (9-inch) pie shell

Place the eggs in a mixing bowl and beat well. Melt the butter in a saucepan over medium-low heat. Whisk in the flour. Whisk in the corn syrup, sherry and sugar. Cook for 3 or 4 minutes, stirring constantly until smooth. Add the hot sherry mixture to the eggs gradually, stirring constantly. Stir in the walnuts. Pour into the pie shell. Bake at 350 degrees for 35 to 45 minutes or until firm. Yield: 6 to 8 servings.

Anna Lindener, Laureate Epsilon Alpha
Panama City, Florida

WHITE CHOCOLATE TART WITH RASPBERRY SAUCE

24 chocolate sandwich cookies, crushed (2 cups)
1/2 cup (1 stick) butter, melted
1 (6-ounce) white chocolate baking bar, chopped
2 cups whipping cream
1 teaspoon vanilla extract
8 ounces cream cheese, softened
1 (10-ounce) package frozen raspberries, thawed
1/3 cup confectioners' sugar

Combine the crushed cookies and melted butter in a small bowl and mix well. Press into the bottom of a 10-inch springform pan. Bake at 375 degrees for 7 to 9 minutes or until set. Cool completely. Heat the white chocolate and 1/2 cup of the cream in a saucepan over low heat, stirring until chocolate is melted. Stir in the vanilla. Cool to room temperature. Beat the cream cheese at medium speed in a large mixing bowl until smooth. Add the chocolate mixture; beat at medium speed until creamy. Beat the remaining 1 1/2 cups whipping cream with chilled beaters at high speed until stiff peaks form. Fold half the whipped cream into the cream cheese mixture until well blended; fold in the remaining whipped cream. Spoon into the prepared pan. Chill, covered, for 3 to 4 hours until set. Purée the raspberries in a blender. Blend in the confectioners' sugar. Press through a strainer to remove the seeds. Chill until serving time. At serving time, cut the tart into wedges and place on individual dessert plates. Drizzle raspberry sauce over the wedges and plates. Yield: 12 servings.

Rose Head, Xi Alpha Iota
Grants Pass, Oregon

Kathi Maxson, Kappa Nu, Westminster, Colorado, has a different take on pie with ***Apple Quesadillas.*** *Mix a can of apple pie filling with a snack box of raisins and 1/2 teaspoon cinnamon. Heat 4 to 6 flour tortillas 1 at a time in a skillet. Spoon about 1/2 cup apple mixture onto half the tortilla and fold over, pressing edges to seal and cool. Arrange on a baking sheet, sprinkle with 1 cup shredded Cheddar cheese, and bake at 350 degrees until the cheese melts. Cool on a wire rack and cut each into 3 pie-shaped pieces.*

APPLE TART

3 apples, peeled and sliced
1 teaspoon cinnamon
2 tablespoons sugar
1/2 cup chopped pecans
1 teaspoon lemon juice
1 tablespoon flour
1 unbaked (9-inch) pie shell
1/2 cup caramel apple dip
2 teaspoons butter
1/4 cup apple jelly

Place the apples, cinnamon, 1 tablespoon of the sugar, pecans, lemon juice and flour in a medium bowl and toss well to combine. If using a purchased pie shell, remove it from the pan and roll it out a little larger. Place on a baking sheet. Spread the caramel dip over the pie shell to within 2 inches of the edge. Place the apple mixture in the center. Dot with butter. Brush water over the edge of the dough and fold the edge up and around the filling. Press to seal. Brush the dough with apple jelly and sprinkle with the remaining 1 tablespoon sugar. Bake at 400 degrees for 20 minutes or until golden brown.
Yield: 4 servings.

Constance M. Orell, Xi Eta Eta
North Huntingdon, Pennsylvania

TAFFY APPLE PIZZA

1 (18-ounce) package sugar cookie dough
2 tablespoons creamy peanut butter
8 ounces cream cheese, softened
1/2 cup packed light brown sugar
1 teaspoon vanilla extract
3 medium Granny Smith apples
2 to 3 teaspoons lemon juice
1 teaspoon cinnamon
2 tablespoons caramel sauce

Place the cookie dough in a well-buttered pizza pan, pressing to spread. Bake at 370 degrees for 14 to 18 minutes or until lightly browned. Cool completely. Combine the peanut butter, cream cheese, brown sugar and vanilla in a mixing bowl and beat until smooth. Spread over the cooled cookie. Peel, core and slice the apples. Dip into a mixture of the lemon juice and 1/2 cup water; drain. Arrange the apple slices over the cream cheese layer. Sprinkle with cinnamon and drizzle with caramel sauce.
Yield: 8 servings.

Judy Manning, Xi Eta Omicron
Great Bend, Kansas

FRUIT PIZZA

1 (18-ounce) package sugar cookie dough
8 ounces cream cheese, softened
1/4 cup confectioners' sugar
8 ounces whipped topping
2 or 3 kiwifruit, peeled and sliced
1 or 2 firm bananas, sliced
1 (11-ounce) can mandarin oranges, drained
1/2 cup red grapes, halved
1/4 cup granulated sugar
1/4 cup orange juice
1 tablespoon lemon juice
1 1/2 teaspoons cornstarch

Press and spread the cookie dough in an unbuttered 14-inch pizza pan. Bake at 375 degrees for 10 to 12 minutes or until lightly browned; cool. Combine the cream cheese and confectioners' sugar in a mixing bowl and beat until smooth. Fold in the whipped topping. Spread over the cooled crust. Arrange the kiwifruit, bananas, mandarin oranges and grapes over the top. Combine the granulated sugar, orange juice, lemon juice, cornstarch and 2 tablespoons of water in a saucepan. Bring to a boil, stirring constantly. Boil for 2 minutes until thickened, stirring constantly. Let cool. Brush the sugar mixture over the fruit. Chill, covered, until serving time.
Yield: 16 to 20 servings.

Nancy Gilmer, Pi Eta
Goodland, Kansas

CHOCOLATE PEANUT BUTTER PIZZA

1/2 cup granulated sugar
1/2 cup packed brown sugar
1/2 cup peanut butter
1/2 cup (1 stick) butter or margarine, softened
1/2 teaspoon vanilla extract
1 egg
1 1/2 cups flour
2 cups miniature marshmallows
1 cup chocolate chips

Combine the granulated sugar, brown sugar, peanut butter, butter, vanilla and egg in a large bowl and mix well. Stir in the flour. Press the dough evenly over the bottom of a 12- or 14-inch pizza pan, making a rim along the edge. Bake at 375 degrees for 10 minutes. Sprinkle with marshmallows and chocolate chips. Bake for 5 to 8 minutes longer or until marshmallows are puffy and lightly browned. Cool and cut into wedges. Store in an airtight container.
Yield: 20 servings.

Linda Kelso, Xi Beta Delta
Maple Grove, Minnesota

BUTTERHORN COOKIES

2 cups flour
1 teaspoon baking powder
1/2 teaspoon salt
1/2 cup (1 stick) butter, softened
1/2 envelope dry yeast
2 eggs, separated
1/4 cup sour cream
1/2 teaspoon vanilla extract
1/2 cup sugar
1/2 cup ground walnuts or pecans
1/2 teaspoon almond extract

Sift the flour, baking powder and salt into a large bowl. Cut in the butter until mixture resembles coarse crumbs. Dissolve the yeast in 2 tablespoons warm water in a separate bowl. Stir in the egg yolks, sour cream and vanilla. Stir the sour cream mixture into the flour mixture. Chill, wrapped in plastic wrap, for at least 1 hour. Beat the egg whites at low speed in a mixing bowl until foamy. Add the sugar gradually, beating constantly at high speed until stiff peaks form. Fold in the walnuts and almond extract. Divide the chilled dough into 4 portions. Roll each portion into a 9-inch circle on a flat surface dusted with confectioners' sugar. Cut each circle into 12 wedges. Spread a rounded teaspoonful of egg white mixture over each wedge. Roll up from the wide ends. Shape into crescents on a lightly buttered cookie sheet. Bake at 400 degrees for 10 to 12 minutes or until lightly browned. Sprinkle with confectioners' sugar. Yield: 4 dozen.

Virginia Smith, Beta Theta Mu
Cleveland, Texas

CHOCOLATE CHERRY COOKIES

2 1/4 cups flour
1/2 teaspoon salt
1 cup (2 sticks) plus 3 tablespoons butter
3/4 cup plus 3 cups confectioners' sugar
1 teaspoon vanilla extract
1 teaspoon almond extract
1/4 cup chopped walnuts
1/4 cup chopped maraschino cherries
1 cup chocolate chips
1/2 cup milk

Sift the flour and salt together into a bowl. Cream the 1 cup butter and the 3/4 cup confectioners' sugar in a mixing bowl until light and fluffy. Beat in the vanilla and almond extracts. Blend in the flour mixture. Stir in the walnuts and cherries. Shape into 3/4-inch balls; arrange on a cookie sheet. Bake at 350 degrees for 12 to 15 minutes; do not brown. Cool. Melt the chocolate chips and 3 tablespoons butter with the milk in the top of a double boiler over hot water. Cool slightly. Blend in the 3 cups confectioners' sugar and beat until smooth. Dip the cookies in the chocolate mixture; arrange on waxed paper to cool. Yield: 5 dozen.

Linda Economon, Preceptor Xi Theta
Lake Forest, California

Nancy Cook, Omega Pi, San Angelo, Texas, makes ***Cherry-Topped Whipped Shortbread Cookies*** *by placing 1 cup softened butter in a mixing bowl and sifting 1/2 cup confectioners' sugar, 1/4 cup cornstarch and 1 1/2 cups flour over the butter. Beat at low speed until blended, then at high speed until the mixture resembles whipped cream. Drop by spoonfuls onto an ungreased cookie sheet; top with a piece of maraschino cherry. Bake at 325 degrees for 20 minutes.*

PECAN CREAMSTONES

1/2 cup (1 stick) butter, softened
1 cup flour
4 tablespoons confectioners' sugar
1 teaspoon vanilla extract
1 cup chopped pecans

Cream the butter in a mixing bowl. Beat in the flour, confectioners' sugar, vanilla and pecans in the order listed, mixing at medium speed after each addition. Chill, wrapped in plastic wrap, for 1 hour. Shape into walnut-size balls and arrange on a nonstick cookie sheet. Bake at 350 degrees for 20 minutes. Roll the warm cookies in additional confectioners' sugar. Cool. Yield: 1 1/2 dozen.

Cathy Dukes, Xi Gamma Rho
Bryan, Ohio

DOUBLE CHOCOLATE ALMOND COOKIES

1 cup (2 sticks) butter or margarine
1/2 cup granulated sugar
2/3 cup packed brown sugar
2 eggs
1 teaspoon vanilla extract
2/3 cup baking cocoa
2 1/4 cups flour
1 teaspoon baking soda
1/4 teaspoon salt
1/2 cup (or more) chocolate chips
1/2 cup (or more) white chocolate chips
1/2 cup (or more) slivered almonds

Cream the butter and sugars in a mixing bowl until light and fluffy. Add the eggs and vanilla and mix well. Add a mixture of the baking cocoa, flour, baking soda and salt; mix well. Stir in the chocolate chips, white chocolate chips and almonds. Shape into balls and arrange on an unbuttered cookie sheet. Bake at 350 degrees for 10 to 12 minutes or until set. Yield: 3 to 4 dozen.

Brenda Hansen, Xi Alpha Nu
Baker, Montana

CHOCOLATE SANDWICH COOKIES

1 (2-layer) package devil's food cake mix
1 (2-layer) package double fudge cake mix
2/3 cup vegetable oil
4 eggs
4 tablespoons butter
8 ounces cream cheese, softened
4 cups confectioners' sugar
1 teaspoon vanilla extract

Combine the dry cake mixes, vegetable oil and eggs in a large bowl and mix well; batter will be stiff. Shape into small balls and arrange on a nonstick cookie sheet; flatten with a buttered glass. Bake at 350 degrees for 10 to 12 minutes or until set; do not overbake. Cool on a wire rack. Cream the butter and cream cheese together in a mixing bowl. Add the confectioners' sugar 1 cup at a time, mixing well after each addition. Beat in the vanilla. Spread butter mixture between two cookies to make a sandwich. Repeat with the remaining butter mixture and cookies. Store in an airtight container; better if made a day ahead. Yield: about 50 cookies.

Gloria Renshaw, Pi Master
Bouton, Iowa

CUT-OUT COOKIES

2 1/4 cups flour
1/2 teaspoon salt
1 cup confectioners' sugar
1 cup (2 sticks) butter, softened
1 egg
2 teaspoons vanilla extract

Sift the flour, salt and confectioners' sugar together into a bowl. Cut in the butter with a pastry blender until mixture resembles coarse crumbs. Add the egg and vanilla and mix well. Shape into a ball. Chill, wrapped in plastic wrap, for 3 to 10 hours. Divide the dough into 4 portions. Roll each portion 1/4 inch thick. Cut out cookies in desired shapes. Sprinkle with colored sugar. Bake at 400 degrees for 5 to 7 minutes or until beginning to brown. Cool on a wire rack. Yield: variable.

Barbara Dunleavy, Beta Psi
Phoenix, Arizona

STRAWBERRY TURNOVER COOKIES

1 cup unsalted butter, softened
12 ounces cream cheese, softened
3 cups flour
Strawberry or pineapple preserves
Confectioners' sugar or cinnamon sugar

Cream the butter and cream cheese together in a mixing bowl. Beat in the flour to make a stiff dough. Shape into 1- to 2-inch balls. Roll into rounds. Place a teaspoon of preserves in the center of each round and fold over as for a turnover, pressing edges to seal. Arrange on a nonstick cookie sheet. Bake at 350 degrees for 5 to 7 minutes or until golden brown. Cool on the cookie sheet. Dust with confectioners' sugar. Yield: 2 to 3 dozen.

Liza Lara, Chi Pi
Bay City, Texas

DATE NUT COOKIES

1 (16-ounce) package pitted dates
1/2 cup chopped walnuts
1/2 cup granulated sugar
1/2 cup shortening
2 cups packed brown sugar
2 eggs
1 teaspoon vanilla extract
3 1/4 cups flour
1/2 teaspoon baking soda
1/2 teaspoon salt

Combine the dates, walnuts, granulated sugar and 2 1/2 cups water in a medium saucepan. Cook over medium-low heat for 20 minutes or until dates are tender. Cool. Cream the shortening and brown sugar in a mixing bowl until smooth and fluffy. Beat in the eggs and vanilla. Beat in a mixture of the flour, baking soda and salt. Roll into a rectangle on a lightly floured surface. Spread with the cooled date mixture. Roll to enclose the filling. Chill, wrapped in plastic wrap, for 3 to 10 hours. Cut into 1-inch slices. Arrange cut side down in a greased 9×13-inch baking dish. Bake at 350 degrees for about 10 minutes or until golden. Yield: variable.

Jan Spooner, Laureate Beta Gamma
Fulton, Illinois

MERRY FRUIT COOKIES

1 1/4 cups glazed mixed fruit
3/4 cup dark raisins
1/2 cup chopped dates
2 1/2 cups flour
1 cup (2 sticks) butter, softened
1 cup granulated sugar
2 eggs
1/2 teaspoon almond extract
1/2 teaspoon baking powder
1/2 teaspoon baking soda
1/2 teaspoon cinnamon

Combine the mixed fruit, raisins, dates and 1/4 cup of the flour in a large bowl; stir to coat the fruit with the flour. Cream the butter and sugar in a mixing bowl until light and fluffy. Add the eggs 1 at a time, mixing well after each addition. Beat in the almond extract. Place the baking powder, baking soda, cinnamon and the remaining flour in a separate bowl; stir to combine. Stir the fruit mixture into the flour mixture. Add to the creamed mixture. Stir until it is too difficult, then work with your hands to mix in the flour. Shape into two or three 1 1/2-inch-diameter logs. Roll each log in waxed paper. Chill for 3 to 10 hours. Cut into 1/4-inch slices. Arrange 1/2 inch apart on a buttered cookie sheet. Bake at 375 degrees for about 10 minutes or until golden brown. Yield: 4 to 5 dozen.

Nancy Munro, Laureate Alpha Delta
Duncan, British Columbia, Canada

GINGERBREAD BOYS AND GIRLS

To make appealing gifts, wrap each cookie in plastic wrap, rose and green. Gather the wrap at the top of the cookie and tie with a ribbon. Fluff the ends of the plastic and trim with scissors.

3/4 cup (1 1/2 sticks) butter or margarine
3/4 cup packed brown sugar
1 egg
1/2 cup molasses
1 teaspoon vanilla extract
3 1/4 cups flour
1/2 teaspoon baking soda
1 teaspoon ginger
1/2 teaspoon salt
1/2 teaspoon cinnamon
1/2 teaspoon ground cloves

Cream the butter and brown sugar in a mixing bowl at medium speed until smooth and fluffy. Beat in the egg. Mix in the molasses and vanilla. Combine the flour, baking soda, ginger, salt, cinnamon and cloves in a separate large mixing bowl. Beat the flour mixture gradually into the sugar mixture until well-blended and a soft crumbly dough is formed. Divide the dough into 3 portions and shape into 3 balls. Chill, wrapped in plastic wrap, until firm, about 2 hours. Roll the dough to 1/4-inch thickness. Cut with 4- or 5-inch cookie cutters and arrange 1 inch apart on a nonstick cookie sheet. Bake at 350 degrees for 10 minutes or until edges are barely browned. Cool on the cookie sheet for 1 minute. Remove to a wire rack to cool completely. Decorate as desired. Yield: 2 1/2 dozen.

Karen Jordan, Preceptor Chi
Surfside, South Carolina

GINGER CRINKLES

2/3 cup vegetable oil
1 cup sugar
1 egg
1/4 cup molasses
1 3/4 cups flour
2 teaspoons ginger
1 teaspoon cinnamon
1 teaspoon baking powder
1 teaspoon baking soda
1/2 teaspoon salt

Combine the vegetable oil and sugar in a bowl and whisk to blend. Whisk in the egg and molasses. Stir in a mixture of the flour, ginger, cinnamon, baking powder, baking soda and salt. Shape the dough into small balls. Roll in additional sugar and arrange on a nonstick cookie sheet. Bake at 350 degrees for 8 to 10 minutes or until golden. Yield: variable.

Sue Emblem, Laureate Alpha Delta
Ladysmith, British Columbia, Canada

MINT SURPRISE COOKIES

1 1/2 cups (3 sticks) butter or margarine
1 1/2 cups granulated sugar
3/4 cup packed brown sugar
2 eggs
1 1/2 teaspoons vanilla extract
4 1/2 cups sifted flour
1 1/2 teaspoons baking soda
3/4 teaspoon salt
72 chocolate mint wafers
3 cups crushed cornflakes

Cream the butter and sugars in a mixing bowl until light and fluffy. Add the eggs, vanilla and 3 tablespoons water; beat until smooth. Sift the flour, baking soda and salt together and stir into the creamed mixture. Chill, wrapped in plastic wrap, for about 2 hours. Shape a spoonful of dough around each chocolate wafer; press to enclose. Dip the top of the cookie in the cornflake crumbs and arrange on an unbuttered cookie sheet. Bake at 375 degrees for 12 minutes or until golden brown. Yield: 6 dozen.

Kathy Beauchamp, Laureate Rho
Jackson, Michigan

ITALIAN CHRISTMAS COOKIES

4 rounded cups unsifted flour
1 cup sugar
4 rounded teaspoons baking powder
1 1/2 cups (3 sticks) butter, softened
1/2 cup plus 2 tablespoons shortening
1 teaspoon salt
3 teaspoons anise seeds
6 eggs
1/4 cup plus 1/2 cup milk
1 (2-ounce) bottle anise flavoring
1 (1-pound) box confectioners' sugar
Pinch of salt
2 tablespoons shortening

Place the flour, sugar, baking powder, butter, the 1/2 cup shortening, salt and anise seeds in a large mixing bowl; mix well. Make a well in the flour mixture. Add the eggs, the 1/4 cup milk and half the bottle of anise flavoring and mix well. Add a little flour if necessary so that dough won't stick to the hands. Shape the dough into balls and arrange on an unbuttered cookie sheet. Bake at 325 degrees for 15 minutes or until golden. Combine the confectioners' sugar, salt and the 2 tablespoons shortening in a bowl and mix well. Mix in the remaining 1/2 bottle anise flavoring and the 1/2 cup milk. Ice the warm cookies, covering all sides with a pastry brush. Place on waxed paper to dry. Yield: 4 dozen.

Nancy Hult-Sims, Xi Mu Epsilon
Princeton, Illinois

NORWEGIAN WISHING COOKIES

Place a cookie in the palm of your hand. Press in the center with one finger of your other hand. If you break the cookie into 3 pieces and can eat all 3 without saying a word, you get to make a wish.

3 1/4 cups flour
1 teaspoon baking soda
1 teaspoon cinnamon
3/4 teaspoon ginger
1/4 teaspoon nutmeg
1 cup (2 sticks) butter
1 1/2 cups sugar
1 egg
2 tablespoons molasses
1/2 teaspoon grated orange zest
Lace Icing

Combine the flour, baking soda, cinnamon, ginger and nutmeg in a bowl; mix well. Cream the butter and sugar in a large mixing bowl until light and fluffy. Add the egg, molasses, orange zest and 1 tablespoon water; beat until smooth. Stir in the flour mixture. Chill, covered, for 2 hours or until dough is easy to handle. Roll the dough into 1/8-inch thickness. Cut with star-shaped cookie cutters and arrange on an unbuttered cookie sheet. Bake at 375 degrees for 8 minutes. Remove to a wire rack to cool. Drizzle with Lace Icing. Yield: about 100 cookies.

LACE ICING

2 cups confectioners' sugar
Light cream or milk
1/2 teaspoon vanilla extract

Blend the confectioners' sugar, enough light cream to make of drizzling consistency and vanilla.

Cheryl Ingeberg, Preceptor Alpha
Regina, Saskatchewan, Canada

CHOCOLATE CHIP SHORTBREAD

1 cup (2 sticks) butter (no substitutes)
1/2 cup confectioners' sugar
1 teaspoon vanilla extract
2 cups flour
2 cups miniature chocolate chips
Melted chocolate for dipping

Cream the butter, confectioners' sugar and vanilla in a mixing bowl until light and fluffy. Blend in the flour. Fold in the chocolate chips. Shape into thin 2-inch-long logs the size of a pinkie finger. Arrange on an unbuttered cookie sheet. Bake at 350 degrees for 10 to 15 minutes or until light golden brown. Remove to a wire rack to cool. Dip the ends of the cooled cookies into melted chocolate. Place on waxed paper to harden. Yield: 2 dozen.

Jill McCormick
Leonard, Michigan

ALMOND STAR COOKIES

1 cup (2 sticks) butter, softened
1/4 teaspoon salt
3/4 cup sugar
1 egg
1 teaspoon vanilla extract
1 1/2 teaspoons almond extract
2 1/2 cups flour

Cream the butter with the salt in a mixing bowl until smooth and creamy. Beat in the sugar 1/4 cup at a time until light and fluffy. Beat in the egg, vanilla and almond extract. Fold in the flour by hand 1/2 to 1 cup at a time. Chill, covered, for about 2 hours. Place the dough in a cookie press fitted with a star tip. Press onto a nonstick cookie sheet. Bake at 400 degrees for 8 to 10 minutes or until set, not brown. Decorate as desired. Yield: 3 dozen.

Marilyn Heinisch, Xi Gamma Alpha
Dubuque, Iowa

LIGHTER-THAN-AIR SUGAR COOKIES

1/2 cup (1 stick) butter, softened
1/2 cup shortening
1/2 cup confectioners' sugar
1/2 cup granulated sugar
1 egg, well beaten
1/2 teaspoon vanilla extract
2 cups flour
1/2 teaspoon cream of tartar
1/2 teaspoon baking soda

Cream the butter, shortening, confectioners' sugar and granulated sugar in a mixing bowl until light and fluffy. Beat in the egg and vanilla. Add a mixture of the flour, cream of tartar and baking soda and mix well. Chill, wrapped in plastic wrap, for about 2 hours or until dough is easy to handle. Shape the dough into 1-inch balls and arrange on a nonstick cookie sheet. Flatten with a glass dipped in additional sugar. Sprinkle additional sugar over each cookie if desired; use colored sugars during the holidays. Bake at 350 degrees for 10 to 13 minutes or until golden. Yield: about 50 cookies.

Donna Svoboda, Xi Epsilon Tau
Thomson, Illinois

GRANDMA'S SUGAR COOKIES

3/4 cup (1 1/2 sticks) butter, softened
1 cup sugar
2 eggs
1 teaspoon baking powder
1 teaspoon vanilla extract
1 teaspoon salt
2 1/2 cups flour
Buttercream Icing

Cream the butter and sugar in a mixing bowl until light and fluffy. Beat in the eggs. Add the baking powder, vanilla and salt; mix well. Beat in the flour. Chill in an airtight container for 8 to 10 hours. Roll 1/4 inch thick on a lightly floured surface. Cut with a cookie cutter. Arrange on a nonstick cookie sheet. Bake in a preheated 350-degree oven for 9 minutes or until light golden. Remove to a wire rack to cool. Frost the cooled cookies with Buttercream Icing. Yield: 2 dozen.

BUTTERCREAM ICING

1/2 cup (1 stick) butter, softened
1/2 cup shortening
1 1/2 teaspoons vanilla extract
1/8 teaspoon salt
5 cups confectioners' sugar
1/4 cup plus 1 tablespoon milk

Beat the butter and shortening in a mixing bowl at medium speed until creamy. Beat in the vanilla and salt. Add the confectioners' sugar 1 cup at a time, beating constantly at medium speed. Add the milk; beat at high speed until light and fluffy. Keep covered with a damp cloth until ready to decorate.

Carla McDaniel, Preceptor Delta
Centralia, Illinois

ROLLED SUGAR COOKIES

1 cup (2 sticks) butter (no substitutes)
1 1/2 cups sifted confectioners' sugar
1 egg
1 teaspoon vanilla extract
1/2 teaspoon almond extract
2 1/2 cups flour
1 teaspoon baking soda
1 teaspoon cream of tartar

Cream the butter and confectioners' sugar in a mixing bowl until light and fluffy. Beat in the egg, vanilla and almond extract. Stir in a mixture of the flour, baking soda and cream of tartar. Chill, wrapped in plastic wrap, for 2 or 3 hours. Roll the dough to desired thickness. Cut with a cookie cutter and arrange on a nonstick cookie sheet. Bake at 350 degrees for about 10 minutes or until light golden. Yield: variable.

Sharlene Guggemos, Laureate Theta Mu
Kingwood, Texas

---

*Elnora Teed, Iota Kappa, Livonia, New York, makes **Quick Cut-Out Cookies** by crumbling 11 ounces pie crust sticks, adding 1 cup confectioners' sugar, 1/2 teaspoon baking soda, 1 egg, 1 tablespoon water and 1 teaspoon vanilla and mixing until dough forms a ball. Roll 1/8 inch thick, cut into shapes, and bake on an ungreased cookie sheet at 350 degrees for 6 to 8 minutes. Frost and decorate as desired.*

SUGAR-FREE COOKIES

1 1/2 cups flour
1 cup margarine
1/2 cup sour cream
Sugar-free jam, flavor of choice

Place the flour in a bowl. Cut the margarine into the flour with a pastry blender until mixture resembles coarse crumbs. Stir in the sour cream with a fork; blend well. Dough will be sticky. Chill, covered, for 8 to 10 hours. Roll a portion of the dough to 1/16-inch thickness on a well-floured surface. Cut into 2-inch rounds. Cut a hole in the center of half the rounds (may use a doughnut cutter). Place a cut round over a plain round. Fill the center with sugar-free jam. Bake at 350 degrees for 20 to 25 minutes or until golden. Yield: 2 dozen.

Mary Lee Heilman, Preceptor Zeta Delta
Medina, Ohio

THUMBPRINT COOKIES

1 cup (2 sticks) butter or margarine, softened
1/2 cup packed brown sugar
2 eggs, separated
1/2 teaspoon vanilla extract
2 1/2 cups flour
1/2 teaspoon salt
1 1/2 cups chopped walnuts
4 tablespoons red currant jelly or raspberry jam

Cream the butter and brown sugar in a mixing bowl until creamy. Beat the egg whites lightly and set aside. Beat the egg yolks and vanilla into the butter mixture. Add a mixture of the flour and salt and mix well. Shape the dough into small balls; dip them in egg whites and roll in chopped walnuts. Arrange on a buttered cookie sheet. Make an indentation in the center of each ball with a thumb. Fill the indentation with jelly or jam. Bake at 375 degrees for 12 to 15 minutes or until golden. Yield: about 3 1/2 dozen.

Susan Smith, Preceptor Chi
Murrells Inlet, South Carolina

COOKIE DOUGH TRUFFLES

1/2 cup (1 stick) butter, softened
1/2 cup firmly packed brown sugar
1/4 cup sugar
1/4 cup thawed egg substitute
1 teaspoon vanilla extract
1 1/4 cups flour
1 cup miniature semisweet chocolate chips
3/4 cup finely chopped pecans
2 cups semisweet chocolate chips
1 1/2 tablespoons shortening

Beat the butter in a mixing bowl at medium speed until creamy. Add the sugars gradually, beating well after each addition. Beat in the egg substitute and vanilla. Add the flour to the butter mixture; beat well. Stir in the miniature chocolate chips and pecans. Chill, covered, for 30 minutes. Shape into 1-inch balls. Chill, covered, until very firm. Combine the chocolate chips and shortening in a 1-quart glass bowl. Microwave until melted using the chocolate chip package directions. Use 2 forks to dip the frozen truffles quickly in the melted chocolate, coating completely. Place on waxed paper to harden. Chill until serving time. Yield: 4 1/2 dozen.

Molly Spruill-Mulkey, Zeta Xi
Clovis, New Mexico

WALNUT REFRIGERATOR COOKIES

1 cup (2 sticks) butter
2 cups packed brown sugar
2 eggs, well beaten
1 teaspoon vanilla extract
3 cups flour
3 1/2 teaspoons baking powder
1/2 teaspoon salt
1 cup chopped walnuts

Cream the butter and brown sugar in a mixing bowl until creamy. Beat in the eggs and vanilla. Sift the flour, baking powder and salt together and add to the creamed mixture. Stir in the walnuts. Shape into 2 rolls. Chill, wrapped in waxed paper, for 8 to 10 hours. Cut the dough into 1/4-inch-thick slices and arrange on a buttered cookie sheet. Bake at 375 degrees for about 8 minutes or until golden.
Yield: 7 to 8 dozen.

Susan Norman, Xi Beta Delta
Richmond, Virginia

ALMOND FLORENTINES

2 1/2 cups sliced almonds
1 cup sugar
1/2 cup unsalted butter, melted
5 tablespoons flour
2 egg whites, beaten
Pinch of salt
1/2 teaspoon vanilla extract

Line a cookie sheet with parchment paper. Combine the almonds and sugar in a bowl and toss to coat. Stir in the melted butter. Add the flour, egg whites, salt and vanilla; stir gently until blended. Drop by teaspoonfuls 2 inches apart on a buttered cookie sheet. Bake at 350 degrees, 1 cookie sheet at a time, for 10 minutes or until golden brown.
Yield: 6 dozen (2-inch) cookies.

Renate Tangren, Laureate Delta
Macon, Georgia

SPICY APPLE COOKIES

1/2 cup (1 stick) butter
1 1/2 cups packed brown sugar
1 egg
2 cups flour
1/2 teaspoon baking soda
1/4 teaspoon ground cloves
1/4 teaspoon nutmeg
1 cup raisins
1 cup walnuts
1 cup shredded peeled raw apple
1/4 cup milk
1 tablespoon butter, softened
2 cups confectioners' sugar
1/8 teaspoon salt
1/2 teaspoon vanilla extract
2 tablespoons milk

Cream 1/2 cup butter and brown sugar in a mixing bowl until smooth and fluffy. Beat in the egg. Sift the flour, baking soda, cloves and nutmeg into a bowl. Add half the flour mixture to the creamed mixture; mix well. Stir in the raisins, walnuts and apple. Stir in 1/4 cup milk. Stir in the remaining half of the flour mixture. Drop by teaspoonfuls 2 inches apart on a buttered cookie sheet. Bake at 350 degrees for 9 minutes or until light brown. Combine the butter, confectioners' sugar, salt, vanilla and 2 tablespoons milk in a mixing bowl and beat until smooth. Spread on the warm cookies. Yield: 4 to 5 dozen.

Marianne Kaiser, Xi Omega
Vincennes, Indiana

HONEY CORNMEAL COOKIES

1 1/4 cups extra-fine cornmeal
3/4 teaspoon baking soda
1/2 teaspoon baking powder
1 1/2 teaspoons cinnamon
1/4 teaspoon nutmeg
1/2 cup (generous) margarine
1/2 cup sugar
1/2 cup honey
2 eggs
1 cup raisins

Combine the cornmeal, baking soda, baking powder, cinnamon and nutmeg in a bowl and mix well. Beat in the next 4 ingredients gradually. Stir in the raisins. Drop by teaspoonfuls 2 inches apart on an unbuttered cookie sheet. Bake at 325 degrees for 13 minutes or until golden brown. Yield: 3 dozen.

Evelyn Tompkins, Xi Theta Tau
Miami, Florida

CHOCOLATE NUT COOKIES

1/2 cup (1 stick) butter
1 cup sugar
2 eggs
1/2 teaspoon vanilla extract
2 cups flour
Pinch of salt
2 teaspoons baking powder
1/2 cup baking cocoa
1/2 cup milk
3/4 cup chopped pecans

Cream the butter and sugar in a mixing bowl until light and fluffy. Beat in the eggs and vanilla. Combine the flour, salt, baking powder and baking cocoa in a separate bowl and stir to mix. Add the flour mixture to the creamed mixture alternately with the milk. Stir in the pecans. Drop by teaspoonfuls 2 inches apart on an unbuttered cookie sheet. Bake at 375 degrees for 8 minutes or until lightly browned. Yield: 3 dozen.

Carol Gregory, Xi Omega
Washington, Indiana

APPLESAUCE OATMEAL COOKIES

1/2 cup vegetable oil
1 cup sugar
1 1/2 cups rolled oats
1/2 cup applesauce
1 egg, beaten
1/2 teaspoon baking soda
1 1/2 cups flour
1 teaspoon cinnamon
1/2 teaspoon ground cloves
1/2 teaspoon nutmeg
1 cup raisins or craisins
1 cup chopped walnuts

Combine the first 10 ingredients in the order listed in a large mixing bowl, mixing at medium speed after the addition of the egg and again after the addition of the nutmeg. Stir in the raisins and walnuts. Drop by teaspoonfuls 2 inches apart on a lightly buttered cookie sheet. Bake at 350 degrees for 12 to 15 minutes or until golden brown. Yield: 3 to 4 dozen.

Sally McGraw, Preceptor Beta Iota
Colorado Springs, Colorado

COCONUT OATMEAL COOKIES

1 cup shortening
1 cup granulated sugar
1 cup packed brown sugar
2 eggs, slightly beaten
1 teaspoon vanilla extract
1 cup flour
1 teaspoon baking soda
1 teaspoon salt
3 1/2 cups quick-cooking oats
1 cup flaked coconut
1/2 cup Post Toasties
1 cup chopped pecans

Cream the shortening and sugars in a mixing bowl until light and fluffy. Beat in the eggs and vanilla. Beat in a mixture of the flour, baking soda and salt. Add the oats, coconut, cereal and pecans; mix well. Drop by teaspoonfuls 2 inches apart onto an unbuttered cookie sheet. Bake at 350 degrees for 12 to 14 minutes or until lightly browned. Yield: 3 dozen.

Sandy Miller, Xi Pi Alpha
Tuscola, Texas

OATMEAL CHOCOLATE CHIP COOKIES

1 cup shortening
3/4 cup granulated sugar
3/4 cup packed brown sugar
2 eggs
1 teaspoon vanilla extract
1 1/2 cups flour
1 teaspoon salt
1 teaspoon baking soda
2 cups rolled oats
1 cup chopped walnuts or pecans
1 cup semisweet chocolate chips

Cream the shortening and sugars in a mixing bowl until light and fluffy. Beat in the eggs and vanilla. Place the flour, salt, baking soda, rolled oats, walnuts, chocolate chips and 1 tablespoon hot water in a separate bowl and stir to combine. Add the flour mixture to the creamed mixture, stirring until well combined. Drop by 1/3 cupfuls onto a cookie sheet, 6 inches apart and 2 inches from the sides of the pan. Flatten to 4-inch-diameter circles with a glass dipped in additional sugar. Bake at 350 degrees for 12 minutes or until golden brown. Remove to a wire rack to cool. Store in an airtight container. Yield: 1 to 1 1/2 dozen.

Jean C. English, Preceptor Theta Delta
Miami Springs, Florida

✣ WHITE CHOCOLATE CHIP OATMEAL COOKIES

1 cup (2 sticks) margarine, softened
1 cup packed light brown sugar
1 cup granulated sugar
2 large eggs
2 teaspoons vanilla extract
3 cups flour
1 teaspoon baking powder
1 teaspoon baking soda
1 teaspoon salt
1 1/2 cups rolled oats
2 cups white chocolate chips
1 cup chopped pecans

Cream the margarine and sugars in a mixing bowl until light and fluffy. Beat in the eggs and vanilla. Add a mixture of the flour, baking powder, baking soda and salt; mix well. Stir in the rolled oats, white chocolate chips and pecans. Drop by tablespoons 2 inches apart onto a buttered cookie sheet. Bake at 350 degrees for 12 minutes or until edges begin to brown. Cool on the baking sheet for 3 minutes. Remove to a wire rack to cool completely.
Yield: 5 dozen.

Mary Anna Minton, Laureate Pi
Hopkinsville, Kentucky

MOLASSES CHEWIES

3 cups sifted flour
1 teaspoon baking soda
1 teaspoon salt
1 teaspoon ground cloves
1 teaspoon ginger
2 cups sugar
1 cup (2 sticks) margarine, softened
2 eggs
1/2 cup dark molasses
1 1/2 cups quick-cooking oats

Sift the first 6 ingredients together into a mixing bowl. Add the margarine, eggs and molasses and beat until smooth. Stir in the oats gently. Drop by level tablespoons 2 inches apart onto an unbuttered cookie sheet. Bake at 375 degrees for 8 to 10 minutes or until beginning to brown; do not overbake. Cool on the cookie sheet for a few minutes; remove to a wire rack to cool completely. Yield: 7 dozen.

Fluff Stephens, Laureate Iota Psi
Banning, California

PEANUT BUTTER BLOSSOMS

1/2 cup shortening
3/4 cup peanut butter
1/3 cup granulated sugar
1/3 cup packed brown sugar
1 egg
2 tablespoons milk
1 teaspoon vanilla extract
1 1/2 cups flour
1 teaspoon baking soda
1/2 teaspoon salt
48 chocolate candy kisses

Beat the shortening and peanut butter in a mixing bowl until smooth. Add the sugars and beat until light and fluffy. Beat in the egg, milk and vanilla. Add a mixture of the flour, baking soda and salt gradually. Shape into 1-inch balls. Roll in additional sugar and arrange on a buttered baking sheet. Bake at 375 degrees for 8 to 10 minutes or until golden. Cool for about 10 minutes. Press a chocolate candy kiss in the center of each cookie. Yield: 4 dozen.

Terri Johnson, Nu Beta
Indianapolis, Indiana

FLOURLESS PEANUT BUTTER COOKIES

4 egg whites
2 cups peanut butter
3/4 cup sugar

Beat the egg whites in a mixing bowl until stiff peaks form. Mix the peanut butter and sugar in a separate bowl. Fold in the stiffly beaten egg whites. Drop by rounded teaspoonfuls 2 inches apart onto a lightly buttered cookie sheet. Flatten slightly with a fork. Bake at 325 degrees for 15 to 20 minutes or until set. Remove to a wire rack to cool. Yield: 6 1/2 dozen.

Henrietta M. Martz, Preceptor Nu Omega
Sutter Creek, California

PEANUT BUTTER CHOCOLATE CHIP COOKIES

1 cup shortening
1 cup granulated sugar
1 cup packed brown sugar
2 eggs, beaten
1 tablespoon milk
2 1/4 cups flour
1/2 teaspoon salt
1 teaspoon baking soda
1 cup peanut butter
1 cup chocolate chips

Cream the shortening and sugars in a mixing bowl until light and fluffy. Beat in the eggs and milk. Sift the flour, salt and baking soda together into a large bowl. Mix in the peanut butter; mix in the chocolate chips. Drop by teaspoonfuls 2 inches apart onto a buttered cookie sheet. Bake at 350 degrees for 10 to 12 minutes or until edges begin to brown.
Yield: 3 dozen.

Melanie Graham, Xi Lambda
Estevan, Saskatchewan, Canada

PEANUT BUTTER HEALTH ROUNDS

1 egg, beaten
1 cup honey
3/4 cup vegetable oil
1 teaspoon salt
1 teaspoon vanilla extract
3 cups quick-cooking oats
1 cup whole wheat flour
3/4 cup wheat germ
1 cup peanut-butter chips
1/2 cup sunflower seeds

Combine the egg, honey, vegetable oil, salt, vanilla and 1/4 cup water in a bowl; mix well. Place the oats, flour and wheat germ in a large bowl and stir to combine. Add the egg mixture to the flour mixture; mix well. Stir in the peanut butter chips and sunflower seeds. Drop by 1/4 cupfuls 2 inches apart onto a buttered cookie sheet. Flatten with a glass dipped in sugar to 3 inches in diameter. Bake at 350 degrees for 15 to 20 minutes or until light brown. Remove to a wire rack to cool. Yield: about 20 cookies.

Gladys Weems, Laureate Eta Iota
Highland, California

PINEAPPLE COOKIES

1 1/2 teaspoons vanilla extract
2 (20-ounce) cans crushed pineapple, drained
1 cup shortening
1 cup packed brown sugar
1 cup granulated sugar
2 eggs
4 cups flour
1/2 teaspoon salt
1 1/2 teaspoons baking soda
1/2 teaspoon baking powder

Stir the vanilla into the pineapple in a bowl. Cream the shortening and sugars in a mixing bowl until light and fluffy. Beat in the eggs. Mix in the pineapple mixture. Sift the flour, salt, baking soda and baking powder over the pineapple mixture. Mix well. Drop by teaspoonfuls onto a buttered cookie sheet. Bake at 350 degrees for 12 to 15 minutes or until beginning to brown. Yield: 4 dozen or more.

Sandy Smith, Mu Tau
Huntingdon, Pennsylvania

POTATO CHIP COOKIES

1 cup (2 sticks) butter, softened
1 cup granulated sugar
1 cup packed brown sugar
1 teaspoon vanilla extract
2 eggs
2 cups crushed potato chips
1 cup butterscotch chips
2 1/2 cups flour
1 teaspoon baking soda

Cream the butter and sugars in a mixing bowl until light and fluffy. Beat in the vanilla and eggs. Stir in the potato chips and butterscotch chips. Sift the flour and baking soda over the potato chip mixture; stir to blend. Drop by teaspoonfuls onto a buttered cookie sheet. Bake at 375 degrees for 10 to 12 minutes or until firm. Yield: 3 to 4 dozen.

Judy Hammond, Laureate Lambda
Tulsa, Oklahoma

PRALINE CREAM COOKIES

1/2 cup (1 stick) butter, softened
2 1/2 cups packed brown sugar
1 large egg
2 teaspoons vanilla extract
1 2/3 cups flour
1 1/2 teaspoons baking powder
1/4 teaspoon salt
1/2 cup heavy cream
1 cup confectioners' sugar
1 cup toasted pecan halves

Cream the butter and 1 1/2 cups of the brown sugar in a mixing bowl until smooth and creamy. Add the egg, 1 teaspoon of the vanilla and a mixture of the flour, baking powder and salt; mix well. Drop by teaspoonfuls 2 inches apart onto a buttered cookie sheet. Bake at 350 degrees for 15 minutes or until beginning to brown. Combine the cream and the remaining 1 cup brown sugar in a saucepan over medium heat. Cook for 2 minutes, stirring constantly. Remove from heat. Stir in the confectioners' sugar, pecan halves and the remaining 1 teaspoon vanilla. Place a teaspoon of the pecan mixture on each cooled cookie. Yield: 3 dozen.

R. Gene Farley, Laureate Gamma Iota
Tallahassee, Florida

APRICOT ALMOND BARS

1 cup (2 sticks) margarine, softened
2 cups flour
1/2 cup sugar
1/2 teaspoon vanilla extract
2 egg whites
1/2 teaspoon almond extract
1 cup confectioners' sugar
1 1/2 cups apricot preserves
Slivered almonds

Combine the margarine, flour, sugar and vanilla in a large mixing bowl and beat until smooth and fluffy. Spread in a buttered 9×13-inch baking dish. Bake at 350 degrees for 15 minutes. Cool completely. Beat the egg whites and almond extract lightly in a small mixing bowl. Beat in the confectioners' sugar; mixture will be thin. Spread the apricot preserves over the cooled crust. Drizzle the egg white mixture over the preserves. Sprinkle with slivered almonds. Cool and cut into bars. Yield: 12 to 16 servings.

Darla Harbison, Xi Omega Delta
Sunray, Texas

BUTTER PECAN TURTLE BARS

2 cups flour
1 1/2 cups firmly packed brown sugar
1/2 cup plus 2/3 cup butter, softened
1 cup pecan halves
1 cup chocolate chips

Combine the flour, 1 cup of the brown sugar and the 1/2 cup butter in a bowl and mix well. Press into a 9×13-inch baking pan. Press pecans in an even layer over the unbaked flour layer. Combine the remaining 1/2 cup brown sugar and the 2/3 cup butter in a saucepan; bring to a boil, stirring constantly. Boil gently for 1/2 to 1 minute, stirring constantly. Pour evenly over the pecan-topped flour mixture. Bake at 350 degrees for 18 to 20 minutes. Remove from oven. Layer the chocolate chips over the top, swirling the chips with a spoon as they melt. Cool and cut into bars. Yield: 30 bars.

Dorothy Wegner, Iota Master
San Marcos, Texas

CINNAMON APPLESAUCE BROWNIES

1/2 cup shortening
1 1/2 cups plus 2 tablespoons sugar
2 cups sweetened cinnamon applesauce
2 eggs, beaten
2 cups flour
2 tablespoons baking cocoa
1/2 teaspoon salt
1/2 teaspoon baking soda
1 cup chopped walnuts or pecans
1 cup semisweet chocolate chips

Combine the shortening, the 1 1/2 cups sugar, applesauce, eggs, flour, baking cocoa, salt and baking soda in a large mixing bowl; beat until well mixed. Pour into a buttered and floured 9×13-inch baking dish. Sprinkle the 2 tablespoons sugar, chopped walnuts and chocolate chips evenly over the top. Bake at 350 degrees for 25 minutes. Cool and cut into squares. Yield: 2 dozen.

Sharon Kennedy Lyster, Laureate Epsilon Chi
DeLand, Florida

BLACK FOREST BROWNIES

1 (20-ounce) package fudge brownie mix
4 ounces cream cheese, softened
1/4 cup sugar
2 eggs
1 teaspoon vanilla extract
2 tablespoons flour
1 (21-ounce) can cherry pie filling
1/4 cup chocolate chips

Prepare the brownie mix using the package directions. Spread half the batter in a buttered 9×13-inch baking dish. Combine the cream cheese and sugar in a mixing bowl and beat until smooth. Add the eggs 1 at a time, mixing well after each addition. Stir in the vanilla. Blend in the flour. Spread the pie filling over the batter in the baking dish. Sprinkle the chocolate chips over the pie filling. Spoon the cream cheese mixture over the chocolate chips. Drop the remaining brownie batter by spoonfuls over the cream cheese mixture. Lightly draw circles in the cream cheese layer and top brownie batter layer with a knife to create a marbled effect. Bake at 350 degrees for 45 to 50 minutes or until set. Cool and cut into bars.
Yield: 3 dozen.

Kerri De Sousa, Beta Zeta
Strathmore, Alberta, Canada

BLONDE BROWNIES

2 cups sifted flour
1 teaspoon baking powder
1/4 teaspoon baking soda
1 teaspoon salt
2/3 cup (1 1/3 sticks) butter, melted
2 cups packed brown sugar
2 eggs, slightly beaten
2 teaspoons vanilla extract
1 cup chopped pecans
2 cups semisweet chocolate chips

Place the flour, baking powder, baking soda and salt in a bowl and stir to combine. Combine the butter and brown sugar in a large bowl and mix well. Cool slightly. Add the eggs and vanilla; mix well. Add half the flour mixture and mix well. Add the remaining 1/2 of the flour mixture; mix well. Batter will be very stiff. Spread in a buttered 9×13-inch baking dish.

Sprinkle pecans and chocolate chips over the top. Press the nuts and chips into the batter slightly. Bake at 350 degrees for 40 to 45 minutes or until brownies pull away from the sides of the pan. Serve warm with ice cream or serve cool. Yield: 2 dozen.

Nancy Parr, Xi Sigma Omicron
San Antonio, Texas

BUTTERMILK BROWNIES

2 ounces unsweetened chocolate
1 1/3 cups butter or margarine
1 teaspoon salt
2 cups plus 1 1/2 cups sugar
2 cups flour
2 eggs
1/2 teaspoon baking soda
1/2 cup buttermilk
2 teaspoons vanilla extract
1/3 cup milk
1 cup semisweet chocolate chips

Combine the chocolate, 1 cup of the butter, salt and 1 cup water in a saucepan; bring to a boil. Remove from heat. Combine the 2 cups sugar, flour, eggs, baking soda, buttermilk and 1 teaspoon of the vanilla in a bowl and mix well. Stir in the chocolate mixture. Pour into a buttered 10 x15-inch cake pan. Bake at 350 degrees for 25 to 30 minutes or until brownies pull away from the sides of the pan. Combine the 1 1/2 cups sugar, milk and the 1/3 cup butter in a saucepan and bring to a boil. Boil gently for 30 seconds. Remove from heat and stir in the chocolate chips and the remaining 1 teaspoon vanilla. Pour evenly over the warm brownies. Cool and cut into bars. Yield: about 3 dozen.

Linda Fae Wiedeman, Xi Gamma
Miles City, Montana

CANDY BAR BROWNIES

3/4 cup (1 1/2 sticks) butter, melted
2 cups sugar
4 eggs
2 teaspoon vanilla extract
1 1/2 cups flour
1/3 cup baking cocoa
1/2 teaspoon baking powder
1/4 teaspoon salt
4 (2-ounce) Snickers bars, cut into 1/4-inch pieces
3 (2-ounce) chocolate candy bars, chopped

Combine the butter, sugar, eggs and vanilla in a mixing bowl and beat until smooth. Place the flour, baking cocoa, baking powder and salt in a separate bowl and stir to combine. Remove 1/4 cup of the flour mixture to a small bowl and set aside. Add the remaining flour mixture to the butter mixture; mix well. Toss the Snickers pieces with the reserved flour mixture in a bowl; stir into the batter. Pour into a buttered 9×13-inch baking dish. Sprinkle with chocolate candy bar pieces. Bake at 350 degrees for 30 minutes or until edges are firm; do not overbake. Cool and cut into bars. Yield: 3 dozen.

Deb Bulloch, Xi Beta Rho
Stuttgart, Arkansas

CHOCOLATE SYRUP BROWNIES

1/2 cup (1 stick) butter or margarine, softened
1 cup sugar
3 eggs
3/4 cup chocolate syrup
1/4 teaspoon vanilla extract
1 cup flour
1 tablespoon chopped nuts or "M & M's" Chocolate Candies, shredded coconut, peanut butter chips

Combine the butter, sugar and eggs in a mixing bowl and beat until smooth. Stir in the remaining ingredients. Pour into a buttered and lightly floured 9×9-inch baking pan. Bake at 350 degrees for 40 minutes or until a wooden pick inserted near the center comes out clean. Cool in the pan on a wire rack. Cut into squares. Yield: 16 brownies.

Marilyn Kelly, Laureate Eta
Clearwater, Florida

DEEP-DISH BROWNIES

3/4 cup (1 1/2 sticks) butter or margarine, melted
1 1/2 cups sugar
1 1/2 teaspoons vanilla extract
3 eggs
3/4 cup unsifted flour
1/2 cup baking cocoa
1/2 teaspoon baking powder
1/2 teaspoon salt

Combine the butter, sugar, vanilla and eggs in a bowl and beat well with a wooden spoon. Add a mixture of the remaining ingredients to the egg mixture gradually, beating until well mixed. Spread in a buttered 8×8-inch baking pan. Bake at 350 degrees for 40 to 45 minutes or until brownies begin to pull away from the edges of the pan. Cool and cut into squares.
Yield: 12 to 16 brownies.

Dottie Friedley, Preceptor Omicron Gamma
Desert Shores, California

Annette Coppetti, Preceptor Xi Psi, Oakdale, California, makes ***Toffee Crunch Cookies*** *by mixing a white cake mix with 1/2 cup melted butter and 1 egg and adding 1 cup crisp rice cereal and 1 cup toffee bits. Mix well and shape into 1-inch balls. Arrange 2 inches apart on a cookie sheet. Bake at 350 degrees for 12 minutes. Do not overbake.*

MARSHMALLOW CRISP BROWNIES

1 (20-ounce) package fudge brownie mix
1½ cups miniature marshmallows
1½ cups semisweet chocolate chips
1 cup creamy peanut butter
1 tablespoon butter or margarine
1½ cups crisp rice cereal

Prepare and bake the brownie mix using the package directions for chewy brownies in a 9×13-inch baking pan. Sprinkle the marshmallows over the hot brownies. Return to the oven and bake for 3 to 5 minutes or until marshmallows are golden. Cool in the pan on a wire rack. Combine the chocolate chips, peanut butter and butter in a saucepan over medium-low heat. Cook until chocolate is melted, stirring frequently. Remove from heat. Stir in the cereal. Pour evenly over the marshmallows. Chill, covered, until the topping is firm. Cut into bars. Serve at room temperature. Yield: variable.

Sarah Kapla, Chi Omicron
Romeoville, Illinois

GERMAN CHOCOLATE BARS

1 (18-ounce) package German chocolate mix
1 cup (2 sticks) cold butter
2 cups semisweet chocolate chips
1 (16-ounce) can coconut-pecan frosting
½ cup milk

Place the dry cake mix in a large bowl. Cut in the cold butter until crumbly. Press 2½ cups of the cake mixture in a buttered 9×13-inch baking dish. Bake at 350 degrees for 10 minutes. Sprinkle the chocolate chips over the hot cake at once. Drop the frosting by tablespoons over the chocolate chips. Stir the milk into the remaining cake mixture. Drop by teaspoonfuls over the frosting layer. Bake for 25 minutes longer or until bubbly around the edges. Cool. Chill, covered, for 4 hours before cutting. Yield: 2 dozen.

Barbara Sabin, Master Alpha Nu
Sedalia, Missouri

FUDGE NUT BARS

1 cup (2 sticks) butter or margarine
2 cups packed light brown sugar
2 eggs
2 teaspoons vanilla extract
2½ cups flour
½ teaspoon baking soda
1 teaspoon salt
5 cups rolled oats
Chocolate Filling

Cream the butter and brown sugar in a mixing bowl until smooth. Beat in the eggs and vanilla. Sift the flour, baking soda and salt into a bowl; stir in the oats. Add the dry ingredients to the creamed mixture and mix well. Prepare the Chocolate Filling. Spread ⅔ of the oats mixture in a buttered 10×15-inch cake pan. Spread Chocolate Filling over the top. Drop the remaining oats mixture by teaspoonfuls over the filling. Bake at 350 degrees for 20 to 25 minutes or until beginning to brown. Cool and cut into bars.
Yield: about 3 dozen.

CHOCOLATE FILLING

2 cups semisweet chocolate chips
1 (14-ounce) can sweetened condensed milk
2 tablespoons butter or margarine
½ teaspoon salt
2 teaspoons vanilla extract

Combine the chocolate chips, condensed milk, butter and salt in a microwave-safe bowl. Microwave until melted, stirring until smooth. Stir in the vanilla.

Maria Mathis, Pi Beta
Clearlake, Iowa

CHOCOLATE SHERRY CREAM BARS

1 cup sifted flour
½ teaspoon salt
4 ounces unsweetened chocolate
1 cup plus 4 tablespoons butter
4 eggs
2 cups sugar
1 teaspoon vanilla extract
Sherry Cream Filling
1 cup semisweet chocolate chips

Sift the flour and salt together. Melt the chocolate and the 1 cup butter in a saucepan over medium-low heat, stirring occasionally. Cool slightly. Beat the eggs in a mixing bowl until light. Add the sugar to the eggs gradually, mixing well after each addition. Add the chocolate mixture, flour mixture and vanilla; beat at medium speed for 1 minute. Pour into a buttered and floured 10×15-inch cake pan. Bake at 350 degrees for 25 minutes. Cool. Spread the Sherry Cream Filling over the cooled base. Chill, covered, for at least 1 hour. Melt the chocolate chips and 4 tablespoons butter with 3 tablespoons water in a saucepan over medium-low heat; mix well. Drizzle the chocolate mixture over the filling. Let the topping harden before cutting into bars. Yield: about 3 dozen.

SHERRY CREAM FILLING

½ cup (1 stick) butter, softened
4 cups confectioners' sugar
4 tablespoons sherry
¼ cup (or up to ½ cup more) heavy cream
1 cup chopped pecans or walnuts

Cream the butter and confectioners' sugar in a mixing bowl until light and fluffy. Add the sherry and cream gradually, beating well after each addition. Mix in the pecans.

Barbara E. Downs, Laureate Alpha Gamma
Bella Vista, Arkansas

COOKIE BRITTLE

1 cup (2 sticks) butter or margarine, softened
1 cup sugar
$1^1/_2$ teaspoons vanilla extract
1 teaspoon salt
2 cups flour
1 cup chocolate chips
$^1/_2$ cup finely chopped walnuts or pecans

Cream the butter and sugar with the vanilla and salt in a mixing bowl or food processor until light and fluffy. Beat in the flour. Mix in the chocolate chips by hand. Pat into an unbuttered 10×15-inch cake pan. Sprinkle with walnuts. Bake at 375 degrees for 20 to 25 minutes or until lightly browned. Cool. Break into irregular pieces and drain on paper towels. Dust with confectioners' sugar. Yield: 20 to 30 pieces.

Billy Jane Gabel, Xi Master
South Bend, Indiana

DUTCH LETTER BARS

A visit to the Dutch community of Pella, Iowa, just isn't complete without a stop at the bakery for a Dutch Letter.

$^1/_2$ cup (1 stick) margarine, melted
$^1/_2$ cup (1 stick) butter, melted
1 cup almond paste
2 eggs, beaten
2 cups flour
2 cups sugar

Combine the margarine, butter, almond paste and eggs in a mixing bowl; mix until smooth. Mix in the flour and sugar. Spread in a buttered 9×13-inch baking dish. Sprinkle additional sugar over the top. Bake at 350 degrees for 30 to 35 minutes or until golden brown. Cut into bars. Yield: about 3 dozen.

Loween Clayberg, Preceptor Delta Beta
Webster City, Iowa

HONEY PECAN TRIANGLES

1 cup (2 sticks) butter, softened
$1^1/_2$ cups packed brown sugar
1 egg yolk
$1^1/_2$ cups flour
$^1/_4$ cup honey
$^1/_2$ cup heavy cream
3 cups chopped pecans

Line a 9×13-inch baking dish or 10×15-inch cake pan with foil; butter the foil. Cream $^1/_2$ cup of the butter and $^1/_2$ cup of the brown sugar in a mixing bowl until smooth. Add the egg yolk and mix well. Add the flour gradually, mixing well after each addition. Press into the prepared baking dish. Bake at 350 degrees for 15 minutes. Combine the remaining 1 cup brown sugar, the remaining $^1/_2$ cup butter and honey in a saucepan over medium heat; bring to a boil. Cook for 3 minutes, stirring constantly. Remove from heat. Stir in the cream and pecans. Pour evenly over the hot base. Bake for 30 minutes longer or until hot and bubbly. Cool completely. Cut into bars; cut each bar in half diagonally. Yield: 36 to 40 triangles.

Georgia Carr, Pi Omicron
Lenexa, Kansas

HONEY-GLAZED BARS

1 cup granulated sugar
$^1/_4$ cup honey
1 egg
$^3/_4$ cup vegetable oil
2 cups flour
1 teaspoon baking soda
1 teaspoon cinnamon
$^1/_2$ teaspoon salt
2 teaspoons vanilla extract
1 cup chopped walnuts or pecans
1 cup confectioners' sugar
2 tablespoons real mayonnaise

Combine the sugar, honey, egg, vegetable oil, flour, baking soda, cinnamon, salt and 1 teaspoon of the vanilla in a large mixing bowl and beat until smooth. Stir in the walnuts. Press in an 11×17-inch baking pan that has been sprayed with nonstick cooking spray. Bake at 350 degrees for 12 to 15 minutes or until beginning to brown. Combine the confectioners' sugar, mayonnaise, the remaining 1 teaspoon vanilla and 1 teaspoon water in a small bowl and whisk until smooth. Spread over the hot base. Cool and cut into bars. Yield: 3 to 4 dozen.

Linda Humphrey, Xi Beta Epsilon
Woodward, Oklahoma

LEMON BARS

$2^1/_4$ cups flour
$^1/_2$ cup sifted confectioners' sugar
1 cup (2 sticks) margarine, softened
2 cups sugar
$^1/_3$ cup lemon juice
4 eggs
$^1/_2$ teaspoon baking powder

Combine 2 cups of the flour, confectioners' sugar and margarine in a mixing bowl and beat until smooth. Press into an unbuttered 9×13-inch baking dish. Bake at 350 degrees for 20 minutes. Combine the sugar, lemon juice and eggs in a mixing bowl and beat until smooth. Mix in the remaining $^1/_4$ cup flour and baking powder. Pour evenly over the hot base and bake for 20 to 25 minutes longer. Cool and cut into bars. Yield: about 4 dozen.

Sue Mattingly, Xi Beta Xi
Paris, Missouri

MACAROON BARS

3 1/4 cups flaked coconut
1 (14-ounce) can sweetened condensed milk
1 teaspoon almond extract
1 (8-count) can crescent rolls

Sprinkle 1 1/2 cups of the coconut evenly into a well-buttered 9×13-inch baking dish. Blend the condensed milk and almond extract. Drizzle half the condensed milk mixture over the coconut layer. Unroll the dough and arrange in a single layer over the top. Drizzle with the remaining condensed milk mixture and sprinkle with the remaining 1 3/4 cups coconut. Bake at 350 degrees for 30 to 35 minutes or until golden brown. Cool completely and cut into bars. Store in the refrigerator. Yield: 3 dozen.

Millissa Duffey, Theta
Vincennes, Indiana

PEANUT BUTTER FINGERS

1/2 cup (1 stick) margarine
1/2 cup granulated sugar
1/2 cup packed brown sugar
1 egg
1/3 cup plus 1/4 cup crunchy peanut butter
1/2 teaspoon baking soda
1/2 teaspoon vanilla extract
1 cup flour
1 cup rolled oats
1 cup semisweet chocolate chips
1/2 cup confectioners' sugar
2 to 4 tablespoons milk

Cream the margarine and sugars in a mixing bowl until light and fluffy. Add the egg, the 1/3 cup peanut butter, baking soda and vanilla; mix well. Mix in the flour and oats. Spread in a greased 9×13-inch baking pan. Bake at 350 degrees for 20 to 25 minutes. Sprinkle the chocolate chips evenly over the hot base. Let stand for 5 minutes; spread the chocolate with a knife over the base. Let cool. Combine the remaining 1/4 cup peanut butter, confectioners' sugar and milk in a bowl; mix well. Drizzle over the chocolate layer. Cool and cut into bars. Yield: 3 to 4 dozen.

Janette Boender, Xi Epsilon Iota
Ottumwa, Iowa

PECAN PIE BARS

2 cups flour
1 cup packed brown sugar
1 cup (2 sticks) butter, softened
5 eggs
1 cup granulated sugar
1 cup light corn syrup
1 teaspoon vanilla extract
1 cup chopped pecans

Combine the flour and brown sugar in a bowl. Cut in the butter until mixture resembles coarse crumbs. Press into a buttered 9×13-inch baking dish. Bake at 350 degrees for 10 to 15 minutes or until edges begin to turn light brown. Combine the eggs, granulated sugar, corn syrup and vanilla in a mixing bowl and beat until foamy. Stir in the pecans. Pour evenly over the base and bake at 275 degrees for 1 hour. Cool and cut into bars. Yield: 3 dozen.

Maggie Shibley, Preceptor Alpha Gamma
Horseshoe Bend, Arkansas

PECAN SLICES

1 cup sifted flour
1/2 cup (1 stick) butter (no substitutes)
2 eggs, beaten
1 1/2 cups packed brown sugar
1/2 cup flaked coconut
1 cup chopped pecans
2 tablespoons flour
1/2 teaspoon baking powder
1/2 teaspoon salt
1 1/2 teaspoons vanilla extract
1 1/2 cups confectioners' sugar
Lemon juice or milk

Place the flour in a bowl. Cut in the butter until mixture resembles coarse crumbs. Press into an unbuttered 9×12- or 8×13-inch baking pan. Bake at 350 degrees for 10 to 12 minutes or until edges begin to turn light brown. Let cool. Combine the eggs, brown sugar, coconut, pecans, flour, baking powder, salt and vanilla in a large bowl and mix well. Pour evenly over the cooled base. Bake at 350 degrees for 25 minutes; let cool. Place the confectioners' sugar in a bowl. Stir in enough lemon juice to make of drizzling consistency. Drizzle over the coconut layer. Let stand until icing is set. Cut into bars and remove from the pan. Yield: 25 to 30 bars.

Nancy B. Pfaff, Xi Nu Theta
Carbondale, Illinois

PUMPKIN BARS

1/2 cup (1 stick) butter, softened
1 cup packed brown sugar
1 egg
1/2 cup canned pumpkin
1 1/2 cups flour
1 teaspoon cinnamon
1/2 teaspoon ginger
1/2 teaspoon allspice
1/2 teaspoon baking soda
2 tablespoons anise seeds
1/2 cup raisins
1/2 cup chopped walnuts or pecans
1 cup confectioners' sugar
5 teaspoons orange juice concentrate

Cream the butter and brown sugar in a mixing bowl until smooth and fluffy. Beat in the egg and pumpkin. Add a mixture of the flour, cinnamon, ginger, allspice and baking soda to the pumpkin mixture; mix well. Add the anise seeds, raisins and walnuts; mix well. Spread evenly in a buttered 11×16-inch baking pan. Bake at 350 degrees for 18 minutes. Cool completely. Frost with a mixture of the confectioners' sugar and orange juice concentrate. Cut into squares. Yield: about 4 dozen.

Jane Barrett, Xi Delta Xi
Seal Beach, California

ALMOND CHOCOLATE BRITTLE

2 cups (4 sticks) butter
2 cups sugar
1 1/2 cups chopped almonds
1 (4-ounce) chocolate candy bar, melted

Combine the butter and sugar in a heavy kettle over medium heat and cook until melted and smooth, stirring constantly. Stir in 1 cup of the almonds. Cook the mixture until it reaches 300 degrees on a candy thermometer, stirring constantly. Pour the mixture into an unbuttered 10×15-inch cake pan. Cool completely. Spread the melted chocolate bar evenly over the hardened candy. Sprinkle with the remaining 1/2 cup almonds. Cool until firm. Break the candy into pieces with the sharp tip of a knife. Yield: variable.

Shana Berry-Buchanan, Laureate Alpha Gamma
Knoxville, Tennessee

DIVINITY FUDGE

2 cups sugar
1/3 cup light or dark corn syrup
2 egg whites
1 teaspoon vanilla extract
1/2 cup chopped walnuts or pecans

Combine the sugar, corn syrup and 1/2 cup water in a 4-cup glass measure. Microwave on High for 3 minutes. Stir well. Microwave on High for 6 to 8 minutes longer or to 250 degrees on a candy thermometer, hard-ball stage; do not leave the thermometer in the microwave while cooking. Beat the egg whites in a large mixing bowl until stiff peaks form. Pour a very thin, slow stream of the syrup into the egg whites, beating constantly at high speed. Add the vanilla; beat for 6 to 8 minutes or until mixture is stiff and has lost its shine. Fold in the walnuts. Drop by teaspoonfuls onto waxed paper; cool. Store in an airtight container. Yield: 36 to 40 pieces.

Charlene Hull, Preceptor Beta Epsilon
Clackamas, Oregon

TEXAS PECAN FUDGE

3 cups sugar
3/4 cup (1 1/2 sticks) butter
1 (5-ounce) can evaporated milk
1 (7-ounce) jar marshmallow creme
1 1/2 (8-ounce) packages semisweet baking chocolate
1 teaspoon vanilla extract
1 cup chopped pecans

Combine the sugar, butter and evaporated milk in a microwave-safe bowl. Microwave on High for 3 minutes; stir. Microwave for 3 minutes longer; stir. Microwave for 4 minutes. Add the remaining ingredients; mix well until chocolate is melted. Spread immediately in a foil-lined 9×9-inch pan. Cool to room temperature. Cut into squares.
Yield: about 3 pounds.

Priscilla Beauregard, Xi Xi Sigma
Copperas Cove, Texas

HOLIDAY FUDGE

4 1/2 cups sugar
1/8 teaspoon salt
4 tablespoons butter
1 (12-ounce) can evaporated milk
2 cups semisweet chocolate chips
12 ounces dark sweet chocolate squares
2 cups marshmallow creme
2 cups chopped walnuts

Combine the sugar, salt, butter and evaporated milk in a saucepan over medium heat and bring to a boil. Boil gently for 6 minutes, stirring constantly. Remove from heat to a large mixing bowl. Add the chocolate chips, chocolate squares, marshmallow creme and walnuts; mix well. Pour onto buttered baking sheets. Cool completely and cut into squares. Yield: variable.

Linda H. Shaver, Kappa Kappa
Valley Falls, Kansas

QUICK FUDGE

3 ounces unsweetened chocolate
3 tablespoons butter
1/3 cup mashed potatoes
1/8 teaspoon salt
1 teaspoon vanilla extract
1 (1-pound) package confectioners' sugar, sifted

Melt the chocolate and butter in the top of a double boiler over simmering water. Remove from heat. Stir in the potatoes, salt and vanilla. Add the confectioners' sugar and mix well. Knead until smooth. Press into a buttered 8×8-inch baking dish. Cool completely and cut into squares. Yield: 1 1/4 pounds.

Robbie Robertson, Gamma Pi Master
Houston, Texas

CHOCOLATE BUTTER FUDGE

3 cups sugar
1 envelope unflavored gelatin
1/2 cup light corn syrup
1 cup milk
1 cup (2 sticks) butter
3 ounces unsweetened chocolate
2 teaspoons vanilla extract
1 cup chopped walnuts

Combine the sugar and dry gelatin mix in a heavy saucepan. Add the corn syrup, milk, butter and chocolate. Cook, uncovered, over medium heat to 238 degrees on a candy thermometer, soft-ball stage. Pour into a mixing bowl; stir in the vanilla. Let stand for 15 minutes. Beat at low speed until thick. Stir in the walnuts. Spread in a buttered pan.
Yield: variable.

Ruth Schwarck, Laureate Gamma
Spencer, Iowa

FRYING PAN FUDGE

2 1/2 cups sugar
1/2 cup (1 stick) margarine, softened
6 ounces evaporated milk
1 cup semisweet chocolate chips
1 cup (or more) chopped pecans or other nuts
1 teaspoon vanilla extract

Combine the sugar and margarine in a heavy skillet and mix until smooth. Stir in the evaporated milk. Place over medium heat; bring to a boil. Reduce heat to low and cook for 6 minutes, stirring occasionally. Remove from heat. Add the chocolate chips and pecans; stir until mixture begins to thicken. Stir the vanilla quickly. Drop by teaspoonfuls onto waxed paper. Cool completely. Store in an airtight container.
Yield: variable.

Betty Yohn, Preceptor Xi
Baxter Springs, Kansas

FANTASTIC FUDGE

1 cup semisweet chocolate chips
1/4 cup margarine
6 large marshmallows
1 cup sugar
1/3 cup evaporated milk
1/2 teaspoon vanilla extract
1/2 cup chopped walnuts (optional)

Combine the first 3 ingredients in a large bowl. Combine the sugar and evaporated milk in a saucepan over medium heat; bring to a boil. Boil for 1 minute and 5 seconds; do not stir. Pour over the ingredients in the large bowl. Stir until melted and smooth. Stir in the vanilla and walnuts. Pour into a buttered pan. Chill, covered, until firm. Yield: variable.

Sylvia Armstrong, Preceptor Beta
Tenants Harbor, Maine

DREAM FUDGE

3 cups sugar
2/3 cup evaporated milk
3/4 cup margarine
1 1/2 cups vanilla chips
1 (7-ounce) jar marshmallow creme
1 tablespoon orange extract
9 drops red food coloring
12 drops yellow food coloring

Combine the sugar, evaporated milk and margarine in a heavy saucepan over medium heat. Bring to a boil, stirring constantly. Boil for 3 minutes, stirring constantly. Remove from heat. Add the vanilla chips and marshmallow creme; stir until chips are melted. Remove 1 cup of the sugar mixture and set aside. Stir the orange extract and red and yellow food coloring into the remaining sugar mixture; mix well. Pour into a buttered 9×13-inch baking dish. Drizzle the reserved 1 cup sugar mixture over the top; swirl with a knife. Chill, covered, until cooled completely. Cut into small squares. Yield: 7 dozen.

Rexie Eaker, Pi Master
Bethalto, Illinois

NEVER-FAIL FUDGE

1 cup (2 sticks) margarine
1 cup creamy peanut butter
4 tablespoons baking cocoa
2 teaspoons vanilla extract
1 (1-pound) package confectioners' sugar

Melt the margarine and peanut butter together in a large saucepan over medium-low heat or in a microwave-safe bowl in the microwave oven. Remove from heat. Mix in the baking cocoa, vanilla and confectioners' sugar. Spread in an unbuttered 8×8-inch baking pan. Chill, covered, for 1 hour. Cut into squares and serve. Yield: 12 to 16 servings.

Beverly Weaver, Xi Alpha Chi
Conway, South Carolina

PEANUT BUTTER FUDGE

1 cup packed brown sugar
3 1/2 cups granulated sugar
1 (12-ounce) can evaporated milk
2 (7-ounce) jars marshmallow creme
1 cup peanut butter, smooth or chunky
2 cups peanut butter chips
2 cups peanuts

Combine the brown sugar, granulated sugar and evaporated milk in a saucepan over medium heat. Cook, uncovered, to 235 degrees on a candy thermometer, soft-ball stage. Remove from heat. Add the marshmallow creme, peanut butter and peanut butter chips; stir until smooth. Stir in the peanuts. Pour into a buttered baking pan or pans. Cool slightly and cut into squares. Wrap with plastic wrap or foil and store in a cool, dry place. Yield: variable.

Betty A. Goforth, Laureate Zeta Iota
Gridley, California

WHITE PECAN FUDGE

1/2 cup (1 stick) butter (no substitutes)
2 1/2 cups miniature marshmallows
2 1/4 cups sugar
1 cup heavy cream
2 cups white chocolate chips
2 teaspoons vanilla extract
2 cups chopped pecans

Cut the butter into small pieces. Combine the butter and marshmallows in a large bowl and set aside. Combine the sugar and cream in a saucepan over medium heat; bring to a boil. Cook, covered, over medium heat for 2 to 3 minutes or until the steam washes the sugar crystals from the side of the pan. Cook, uncovered, over medium heat to 234 degrees on a candy thermometer, soft-ball stage; do not stir. Remove from heat. Pour the hot cream mixture over the ingredients in the large bowl and stir until melted and smooth. Stir in the white chocolate chips; stir until smooth. Stir in the vanilla and pecans. Pour into a buttered 8×11-inch baking pan. Chill until firm. Yield: 4 pounds.

Karla G. Wheeler, Laureate Alpha Theta
Rifle, Colorado

WHITE FUDGE

4 1/2 cups granulated sugar
1 cup sour cream
1/2 cup milk
1/2 teaspoon salt
1/4 cup real butter
2 tablespoons light corn syrup
4 teaspoons real vanilla extract
2 cups broken walnuts
2/3 cup candied cherries

Combine the first 6 ingredients in a heavy saucepan over medium heat. Bring to a boil, stirring constantly. Cook, uncovered, over medium heat to 238 degrees on a candy thermometer, soft-ball stage; do not stir. Remove from heat. Let stand until lukewarm (110 degrees), about 1 hour and 15 minutes. Stir in the vanilla. Beat until the mixture thickens and loses its luster. Stir in the walnuts and cherries at once. Pour into a buttered 9×13-inch baking dish. Let stand until firm. Cut into squares. Yield: 4 dozen.

Dorothy Bogue, Preceptor Xi
Aberdeen, South Dakota

ORANGE JOY BALLS

1 cup confectioners' sugar
2 1/2 cups crushed vanilla wafers
1/2 teaspoon cinnamon
2 tablespoons grated orange zest
1/2 cup flaked coconut
1/2 cup chopped pecans
3 tablespoons light corn syrup
1/3 cup frozen orange juice, thawed

Combine the confectioners' sugar, vanilla wafer crumbs, cinnamon, orange zest, coconut, pecans, corn syrup and orange juice concentrate in a large bowl; mix well. Sift additional confectioners' sugar onto a 12×12-inch piece of foil. Shape the orange mixture into teaspoon-size balls; roll each in the confectioners' sugar. Place in an airtight plastic container. Let stand for 2 or 3 days before serving. Will keep for several weeks. Yield: 3 1/2 dozen.

Jeanette E. Felger, Iota Master
New Braunfels, Texas

MOUNDS CANDIES

1 (14-ounce) package shredded coconut
1 (1-pound) package confectioners' sugar
1 (14-ounce) can sweetened condensed milk
1/2 cup (1 stick) butter, melted (no substitutes)
4 cups semisweet chocolate chips
1 bar paraffin

Combine the coconut, confectioners' sugar, condensed milk and butter in a large bowl and mix well. Pat into a buttered 9×13-inch baking dish. Freeze, covered, for 30 minutes to 1 hour. Melt the chocolate chips and paraffin together in the top of a double boiler over simmering water. Cut the frozen candy into very small pieces; you may use a pizza cutter to cut into rows, about 15 across and 10 down. Use a spatula to remove the candy pieces from the dish. Poke a wooden pick into the end of each piece of candy and dip into the chocolate mixture. Place on waxed paper to dry. Twist the wooden pick from each piece of candy. Arrange the candy on a tray. Refrigerate, or serve at room temperature.
Yield: about 150 pieces.

Diana Neil, Epsilon Alpha
Garland, Texas

Elizabeth Walden, Laureate Eta, Warner Robins, Georgia, makes ***Pretzel Goodies*** *by arranging round flat pretzels on a cookie sheet and topping each with an unwrapped chocolate kiss. Bake at 400 degrees for 1 minute and press an M&M on each softened kiss.*

SLOW-COOKER PEANUT CLUSTERS

1 (16-ounce) jar dry-roasted unsalted peanuts
1 (16-ounce) jar salted peanuts
16 ounces German's sweet chocolate, cut into small pieces
2 cups semisweet chocolate chips
2 (24-ounce) packages white almond bark, cut into small pieces

Layer the dry-roasted unsalted peanuts, salted peanuts, German's chocolate, chocolate chips and almond bark in a slow cooker. Cook on Low for 3 hours; do not lift the lid while cooking. Stir the mixture. Drop by teaspoonfuls or tablespoonfuls onto waxed paper. Let cool. Yield: 100 or more pieces.

Dottie Inman, Laureate Alpha Pi
Sedona, Arizona

PEANUT BRITTLE

1 cup sugar
1/2 cup light corn syrup
1/8 teaspoon salt
2/3 cup dry-roasted salted peanuts
1 tablespoon butter
1 teaspoon vanilla extract
1 teaspoon baking soda

Combine the sugar, corn syrup and salt in a 2-quart microwave-safe bowl. Microwave on High for 5 minutes. Stir in the peanuts. Microwave for 6 minutes longer or until syrup and nuts are lightly browned, stirring occasionally after 2 to 4 minutes. Add the butter, vanilla and baking soda and stir until foamy. Spread over a well-buttered baking sheet to desired thickness. Cool and break into pieces. Yield: variable.

Dee Hoisington, Preceptor Xi
Aberdeen, South Dakota

CARAMEL CHOCOLATE BARS

2 cups semisweet chocolate chips
2 cups milk chocolate chips
1/4 cup shortening
1 (28-ounce) package caramels
2/3 cup (1 1/3 sticks) butter
2 1/2 cups party peanuts

Microwave the chocolate chips and shortening on High in a microwave-safe bowl for 1 1/2 minutes; stir. Microwave for 1 1/2 minutes longer; stir. Spread half the chocolate mixture in a buttered 9×13-inch baking dish. Let cool. Combine the caramels, butter and 1/4 cup water in a bowl. Microwave for 2 minutes; stir. Microwave for 2 minutes longer; stir in the peanuts. Pour the peanut mixture over the cooled chocolate layer. Let cool. Spread the remaining half of the chocolate mixture over the top. Let stand, covered, in a cool place for 24 hours. Cut into 1×1 1/2-inch pieces. Do not refrigerate. Yield: 4 dozen.

Diane A. Golden, Preceptor Xi
Aberdeen, South Dakota

COCONUT STRAWBERRIES

3 (3-ounce) packages strawberry gelatin
Pinch of salt
Pinch of cream of tartar
1 (18-ounce) package finely chopped coconut
1 (14-ounce) can sweetened condensed milk
Tube of green icing

Combine 2 packages of the dry gelatin mix, salt, cream of tartar, coconut and condensed milk in a large bowl and mix well. Chill, covered, for 3 hours. Shape into small strawberry shapes. Roll in the remaining dry gelatin mix to coat. Insert green wooden picks in the strawberries to make stems. Make leaves with green icing. Let stand at room temperature for 1 hour. Store in an airtight container in the refrigerator. Yield: 2 dozen pieces.

Pat Rohach, Xi Delta Nu
Lexington, Kentucky

SWEETHEART PRETZEL STICKS

1 (14-ounce) package caramels
18 large pretzel sticks
1 cup chopped pecans
1 cup chocolate chips
6 ounces chocolate candy coating
2/3 cup vanilla baking chips
4 ounces vanilla candy coating

Line a baking sheet with buttered waxed paper. Combine the caramels and 3 tablespoons water in a heavy saucepan over low heat. Cook for about 15 minutes, stirring frequently. Hold a pretzel over the saucepan and spoon the caramel mixture over 2/3 of the pretzel. Roll in pecans to coat the caramel area; chill for 15 minutes. Melt the chocolate chips and chocolate candy coating together in a saucepan over low heat. Drizzle over the pecan-coated pretzel area. Chill for 10 minutes. Melt the vanilla baking chips and vanilla candy coating together and drizzle over the chocolate-coated pretzel area. Chill for 10 minutes. Store in an airtight container. Yield: 1 1/2 dozen.

Norma McCrary, Alpha Epsilon
Washington, Indiana

Desserts

✣ TRIPLE CHIP CHEESECAKE

1½ cups crushed vanilla wafers or graham crackers
½ cup confectioners' sugar
¼ cup baking cocoa
⅓ cup butter or margarine, melted
24 ounces cream cheese, softened
¾ cup granulated sugar
⅓ cup sour cream
3 tablespoons flour
1 teaspoon vanilla extract
3 large eggs
1 cup plus 1 tablespoon butterscotch chips
1 cup plus 1 tablespoon semisweet chocolate chips
1 cup plus 1 tablespoon white vanilla chips

Combine the wafer crumbs, confectioners' sugar, baking cocoa and melted butter in a small bowl; mix well. Press over the bottom and 1½ inches up the side of a buttered 9-inch springform pan. Bake in a preheated 300-degree oven for 7 to 9 minutes. Cool in the pan on a wire rack. Combine the cream cheese and granulated sugar in a large mixing bowl and beat until creamy. Beat in the sour cream, flour and vanilla. Add the eggs and beat until combined. Microwave the 1 cup butterscotch chips on Medium-High (70%) in a medium microwave-safe bowl for 1 minute; stir. The chips may partially retain shape. Microwave for additional 10- to 15-second intervals or until chips are melted when stirred. Stir 1½ cups of the cream cheese mixture into the melted chips. Pour into the crust in the springform pan. Repeat the procedure with the 1 cup semisweet chocolate chips; spoon them carefully over the butterscotch layer. Repeat with the 1 cup white vanilla chips; spoon carefully over the semisweet chocolate layer, covering it completely. Bake at 300 degrees for 1 hour and 10 to 15 minutes or until edge is set and center moves slightly. Cool in the pan on a wire rack for 10 minutes. Loosen the cheesecake from the side of the pan with a knife. Let stand at room temperature for 1 hour. Place the 1 tablespoon butterscotch chips in a small heavy-duty plastic bag. Microwave on Medium-High for 20 seconds; knead the plastic bag. Microwave for additional 10- to 15-second intervals, kneading until smooth. Cut a tiny corner from the bag; squeeze to drizzle the melted butterscotch over the cheesecake. Repeat the procedure with 1 tablespoon chocolate chips and 1 tablespoon vanilla chips. Chill, covered, for 3 to 10 hours. Remove the pan and serve. Yield: 16 servings.

Maria Sandy, Zeta Lambda
Russell, Iowa

OREO CHEESECAKES

24 ounces cream cheese, softened
¾ cup sugar
3 eggs
24 chocolate sandwich cookies
Chocolate sprinkles, chocolate chips, berries

Beat the cream cheese, sugar and eggs in a mixing bowl until smooth. Line 2 dozen muffin cups with paper liners. Place a cookie in each lined muffin cup. Spoon the cream cheese mixture over the cookies. Bake at 350 degrees for 15 to 20 minutes or until set. Remove from oven. Garnish with chocolate sprinkles, chocolate chips or berries. Let cool. Chill, covered, until serving time. Yield: 2 dozen.

Barbara Buroker, Epsilon Sigma
Ville Platte, Louisiana

CHOCOLATE CHUNK CHEESECAKE

1½ cups chocolate sandwich cookie crumbs
¼ cup butter, melted
12 ounces semisweet chocolate
24 ounces cream cheese, softened
¾ cup sugar
3 eggs
½ cup sour cream
½ cup heavy cream

Press a mixture of the cookie crumbs and melted butter over the bottom of a 9-inch springform pan. Chop 8 ounces of the semisweet chocolate. Combine the cream cheese and sugar in a large mixing bowl and beat until smooth. Add the eggs 1 at a time, mixing well after each addition. Beat in the sour cream. Mix in the chopped chocolate. Pour into the prepared springform pan. Bake at 325 degrees for 45 to 50 minutes or until set. Loosen the cheesecake from the side of the pan. Cool completely. Place the heavy cream in a saucepan over low heat and bring to a simmer. Add the remaining 4 ounces semisweet chocolate and cook until melted, stirring constantly. Drizzle over the cheesecake. Chill, covered, for 8 to 10 hours. Remove the side of the pan. Cut into small pieces. Yield: variable.

Susan Secoy, Preceptor Sigma
Bryan, Ohio

RASPBERRY CHEESECAKE

1½ cups graham cracker crumbs
¼ cup butter or margarine, melted
1 cup sugar
20 ounces cream cheese, softened
1½ tablespoons flour
½ teaspoon vanilla extract
¼ teaspoon peach flavoring (optional)
3 eggs
¼ cup heavy cream
1 cup raspberries (optional)

Combine the graham cracker crumbs, melted butter and ¼ cup of the sugar in a small bowl and mix well. Press the mixture into a 9-inch springform pan that has been sprayed with nonstick cooking spray. Bake at 325 degrees for 8 to 10 minutes. Remove from the oven and let stand until cool. Reduce oven temperature to 250 degrees. Place the cream cheese in a large mixing bowl and beat until fluffy. Beat in the remaining ¾ cup sugar gradually. Add the flour, vanilla, peach flavoring, eggs and cream; beat well. Stir in the raspberries. Pour over the crust in the springform pan. Place a shallow pan of water on the bottom rack of the oven. Place the springform pan on a baking sheet on a rack in the top half of oven. Bake for 1 hour and 15 minutes or until edge is set but center moves slightly. Turn off the oven. Let cheesecake stand in the oven with door slightly ajar for 1 hour. Cool completely in the pan on a wire rack. Chill, covered, for at least 4 hours. Garnish with raspberries.
Yield: 12 to 16 servings.

Ellen Jenson, Kappa Sigma
Charlevoix, Michigan

COCONUT SNOWBALLS

¾ cup margarine
2 cups packed brown sugar
1 (8-ounce) can crushed pineapple, drained
1 cup chopped walnuts or pecans
1 (16-ounce) package vanilla wafers, crushed
Whipped cream
Shredded coconut

Cream the margarine and brown sugar in a mixing bowl until smooth and creamy. Add the pineapple, walnuts and wafer crumbs and mix well. Shape into 6 to 8 balls. Chill, wrapped in plastic wrap, for 8 to 10 hours. Roll the balls in whipped cream to coat. Roll in coconut to coat. Freeze until serving time.
Yield: 6 to 8 servings.

Sherry Doctor, Gamma Nu
Wellington, Kansas

HOT FUDGE ICE CREAM BAR DESSERT

1 (16-ounce) jar chocolate syrup
¾ cup creamy peanut butter
19 ice cream sandwiches
12 ounces whipped topping
1 cup salted peanuts

Microwave the chocolate syrup on High in a medium microwave-safe bowl for 2 minutes; do not allow to boil. Add the peanut butter and stir until smooth. Cool to room temperature. Line the bottom of a 9×13-inch baking dish with 9½ ice cream sandwiches. Layer the whipped topping, chocolate mixture and peanuts ½ at a time over the ice cream sandwiches. Repeat the layers. Freeze for 1 hour or until firm. Cut into squares and serve. Yield: 18 servings.

Mary Ann Williams, Chi Iota
Summerfield, Illinois

ICE CREAM PIE WITH HOT FUDGE SAUCE

½ cup melted butter or margarine
1 cup firmly packed brown sugar
1½ cups crushed cornflakes
1 cup chopped walnuts or pecans
1 quart vanilla ice cream
Hot Fudge Sauce

Combine the butter and brown sugar in a bowl and mix well. Stir in the cornflakes and walnuts. Press

2/3 of the cornflakes mixture in a large square or oblong baking dish. Fill with ice cream. Sprinkle with the remaining cornflakes mixture. Freeze until serving time. Serve with Hot Fudge Sauce.
Yield: 8 to 10 servings.

HOT FUDGE SAUCE

1 cup chocolate chips
1/2 cup (1 stick) butter
2 cups confectioners' sugar
11/2 cups evaporated milk
1 teaspoon vanilla extract

Melt the chocolate chips and butter in a saucepan over medium-low heat. Stir in the confectioners' sugar and evaporated milk. Cook until thickened and smooth, stirring constantly. Remove from heat. Stir in the vanilla.

Marlene Markey, Laureate Epsilon Theta
St. Petersburg, Florida

FAMILY REUNION VANILLA ICE CREAM

8 cups milk
8 teaspoons cornstarch
2 cups sugar
1/2 teaspoon salt
4 eggs, beaten
4 cups heavy cream
2 tablespoons vanilla extract

Scald 6 cups of the milk in the top of a double boiler over hot water. Combine the cornstarch, sugar and salt in a bowl. Add the scalded milk, stirring until sugar is dissolved. Return the mixture to the top of the double boiler and cook over boiling water for 20 minutes, stirring constantly. Combine the eggs and the remaining 2 cups milk in a large bowl and beat until smooth. Stir the hot milk mixture gradually into the egg mixture. Return to the double boiler and cook over boiling water for 10 minutes, stirring constantly. Cool. Stir in the cream and vanilla. Chill for at least 5 hours. Pour into a 1-gallon ice cream freezer container. Freeze using manufacturer's directions.
Yield: 1 gallon.

Shan Stover, Preceptor Delta
Centralia, Illinois

PUMPKIN ICE CREAM FREEZE

21/2 cups fine gingersnap crumbs
1/2 cup chopped walnuts or pecans (optional)
1/2 cup granulated sugar
1/2 cup (1 stick) butter or margarine, melted
8 cups (1 quart) vanilla ice cream, softened
2 cups cooked pumpkin
1 cup firmly packed brown sugar
1 teaspoon salt
2 teaspoons cinnamon
1/2 teaspoon ginger
1/2 teaspoon nutmeg
2 teaspoons vanilla extract

Combine the gingersnap crumbs, chopped walnuts, granulated sugar and butter in a bowl and mix well with a fork. Remove 1 cup of the crumb mixture and set aside. Press the remaining crumb mixture into a 9×13-inch dish. Combine the ice cream, pumpkin, brown sugar, salt, cinnamon, ginger, nutmeg and vanilla in a large bowl and mix quickly until well blended. Pour evenly over the crumb layer. Sprinkle with the reserved crumb mixture. Freeze until firm. Let stand at room temperature for a few minutes before serving. Yield: 18 servings.

Joan C. Bower, Master Iota
Lockport, New York

STRAWBERRY DESSERT

1 cup flour
1/4 cup light brown sugar
1/2 cup chopped pecans
1/2 cup (1 stick) margarine, softened
2 egg whites
2/3 cup sugar
2 tablespoons lemon juice
1 (16-ounce) package frozen sliced strawberries, thawed
8 ounces whipped topping

Combine the flour, brown sugar, pecans and margarine in a bowl and mix well. Pat into a 9×13-inch dish. Bake at 350 degrees for 20 minutes or until lightly browned. Remove from the oven. Cool and break into crumbs. Return 2/3 of the crumb mixture to the dish and pat evenly over the bottom. Beat the egg whites in a mixing bowl until frothy. Add the sugar gradually, beating until stiff peaks form. Add the lemon juice and strawberries. Beat at medium speed for 5 to 8 minutes or until the consistency of meringue. Fold in the whipped topping. Pour into the crumb-lined dish. Sprinkle with the remaining crumb mixture. Freeze until firm. Cut into squares. Top each serving with a whole strawberry if desired.
Yield: 15 servings.

Margie Hungate, Laureate Gamma Theta
Macon, Missouri

Mary L. Reardon, Omicron Master, Maryville, Missouri, makes a color and delicious ***Rainbow Freeze.*** *Place a 16-ounce carton of whipped topping in a large bowl. Crumble 2 packages of coconut macaroons. Fold the crumbled macaroons and 1 cup pecans into the whipped topping. Spread a layer half the mixture in a 9×13-inch dish. Add a layer of spoonfuls of rainbow sherbet over the sherbet. Use as much sherbet as you wish. Spread the remaining macaroon mixture. Freeze until firm.*

APPLE DUMPLINGS

2 cups flour
1 teaspoon salt
2/3 cup shortening
8 medium apples, peeled and cored
1/2 cup sugar
1 1/2 teaspoons cinnamon
Butter or margarine
Cinnamon Syrup

Measure the flour and salt together into a bowl. Cut in half the shortening until mixture resembles coarse crumbs. Cut in the remaining shortening until particles are the size of large peas. Sprinkle 4 tablespoons cold water over the mixture to moisten it. Gather the pastry into a ball. Roll into eight 7-inch squares on a lightly floured surface. Fill the apple cavities with a mixture of the sugar and cinnamon; dot with butter. Place an apple in the center of each pastry square. Pull the pastry up around the apple; seal at the top to enclose. Arrange the wrapped apples in a baking pan. Pour the Cinnamon Syrup evenly over the wrapped apples. Bake at 350 degrees for 1 hour. Yield: 8 servings.

CINNAMON SYRUP

1 cup sugar
3 tablespoons butter
1 teaspoon vanilla extract
1/2 teaspoon cinnamon
2 or 3 drops red food coloring

Combine the sugar, butter, vanilla, cinnamon, food coloring and 2 cups of water in a saucepan over medium-high heat. Bring to a boil.

Beverly McDaniel, Preceptor Beta Theta
Blue Springs, Missouri

FRESH APPLE PASTRY SQUARES

2 1/2 cups flour
1 teaspoon salt
1 cup plus 2 tablespoons butter
1 egg, separated
Milk
1 cup crushed cornflakes
8 cups sliced peeled tart apples
2/3 cup granulated sugar
1/2 teaspoon ginger
1/2 teaspoon cinnamon
1 cup sifted confectioners' sugar
1/2 teaspoon pure vanilla extract

Combine the flour and salt in a large bowl and stir. Cut in the butter until mixture resembles coarse crumbs. Place the egg yolk in a measuring cup and beat lightly with a fork; beat in enough milk to make 2/3 cup liquid. Add the egg mixture to the flour mixture and stir with a fork to make a soft crumbly dough. Roll half the dough into a rectangle large enough to line a 10x15-inch cake pan. Press the dough across the bottom and up the sides of the pan. Sprinkle evenly with cornflakes. Combine the apples, granulated sugar, ginger and cinnamon in a large bowl and stir to mix. Spread the apple mixture evenly over the cornflake layer. Roll the remaining dough half into a rectangle large enough to cover the pan. Place it over the apple layer. Pinch the edges to seal. Brush stiffly beaten egg white over the top. Bake at 400 degrees for 50 to 60 minutes or until browned. Cool slightly. Combine the confectioners' sugar, vanilla and 1 to 2 tablespoons water in a small bowl; whisk until smooth. Frost the slightly cooled top pastry. Cut into squares. Yield: 16 servings.

Betty I. Storsberg, Alpha Omega Master
Longwood, Florida

BLUEBERRY APPLE CRUNCH

1 (21-ounce) can apple pie filling
1 (14-ounce) package frozen blueberries
1 cup sugar
1 (2-layer) package white cake mix
1/2 cup (1 stick) butter, melted
1 cup chopped walnuts or pecans
Vanilla ice cream

Spread the apple pie filling in a lightly buttered 9x13-inch baking dish. Toss the blueberries with 3/4 cup of the sugar and spoon evenly over the pie filling. Layer the dry cake mix over the blueberries. Drizzle with melted butter. Sprinkle with the walnuts and the remaining 1/4 cup sugar. Bake at 350 degrees for 45 to 50 minutes or until golden brown and bubbly. Serve with ice cream. Yield: 6 to 8 servings.

Cindy Julian, Pi Omicron
Overland Park, Kansas

BERRY COOKIE COBBLER

2 (12-ounce) packages frozen mixed berries, thawed
1 (21-ounce) can apple pie filling
1/3 cup sugar
1 1/2 teaspoons cinnamon
1 (18-ounce) roll prepared sugar cookie dough

Combine the berries, apple pie filling, sugar and cinnamon in a large bowl and mix well. Spoon into individual ovenproof bowls or an 8x8-inch baking dish. Crumble the cookie dough over the fruit mixture, covering thickly and completely. Bake at 350 degrees for 45 minutes or until cookie layer is golden and crisp and juices bubble thickly. Serve warm with ice cream. Yield: 6 servings.

Mabel Hickey, Xi Upsilon Psi
Yoakum, Texas

ELEGANT CHERRY CRISP

2/3 cup packed brown sugar
1/2 cup flour
1/2 cup rolled oats, or 1 envelope honey-nut instant cereal
1/4 cup chopped pecans or walnuts
3/4 teaspoon cinnamon
3/4 teaspoon nutmeg
1/3 cup butter, softened
2 (21-ounce) cans cherry pie filling
8 scoops vanilla ice cream

Combine the brown sugar, flour, oats, pecans, cinnamon and nutmeg in a large bowl. Cut in the butter until crumbly. Pour the cherry pie filling into a buttered 9×9-inch baking dish. Sprinkle the brown sugar mixture evenly over the top. Bake at 375 degrees for 30 minutes or until golden brown. Cool. Spoon into water goblets or large wine glasses. Top each with a scoop of vanilla ice cream. Yield: 8 servings.

Denise Balsama, Laureate Zeta Lambda
Stroudsburg, Pennsylvania

LEMON FLUFF SQUARES

1 cup flour
1/2 cup (1 stick) butter, softened
1/2 cup chopped walnuts
8 ounces cream cheese, softened
1 cup confectioners' sugar
1/2 cup whipped topping
1 (22-ounce) can lemon pie filling

Combine the flour, butter and walnuts in a bowl and mix well. Pat into a 9×13-inch baking dish. Bake at 350 degrees for 10 to 12 minutes or until edges begin to brown. Cool. Combine the cream cheese and confectioners' sugar in a mixing bowl and beat until smooth. Fold in the whipped topping. Spread over the cooled walnut crust. Pour the lemon pie filling evenly over the top. Chill, covered, until serving time. Top with additional walnuts and whipped topping; cut and serve. Yield: 15 servings.

Diane L. Pruett, Preceptor Alpha Upsilon
Tamaqua, Pennsylvania

PUMPKIN CRISP

1 (15-ounce) can pumpkin
1/2 cup sugar
1 (14-ounce) can sweetened condensed milk
3 eggs
1 1/2 teaspoons pumpkin pie spice
1 (2-layer) package yellow cake mix
1 cup chopped pecans
1 cup melted margarine

Mix the first 6 ingredients in a large mixing bowl until smooth. Pour evenly into a 9×13-inch baking dish that has been sprayed with nonstick cooking spray. Layer the dry cake mix over the top. Sprinkle with pecans and pat the pecans into the cake mix layer. Drizzle with the melted margarine. Bake at 350 degrees for 50 to 60 minutes or until a wooden pick inserted in the center comes out clean. Cool slightly. Serve with whipped topping. Yield: 24 servings.

F. Jewell Patton, Laureate Epsilon Iota
Melbourne, Florida

CHERRY RHUBARB DESSERT

1 cup quick-cooking oats
1 cup packed brown sugar
Pinch of salt
1 cup flour
1 cup (2 sticks) butter or margarine, softened
4 cups chopped rhubarb
1 cup granulated sugar
2 tablespoons cornstarch
Red food coloring
1 (21-ounce) can cherry pie filling
1 teaspoon almond extract
1/2 cup chopped walnuts or pecans

Combine the oats, brown sugar, salt, flour and butter in a bowl and mix well. Press half the oats mixture into a 9×13-inch baking dish. Layer the rhubarb over the oats layer. Combine the sugar, cornstarch and 1 cup water in a saucepan over medium-low heat. Whisk to blend. Cook until thickened, stirring constantly. Stir in the food coloring, cherry pie filling and almond extract. Pour evenly over the rhubarb layer. Stir the walnuts into the reserved oats mixture and sprinkle evenly over the top. Bake at 350 degrees for 45 minutes or until browned and bubbly.
Yield: 15 servings.

Jane Eisma, Epsilon Eta
Hawarden, Iowa

BANANA PUDDING

3/4 cup sugar
3 tablespoons flour
Dash of salt
1 whole egg
3 eggs, separated
2 cups milk
1/2 teaspoon vanilla extract
1 (12-ounce) package vanilla wafers
5 bananas, sliced

Combine 1/2 cup of the sugar, flour, salt, whole egg, 3 of the egg yolks, milk and vanilla in a large microwave-safe bowl. Microwave on High in 30-second intervals until slightly thickened, stirring after each interval. Layer the vanilla wafers, bananas and pudding 1/2 at a time in a 9 1/2×11-inch baking dish. Beat the egg whites and the remaining 1/4 cup sugar in a mixing bowl until stiff peaks form. Spread over the pudding, sealing to the edge. Bake at 350 degrees for 5 minutes or until golden brown.
Yield: 15 to 18 servings.

Ann Levingston, Theta Chi
Steinhatchee, Florida

BLACKBERRY PUDDING

1/3 cup margarine
2 cups sugar
1 cup milk
2 cups flour, sifted
1 teaspoon salt
2 teaspoons baking powder
2 cups blackberries

Cream the margarine and 1 cup of the sugar in a mixing bowl until light and fluffy. Add the milk and a mixture of the flour, salt and baking powder; mix well. Pour into a buttered 3-quart baking pan. Layer the blackberries over the top. Drizzle a mixture of 2 cups boiling water and the remaining 1 cup sugar over the blackberries. Bake at 350 degrees for about 50 minutes or until top is golden brown.
Yield: at least 12 servings.

Maxine Johnson, Xi Alpha Omega
Foley, Alabama

AMARETTO BREAD PUDDING

12 slices white bread
4 cups milk
3/4 cup butter
3 eggs, beaten
1 teaspoon almond extract
1 1/2 cups sugar
1/2 cup sliced or slivered almonds
1 cup confectioners' sugar
1 egg
1/4 cup amaretto

Tear the bread into medium pieces and place in a buttered large baking dish. Combine the milk and 1/4 cup of the butter in a large saucepan over low heat; heat until butter is melted, stirring occasionally. Pour the milk mixture evenly over the bread layer. Combine the eggs, almond extract and sugar in a mixing bowl and beat until smooth. Pour the egg mixture over the bread and stir to combine. Sprinkle with almonds. Bake at 350 degrees for 40 minutes or until set. Cut into squares. Combine the remaining 1/2 cup butter and confectioners' sugar in a saucepan over medium-low heat. Heat until butter is melted, stirring frequently. Remove from heat and quickly whisk in the egg. Stir in the amaretto; beat until smooth. Serve warm over the warm bread pudding with whipped cream. Yield: 15 servings.

Wendy Bennett, Xi Pi Rho
Napa, California

APPLE AND RAISIN BREAD PUDDING

4 apples, peeled and cubed
8 to 10 end slices of bread, torn into pieces
1 cup granulated sugar
1/2 cup raisins
2 eggs, beaten
2 cups milk
1 teaspoon vanilla extract
1/2 cup packed brown sugar
1/4 cup butter or margarine, softened
1 teaspoon cinnamon

Combine the apples, bread, sugar and raisins in a bowl and mix well. Combine the eggs, milk and vanilla in a separate bowl and beat until smooth. Stir the egg mixture into the apple mixture; mix well. Spread in a buttered 8×8-inch baking pan. Combine the brown sugar, butter and cinnamon in a small bowl and mix well with a fork. Sprinkle evenly over the top of the bread pudding. Bake at 350 degrees for 45 minutes to 1 hour or until browned. Serve warm with cream or ice cream. Yield: 12 servings.

Vanette Allen, Laureate Zeta Eta
Bryan, Texas

JAMBALAYA BREAD PUDDING

1 large loaf French bread
4 cups whole milk
3 eggs, beaten
2 cups sugar
2 tablespoons vanilla extract
1 teaspoon cinnamon
1 cup white raisins
3 tablespoons butter
Whiskey Sauce

Break the bread into bite-size pieces into a large bowl. Add the milk to cover; soak for 1 hour. Mix well. Add the eggs and sugar. Stir in the vanilla, cinnamon and raisins. Melt the butter in a 9×13-inch baking dish, tilting to coat the sides. Pour in the pudding mixture. Bake for 1 hour or until browned. Serve warm with Whiskey Sauce. Yield: 15 servings.

WHISKEY SAUCE

1/2 cup (1 stick) butter, melted
1 cup sugar
1 egg
1/4 cup whiskey, or 1/4 cup hazelnut or other liqueur

Place the butter and sugar in a mixing bowl and mix well. Beat in the egg and whiskey.

Sally Lund, Preceptor Alpha Chi
Fayetteville, Arkansas

RASPBERRY BREAD PUDDING

3 tablespoons butter, softened
1/2 cup raspberry jam
8 slices firm bread, crusts trimmed
2 large eggs
1 cup milk
1/2 cup heavy cream
1/2 teaspoon vanilla extract

Butter five 1-cup loaf pans. Spread butter and jam over one side of each bread slice. Line each loaf pan with 1 1/2 bread slices, jam side up. Combine the eggs, milk, cream and vanilla in a bowl and whisk to blend. Pour 1/5 of the egg mixture evenly over the contents of each loaf pan. Place the pans on a baking sheet. Bake at 375 degrees for 20 to 25 minutes or until puffed and golden. Cool for 10 minutes and serve. Yield: 5 servings.

Pat Shamroy, Xi Beta Eta
East Setauket, New York

CREAM CHEESE BREAD PUDDING

Butter or margarine, softened
6 slices white bread
4 eggs
1 cup sugar
1 teaspoon vanilla extract
Dash of salt
1½ to 2 cups milk
1 (14-ounce) can sweetened condensed milk
1 teaspoon cinnamon
8 ounces cream cheese, softened

Spread the butter over both sides of each bread slice; cut into 1-inch squares. Layer in a lightly buttered 8×12×2-inch baking dish. Place 3 of the eggs in a large bowl and beat slightly. Add ½ cup of the sugar, vanilla and salt; mix well. Add the milk and condensed milk; mix well. Pour the milk mixture evenly over the bread layer. Sprinkle with cinnamon. Combine the cream cheese and the remaining ½ cup sugar; blend until smooth. Beat in the remaining egg. Spread the cream cheese mixture evenly over the soaked bread. Bake at 350 degrees for 45 minutes or until firm. Cool slightly and serve. Yield: 8 servings.

Sheryl Tyler, Beta Theta Delta
Houston, Texas

WHITE CHOCOLATE MOUSSE

8 ounces white chocolate
½ cup unsalted butter
6 eggs, separated, at room temperature
1 cup sifted confectioners' sugar
1 cup Frangelico (hazelnut liqueur)
2 cups whipping cream
Pinch of cream of tartar

Melt the white chocolate and butter in a small saucepan over low heat, stirring constantly. Mix with a hand or electric mixer if the mixture separates. Combine the egg yolks, confectioners' sugar and Frangelico in a mixing bowl and beat until the mixture forms a slowly dissolving ribbon when the beaters are lifted. Pour into the top of a double boiler and cook over simmering water for about 30 minutes or until very thick, whisking constantly. Pour into a large mixing bowl. Whisk in the chocolate mixture; stir until smooth. Cool. Beat the whipping cream in a chilled mixing bowl until stiff peaks form. Beat the egg whites with the cream of tartar in a separate mixing bowl until stiff peaks form. Fold the egg whites into the chocolate mixture; fold in the whipped cream. Chill, covered, until firm, about 3 hours. Spoon into crystal goblets. Top with raspberries or baking cocoa. Yield: 6 servings.

Marge Bayles, Alpha Epsilon
Tallahassee, Florida

CREME BRULEE

4 cups heavy cream
4 egg yolks
½ cup sugar
1 teaspoon vanilla extract
¼ teaspoon salt
8 tablespoons brown sugar

Heat the cream in a saucepan over low heat; do not scald. Combine the egg yolks and sugar in a mixing bowl and mix well. Beat in the vanilla and salt. Add the hot cream to the mixture gradually, mixing as you pour. Fill small custard cups ¾ full. Place the custard cups in a large baking pan. Add water to the pan to reach halfway up the sides of the custard cups. Bake at 325 degrees for 40 minutes or until set. Chill, covered, for at least 3 hours. Sprinkle brown sugar evenly over the tops. Broil 4 inches from the heat source until brown sugar is caramelized. Chill, covered, until caramelized topping hardens, about 2 hours. Yield: 8 servings.

Lin Kobsey, Preceptor Pi
Tulsa, Oklahoma

DATE PUDDING

1½ cups flour
2 tablespoons baking powder
1 teaspoon salt
1 cup packed brown sugar
⅔ cup boiling water
1 teaspoon butter
1 cup chopped dates
1 cup chopped walnuts
2 cups packed brown sugar
1 tablespoon butter
2 cups boiling water

Combine the flour, baking powder, salt and 1 cup brown sugar in a large bowl; mix well. Add ⅔ cup boiling water and 1 teaspoon butter; stir. Stir in the dates and walnuts; mixture will be stiff. Spread in a 9×13-inch baking dish that has been sprayed with nonstick cooking spray. Combine the remaining 2 cups brown sugar, the 1 tablespoon butter and 2 cups boiling water in a large bowl; mix well. Pour evenly over the top of the flour mixture. Bake at 375 degrees for 30 minutes or until golden brown. Cool and serve with whipped cream.
Yield: 10 to 12 servings.

Judy Caldwell, Xi Omega
Washington, Indiana

PINEAPPLE PUDDING

3/4 cup flour
Dash of salt
2 cups nonfat dry milk powder
2 cups sugar
2 eggs
3 tablespoons margarine
1 tablespoon vanilla extract
1 (12-ounce) package vanilla wafers
1 (20-ounce) can crushed pineapple, well drained

Place the flour, salt, dry milk powder and sugar in a large bowl and stir to combine. Place the eggs in a small bowl and beat well. Combine the margarine, vanilla and 2 cups water in a saucepan over medium-high heat and bring to a boil. Add the flour mixture to the boiling liquid gradually, whisking to blend. Cook for 2 to 3 minutes or until thickened, stirring constantly. Remove from heat. Add a small amount of the hot mixture to the eggs and beat well. Return the egg mixture to the hot pudding mixture and mix well. Layer vanilla wafers 1/3 at a time, pineapple 1/2 at a time and pudding 1/2 at a time in a 9×13-inch baking dish, ending with a layer of vanilla wafers. Chill, covered, until serving time. Yield: 10 to 15 servings.

Linda Edwards, Beta Kappa Sigma
Hilltop Lakes, Texas

PUMPKIN PUDDING

1 (32-ounce) can pumpkin
3 eggs, beaten
1 cup milk
1/2 teaspoon salt
1/2 teaspoon ginger
1/2 teaspoon ground cloves
1 teaspoon cinnamon
1 cup sugar
1 (2-layer) package spice cake mix
3/4 cup (1 1/2 sticks) butter, melted
1 cup chopped walnuts or pecans

Combine the pumpkin, eggs, milk, salt, ginger, cloves, cinnamon and sugar in a large bowl and mix well. Pour into a buttered 9×13-inch baking dish. Combine the cake mix, melted butter and walnuts in a bowl and mix well. Sprinkle evenly over the pumpkin mixture. Bake at 350 degrees for 1 hour. Serve with whipped topping or vanilla ice cream. Yield: 12 servings.

Carol Neel, Gamma Beta Master
San Rafael, California

RICE PUDDING

1 cup quick-cooking rice
1 cup sugar
3 eggs, beaten
2 quarts milk
5 ounces heavy cream
1/2 teaspoon cinnamon
1/2 cup raisins
1/2 teaspoon pure vanilla extract

Combine the rice, sugar, eggs, milk, cream, cinnamon, raisins and vanilla in a heavy saucepan over low heat. Bring to a full boil, stirring frequently. Boil for 5 minutes, stirring frequently. Pour into a serving dish. Dust with additional cinnamon. Chill, covered, until serving time. Yield: 8 to 10 servings.

Janice Moore, Xi Gamma Tau
Pottstown, Pennsylvania

RICE CUSTARD

3 eggs, beaten
1/3 cup sugar
1/4 teaspoon salt
1/4 teaspoon nutmeg
2 cups milk
1 1/2 cups cooked rice
1 teaspoon vanilla extract

Combine the eggs, sugar, salt and nutmeg in a large bowl and mix well. Add the milk, rice and vanilla; mix well. Pour into a buttered 9×9-inch baking dish. Bake at 325 degrees for 45 minutes or until set. Yield: 6 to 8 servings.

Doris Kane, Xi Omega
Washington, Indiana

RUSSIAN CREAM

1 cup sugar
1 envelope unflavored gelatin
1 cup low-fat sour cream
1 1/2 teaspoons vanilla or almond extract
1 cup light whipped topping

Combine the sugar, gelatin and 1 1/2 cups water in a saucepan over low heat; cook until sugar and gelatin are dissolved, stirring constantly. Remove from heat. Stir in the sour cream and vanilla. Pour into a glass dish. Chill, covered, until very thick, about 3 hours. Add the whipped topping and whisk to blend. Chill for at least 3 more hours. Serve plain or with fresh fruit or your favorite sauce. Yield: 7 to 8 servings.

Nettie Ruth Brown, Alpha Upsilon Master
Saint Augustine, Florida

CLASSIC TIRAMISU

6 egg yolks
1 1/4 cups sugar
1 1/4 cups mascarpone cheese
1 3/4 cups whipping cream
2 (3-ounce) packages ladyfingers
1/3 cup coffee liqueur

Combine the egg yolks and sugar in a mixing bowl and beat for about 1 minute or until thick and pale yellow. Scrape into the top of a double boiler and cook over simmering water for 8 to 10 minutes, stirring constantly. Remove from heat. Combine the egg mixture and mascarpone in a mixing bowl and beat

well. Beat the whipping cream in a mixing bowl until stiff peaks form; fold into the egg mixture. Line the bottom and side of a 3-quart bowl with ladyfinger halves. Brush the ladyfingers with coffee liqueur. Spoon half the egg mixture over the ladyfingers. Repeat the ladyfinger, liqueur and egg mixture layers. Garnish with baking cocoa and chocolate curls. Chill, covered, until serving time.
Yield: 10 to 12 servings.

Shirley Peak, Epsilon Master
Duluth, Minnesota

TIRAMISU TORTE

1 (18-ounce) package white cake mix
1 cup strong coffee, at room temperature
4 egg whites
5 (7-ounce) candy bars, chopped
Tiramisu Frosting

Combine the cake mix, coffee and egg whites in a large mixing bowl and beat at low speed until moistened. Beat at high speed for 2 minutes. Fold in 4 of the chopped candy bars. Pour into 2 buttered and floured 9-inch cake pans. Bake at 350 degrees for 25 to 30 minutes or until the cake tests done. Cool in the pan. Remove to a wire rack. Cut each layer in half horizontally. Spread the frosting between each layer and over the top. Sprinkle with the remaining chopped candy bar. Yield: 10 to 12 servings.

TIRAMISU FROSTING

4 ounces cream cheese, softened
2/3 cup sugar
1/2 cup plus 2 tablespoons strong coffee, cooled
2 cups heavy cream
1/3 cup chocolate syrup
2 teaspoon vanilla extract

Combine the cream cheese and sugar in a mixing bowl and beat until smooth. Add the coffee, cream and chocolate syrup; beat until thick and creamy. Blend in the vanilla.

Marcene M. Pederson, Epsilon Delta
Benson, Minnesota

EASY TIRAMISU

1 (11-ounce) frozen pound cake, thawed
3/4 cup strong brewed coffee
1 cup sugar
1/2 cup chocolate syrup
8 ounces cream cheese, softened
2 cups heavy cream
2 (7-ounce) chocolate candy bars, chopped

Cut the pound cake lengthwise into 9 slices. Arrange the slices in a single layer in a 9×13-inch baking dish, cutting slices if necessary to fit. Drizzle the coffee over the cake. Combine the sugar, chocolate syrup and cream cheese in a large mixing bowl and beat at medium speed until smooth. Add the cream; beat at medium speed until light and fluffy. Spread the cream mixture over the cake. Sprinkle with chopped candy bars. Chill, covered, until firm and flavors are enhanced, at least 1 hour. Yield: 24 (2-inch) squares.

B.J. Ness, Preceptor Gamma Alpha
Cedaredge, Colorado

OLD-FASHIONED CHARLOTTE

2 tablespoons unflavored gelatin
1 1/2 cups milk
3 eggs, separated
1 cup sugar
7 tablespoons sherry
2 cups whipping cream

Soften the gelatin in a small amount of water in a large bowl. Heat 3/4 cup of the milk in a saucepan over low heat or in the microwave oven. Add the hot milk to the gelatin mixture. Combine the egg yolks and sugar in a mixing bowl and beat until well mixed. Beat in the remaining 3/4 cup milk and sherry. Stir into the gelatin mixture. Beat the egg whites in a mixing bowl until stiff peaks form. Fold into the cooled gelatin mixture. Beat the whipping cream in a mixing bowl until stiff peaks form. Fold into the gelatin mixture. Chill, covered, until set.
Yield: 6 to 8 servings.

Dorothy Holbrook, Alpha Omega Master
Winter Park, Florida

BUTTERSCOTCH LAYERED DESSERT

1 cup flour
1/2 cup (1 stick) butter or margarine, melted
1/4 cup brown sugar
8 ounces cream cheese, softened
16 ounces whipped topping
1 cup confectioners' sugar
2 (4-ounce) packages butterscotch or chocolate instant pudding mix
3 cups milk

Combine the flour, melted butter and brown sugar in a bowl and mix well. Pat into a 9×13-inch baking dish. Bake at 350 degrees for 15 minutes or until golden brown. Cool. Combine the cream cheese, half the whipped topping and confectioners' sugar in a bowl and mix well. Spread over the cooled crust. Combine the dry pudding mix and milk in a mixing bowl and beat at medium speed for 2 minutes. Spread over the cream cheese layer. Spread the remaining whipped topping over the top. Chill, covered, until serving time. Yield: 10 to 15 servings.

Cathy Gilliland, Alpha Kappa
Rose Hill, Iowa

CREAM PUFF CAKE

1/2 cup (1 stick) butter or margarine
1 cup flour
4 eggs
12 ounces French vanilla instant pudding mix (4 small packages)
4 cups milk
8 ounces cream cheese, softened
8 ounces whipped topping
Fudge Sauce

Combine the butter and 1 cup of water in a saucepan over medium heat; bring to a boil. Add the flour and whisk until smooth. Remove from heat. Cool for 2 minutes. Add the eggs 1 at a time, mixing well after each addition. Spread in an unbuttered 9×13-inch baking dish. Bake at 400 degrees for 30 to 35 minutes or until pastry is dry. Cool. Combine 1 package of the dry pudding mix, 1 cup of the milk and the cream cheese in a large mixing bowl and beat until smooth. Add the remaining pudding mix and milk 1 package and 1 cup at a time, mixing well after each addition. Spread evenly over the cooled pastry. Spread the whipped topping over the top and drizzle with Fudge Sauce. Yield: 10 to 15 servings.

FUDGE SAUCE

Multiply the amounts by 1 1/2 if you like lots of fudge sauce.

1 cup sugar
1/2 teaspoon salt
3 tablespoons baking cocoa
3/4 cup evaporated milk
1 teaspoon vanilla extract
2 tablespoons butter

Combine the sugar, salt and baking cocoa in a medium saucepan; whisk to mix and to eliminate lumps. Whisk in the evaporated milk. Bring to a boil over medium-high heat. Boil for 2 minutes. Remove from heat. Stir in the vanilla and butter. Cool completely before drizzling over the cake.

Mary Ann Cowenhoven, Laureate Kappa Theta
Fremont, California

COOKIES AND CREAM CHEESE SENSATION

1 (16-ounce) roll chocolate chip cookie dough, at room temperature
8 ounces cream cheese, softened
1/3 cup sugar
2 cups half-and-half
1 (4-ounce) package chocolate instant pudding mix
8 ounces whipped topping

Press the cookie dough in an even layer on a baking stone. Bake at 375 degrees for 12 to 15 minutes or until browned. Cool for 10 minutes. Loosen from the stone. Combine the cream cheese and sugar in a bowl and mix until smooth. Combine the half-and-half and dry pudding mix in another bowl and mix well; let stand for about 5 minutes or until thickened. Spread the cream cheese mixture evenly over the cookie crust. Spread the pudding over the cream cheese layer. Spread whipped topping over the pudding layer. Chill, covered, until serving time.
Yield: 16 to 20 servings.

Annette Decker, Delta Delta
Ellicott City, Maryland

BANANA SPLIT DESSERT

3 cups graham cracker crumbs
3/4 cup (1 1/2 sticks) butter, melted
11 ounces cream cheese, softened
1 1/2 cups sugar
4 bananas
1 (20-ounce) can crushed pineapple, drained
16 ounces whipped topping
Chocolate syrup to taste
Chopped nuts to taste
Maraschino cherries to taste

Mix the crumbs and melted butter together and press into a 9×13-inch baking dish. Bake at 350 degrees for 5 minutes. Let cool. Combine the cream cheese and sugar in a mixing bowl and beat until smooth. Spread the cream cheese mixture over the cooled crumb layer. Slice the bananas evenly over the top. Spoon the pineapple evenly over the bananas. Top with whipped topping. Drizzle with chocolate syrup and sprinkle with nuts and cherries.
Yield: 6 servings.

Jodi Testa, Zeta Zeta
Junction City, Kansas

SODA CRACKER DESSERT

3 egg whites
1/2 teaspoon cream of tartar
1 cup sugar
18 saltine crackers, crushed
1 cup pecans, chopped
1 teaspoon vanilla extract
3 bananas, sliced
8 ounces whipped topping
Toasted shredded coconut (optional)

Beat the egg whites with the cream of tartar in a mixing bowl until foamy. Add the sugar gradually, beating until stiff peaks form. Mix in the saltines. Mix in the pecans. Mix in the vanilla. Pour into a buttered 9×13-inch baking dish. Bake at 325 degrees for 20 minutes or until lightly browned. Cool completely. Arrange the banana slices over the crust. Garnish with whipped topping and coconut.
Yield: 12 servings.

Melody Johnson, Theta Rho
Clarksville, Arkansas

BLUEBERRY TORTE

1 1/4 cups graham cracker crumbs
1/4 cup melted butter
1 1/4 cups sugar
6 ounces cream cheese, softened
2 eggs, beaten
1 (15-ounce) can blueberries, drained, juice reserved
1 1/2 tablespoons cornstarch
1/4 teaspoon cinnamon
1/4 teaspoon almond extract
1 tablespoon lemon juice
1 tablespoon butter

Combine the graham cracker crumbs, melted butter and 1/4 cup of the sugar in a bowl and mix well. Pat into a buttered 9-inch springform pan. Combine the cream cheese, eggs and 1/2 cup of the sugar in a mixing bowl and beat until smooth. Spread evenly over the crumb layer. Bake at 350 degrees for 20 minutes. Combine the blueberry juice, cornstarch and the remaining 1/2 cup sugar in a saucepan over medium-low heat. Cook until thickened, stirring constantly. Stir in the blueberries, cinnamon, almond extract, lemon juice and butter. Cool. Spread the blueberry mixture over the cooled cream cheese layer. Chill, covered, until serving time. Serve with whipped cream. Yield: 12 to 16 servings.

Sharon Chalmers, Preceptor Gamma Omicron
Lynchburg, Virginia

CRACKERS AND BERRIES

Try strawberries, blackberries, or a type of serviceberry called "saskatoon."

84 unsalted soda crackers
2 (4-ounce) packages vanilla instant pudding mix
4 cups milk
4 cups whipped topping
2 cups fresh or frozen (thawed) sliced berries
1/2 cup sugar
2 tablespoons cornstarch

Line a buttered 9×13-inch baking dish with 1/3 of the soda crackers. Combine the dry pudding mix and milk in a large mixing bowl and beat until smooth. Spread 1/3 of the pudding mixture over the cracker layer. Spread 1/3 of the whipped topping over the pudding layer. Repeat the cracker, pudding and whipped topping layers twice. Chill, covered, for at least 24 hours. Combine the berries, sugar, cornstarch and 1 cup water in a saucepan over medium heat. Bring to a boil and cook until thickened, stirring constantly. Cool. Drizzle over the layered dessert and serve. Yield: 24 servings.

Bev Scarcelli, Preceptor Delta Alpha
Revelstoke, British Columbia

COOKIES AND CREAM TORTE

1 cup (2 sticks) butter, softened
1 1/4 cups sugar
2 eggs
2 cups flour
1 teaspoon grated lemon zest
2 teaspoons baking powder
1/2 teaspoon salt
1 teaspoon unflavored gelatin
3 cups whipping cream
7 cups sliced strawberries, or 2 (10-ounce) packages frozen strawberries, thawed

Cream the butter and sugar in a mixing bowl until light and fluffy. Add the eggs 1 at a time, mixing well after each addition. Mix the flour, lemon zest, baking powder and salt together and add to the creamed mixture gradually, beating well after each addition. Place a 9-inch round of parchment paper on a baking sheet. Spoon the batter over the round of paper, making an uneven edge. Bake at 350 degrees for 12 to 15 minutes or until lightly browned. Repeat the procedure with the remaining batter; bake 1 at a time. There will be 4 layers. Let cool. Soften the gelatin in 1/4 cup cold water. Combine the gelatin mixture and whipping cream in a mixing bowl and beat until stiff peaks form. Layer the baked layers, strawberries and whipped cream mixture 1/4 at a time on a serving plate. Chill until serving time or freeze. Cut into wedges and serve.Yield: 12 to 16 servings.

Carol Langworth, Theta Beta
Sicamons, British Columbia

THREE-FRUIT FLUFF

1 cup crushed pineapple
1 cup mandarin oranges
8 ounces fat-free strawberry yogurt
8 ounces fat-free whipped topping
1 small package white chocolate fat-free sugar-free instant pudding mix
Maraschino cherries (optional)

Combine the undrained pineapple, undrained mandarin oranges, yogurt, whipped topping and dry pudding mix in a bowl; mix well. Chill, covered, until serving time. Spoon into a chilled trifle bowl. Top with maraschino cherries. Yield: 6 to 8 servings.

Betsy Johnston, Xi Beta Kappa
Greensboro, North Carolina

Chris Stafford, Laureate Omicron, Sterling, Colorado, prepares ***Peaches in Wine*** *by slicing enough peeled fresh peaches to measure 4 cups. Place in a glass bowl and cover with a mixture of 2 cups white zinfandel, 1/2 cup amaretto and 3 tablespoons sugar. Refrigerate, covered, for 6 hours or longer.*

PEPPERMINT DREAM DESSERT

Be sure to use real whipped cream.

2 cups graham cracker crumbs
1 cup crushed peppermint candy canes
1 cup miniature marshmallows
1/2 cup chopped walnuts
2 cups whipping cream
2 teaspoons vanilla extract

Layer half the graham cracker crumbs over the bottom of a lightly buttered 8×8-inch or 9×9-inch baking pan. Combine the candy canes, marshmallows and walnuts in a bowl. Combine the whipping cream and vanilla in a chilled mixing bowl and beat until stiff peaks form. Fold into the candy cane mixture. Pour evenly over the crumbs in the baking pan. Layer the remaining crumbs over the top. Chill, covered, until serving time. Yield: about 12 servings.

Carol Ann Gearner, Delta Gamma Master
Desoto, Texas

RHUBARB TORTE

1 cup (2 sticks) butter, softened
2 cups plus 7 tablespoons flour
4 tablespoons plus 2 3/4 cups sugar
6 egg yolks
1/4 teaspoon salt
1 cup heavy cream or milk
5 cups chopped rhubarb
6 egg whites
1/4 teaspoon cream of tartar
1 teaspoon vanilla extract

Combine the butter, the 2 cups flour and the 4 tablespoons sugar in a bowl and mix well. Pat into a 9×13-inch baking dish. Bake at 350 degrees for 10 minutes. Beat the egg yolks. Combine the egg yolks, 2 cups of the sugar, the 7 tablespoons flour, salt, cream and rhubarb in a mixing bowl and mix well. Pour over the crust. Bake at 350 degrees for 45 minutes or until set. Beat the egg whites with the remaining 3/4 cup sugar, cream of tartar and vanilla in a mixing bowl until stiff peaks form. Spread over the torte, sealing to the edges. Bake at 350 degrees for 15 minutes or until lightly browned. Yield: 15 servings.

Norma Borgmann, Preceptor Delta
Patoka, Illinois

NO-PEEK MERINGUE DESSERT

6 egg whites
1/2 teaspoon cream of tartar
2 cups sugar
6 (2-ounce) Skor toffee bars, crushed
Dash of salt
2 cups whipping cream, whipped

Preheat the oven to 400 degrees. Line 2 baking sheets with brown paper. Draw two 5-inch circles, or make circles 1 inch smaller than the serving plate. Beat the egg whites with the cream of tartar until frothy. Add the sugar 1 tablespoon at a time, beating well after each addition; stiff glossy peaks will form. Spread half the meringue evenly over each paper circle. Place in the oven. Close the oven door and turn off the heat. Let stand in the oven for 8 to 10 hours; do not peek. Fold the toffee bars and salt into the whipped cream. Spread 1/3 of the whipped cream mixture between the meringues. Cover the side and top with the remaining whipped cream mixture. Chill, covered, for at least 8 hours. Yield: 16 servings.

Chris McGoun, Alpha Upsilon Master
Ottawa, Ontario, Canada

PEACHES AND CREAM

3/4 cup flour
1 teaspoon baking powder
1/2 teaspoon salt
1 (4-ounce) package vanilla cook-and-serve pudding
3 tablespoons margarine
1 egg
1/2 cup milk
1 (15- to 20-ounce) can sliced peaches, drained well, juice reserved
8 ounces cream cheese, softened
1/2 cup sugar

Combine the flour, baking powder, salt, dry pudding mix, margarine, egg and milk in a large mixing bowl. Beat at medium speed for 2 minutes. Pour into a buttered 9-inch pie plate. Arrange the peaches over the batter. Combine the cream cheese, 3 tablespoons reserved peach juice and sugar in a mixing bowl and beat at medium speed for 2 minutes. Spoon evenly over the peaches to within 1 inch of the edge. Sprinkle with a mixture of 1 tablespoon sugar and cinnamon to taste. Bake at 350 degrees for 30 to 35 minutes or until set around the edge. Chill, covered, until serving time. Yield: 6 servings.

Nancy Creech, Preceptor Gamma Epsilon
Plainwell, Michigan

PEACHY PUDDING DESSERT

1 cup flour
1/2 cup (1 stick) butter, softened
1 cup chopped walnuts or pecans
8 ounces cream cheese, softened
16 ounces whipped topping
1 cup sugar
3 cups milk
2 (4-ounce) packages French vanilla instant pudding mix
6 peaches or nectarines, pitted, sliced, peeled

Combine the flour, butter and walnuts in a bowl and mix well. Pat the mixture evenly into a 9×13-inch baking dish. Bake at 350 degrees for 15 minutes. Cool completely. Combine the cream cheese, half the whipped topping and sugar in a mixing bowl and mix until smooth. Spread evenly over the cooled crust. Combine the milk and dry pudding mix in a bowl and stir until smooth. Spread evenly over the cream cheese layer. Arrange the peach slices over the top. Spread the remaining whipped topping over the peaches. Chill, covered, for at least 3 hours before serving. Top with additional nuts and peach slices and serve. Yield: 20 to 25 servings.

Judy Jackson, Preceptor Nu Omega
Ione, California

CHOCOLATE TRIFLE

1 (2-layer) package devil's food cake mix
2 tablespoons vegetable oil
2 large egg whites
1 large egg
1 (6-ounce) package chocolate instant pudding mix
3 cups cold milk
1/2 cup Kahlúa or strong brewed coffee
8 ounces whipped topping
1 cup chopped Snickers bars

Combine the dry cake mix, vegetable oil, egg whites, egg and 1 1/3 cups water in a large mixing bowl; beat at medium speed until well blended. Spoon the batter into a 9×13-inch baking dish that has been sprayed with nonstick cooking spray. Bake at 350 degrees for 25 minutes or until the cake tests done. Remove to a wire rack to cool completely. Tear the cooled cake into 1-inch pieces. Prepare the pudding mix with 3 cups cold milk using the package directions. Layer the cake, Kahlúa, pudding, whipped topping and Snickers bars 1/2 at a time in a trifle bowl or other 3-quart bowl. Chill, covered, for at least 4 hours before serving. Yield: 16 servings.

Susanne G. Muffley, Zeta Xi
Clovis, New Mexico

ANGEL SOUFFLE

1 (16-ounce) package angel food cake mix
8 ounces cream cheese, softened
1 cup sugar
1 teaspoon vanilla extract
2 cups chilled whipping cream
1 cup miniature marshmallows
1 (10-ounce) jar maraschino cherries, drained
Sliced almonds (optional)

Prepare and bake the cake mix using the package directions. Combine the cream cheese, sugar and vanilla in a mixing bowl; beat at medium speed until smooth and creamy, scraping bowl occasionally. Beat the whipping cream in a chilled bowl until stiff peaks form. Fold the whipped cream, marshmallows and cherries gently into the cream cheese mixture. Tear the cake into 1-inch pieces. Add the cake pieces to the cream cheese mixture and toss gently to combine. Make a 4-inch band of foil 2 inches longer than the circumference of a 1 1/2-quart soufflé dish. Extend the height of the dish by securing the foil band around the outside of the dish. Pour the cake mixture into the dish. Garnish with sliced almonds. Chill until set, for at least 8 hours. Refrigerate any leftovers.
Yield: 12 to 16 servings.

Robin Fiebrich, Xi Alpha Eta
New Braunfels, Texas

BLUEBERRY ORANGE TRIFLE

1/2 cup orange juice
1 envelope unflavored gelatin
1 1/2 cups non-fat plain yogurt
1/2 teaspoon vanilla extract
1/4 cup light brown sugar or Splenda
Grated zest of 1 orange
1 angel food cake
1/2 cup orange juice
8 ounces whipped topping
1 cup chopped pecans or walnuts
4 cups fresh or frozen (thawed) blueberries
2 tablespoons granulated sugar or 3 packages Splenda
Juice of 1/2 lemon
Fresh mint leaves

Heat 1/2 cup orange juice in a small saucepan over medium heat. Remove from the heat. Sprinkle the gelatin over the hot orange juice; stir. Let stand for 5 minutes. Combine the yogurt, vanilla, brown sugar, orange zest and gelatin mixture in a bowl and mix well. Tear the angel food cake into 1-inch pieces. Place the cake pieces in a large bowl and toss with 1/2 cup orange juice to moisten. Spoon the yogurt mixture over the cake. Layer the whipped topping and chopped pecans over the top. Combine the blueberries, granulated sugar and lemon juice in a saucepan over medium heat. Cook until heated through, stirring gently until the sugar is dissolved; consistency will remain a little chunky. Cool. Spread over the trifle. Chill, covered, for 8 to 10 hours. Garnish with fresh mint and serve. Yield: 8 servings.

Susan Bryhn, Alpha Beta Master
Williamsburg, Virginia

LEMON BERRY TRIFLE

2 (16-ounce) cans lemon pie filling
16 ounces lemon yogurt
1 angel food cake
3 cups blueberries, strawberries or other berries
8 ounces whipped topping

Combine the lemon pie filling and lemon yogurt in a bowl and blend well. Tear the cake into 1-inch pieces. Layer 1/3 of the cake pieces, 1/3 of the lemon mixture and 1/4 of the berries in a trifle bowl. Repeat the layers twice. Spread whipped topping over the top. Decorate with the remaining berries. Chill, covered, for at least 3 hours. Yield: 12 servings.

Judy Newlan, Laureate Iota
Sun City West, Arizona

LIGHT SCOTTISH TRIFLE

1 (8-ounce) can fruit cocktail
3 (3-ounce) packages gelatin, any flavor
1 small sponge cake, cut into 1-inch pieces
3 small bananas, sliced
1 (8-ounce) can mandarin oranges
1 (4-ounce) package vanilla instant pudding mix
2 cups milk
2 cups whipped cream

Drain the fruit cocktail, reserving the juice. Combine the reserved fruit cocktail juice with enough cold water to make 1 cup liquid. Prepare one of the packages of gelatin using the directions for 1 cup boiling water and 1 cup cold water, substituting the fruit cocktail liquid mixture for the cold water. Stir in the fruit cocktail and cake pieces. Pour into a 2- to 3-quart bowl or trifle dish; chill until firm. Prepare the second package of gelatin using 1 cup boiling water and 1 cup cold water; stir in the banana slices. Pour over the fruit cocktail layer. Chill until firm. Drain the mandarin oranges, reserving the juice. Combine the reserved mandarin orange juice with enough cold water to make 1 cup liquid. Prepare the third package of gelatin, substituting the mandarin orange liquid mixture for the cold water. Stir in the mandarin oranges. Pour over the banana layer. Chill until firm. Prepare the pudding with whole or 2% milk using the package directions. Spread over the mandarin orange layer. Top with whipped cream. Decorate as desired. When serving, scoop carefully through all the layers so that each serving has some of each layer. Yield: 20 servings.

Hazel Hanson, Preceptor Mu
Kamloops, British Columbia, Canada

BLACK FOREST TRIFLE

1 (4-ounce) package chocolate instant pudding mix
1 (3-ounce) package chocolate mousse mix
1 (9×13-inch) chocolate sheet cake
8 ounces whipped topping
1 (15-ounce) can cherry pie filling
1/4 to 1/2 cup cherry liqueur (optional)
1 (7-ounce) chocolate bar, shaved

Prepare the pudding mix using the directions on the package. Prepare the mousse using the directions on the package. Dice or crumble 1/3 of the cake into a large glass bowl or trifle bowl. Layer the whipped topping and cherry pie filling over the cake layer. Dice or crumble another 1/3 of the cake evenly over the whipped topping. Layer the chocolate pudding over the cake layer. Dice or crumble the remaining cake over the pudding. Drizzle with cherry liqueur. Spread the chocolate mousse over the top. Sprinkle with shaved chocolate. Chill, covered, for at least 2 hours. Spoon into bowls to serve.
Yield: 8 to 10 servings.

Jacqueline Schamber, Sigma Eta
Chesterfield, Missouri

ANGEL PINEAPPLE DESSERT

1 (16-ounce) package angel food cake mix
2 envelopes unflavored gelatin
1 cup pineapple juice
1 cup sugar
1 cup fresh orange juice
Juice of 1 lemon
Dash of salt
1 (20-ounce) can crushed pineapple, drained
1 (10-ounce) jar maraschino cherries, drained and chopped
2 cups whipping cream, whipped, or 16 ounces whipped topping

Prepare and bake the cake mix using the package directions. Soften the gelatin in 1/4 cup cold water. Bring the pineapple juice to a boil in a saucepan over medium-high heat. Stir in the sugar and the gelatin mixture. Remove from heat. Stir in the orange juice, lemon juice and salt. Chill until partially set. Tear or cut the cooled cake into bite-size pieces. Stir the pineapple, cherries and whipped cream into the partially set gelatin mixture. Layer the cake pieces and pineapple mixture 1/2 at a time in a 9×13-inch baking dish. Sprinkle with shredded coconut and chopped nuts. Serve with additional whipped cream and a cherry. Yield: 12 to 16 servings.

Louise M. Burns, Iota Master
Quincy, Illinois

Merit Winners

Catherine Ariemma, page 28
Basil Cheese Terrine
Juanita Bean, page 172
Tiramisu Cake
Joyce Boor, page 131
Apricot Coconut Coffee Cake
Eileen Cockburn, page 118
Crunchy Granola
Dianne Daniel, page 14
Cajun Pork Soutache
Carol Darlington, page 17
Pecan-Topped Artichoke Dip
Sharon Haworth, page 9
Mushroom Croustades
Jane Humphrey, page 19
Mexican Chicken Scoops
Tommie May, page 163
Chocolate Italian Cream Cake
Lois M. McAleer, page 84
Puerto Rican Pot Roast
Deborah A. Miller, page 91
Champagne Chicken
Mary Anna Minton, page 188
White Chocolate Chip Oatmeal Cookies
Jessie Neighbors, page 80
Cheesy Grilled Pork Loin
Kay Nelson, page 178
Chocolate Raspberry Pie
Bonnie Pearson, page 127
Pecan Sandwich Mix
Debra Pellett, page 58
Creamy White Chili
Sharon Ann Robinson, page 152
Mock Potato Bake
Maria Sandy, page 199
Triple Chip Cheesecake
Patricia Soard, page 145
Six-Cheese Penne Pasta
Lina Steel, page 40
Mandarin Salad
Dorothy Steger, page 81
Stuffed Holiday Roll
Karen Stowers, page 138
Jalapeño Pull-Apart Bread
Mary Ann Valley, page 113
Tomato Shrimp with Fettuccine
Misty Wells, page 122
Cheesy Spinach Breakfast Bake
Fawn Wright, page 40
Craisin Salad

Honorable Mention

Abernathy, Rose Ann, page 41
Andriesian, Lori, page 145
Artalejo, Diana G., page 167
Auger, Joyce, page 10
Behrens, Gloria, page 123
Benzon, Shelly, page 134
Bertram, Linda, page 155
Bryhn, Susan, page 211
Bulloch, Deb, page 191
Burke, Evelyn, page 177
Buttman, Mary Helen, page 95
Clemons, Linda, page 95
Copeland, Anne M., page 12
Cramer, Mary Ellen, page 99
DeMond, Nancy, page 111
Esposito, Marcia, page 107
Evans, Judy Ann, page 19
Farley, R. Gene, page 189
Fitzsimmons, Tish, page 48
Franz, Lois, page 120
Fred, Joyce, page 44
Furlong, Doris, page 20
Gabrielli, Shirley, page 45
Helle, Florence, page 33
Johnson, Jane, page 49
Johnson, Paula, page 67
Johnston, Beth, page 92
Juch, Judene, page 83
Knapp, Carole S., page 133
Knickerbocker, Val, page 50
Kruse, Myrt, page 160
Liggett, Marge, page 76
McNamara, Catherine, page 50
Meredith, Jan, page 171
Moore, Phyllis G., page 22
Osborne, Donna, page 129
Ouellette, Ellen, page 137
Pederson, Marcene M., page 207
Perry, Jacqueline V., page 82
Petru, Brenda, page 112
Povlot, Rhonda, page 117
Pruett, Diane L., page 203
Reinhart, Mary Elizabeth, page 117
Robinson, Sharon, page 50
Rochford, LouAnn, page 22
Rohleder, Patty, page 96
Rosenthal, Eileen, page 97
Samsel, Charlene, page 28
Schmidt, Joyce, page 80
Scott, Beverly, page 100
Shannon, Gail, page 162
Spence, Sharon, page 54
Thompson, Janet, page 116
Throgmorton, LuAnn, page 13
West, Betty, page 139
Williams, Marilyn A., page 144
Williams, Vicky, page 171
Wilson, Verlyne, page 135

Metric Equivalents

Although the United States has opted to postpone converting to metric measurements, most other countries, including England and Canada, use the metric system. The following chart provides convenient approximate equivalents for allowing use of regular kitchen measures when cooking from foreign recipes.

Volume

These metric measures are approximate benchmarks for purposes of home food preparation.
1 milliliter = 1 cubic centimeter = 1 gram

Liquid	Dry
1 teaspoon = 5 milliliters	1 quart = 1 liter
1 tablespoon = 15 milliliters	1 ounce = 30 grams
1 fluid ounce = 30 milliliters	1 pound = 450 grams
1 cup = 250 milliliters	2.2 pounds = 1 kilogram
1 pint = 500 milliliters	

Weight

1 ounce = 28 grams
1 pound = 450 grams

Length

1 inch = 2 1/2 centimeters
1/16 inch = 1 millimeter

Formulas Using Conversion Factors

When approximate conversions are not accurate enough, use these formulas to convert measures from one system to another.

Measurements	Formulas
ounces to grams:	# ounces x 28.3 = # grams
grams to ounces:	# grams x 0.035 = # ounces
pounds to grams:	# pounds x 453.6 = # grams
pounds to kilograms:	# pounds x 0.45 = # kilograms
ounces to milliliters:	# ounces x 30 = # milliliters
cups to liters:	# cups x 0.24 = # liters
inches to centimeters:	# inches x 2.54 = # centimeters
centimeters to inches:	# centimeters x 0.39 = # inches

Approximate Weight to Volume

Some ingredients which we commonly measure by volume are measured by weight in foreign recipes. Here are a few examples for easy reference.

flour, all-purpose, unsifted	1 pound = 450 grams = 3 1/2 cups
flour, all-purpose, sifted	1 pound = 450 grams = 4 cups
sugar, granulated	1 pound = 450 grams = 2 cups
sugar, brown, packed	1 pound = 450 grams = 2 1/4 cups
sugar, confectioners'	1 pound = 450 grams = 4 cups
sugar, confectioners', sifted	1 pound = 450 grams = 4 1/2 cups
butter	1 pound = 450 grams = 2 cups

Temperature

Remember that foreign recipes frequently express temperatures in Centigrade rather than Fahrenheit.

Temperatures	Fahrenheit	Centigrade
room temperature	68°	20°
water boils	212°	100°
baking temperature	350°	177°
baking temperature	375°	190.5°
baking temperature	400°	204.4°
baking temperature	425°	218.3°
baking temperature	450°	232°

Use the following formulas when temperature conversions are necessary.

Centigrade degrees x 9/5 + 32 = Fahrenheit degrees
Fahrenheit degrees - 32 x 5/9 = Centigrade degrees

American Measurement Equivalents

1 tablespoon = 3 teaspoons	12 tablespoons = 3/4 cup
2 tablespoons = 1 ounce	16 tablespoons = 1 cup
4 tablespoons = 1/4 cup	1 cup = 8 ounces
5 tablespoons + 1 teaspoon = 1/3 cup	2 cups = 1 pint
8 tablespoons = 1/2 cup	4 cups = 1 quart
	4 quarts = 1 gallon

Index